OSWALD, THE CIA and the WARREN COMMISSION:

The Unanswered Questions

Peter Kross

ISBN: 978-0-9844733-6-6

Published By:
Bridger House Publishers, Inc.
PO Box 599, Hayden ID, 83835
1-800-729-4131
www.nohoax.com

Printed in the United States of America

Cover Design / Typesetting:
Julie Melton, The Right Type, (www.therighttype.com) USA

10 9 8 7 6 5 4 3 2 1

To my old friend,
Mark Winnegrad

"Now then, that is the tale. Some of it is true."

— Mark Twain Autobiography

Table of Contents

INTRODUCTION

Months before Oliver Stone's blockbuster film, JFK, hit the movie theaters across America, most of the mainstream press in this country began its massive assault on Stone's version of the Kennedy assassination. They called Stone a liar, a man who played fast and loose with history, a person who was out just to make a buck. Despite the cry to arms concerning JFK, the film was a nationwide success, reopening the JFK case to millions of Americans, especially generation X'ers who only had a fleeting knowledge of the 35th President of the United States and the events of November 22, 1963 (mostly from the mainstream press).

One of the positive ramifications to come out of the movie was the overwhelming cry from an already skeptical American public who, in all polls, believed in a conspiracy in the Kennedy assassination. The hue and cry was so loud that the Congress of the United States, over the reluctance of the Bush administration, passed the 1991 JFK Records Act, which mandated that any federal and local administrative bodies that had any records on the Kennedy assassination be turned over for eventual release. The JFK Records Act set up a panel of experts who would evaluate the records, mostly from the CIA and the FBI, and release them to the National Archives where they would be available to the public for inspection. (The Review Board went out of business in the Fall of 1998).

Since the Review Board has been in business, hundreds of

thousands of pages of previously classified documents on the Kennedy case have been released. One author to use these files (especially CIA files) is John Newman in Oswald and the CIA, a dramatic and detailed study of the intelligence agencies and their relationship to the president's alleged assassin, Lee Harvey Oswald. These CIA files help to fill in the blank concerning the government wide interest among the various branches of US intelligence in Oswald, whom the Warren Commission labeled as the "lone nut," the man who without a doubt, assassinated President Kennedy.

While these files do not shed new light on the events in Dealey Plaza, they do however, cast information on the Kennedy administrations relationship with Cuba, on the CIA-Mafia plots to assassinate Fidel Castro, and the strong possibility that Lee Oswald was part of some sort of US intelligence gathering operation of which he may or may not have had direct knowledge.

This study will show the relationship, based primarily on the new files, and information already in the public domain, between the Warren Commission's investigation of the JFK assassination, the Central Intelligence Agency, and Lee Harvey Oswald.

This investigation will not just cover the above mentioned topics but a whole host of other issues, people, and events surrounding the Kennedy assassination, most of which will already be known to the serious JFK assassination researcher. Among the new information in this report are the following: the once secret testimony of "John Scelso" who wrote a report on the CIA's investigation of the assassination, new material on AMLASH, the second invasion of Cuba to be held in the last week of November, 1963, Howard Hunt's secret investigation of the assassination, and the Kennedy administration's two track policy toward Castro's Cuba. The last section contains new material that has been released since 2000 and adds even more to the story of Oswald and the CIA.

What is obvious is that the Warren Commission failed to investigate all of the relevant facts surrounding the assassination, had its mind made up from the beginning, and wanted to end the "investigation" as soon as politically possible. Had they known about the events concerning the relationship between the CIA and Lee Oswald, the CIA-Mafia plots to kill Castro, and other material now available via the 1991 JFK Records Act, would their conclusion have been the same?

Chapter 1

The Warren Commission And The Search For The "Truth"

"The thing I am concerned about, and so is (Deputy Attorney General Nicholas D.J.) Katzenbach, is having something issued so we can convince the public that Oswald is the real assassin. Mr. Katzenbach thinks that the President might appoint a Presidential Commission of three outstanding citizens to make a determination."

– Memo from FBI Director J. Edgar Hoover to Walter Jenkins, aide to President Lyndon Johnson, dated November 24, 1963.

It was quiet once again. The haunting beat of the drums echoing across Arlington National Cemetery had ended. The plaintive sounds of "taps," the bugler missing his rhythm was gone. The only difference was the bright, eternal flame that burned forever more on the gentle hillside below the stately Custis-Lee Mansion, at the grave of the 35th president of the United States, John Fitzgerald Kennedy. Drivers leaving Washington via the Memorial Bridge near the Lincoln Memorial could see the bright light illuminating the grave of John Kennedy, another martyred president who paid the ultimate sacrifice for his country.

Now, the country began to get back to normal; businesses reopened, schools were in session once again, and the horrible events of the past weekend, though not to be forgotten, were to take a back seat to living.

It was less than a week after the events in Dealey Plaza when FBI Director J. Edgar Hoover sent his memo to Deputy Attorney General Nicholas Katzenbach. The president's alleged assassin, Lee Harvey Oswald, a 24-year-old former Marine, a "defector" to the Soviet Union, a loner with pro-Castro, pro-Communist leanings, had been brutally murdered in the basement of the Dallas Police Department as he was being transferred to await trial for the murders of the president and of Dallas Police Officer, J.D. Tippit. Oswald was shot by a petty gangster with ties to the criminal underworld, the owner of a local strip tease club, a man with ties to the FBI, and interests in Castro's Cuba, Jack Rubenstein, a.k.a., Jack Ruby.

Oswald was dead, there could be no trial, case closed. But even as John Kennedy was laid to rest next to his two young children, (and eventually his wife, Jackie), questions as to the actual events of Dealey Plaza were beginning to percolate. In Europe, where conspiracies were as common as the change in governments, there was talk of a right wing conspiracy in the assassination of the president

In the United States, the FBI was given responsibility of "investigating" the events surrounding the assassination, despite ample warnings by informants in the weeks prior to November 22, 1963 that a plot against JFK was afoot.

As far as J. Edgar Hoover was concerned, they had got their man and no further investigation was required. On November 25, the new president, Lyndon Johnson, ordered the FBI Director to prepare a detailed report on the circumstances surrounding Kennedy's death. That same day, Nick Katzenbach wrote a letter to another of Johnson's aides, Bill Moyers going over the details of any assassination study:

It is important that all of the facts surrounding President Kennedy's assassination be made public in a way which will satisfy people in the United States and abroad, That all the facts have been told and that a statement to this effect be made now.

1. *The public must be satisfied that Oswald was assassin; that he did not have confederates who are still at large, that the evidence was such that he would have been convicted at trial.*

2. *Speculation about Oswald's motivation ought to be cut off, and we should have some basis for rebutting thought that this was a Communist conspiracy.*

3. *The matter has been handled thus far with neither dignity nor conviction... I think this objective may be satisfied and made public as soon as possible with the completion of a thorough FBI report on Oswald and the assassination. This may run into the difficulty of pointing to inconsistency between this report and statements by Dallas Police officials; but the reputation of the Bureau is such that it may to the whole job... The only other step would be the appointment of a Presidential Commission of unimpeachable personnel to review and examine the evidence and announce its conclusions...*

At the time of the president's assassination, it was not a federal crime to kill a president of the United States. Since the murder took place in Texas, the inquiry into the event was relegated to a state level. The Lone Star state of Texas would carry out the investigation into John Kennedy's murder, and to that effect, on November 25, Texas Attorney General Waggoner Carr announced his intention to begin an official state inquiry.

After all, President Kennedy's fatal trip to Dallas was purely political. He had gone to Texas to help heal a rift among the members of the Texas political establishment; Texas Governor John Connally (who was severely wounded in the assassination attempt) and Senator Ralph Yarborough were bitter enemies, each man jockeying for position as the head of the Democratic Party in Texas. The other mainstay of Texas politics was Kennedy's beleaguered Vice President, Lyndon Johnson. Johnson had been instrumental in Kennedy's razor slim margin of victory in Texas (and in the national election) in 1960 and JFK owed Johnson big. But Johnson had his own political troubles brewing up on Capitol Hill. LBJ's most trusted political aid, Bobby Baker, who LBJ had appointed to the post of secretary to the Senate Democrats in 1955, was being investigated for questionable campaign dealings. As Senate investigators began looking into Baker's business dealings they found links to organized crime figures, mostly located in Las Vegas. One of Baker's mob pals was Edward Levinson, a top member of Meyer Lansky's Florida underworld. There were also rumors going around that LBJ had a secret connection to Louisiana mob boss Carlos Marcello. There were even suggestions by some members of Kennedy's inner circle that the president had decided to drop LBJ from the national ticket in 1964. In 1967, Baker was convicted of tax evasion.

Before landing in Dallas, President Kennedy had two other highly successful stops in Texas; Houston and Fort Worth. Accompanying President Kennedy on the trip was his wife Jackie who, only, a few months previously, had lost her baby. This was her first political foray into the 1964 presidential campaign.

But President Kennedy's trip to Texas was not without warning signs. A few weeks before, UN Ambassador Adlai Stevenson was roughed up and spat upon by anti-Kennedy hecklers when he arrived in Dallas. Kennedy and his liberal policies were not welcomed in conservative Dallas and on the very day that Kennedy arrived in Dallas, the local paper, the Dallas Morning News, published a full-page ad charging that JFK was soft on Communism and was a traitor to the country.

All this was on his mind when the presidential limousine

turned the corner into Dealey Plaza at 12:30 P.M. Less than five minutes later, John F. Kennedy was dead.

Not to be outdone by local officials, the United States Congress began plans to start its own investigation into the assassination. On November 26, Republican Senator Everett Dirksen reported that a special Senate panel was being given permission to start up its own plans to look into the events of Kennedy's murder. Heading the special panel was Senator James Eastland who was chairman of the Judiciary Committee. The House of Representatives too began to make rumblings concerning their part in any investigation.

While Robert Kennedy was not consulted, nor wanted to be, other top men in the new administration began behind the scenes planning to get an official government sponsored inquiry on track. Among those who convinced President Johnson to stop a Texas examination, fearing that it would only convince the public that there was a home grown cover-up taking place, were Yale Law Professor Eugene Rostow, Secretary of State Dean Rusk, and the influential columnist, Joseph Alsop.

Not known at the time, but revealed years later, was the fact that President Johnson himself had doubts about Oswald's true role in the assassination. Johnson would later say that Oswald was a very mysterious young man, who may have had help in planning the murder. Johnson was also very concerned about the possible role of foreign powers in Kennedy's death, particularly, the possible parts of either Cuba or Russia. It was Cuba and the regime of Fidel Castro that most troubled LBJ. Johnson feared that if it were revealed that either country had a hand in Kennedy's assassination, the consequences of such bombshell might lead to nuclear war.

To finally end such fears and speculation, Johnson, on November 29, 1963, one week after JFK's death, officially appointed a body of distinguished men to officially investigate the death of the president. After all, 52% of the American public, one week after the event, believed that Oswald did not act alone. Thus, the

"Warren Commission" was born to seek out the "truth" into the crime of the century. But what it turned out to be was not the "truth," nor the full cover-up that conspiracy theorists said it was, but an investigation that was flawed from the start, of men lacking the deep instinct to look wherever the facts could have lead them, consciously not requiring the testimony of witnesses who were on hand at Dealey Plaza, not pursuing leads and information that would have materially changed the conclusion they reached only nine months later.

The same day that LBJ decided on the appointment of a governmental investigative committee, Deputy Attorney General Nicholas Katzenbach and Solicitor General Archibald Cox (later of Watergate fame) paid a visit to Supreme Court Justice Earl Warren. When the talk of a commission to investigate Kennedy's death came up, Warren said that he opposed any of his Associate Justices as members of the panel. Warren was shocked when the men told him that LBJ wanted him to serve as chairman of the body. Warren refused; saying that he thought it would be improper for a member of one branch of the executive to work for another. A few hours after Katzenbach and Cox left, the Chief Justice received a call from a very distressed President Johnson. Johnson turned on the "charm" that had won over so many political opponents over the years. Johnson told Warren that public trust in the governments possible role in the assassination was beginning to gel, that there were hints of foreign conspiracies behind the assassination, and more important, that Johnson needed Warren's ok and would not take no for an answer. Warren reluctantly accepted President Johnson's request.

After Johnson's call to the Chief Justice, he issued Executive Order 11,130 creating the seven member "Warren Commission."

Over the next few days, both Katzenbach and Johnson's old friend, lawyer Abe Fortas, drafted a list of possible men to serve on the panel. The men who made up the Warren Commission were:

- **Representative Hale Boggs, (D. La)** Over time, Boggs was to become one of the most critical members of the commission, finding fault with the over reliance by the Commission on information supplied by the FBI. Boggs was also a critic of the so-called "single bullet theory" adopted by the panel concerning the wounds to Kennedy's body. Boggs held a very powerful place in Congress and in time, was positioned to take on a leadership role in the House. But he died under mysterious circumstances when his military plane crashed over Alaska on October 16, 1972.

- **Senator John Sherman Cooper, (R. Ky).** A former military lawyer in World War II, Cooper also served as US Ambassador to India and Nepal during the Eisenhower administration.

- **Allan Dulles:** Dulles was CIA Director under Kennedy and was fired from his post after the failed Bay of Pigs invasion of April 1961. Dulles had a long history in intelligence, having served in the wartime OSS as America's chief spy master in neutral Switzerland during World War II. Not known at the time of his appointment was that he deliberately withheld critical information from the commission concerning the CIA-Mafia plots against Fidel Castro (see more biographical information on Dulles in Chapter 2).

- **Representative Gerald Ford, (R. Mi).** Ford has been called the "FBI's spy" on the Warren Commission due to his close association with the FBI during the time of the commission's work. Ford also had a close relationship with the CIA and would later write a book on Lee Harvey Oswald. A firm believer in the lone gunman theory, Ford would later become President of the United States after the resignation of President Richard Nixon (it was Nixon who recommended that Ford be appointed to the panel).

- **John J. McCloy:** McCloy had a long career in government. During World War 11, he served as an assistant secretary of war, was president of the World Bank, and was high commissioner of Germany after the war ended. During the Kennedy administration, he helped make disarmament policy. During the commission's work, he was an advocate of the "single bullet theory."

- **Senator Richard Russell (D. Ga)** At the time of the assassination of President Kennedy's, Russell served as chairman of the important Senate Armed Services Committee, was much admired by the Pentagon brass, and had wide contacts in the domestic arms industry. By 1970, long after the commission had gone out of business, Russell criticized the Warren Report by saying that he believed that a criminal conspiracy had organized Kennedy's death.

As the commissioners got down to work, they divided themselves up into working groups. The areas they were to investigate were the following:

- **Area 1:** The Basic Facts of the Assassination.
- **Area 2:** The Identity of the Assassin.
- **Area 3:** Oswald's Background.
- **Area 4:** Possible Conspiratorial Relationships.
- **Area 5:** Oswald's Death.
- **Area 6:** Presidential Protection.

The commission members themselves did not do most of the day-to-day work and failed to attend a majority of the interviews and meetings. They hired as their General Counsel, attorney, J. Lee Rankin whose views on the assassination mirrored those of J. Edgar Hoover. In fact, the commission relied almost entirely at first on the investigative talents (or lack thereof) of the FBI. Hoover did not want to see the commission established believing that 1) Oswald was the lone assassin of President Kennedy and

2) if the commission looked deep enough they might uncover the bureau's bumbling in its clandestine contacts with Oswald in Dallas in the months prior to the assassination.

Even more critical to the FBI's pre-assassination performance concerns an FBI teletype dated November 17, 1963 that went out to all FBI offices around the country. The memo directed all of the bureau's CI's (confidential informers) to find out if a militant revolutionary group had any plans to assassinate the president during his trip to Texas. What is most interesting is that FBI headquarters received no replies to its nation wide inquiries.

This wasn't the only incident of the FBI's foreknowledge that a threat on President Kennedy's life was in the works. Through various bureau informers, Hoover had received reports that Louisiana mob boss Carlos Marcello, had made threats against President Kennedy. Instead of alerting the Secret Service, he filed the information away.

Conspiracy theorists have had a field day trying to implicate Hoover in the assassination of President Kennedy and they may be right. To a greater degree, Hoover was an accessory before the fact, knowing that clandestine plans were afoot to kill Kennedy. On the evening of November 21, 1963, the day before the assassination, Hoover had a private dinner in Dallas at the home of the Murchison family, whose oil business and right wing politics flew right in the face of the liberal president, John Kennedy. Another person attending the dinner was Vice President Lyndon Johnson. Hoover returned to Washington on the morning of the 22nd. What went on at that meeting at the Murchison home that night is not known but speculation is ripe.

Hoover tried with all his power to hamper the initial investigation of the assassination by the Warren Commission. Hoover bombarded the commission members with daily reports saying that Oswald was the lone assassin, he had no confederates lurking behind hidden walls, and that the FBI was on the case. But for all of Hoover's cajoling, and to the commissioner's credit, they refused to take Hoover's bait. They told the esteemed director that they believed that there were serious flaws in the FBI's initial investigation and that their work would continue. But Hoover wasn't done. He had the FBI prepare a 5-volume report on the assassination in December 1963, two months before the first witness appeared before the committee. The account found that Lee Harvey Oswald acted alone in killing the president. In order to cement his power base over the Warren panel, Hoover ordered his agents to dig up dirt, political and otherwise, on the 7 Warren Commissioners.

Hoover also had his friend, President Lyndon Johnson over a barrel. Even though both men had known each other for years in Washington's power circle, Hoover trusted no one, including his buddy, the new chief executive. Hoover was aware of the two growing political scandals that were engulfing the life of the Vice President; the case of his political crony, Billy Sol Estes, and the ongoing Bobby Baker affair. Estes was a political wheeler-dealer who had close ties to Johnson. The Estes case gets murkier and deadlier when a man by the name of Henry Marshall, who was a top Agriculture Department official investigating Estes' affairs, was killed on June 3, 1961. Marshall was shot five times by a rifle but his death was called a suicide by the local coroner.

On May 8, 1964, President Johnson appointed his good friend, J. Edgar Hoover, Director of the FBI for life.

If the commission had its doubts about Hoover's FBI and their hurried up investigation of the events of November 22, 1963, they had an even harder time when it came to a possible conspiracy in the murder of John Kennedy. When the Warren Commission's final verdict came out in September 1964, there was no mention of a possible conspiracy; Oswald was the lone gunman. But through de-classified papers that have recently come to light, there were heated discussions among the members of the group as to any possible accomplices that Oswald may have had, especially foreign ones.

The question of conspiracy was debated among the commissions' lawyers one afternoon in early 1964 over lunch in

Washington's Monocle restaurant, near Capitol Hill. The talk among the attorney's, including David Slawson, who was given the job of searching for foreign plots, lead to a disturbing scenario. What Wit was learned that the Russians were responsible for the crime? Would it lead to World War III? What if was proven that LBJ had a hand in the plot (as some conspiracy theorists today believe)? Could they say so in public?

Rankin had instructed his staff attorney's to look into the role of the CIA in the assassination. As it turned out, they didn't have to look far. The CIA only gave the Warren Commission that much information, as they were willing to give up, and nothing more. For example, the CIA never reported to the Commission the fact that a high-ranking Soviet defector from the KGB, Yuri Nosenko, had come over to the west shortly after the assassination. It seems that Nosenko had been in charge of the Oswald file while the ex-Marine spent over two years in the Soviet Union. Furthermore, said Nosenko, the Soviet Union had no operational interest in Oswald and that he was not working in any capacity for the Russians at the time of Kennedy's death. That fact would absolve the Russians in any way in Kennedy's murder, leaving the Hoover-Warren theory complete; Oswald was the lone assassin.

In order to get the other side of the conspiracy coin, certain members of staff met with skeptics who were trying to prove a conspiracy. One of the men who filled this description, and who was interviewed by the panel was Thomas Buchanan, who wrote one of the early conspiracy books on the assassination. Buchanan's theories were rejected out of hand.

In a rather unusual move, the CIA secretly flew two Commission staffers, David Slawson and William Coleman to Mexico City where they were given a secret briefing from agency officials on information supplied by a CIA asset stationed in the Cuban Embassy. One of the areas that the Commission had a hard time reconciling was Oswald's (or an impostors) one-week trip to the Mexican capital in late September, early October 1963. Oswald's trip to Mexico is filled with confusion and the overt hint of an intelligence operation (as newly released documents show). Both men urged the Commission to investigate the anti-Castro angle in the assassination and believed that Oswald was being set up in some way to be used as a tool of these militant groups to take the fall as the pro-Castro "nut" that killed the president. But the Commission ran out of time before they could pursue this matter.

But all these activities were all just a smoke screen for the final judgment, which had been, preordained right from the start. When the Warren Report was put to bed and given to President Johnson in September 1964, the 7 commissioners had come up with their final verdict. 1) Lee Harvey Oswald alone killed President John Kennedy. 2) Lee Harvey Oswald alone killed Dallas Police Officer J.D. Tippit. 3) Jack Ruby alone killed Lee Harvey Oswald and neither man had prior knowledge of each other. 4) There was no evidence of a conspiracy, either foreign or domestic in the assassination of President Kennedy. 5) All of the shots came from the sixth floor of the Texas School Depository Building and came from the rifle that was owned by Lee Harvey Oswald. 6) Three shots, and three shots only, were fired at President Kennedy, one which hit him in the neck, which then passed through the body of Texas Governor John Connally, the second shot missed the car completely, and the third, and fatal shot, hit the president in the back of the head, killing him instantly. And that was that. (There was never any consideration, despite eyewitnesses on the ground in Dealey Plaza that shots came from the front, on the so called, Grassy Knoll.)

But what about the bullet fragment that struck bystander James Tague who was standing near the triple underpass and was hit by a bullet fragment? What about the dozens of people who saw and heard shots being fired from the area of the grassy knoll? What about Gordon Arnold, a young soldier on leave from the army who was standing near the knoll and felt a bullet come flying over his shoulder? Arnold was never deposed by the commission. And what about the mysterious Secret Servicemen who were deployed around the knoll when all of the real Secret Service Agents were nowhere near Daley Plaza at the time of the assassination?

These questions, and others, were not investigated by the Warren Commission, or were given short shrift. In all, 26 volumes were published, along with a separate report, which was an immediate best seller across America.

Most Americans read the report and praised its content. The commissioners were honorable men who had a most difficult task to perform under tragic conditions and did it well. It wasn't until a few years later that critics of the report were to begin chipping away at the story, and a skeptical American public who originally thought Oswald could not have done the deed alone became even more dubious.

Walt Brown, the author of several successful books on the Kennedy assassination, *The People vs. Lee Harvey Oswald, Treachery in Dallas, The JFK Assassination Quiz Book* spoke to the author on the historical significance of the Warren Commission. "At the time of the assassination, the people of the United States had to be told that there was no conspiracy. He's dead, let's not make things worse. They (the commissioners) had to bend the truth. The report had to happen at the time it was written to maintain the lie that there was no conspiracy. If it were admitted that there was a conspiracy, the fabric of our society would have been ripped apart. The admitted goal of the Warren Commission was to convict Oswald. That should trouble all of us. It was a lie from the start. If the full truth of what happened came out we could not deal with it." [1]

Years later, the Warren Commission report would fall like a house of cards. In the ensuing thirty years, information would come to light proving just how hollow and historically inaccurate the report truly was.

1 Interview with Walt Brown 3/6/97

Chapter 2

The Warren Commission and the CIA

From its inception, the Warren Commission was almost exclusively dependent on the FBI and the CIA for its information. Hoover gave the commission only that material that he wanted it to have, and as the Kennedy investigation got underway, the CIA would do likewise.

FBI's main duty was to counter domestic crime on a national level; the fight against organized crime (which J. Edgar Hoover said did not exist), battling crimes in interstate commerce, etc. The CIA had no such domestic mandate and wasn't supposed to operate inside the U.S. (that was to change dramatically, especially in the early 1960's during the CIA's covert war against Fidel Castro). The CIA's job was to counter foreign penetration of our spy agency and keep a watch on all hostile countries or groups that were targeting the United States.

By the time of John F. Kennedy's death, the CIA had been in operation sixteen years, just long enough to get its feet wet as far as covert operations against foreign countries were concerned. By the early 1960's, the CIA had already overthrown the governments of Guatemala, ban, helped in the assassination of Dominican Republic leader Rafael Trujillo, played a massive role in the ill fated Bay of Pigs invasion of Cuba in April, 1961, and most importantly as far as this story is concerned, conducted a huge, clandestine war out of the Miami area, dubbed "Operation Mongoose," in a comic-opera operation with the American mafia to kill Fidel Castro.

The CIA that we know today was not the instrument of policy that President Harry Truman had in mind when he signed the law in 1947 creating the successor vehicle to Bill Donovan's OSS. The birth of the CIA had its roots in the last days of World War II when President Roosevelt asked Bill Donovan to give him a proposal for a unified American intelligence agency after the war was over. His proposal to unify the various intelligence functions among the State Department, Army and Navy Departments met with heated resistance. Added to that fact was the detailed reports in the press of an "American Gestapo" eventually doomed FDR's plan. When FDR died on April 12, 1945, any immediate hope of a successor group to the OSS died with him. The new president, Harry S. Truman, a man who was kept in the dark on even the most vital intelligence function, i.e. the Manhattan Project, had more on his mind then who was to get the American espionage pie. Truman, unlike Roosevelt, had no interest or liking for Bill Donovan or his OSS, and on September 20, 1945, he signed an executive order eliminating the OSS. Most of the OSS's branches were transferred to the various government agencies like the State Department and others, including the Army. The OSS's spy arm, the Counter-Espionage Branch was given to the Army as the newly renamed Strategic Services Unit commanded by General John Magruder. President Truman asked Secretary of State James Byrnes to investigate the possibilities of creating a new group that would be responsible for collecting foreign intelligence for the president's use. On January 22, 1946, President Truman signed an order creating a centralized intelligence service called the National Intelligence Authority, which comprised the Secretaries of State, War, and the Navy. One of the most important aspects of the NIA was the creation of the CIG, Central Intelligence Group whose job it was to integrate all intelligence information from all other government departments. Another part of the NIA was the appointment of a Director of Central Intelligence (DCI) who would be directly responsible to the president. The first DCI was Admiral Sidney Souers who lasted only a short period of time. Souer's successor was General Hoyt Vandenberg who took over in June 1946. By 1947, Vandenberg resigned and was replaced by Rosoce Hillenkoetter. It was also in that pivotal year that President Truman signed a bill that created the CIA as an independent agency. Truman signed the National Security Act of 1947 that created the Department of Defense under its own Secretary. The NSA brought all the armed forces under one umbrella. Also signed into law was the National Security Council. The new DCI's job was to be responsible for all government wide intelligence activities. The CIA's charter forbad it from operating at home, had no police power, no law enforcement power, and would advise the NSC on any matters concerning intelligence that might be of interest to the president. This was a far cry from what the CIA has turned into since its inception, almost fifty years ago.

The CIA's Investigation

Before getting into the history of the CIA's relationship with the Warren Commission, and more to the point, its belief in the Oswald as the lone assassin theory, it is important to see the mindset of the CIA in relation to the commission's work and to the critics of the CIA's investigation of the assassination.

The below, lengthily account comes from a CIA document that sums up the agency's attitude toward its accusers in the media.

RE: Concerning Criticism of the Warren Report:

1. *Our Concern. From the day of President Kennedy's assassination on, there has been speculation about the*

responsibility for his murder. Although this was stemmed for a time by the Warren Commission report, various writers have now had time to scan the Commission's published report and documents for new pretexts for questioning, and there has been a new wave of books and articles criticizing the Commission's findings.

2. *This trend of opinion is a matter of concern to the U.S. government, including our organization. Moreover, there seems to be an increasing tendency to hint that President Johnson himself, as the one person who might be said to have benefited, was in some way responsible for the assassination. Our organization itself is directly involved; among other facts, we contributed information to the investigation. Conspiracy theorists have frequently thrown suspicion on our organization, for example by falsely alleging that Lee Harvey Oswald worked for us. The aim of this dispatch is to provide material countering and discrediting the claims of the conspiracy theorists, so as to inhibit the circulation of such claims in other countries. Background information is supplied in a classified section and in a number of unclassified attachments.*

3. *Action. We do not recommend that discussion of the assassination question be initiated where it is not already taking place. Where discussion is active addresses are requested:*

   A. *To discuss the publicity problem with deleted and friendly elite contacts, pointing out that the Warren Commission made as thorough as investigation as humanly possible, that the charges of the critics are without foundation, and that further speculative discussion only plays into the hands of the opposition...*

B. *To employ propaganda assets to negate and refute the attacks of the critics...*

4. *In private to media discussions not directed at any particular writer, or in attacking publications which may be yet forthcoming, the following arguments should be useful:*

   A. *No significant new evidence has emerged which the Commission did not consider...*

   B. *Critics usually overvalue particular items and ignore others...*

   C. *Conspiracy on the large scale often suggested would be impossible to conceal in the United States, esp., since informants could expect to receive large royalties...*

   D. *Critics have often been enticed by a form of intellectual pride; they light on some theory and fall in love with it; they also scoff at the Commission because it did not always answer every question with a flat decision one way or another...*

   E. *As to charges that the Commission's report was a rush job, it emerged three months after the deadline originally set...*

5. *Where possible, counter speculation by encouraging reference to the Commission's Report itself...*"[2]

---

2 CIA Document #1035-960. RE; Concerning Criticism of the Warren Report.

What this report amply shows is that the CIA did not go into the investigation of the assassination with an open mind. Rather, they, like the FBI, were interested in protecting their own turf, as far as any prior agency involvement with Lee Harvey Oswald was concerned. What was not known in 1963, and not given to the Warren Commission, was the agency's extensive "paper chase" on Oswald from 1959, up until, and including his "defection" to the Soviet Union and his return to the United States two years later.

As the commission began its work in January 1964, one of the primary areas that they began looking into was the possibility of a foreign conspiracy. The two point men on the commission who were tasked with looking into the foreign intrigue angle were W. David Slawson, the commissions counsel and William Coleman Jr. As time went on, Slawson would lament that he was at the mercy of the CIA in regards to the type and amount of classified information being supplied to him by the boys at Langley. As he delved deeper into the assassination investigation, Slawson became convinced that a foreign hand had a role in Kennedy's death. In the late 1970's, when the Senate began looking into the Kennedy assassination, Slawson would say this in regards to a possible role of the CIA in the JFK assassination, "Also, and I don't think I thought of this at the time, but in retrospect an agency that sanctions an attempt to kill somebody else's head of state is not in a very good position to be outraged when ours is killed."

Slawson was of course; speaking about the CIA-Mafia plots to kill Castro, which it withheld from the Warren Commission.

The initial CIA probe of the assassination was centered on Oswald's trip to Mexico City in September-October 1963, and later, the possible Cuban connection to the assassination. While the commission did indeed spend a considerable amount of time detailing Oswald's (or someone else's) sojourn south of the border, they passed over the considerable amount of information that may have tied either the anti-Castro exiles based in Florida or Louisiana, and possibly, the government of Fidel Castro to the president's death.

From an outward appearance, all was cozy between the Commission and the CIA. After all, one of the members of the commission was Allan Dulles, the former Director of the CIA (DCI). But Dulles' appointment to the panel was filled with controversy. Dulles was fired by President Kennedy after the Bay of Pigs failure in which over 1,000 Cuban exiles, backed to the hilt by the CIA, failed to overthrow the Castro regime. Another man who was fired by President Kennedy after the Bay of Pigs was Richard Bissell, one of the rising stars in the agency, and friend of the Kennedy brothers.

Right from the start, Dulles was certain that Oswald was the lone assassin of President Kennedy and when the commissioners had a heated discussion on the possibility that Oswald was an informant for the FBI, Dulles' true colors began to show. Below is an excerpt of a dialogue between Dulles and Congressman Hale Boggs, among others on this matter:

Boggs: You could disapprove it, couldn't you?

Dulles: No.

Boggs: Let's take a specific case: that fellow Powers (U-2 pilot Gary Francis Powers) was one of your men.

Dulles: Not an agent. He was an employee.

Boggs: Let's say Powers did not have a signed contract but was recruited by someone in the CIA. The man who recruited him would know, wouldn't he?

Dulles: Yes, wouldn't tell.

Warren: Wouldn't tell it under oath?

Dulles: I wouldn't think he would tell it under oath, no.. He ought not to tell it under oath.

McCloy: Suppose the President of the United States comes to you and says, "Will you tell me, Mr. Dulles?"

Dulles. I would tell the President of the U.S. anything, yes; I am under his control. He is my boss. I wouldn't necessarily tell anybody else, unless the President authorized me to do it.

The rumor that Oswald was a paid employee of the FBI was "checked out" and found to be just that.

But Dulles' discourse with his fellow commissioners stipulated that the CIA could lie if it had to on any aspect of national security as it effected the commissions' investigation.

The CIA probe of the Kennedy assassination was focused, as stated before, on Oswald's trip to Mexico City. It was managed at CIA headquarters by an agency employee who was the desk officer responsible for CIA activities concerning operations in Mexico. This officer's name has just recently come to light, as well as a 200-page report concerning his investigation of Oswald and the assassination. He is "John Scelso," most likely a pseudonym. The Scelso document is revealing and will be given an extensive examination later in this chapter.

Another area of Oswald's life that the Commission studied was his 2-year stay in the Soviet Union. Like Oswald's trip to Mexico City, his time in Russia, in which he married a young Russian woman, was hotly debated. There were rumors going around that the Soviet's were somehow involved in Kennedy's murder, that Oswald was a Russian agent sent to kill the president, and that an Oswald "double" was sent back to the U.S. to do the deed.

This part of the inquiry was headed by the CIA's counterintelligence branch, which was responsible for the agency's world-wide actions regarding sabotage, guerilla activities and counterespionage. At the time of the Kennedy assassination, the CI branch was headed by the legendary CIA officer James Jesus Angleton who was one of the most gifted, yet paranoid men to hold a top post in the agency (more about Angleton later).

Another CIA officer who worked out of the CI branch, and who had a major part in the Warren Commissions liaison with the CIA was Raymond Rocca, Chief of Research and Analysis. Rocca was appointed "point of record" officer and he drafted a long report on Oswald's years in the Soviet Union. The CI/R & A, "Rocca was the CIA's working level contact point with the Warren Commission; consequently he was in a position to review most CIA information pertaining to the assassination, which comprised a heavy volume of incoming cable traffic. Due to compartmentalization, however, Rocca did not have access to all materials potentially relevant to the Warren Commission investigation. For example, Rocca had no knowledge of efforts by the CIA to kill Fidel Castro in the early 1960's."[3]

As Slawson and Coleman began to dig deeper into the Kennedy assassination's foreign conspiracy angle, they found their way into a morass of CIA stonewalling as far as what secret files the agency was willing to share. The CIA gave the commission only that information that they wanted to put forth, nothing more, nothing less.

The man most responsible for the CIA stonewalling was Deputy Director of Plans, Richard Helms. Helms knew of the CIA plots to kill Castro yet failed to inform the Warren Commission. In the 1970's, when the Senate of the United States conducted its own investigation of the Kennedy assassination, Helms was called to testify concerning his role with the Warren Commission. Helms said that at the time of the commission's work, the CIA would only send along files only in response to specific inquires by the commission's staff.

On November 23, 1963, one day after the assassination, Helms called a meeting of senior level CIA officials to outline the agency's responsibility concerning the assassination. During that meeting, Helms appointed John Scelso, a desk officer in the Western Hemisphere Division's and headquarters branch chief, in charge of the CIA's first look into the Kennedy murder.

3 Final Assassinations Report, NY Times edition, 1979, pg. 325-26.

While the Scelso investigation was going under way in secret, the Warren Commission's investigators were setting the parameters for cooperation with the CIA.

John McCone was the DCI at the time of the president's assassination, having taken the place of the fired Allan Dulles. What would come out years later, and in retrospect, would probably have had an effect on the final outcome of the Warren Report if known, was that McCone did not have knowledge of the CIA-Mafia plots against Castro. McCone assured J. Lee Rankin, the General Counsel for the Committee that the CIA was prepared to cooperate fully with any information request that they needed. Unfortunately, this was not the case.

McCone would later testify to the Senate panel investigating the case in the late 1970's, "The policy of the CIA was to give the Warren Commission everything that we had. I personally asked Chief Justice Warren to come to my office and took him down to the vault of our building where our information is microfilmed and stored and showed him the procedures that we were following and the extent to which we were giving him-giving his staff everything that we had, and I think he was quiet satisfied."

Ray Rocca too said that he ordered his section to fully cooperate with the Commission. Rocca said that Helms told him to pass along all material in the possession of the CI R&A staff to the Warren panel. Rocca said that Helms' orders were followed to the letter by the CIA.

But when the Senators investigating the Kennedy assassination in the 1970s' quizzed Helms about his relationship with the Warren Commission, they got a different view than that of the historical record.

Helms testified that the CIA was cooperating as much as possible with the WC but at a certain point, collaboration had to be held in check. According to Helms, "An inquiry would come over. We would attempt to respond to it. But these inquiries came in individual bits and pieces or as individual items... Each individual item that came along we took care of as best we could."

According to Helms, the CIA provided the WC only on requests for specific information.

Staff Counsel. In summary, is it your position that the Agency gave the Warren Commission information only in response to specific requests by the Warren Commission?

Mr. Helms. That is correct. I want to modify that by saying that memory is fallible. There may have been times or circumstances under which something different might have occurred, but my recollection is that we were attempting to be responsive and supportive to the FBI and the Warren Commission. When they asked for something we gave it to them. As far as our volunteering information is concerned, I have no recollection of whether we volunteered it or not.

According to the Senate Report on the Helms-WC connection, they would say, "Helms' characterization of fulfilling the Warren Commission requests on a case-by-case basis rather than uniformly volunteering relevant information to the Warren Commission stands in direct opposition to Rankin's perception of the CIA's investigative responsibility." Rankin was asked by staff counsel whether he was under the impression that the Agency's responsibility was simply to respond to questions addressed it by the Warren Commission. In response, Rankin testified:

"Not at all and if anybody had told me that I would have insisted that the Commission communicate with the President and get a different arrangement because we might not ask the right questions and then would not have the information and that would be absurd."

Oswald, Cuba and Russia

While the WC staff and the CIA bickered over what materials they would be provided with, the so-called second phase of the CIA's investigation of the assassination took shape.

The two areas in which the CIA looked into were Oswald's trip to Russia, any possible Soviet intelligence involvement with him, and the possible Cuban connection to the president's death. The man given primary responsibility for this study was Raymond Rocca, the chief of research and analysis for the CIA's Counterintelligence Staff. As head of R&A, Rocca worked closely with James Angleton, who was in charge of the mole hunting unit of the CIA, the CI branch. It would be later learned that the CI branch had a huge file on the "defector," Lee Harvey Oswald, and the Oswald paper trail that was later to be unearthed via the JFK Records Act, lead directly to Angleton's office.

Rocca was suspicious of Oswald's two-year stint in the Soviet Union saying of Oswald's time there, "...because the people he (Oswald) was in touch with in Mexico had traces, prior traces, as KGB people. They were under consular cover and obviously could have been doing and were undoubtedly doing a consular job in those earlier contacts."

All three men, Helms, Rocca and Angleton were all concerned about possible Cuban involvement with Oswald in the assassination. But Helms said years later that it was virtually impossible to develop factual leads concerning this aspect of the case. In light of the CIA-Mafia assassination plots against Castro, and the CIA' secret finding and cooperation of various anti-Castro Cuban exile groups in the United States, i.e., Alpha 66, etc., this explanation rings hollow.

By late December 1963, early January 1964, Angleton's CI staff was given responsibility in assisting the Warren Commission in its investigation. Rocca's team coordinated all cable traffic concerning the assassination, studied it, and passed it on to the WC. Even though Rocca's R& A staff did most of the paper work, it was still Richard Helms who called the shots and Rocca had to divert to Helms if there were any major questions or problems that needed to be answered. As an example of Rocca's lack of power, he did not have any access to CIA discussions concerning the Soviet defector, Yuri Nosenko whose sudden flight to the west caused a firestorm of controversy inside US intelligence (more about Nosenko later). Another area in which Rocca was kept in the dark concerned the CIA's secret mail interception program called HT-Lingual. This was a clandestine mail opening project carried out by the CIA, targeting a small group of American citizens including Lee Harvey Oswald. The CIA would read the mail coming and going from this select group, gleam its information, and send the letters back to their original destination.

One of the most vital areas in which the CIA failed to come clean with the WC was the ongoing secret CIA-Mafia plots to kill Fidel Castro of Cuba. Richard Helms and Allan Dulles, one of the WC's members, knew of the plots to kill the "beard." But they successfully kept this knowledge from the full WC, including John McCone, the DCI at the time of the Kennedy murder until August 1963. Others not familiar with the Castro plots were Ray Rocca and "John Scelso."

The following exchange between Helms and the WC Staff Counsel regarding the Castro plots is most revealing:

Staff Counsel: Mr. Helms, I take it from your testimony that your position is that the anti-Castro plots, in fact, were relevant to the Warren Commission's work; and in light of that, the Committee would like to be informed as to why the Warren Commission was not told by you of the anti-Castro plots.

Mr. Helms: I have never been asked to testify before the Warren Commission about our operations.

Staff Counsel: If the Warren Commission did not know of the operation, it certainly was not in a position to ask you about it. Is that not true?

Mr. Helms: Yes, but how do you know they did not know about it? How do you know Mr. Dulles had not told them? How was I to know that? And besides, I was not the Director of the Agency and in the CIA, you did not go traipsing around to the Warren Commission or to Congressional Committees or to anyplace else without the Director's permission.

Staff Counsel: Did you ever discuss with the Director whether the Warren Commission should be informed of the anti-Castro assassination plots?

Mr. Helms: I did not, as far as I can recall.

DCI McCone said that he learned of the anti-Castro plots in August 1963, over two years after he took over as head of the CIA. McCone immediately ordered a stop to the plot but as history shows, his directive was ignored. When asked whether or not the CIA desired to hold back information on the anti-Castro plots to avoid embarrassing the agency, he said, "I cannot answer that since they (CIA employees knowledgeable of the continuance of the plots) withheld the information from me. I cannot answer that question. I have never been satisfied as to why they withheld the information from me."

When the anti-Castro plots were revealed in the 1970s Rocca said that had he known about them at the time, he would have explored the possibility that Castro might have retaliated against President Kennedy in a more thorough fashion. (This line of information concerning the Castro plots was first offered by mobster Johnny Rosseli and will be explored later on).

One area in which the WC took strong exception to the CIA's cooperation was in relation to the agency's protection of sensitive sources and methods. One of the responsibilities of the DCI is to protect its methods of gathering information and protecting its sources and methods as to how this is done. As the WC's study of the assassination got under way, Counsel Rankin raised hackles about the lack of the quality of information being supplied to it by the CIA. Two of the areas of most concern by the WC were the following: – initially not providing the Commission with original source materials pertaining to Oswald's trip to Mexico – the agency's reluctance to reveal the origin of a photograph of an unidentified man who had mistakenly been linked to Oswald.

The first major report that went to the WC that reflected this lack of sensitive source material was a CIA study dated January

31, 1964, regarding Oswald's trip to Mexico. Most of the information in the report was based on top-secret sources and methods and were subsequently purged from the account.

The agency's policy of limiting what information regarding sources and methods to be made available to the WC says in a December 20, 1963 cable, "Our present plan is passing information to the Warren Commission is to eliminate mention of (sensitive sources and methods) in order to protect continuing ops. Will rely instead on statements of Silvia Duran and on contacts of Soviet consular file which Soviets gave State Department."

The CIA refused to provide to the WC, its sources and methods on Oswald's trip to Mexico City but, in order to get some written report to them, provided them with a narrative minus this vital information. On February 10, 1964, J. Lee Rankin sent a letter to the CIA asking them if Oswald was in direct communication with anyone at the Soviet Embassy in Mexico City based on any sensitive sources. The agency failed to give Rankin a satisfactory answer. Later, Ray Rocca would state that in the January-February 1964, time frame, several representatives from the WC were shown some information gleamed from these sensitive sources and methods at CIA headquarters. But Rocca insisted that he personally did not make this material available to the staff.

On February 10, 1964, the CIA sent a letter to Rankin saying that Oswald had contacted the Soviet consulate and was interviewed by someone there. But the letter did not reveal the sources of this information.

Almost immediately after the assassination, the CIA began to collect a large amount of data on Oswald's trip to Mexico and other aspects of the president's death from various sources, including overt and covert, i.e., sensitive sources and methods. WC members most concerned in obtaining this information were Slawson, Coleman and Willens, and it wasn't until April 9, 1964, that these three men met with a representative of the CIA who provided them with some of this material. But little by little the WC staffers were able to piece together part of the story of Oswald's meetings with workers at the Soviet embassy.

"Nevertheless, by March 12, 1964, the record indicates that the Warren Commission had at least become aware of the CIA (sensitive operations) that had generated information concerning Oswald. Slawson's memorandum of March 12 reveals that the Warren Commission had learned that the CIA possessed information concerning conversations between the Cuban Ambassador to Mexico, Hernandez Armas, and Cuban President Dorticos. The Dorticos-Armas conversations, requested by the Warren Commission representatives at a March 12 meeting with CIA officials, including Richard Helms, concerned Silvia Duran's arrest and interrogation by the Mexican Federal Police. Helms responded to the Commission's request for access that he would attempt to arrange for the Warren Commission's representatives to review this material."

To show just how little cooperation the WC staffers received as far as sensitive sources and methods is concerned, revolves around the WC's investigation of Oswald's trip to Mexico City. Slawson wrote that the their conclusions about this aspect of Oswald's pre-assassination life were based on reports from the Mexican Federal Police summaries of interrogations with Silvia Duran, her brother, Ruben, and her husband, Horacio.

Silvia Duran was a secretary to the Cuban consul in Mexico City at the time that Oswald (or the impostor) was there. Duran processed a visa request by Oswald, or someone using his name. The newly declassified Lopez Report on Oswald in Mexico City, hints of a broader, more secretive relationship between Oswald and Duran-sexual in nature.

As in other areas of its investigation, the WC got precious little sensitive information from CIA covert means on Duran and her relationship with Oswald (if any).

WC Staffers Coleman and Slawson summed up their thinking on getting access to CIA materials concerning Oswald's Mexico City in a revealing April 3, 1964 cable:

"The most probable final result of the entire investigation of Oswald's activities in Mexico is a conclusion that he went there for the purpose of trying to reach Cuba and that no bribes, conspiracies, etc. took place."

Both Coleman and Slawson's investigation of a foreign conspiracy in the president's death were hampered on a continuing basis by the lack of vital, sensitive intelligence by the CIA, especially as it related to Oswald's Mexico City trip.

In order to placate Coleman and Slawson, on April 8, 1964, both men flew down to Mexico City to meet with representatives of the State Department, FBI, CIA and the Government of Mexico. When they got down to business, a CIA agent finally gave them some of the raw materials gathered by US intelligence concerning Oswald's journey to the Mexican capital. What they learned was that immediately after the assassination agency officers in Mexico City had complete files on Oswald, Duran and anyone else that had any contact with Oswald during his one week stay. Also, said the CIA man, all known Cuban and Russian intelligence agents were immediately put under close surveillance.

The WC's final thought on how it was treated concerning the Mexican aspect of the investigation is summed up as follows:

"The (CIA representative's) narrative plus the material we were shown disclosed immediately how incorrect our previous information had been on Oswald's contacts with the Soviet and Mexican embassies. Apparently the distortions and omissions to which our information had been subjected had entered some place in Washington because the CIA information that we were shown by the CIA representative was unambiguous on almost all the crucial points. We had previously planned to show the CIA representative Slawson's reconstruction of Oswald's probable activities at the embassies to get the CIA's representative's opinion, but once we saw how badly distorted our information was we realized that this would be useless..."

The Unidentified Man Dilemma

Another area in which the Warren Commission had its informational problems with the CIA concerned a photograph of an "identified man" in Mexico City whom the agency mistakenly took for the real Lee Harvey Oswald. This man, whose picture has been known and seen by researchers for years, is still a secret (maybe not to the CIA) and what, if any, his relationship to Oswald and the assassination, is still in doubt.

The origins of this unidentified man photograph goes back to November 23, 1963, when the FBI, after getting it from the CIA, showed it to Marguerite Oswald, Lee Oswald's mother. This photograph was said to be the real Lee Harvey Oswald but it clearly is not. This man was beefy, with broad shoulders, a receding hairline and older than the 24 year old Oswald. When she testified before the Warren Commission on February 10, 1964, Mrs. Oswald said that the man in the photograph was Jack Ruby.

When the unidentified man photograph became known to the Warren Commission, they began immediate steps to ascertain who the man was and how the CIA had obtained it. On February 12, 1964, Lee Rankin wrote to Thomas Karramesiness, the assistant deputy director for plans (DDP) asking for the identity of the man and the circumstances on how the CIA came into possession of it. On the same day he also sent a letter to DCI McCone requesting CIA materials that the agency had sent to the Secret Service but not the Warren Commission concerning the unidentified man photo.

John Scelso, the CIA officer who did a study on the assassination said that the CIA did not inform the Warren Commission that it had this photo because it concerned a covert intelligence mission in Mexico City that it wanted to keep secret. Soon, what actions the CIA should take in informing the Warren Commissioners about this problem spread to the top of the covert action branch (CI). On March 5, 1964, Ray Rocca wrote an internal memorandum to Richard Helms stating, "We have a problem here for your determination." The "problem" was what to do about a photo of a man whom the CIA said was the presidential assassin, but was clearly not. If, as many people suspect, this man was part of some covert operation in Mexico at the time of the Oswald visit, was he in fact a part of the assassination conspiracy? Was he in fact linked in some way with Oswald in a possible framing of the ex-Marine?

During the time of the cold war, Mexico City was one of the hot spots of international espionage. Located between the United States and Latin and South America, it was a vital listening post for spies of both the NATO and Warsaw Pact blocks. In his book, *Confessions of a Spy, The Real Story of Aldrich Ames,* author Pete Earley gives a vivid description of how the spy game was played in Mexico City. During the 1980s, says Earley, the US Defense Intelligence Agency (DIA) began flooding the Soviet embassy with dozens of double agents, i.e., volunteer spies, to gleam any information that they could get. At that time, the US had over one hundred double agent programs going on a worldwide basis with a majority of them taking place in Mexico City.

"...But the main benefit was that it helped US intelligence identify which Soviets in the embassy (Russian) were KGB or GRU officers, and what procedures the Soviets used when someone volunteered. The constant turnover in volunteers also wasted the Soviets' resources and kept them confused."[4]

Was this "unidentified man" a part of a CIA covert operation that pre-dated the DIA double agent program, twenty years later? It is apparent that this man was not there just for the sights. He was part of some sort of operation, probably in the employ of one of the US intelligence agencies. But which one? This is one area in which the Assassinations Review Board must look into before it goes out of business (maybe we'll be lucky and the "unidentified man" or someone who knows him, will come forward?

4 Confessions of a Spy: The Real Story of Aldrich Ames. Pete Earley. Pg. 92.

Rocca stated in his memo, James Angleton's desire not to respond directly to the WC's request for information on the photo... "Unless you feel otherwise, Jim would prefer to wait out the Commission on the matter covered by paragraph 2 (letter to McCone). If they come back on this subject he feels that you, or someone from here, should be prepared to show the Commission the material rather than pass it to them in copy... We have either passed the material in substance to the Commission in response to earlier levies or the items refer to aborted leads, for example, the famous six photographs, which are not of Oswald." (emphasis mine). From this passage it is obvious that the CIA knew that the man in the photo was not Lee Harvey Oswald. But did they know who he really was?

If the CIA knew that the mystery man was not Lee Harvey Oswald, so did the Warren Commission and they took the CIA to task over it. In late March 1964, William Coleman wrote a memo on this subject:

"As you know, we are still trying to get an explanation of the photograph which the FBI showed to Marguerite Oswald soon after the assassination. I hope that... memorandum of March 24, 1964, (CD 63 1) sent Mr. Rankin by the CIA is not the answer which the CIA intends to give us as to this inquiry."

The next day, WC Staffer Samuel Stern made a trip to CIA headquarters to view the materials in the Oswald file. Ray Rocca showed Stern the file that the agency had on Oswald, which contained materials already, furnished to the Commission. Among the documents that Stem reviewed were, a) cable reports from the CIA dated November 22 and 23, 1963, of a man who visited the Cuban and Soviet Embassies during October-November 1963 (it should be noted that Oswald was not in Mexico City in November, 1963. So who were these cables referring to?) and b) reports on these cables given to the Secret Service on November 23.

Also seen by Stern were agency cables concerning Oswald's contact with employees of the Soviet embassy and detailed background information on Oswald. Before leaving, Rocca give Stern a computer printout from the CIA's electronic database on references to President Kennedy's assassin. Later, Stern would comment that he had been provided with all relevant materials on Lee Oswald by the CIA, either in full or paraphrased text.

It seems obvious that before Stern's trip to CIA headquarters, there was some doubt on behalf of the certain members of the commission regarding who the mystery man was. But after meeting with Rocca and his colleagues, and having been provided with primary source documents by the CIA on Oswald and the mystery man, their minds had been changed.

What Stern and the rest of the Warren Commission did not know in relation to the investigation of the CIA's sensitive sources and methods concerning the mystery man, was that the CIA had three sources of covert intelligence coming from the Soviet Embassy; a human mole inside the building, hidden microphones, and surveillance cameras outside the building, taking pictures of everyone who entered an left. The only time that the cameras were not working was when the real Oswald (it he was there at all) paid a visit.

The absence of a CIA photograph of the real Oswald is striking. If they had a picture of the Oswald arrested after the assassination, and produced it for the world to see, then their case against Oswald as a Communist agent, or left wing nut making a trip to Mexico before the assassination for some sinister reason, would play right into their hands. On the other hand, if they did not have a picture of the real Oswald, or happened to lose it at a convenient time, than there is no concrete proof that the real Oswald was in Mexico City, (and if he was there, his picture was purposely not taken), than it seems clear that Oswald was either being framed, or he was there on some other matter of which we don't know about.

Years later, the late CIA Director, William Colby would comment on the unidentified man, "To this day we don't know who he is."

The Luisa Calderon Statement

Another area of contention between the CIA and the WC was a statement made by Luisa Calderon Carralero, a Cuban employee of the Cuban Embassy in Mexico City at the time of President Kennedy's death. The CIA received information from a "reliable source" that Luisa Calderon, who was believed to be a possible agent of the Cuban intelligence service, DGI, had made possible incriminating statements concerning the assassination of the president before the event took place. The CIA report on Calderon says that when she was asked if she had heard the news of the assassination, she replied to the effect that, "yes, of course, I knew almost before Kennedy." She also reported that her colleagues in the Cuban embassy learned about the assassination, "a little while ago."

While these statements in and of itself, bear little meaning in the overall scheme of the JFK assassination, it does have some relevance when one considers the possibility by some people in the CIA, the FBI, and other organs of US intelligence, that Oswald was possibly involved with the Cubans in the Kennedy murder.

When Calderon's supposed remarks hit the fan at CIA headquarters shortly after the assassination, Ray Rocca wrote a memo stating that this was, "Latin hyperbole! Boastful ex post facto suggestion of foreknowledge. This is the only item in the (sensitive operation) coverage of the Cubans and Soviets after the assassination that contains the suggestion of foreknowledge or expectation."

As the Calderon account made its way through the CIA, they boys at Langley hq, tossed around what to do with it and passed it along to the warren Commission to consider its validity.

The first official account of Calderon's remarks from the US government's standpoint came on November 27, 1963, four days after the assassination, in a cable sent by Ambassador Thomas Mann to the State Department. Mann wrote... "Washington should urgently consider feasibility of requesting Mexican authorities to arrest for interrogation; Eusebio Azcue, Luisa Calderon, and Alfredo Mirabal. The two men are Cuban national and Cuban consular officers. Luisa Calderon is a secretary in the Cuban Consulate here."

The unofficial reason for this request was to forestall a return trip to Cuba by the above-mentioned people in order to escape interrogation by either Mexican or American officials in the Kennedy assassination investigation. They may have been right concerning Calderon who made reservations to go back to Cuba via Cubana Airlines on December 11, 1963.

Calderon, Azcue and Mirabal were not arrested in the Oswald investigation by local police authorities. But Silva Duran, a name that would come to play a large part in the entire Mexico City angle of the assassination, and any Oswald part in it, was arrested and questioned repeatedly by Mexican police on two different occasions.

Calderon's relationship with Duran when they both worked at the Cuban Embassy were given to the Warren Commission by the CIA on February 21, 1964, over two months after Calderon had returned to Cuba.

If the Luisa Calderon confession was bizarre enough, events from a CIA secret source would only tend to complicate the matter even more. In May 1964, the CIA received information from one of its sensitive and reliable sources, code named "A-1," a defector, who once worked for the DGI, the Cuban intelligence service. "A-1's" debriefing was conducted by Joseph Langosch, the Chief of Counterintelligence for the Special Affairs Staff (SAS) in Jim Angleton's department. In his report to Angleton, Langosch said that A-1 said that he had no direct knowledge of Lee Harvey Oswald or his activities in Mexico City, However, he did say that he had information about the assassination coming from various members of the DGI. Among the most important information from A-1 was the following concerning Oswald and his possible association with the Cuban's; "Prior to October, 1963,

Oswald visited the Cuban Embassy in Mexico City on two or three occasions. Before, during, and after these visits, Oswald was in contact with the DGI, specifically with Luisa Calderon, Manuel Vega Perez, and Rogelio Rodriquez Lopez."

Langosch said that he wasn't sure what, if any relationship Luisa Calderon had with the DGI. A-1 was later to tell Langosch concerning Oswald and the DGI, "Luisa Calderon, since she returned to Cuba has been paid a regular salary by the DGI even though she has not performed any services..."

A-1 later told Langosch more information on Calderon, and the CIA officer described what he said in part, in the following May 8, 1964, report:

"I thought that Luisa Calderon might have had contact with Oswald because I learned about 17 March, 1964, shortly before I made a trip to Mexico, that she had been involved with an American in Mexico. The information to which I refer was told to me by a DGI case officer...I had commented to him that it seemed strange that Luisa Calderon was receiving a salary from the DGI although she apparently did not do any work for the Service. The case officer told me that hers was a peculiar case and that he himself believed that she had been recruited in Mexico by the CIA although Manuel Pineiro, the head of the DGI, did not agree. As I recall, the case officer had investigated Luisa Calderon. This was because, during the time she was in Mexico, the DGI, had intercepted a letter to her by an American who signed his name OWER (phonetic) or something similar...I do not know if this could have been Oswald."

Clearly, A-1's allegation about a possible Oswald connection with Luisa Calderon fit the category of a "sensitive source and method" which the agency was reluctant to discuss in public. On May 11, 1964, Rocca wrote the following memo to Helms regarding A-1's news:

"The DDP in person or via a designee, preferably the former, discuss the A-1 situation on a very restricted basis with Mr. Rankin at his earliest convenience either at the Agency or at the

Commission headquarters. Until this takes place, is not desirable to put anything in writing."

On May 15, Helms wrote a memo to Rankin telling him of A-1's details of Manuel Vega Perez and Rogelio Rodriguezs' association with the DGI but not with Luisa Calderon. Why? If, as many high ranking officers in Angleton's CI branch believed that Oswald was associated with a foreign power, i.e., the Cubans or the Soviet's, a foreign tie to the assassination could be ascertained. If that was proven to be the case, then the lone assassin theory postulated by J. Edgar Hoover would be debunked, and a conspiracy in the killing of the president would be a reality. And that could not be tolerated, given the many peculiarities to the Oswald case.

In June, a member of Rocca's Counterintelligence Staff, gave Howard Willens of the Warren Commission access to the questions used in interrogation of A-1. But only one mention of Luisa Claderon was found in these papers. "The precise relationship of Luisa Calderon to the DGI is not clear. She spent about six months in Mexico from which she returned to Cuba in early 1964." Willens was not supplied any of the detailed reports supplied to the CI branch by A-1 concerning Calderon, her possible relationship with Cuban intelligence and possibly, with Oswald.

When the Senate investigated the Kennedy assassination in the 1970's, they said of the CIA-Warren Commission relationship regarding the Calderon case:

"The evidence indicates that the CIA did not provide a report of Calderon's conversation of November 22 to the Warren Commission. Consequently, even though the Warren Commission was aware that Calderon reportedly had connections to intelligence work, as did other Cuban Embassy officers, the vital link between her background and her comments was never established for the Warren Commission by the CIA. The agency's omission in this regard may have foreclosed the Commission's actively pursuing a lead of great significance."

The House Select Committee on Assassinations, in their 1977

study on the Kennedy assassination, found the Calderon incident most disturbing vis-a-vi the CIA and posed more questions to the agency. They asked the CIA the following questions concerning the Calderon case.

1) "Was the Warren Commission or any Warren Commission staff member ever given access to the raw data of Calderon's conversation dated November 22, 1963?"

2) "Was the Warren Commission or any member of the Warren Commission staff ever informed orally or in writing of the substance of the above referenced conversation of November 22, 1963? If so, please indicate and in what form this information was provided, and which CIA official provided it."

The CIA responded thus:

"Although the (Mexican unit) considered the conversation of sufficient possible interest to send a copy to headquarters, the latter apparently did nothing with it, for there appears to be no record in the Oswald file of such action as may have been taken. A review of those Warren Commission documents containing information provided by the agency and still bearing a Secret or Top Secret classification does not reveal whether the conversation was given or shown to the Commission."

In the end, the mystery of Luisa Calderon's statement about a possible link with the Cuban government and the president's alleged assassin, Lee Oswald, was not clearly determined. What is beyond doubt is that the CIA, for whatever reasons, i.e., an ongoing covert operation in Mexico City possibly using Luisa Calderon, or something else, deliberately withheld certain pertinent information on her from the Warren Commission. They CIA countered by saying that they gave the Warren Commission its information that possibly linked Calderon to the Cuban DGI, and potentially, to their own organization. When the HSCA wrote their report they concluded that Luisa Calderon had no CIA connections.

The HSCA concluded that while the CIA acted in a competent way in its dealings with the Warren Commission's investigation of the Kennedy assassination, there were indeed a number of deficiencies that had a great bearing on the overall case.

The first instance concerned the CIA's failure to inform the Warren Commission of the on-going CIA-Mafia plots to assassinate Fidel Castro. The second dealt with the CIA's highly covert means of obtaining secret sources and methods, which they held as tightly as a mother to a newborn baby. The third category of dispute was the agency's failure to come clean with the WC concerning Luisa Calderon's allegations.

Chapter 3

The Scelso Document

As mentioned in the last chapter, when the CIA began its probe into the assassination of the President, the man asked to conduct the study was a CIA officer named "John Scelso." Scelso is not his real name and the true identity of the man is still unknown (It was revealed many years later that this real name was John Whitten). According to the Assassinations Records Review Board, a federally mandated investigative body that is currently responsible for the release to the National Archives of all government held documents on the Kennedy assassination, there is much interest in who John Scelso really is. According to the ARRB's Fiscal Year 1996 Report on its work in releasing Kennedy assassination documents, "The Review Board voted to release the individual's name in 188 "Scelso" documents on either May 1, 2001, or three months after the death of the individual whose name is postponed, whichever occurs first. The Review Board is very much aware of the research community's interest in knowing the identity of the person in the records under the pseudonym of "John Scelso." The Review Board received extensive information about the true identity of Scelso. Because of issues related to his identity, the Review Board decided that Scelso should be protected for five years, after which his true name will be revealed."[5]

5 Assassination Records Review Board. Fiscal Year 1996 Report. Pages 13-14.

This chapter will analyze and report on the Scelso Document that was released by the National Archives earlier this year. The reader will find it most revealing and interesting, especially concerning Mr. Scelso's comments on the assassination, as well as his impressions of certain members of the intelligence community who played a vital role in the assassination investigation.

John Scelso worked for the CIA for twenty-three years as an officer in the clandestine operations organization. When he retired from the agency he was on the foreign intelligence staff in charge of the operations branch responsible for reviewing all of the foreign intelligence and counter-intelligence operations of the CIA and of formulating rules for such operations. He also was a member of a panel, which looked into the programs that the CIA ran on a worldwide basis.

At the time of President Kennedy's death, Mr. Scelso was chief of a branch responsible for operations in Mexico and Central America, including Panama. His branch was called WH-3, or Western Hemisphere 3.

This area is most important in the investigation of the Kennedy assassination, as Lee Harvey Oswald spent a short, yet eventful period of time in Mexico City in late September, early October 1963.

Mr. Scelso's earliest knowledge of the assassination came by reading hundreds of papers and summaries of reports generated by the CIA on their investigation of the president's death, including the book Legend. *"The Secret World of Lee Harvey Oswald,"* by Edward Jay Epstein. Scelso stated that he did not know that there had ever been any involvement between the domestic branch of the CIA (which was then called the Office of Operations) and their offices in the US. When asked by his interviewer if he knew that a CIA officer named J. Walton Moore, who was a friend of George de Mohrenschieldt, another friend of Lee Harvey Oswald in Dallas, had been in touch with Oswald in the months prior to the assassination, he said he wasn't informed by his superiors in the agency.

Mr. Goldsmith: Does that surprise you?

Mr. Scelso: Yes, because that should have shown up in the traces and it was, of course, a vital factor in the investigation.

Mr. Goldsmith: When I say does that surprise you, does the fact that no officer from the domestic contacts division, or domestic contacts service, ever contacted Oswald? Does the fact of the absence of such a contact surprise you?

Mr. Scelso: No, it would not have surprised me, because Oswald was a security suspect and was a proper subject for handling by the Office of Naval Intelligence and the Federal Bureau of Investigation not with the CIA.[6]

Along these same lines, Scelso also said that he thought it was odd that the CIA did not interview Oswald after his return to the United States due to the fact that he worked in the Minsk Radio Factory while living in the Soviet Union.

In his early testimony by the Senate Committee Mr. Scelso gives the first hint (and a name) of a CIA officer from the Domestic Contacts Service who was in Moscow at the same time as Lee Oswald and may have been in on an interview with him. The CIA officer whom Scelso is talking about is a man named Hugh Montgomery. Scelso had a conversation with Montgomery about two months after the assassination in which Montgomery told Scelso that he might have been present in Moscow when the US Counsel was interviewing Oswald before his return to the US. But, said Montgomery, he made no comments to Scelso about the Oswald case.

When questioned about the Oswald file at the CIA, Mr. Scelso's remarks were more than interesting. He told how the CIA did not have a substantial file on Oswald (not true) before the assassination (he called it a "scan file") made up mostly of

6 Scelso Report Pg. 1-8 & 1-9. All future references to this report will be known as Scelso.

information given to the agency by the Navy, the Marine Corps, and information provided by the agency from Mexico City. He said that he had previously dealt with many other defector cases in the past and that the Oswald incident was just "a typical defection case."

During his tenure at CIA, Scelso was the first polygraph operator in the agency and had polygraphed hundreds of people who were suspected as being security suspects. He had also been a prisoner of war interrogator in World War II and had interrogated thousands of German prisoners. After the birth of the CIA, he had been the counterespionage officer for the European Division in the 1950's and had dealt with dozens of defection cases.

"So, Oswald just seemed to me to be a small potatoes defector."

Whether or not Oswald was a "small potatoes defector" as relayed by Scelso, he was a man who had considerable influence within the CIA. As Chief of the Division, WH-3, Scelso had control of the Mexico City Station (CIA), at that time. He first became Chief of the Mexico desk in 1962, and later added on branches, which included Mexico and several other countries. At the time of the assassination, Winston Scott was the Chief of Station in Mexico City, serving directly under Scelso.

Mr. Scelso: Winn Scott was, at that time – probably in view of my later experience surveying all of the stations in the world, as good a Station Chief as we had, and you could fairly say that he had the best station in the world.

Mr. Goldsmith: Why would you say that he had the best in the world?

Mr. Scelso: Because of the breadth and depth of their operations, both in the counter-intelligence field and the political action field, and in the espionage field.[7]

---

7 Scelso. Pg. 1-18

Mr. Scelso also had some very interesting comments to make concerning another man whose name is prominently mentioned as possibly playing a role in the events leading up to the president's death; David Phillips.

According to Scelso, who was related to Phillips through marriage, Phillips was "one of the most brilliant, capable officers that I have ever known, and nothing has happened since then that has changed by judgment."

When asked if it were possible that David Phillips ever sent out disinformation concerning the JFK assassination, Mr. Scelso stated:

"No, but I can conceive that it might have happened in the Mexico station. Perhaps they did, in their propaganda efforts, which were going full-blast all the time, put in newspaper articles and so on to discredit somebody, some foreign power, in connection with the operation. I do not believe that it was ever a policy to do so, but they were pretty much independent in formulating their propaganda."[8]

What Scelso failed to say, or maybe he wasn't aware of the fact, that many researchers believed that his relative, Mr. Phillips, may have been the mysterious CIA officer called "Maurice Bishop" Bishop, it is noted, is said to have been Lee Harvey Oswald's case officer and met him in Dallas a few months prior to the assassination.

According to Scelso, the CIA first learned of Lee Oswald on the day of the assassination when his name was broadcast on the television and radio, and "an officer of my branch came running in and said, with the telegrams on Lee Harvey Oswald which we had sent, those telegrams which had gone out some weeks before the assassination."

8 Scelso. Pg. 1-21 & 1-22

Mr. Goldsmith: When the name Oswald first came to your attention after the assassination, what action, if any, did you take?

Mr. Scelso: When it came in, I was not sitting in my office. I was up in the Division front offices. I happened to be up there on another matter when the thing came in over the radio and within minutes, people from my office were up there with the cables. And I do not know exactly what we did, but within minutes we had notified the Division Chief and the DDP that is, the DDO.

Mr. Goldsmith: How soon after the assassination did this officer come on with the Oswald cables?

Mr. Scelso: About a half hour after the assassination or fifteen minutes later, then we were all listening to this. I do not know how long after the actual shooting it was that Oswald's name became known, perhaps an hour, hour and a half. Within minutes after that, they were out with the cables in their hands.[9]

According to Scelso, a woman CIA officer by the name of Charlotte Bustos, who was the "major domo of the branch," was the one who brought in the original CIA cables on Oswald that had been collected prior to November 22, 1963. Bustos managed all records, and handled all of the cables from Mexico that dealt with security suspects, etc.

Scelso then turned his attention to the famous "mystery man" photograph that the CIA took in Mexico City that proved not to have been Oswald. He told his interviewer that the CIA had not received this photograph prior to the assassination, and when it was finally received, he did not know if the picture was the real Lee Harvey Oswald. While it seems that Scelso was kept out of the loop of information concerning whom the mystery man was he did say that he was certain that the CIA surveillance team did not photograph everyone who entered and exited the Soviet

---

9 Scelso. Pg. 1-30 & 1-31

Embassy. He said that the case officers whom he personally spoke to regarding the mystery man photo were Winn Scott and David Phillips but cannot recall if Phillips was physically in Mexico City at the time of the assassination. The only clue to this man's identity, according to Scelso, was that the CIA 'conjectured that it (he) was a Mexican seaman.

Scelso further stated that there was a fair amount of intelligence sharing cooperation between the CIA and the FBI and other US intelligence agencies in Mexico City in the months preceding President Kennedy's death. The CIA passed on all information to J. Edgar Hoover's G-Men on leads on any American citizen in Mexico City who appeared around the Soviet and Cuban Embassies, and anybody who was possibly trying to defect. A similar arrangement was formalized with military intelligence.

When one reads the Scelso interview, the person is struck by just how frustrating a job he had to contend with. While he was given this sensitive job of reviewing the Oswald case, he wasn't privy to some of the most vital information concerning Oswald; his stay in the Soviet Union.

Mr. Goldsmith: The fact of Oswald's appearance at the Soviet Embassy in Moscow would not have been considered an insignificant matter?

Mr. Scelso: No. But, as I say, what went on in the Soviet Union and what the CIA officers in the Soviet Union did, is something that completely escaped my knowledge and scope and view at that time... Even when I was in my later positions where I saw everything in the world, I did not see that.

As far as Oswald contacting the Soviet and Cuban embassies was concerned, Scelso said that action sent red flags flying at CIA.

Mr. Scelso: The fact that he was an American contacting the Cubans and the Russians, especially in the context of which they knew it, because they had details of the telephone conversations, signaling this to them, that this was a very important case.

Mr. Goldsmith: Americans frequently contacting either the Soviet or Cuban Embassy?

Mr. Scelso: I do not know about the Cuban Embassy. Not many cases like – of course they were. On the Soviet Embassy, a significant number of American military people involved in sensitive, highly-classified military people involved in sensitive, military activities in the southwestern United States attempted to defect to the Russians in order to pass information to them and were detected by our surveillance means and were apprehended. That happened before.[10]

Scelso revealed that once the CIA had learned of Oswald's first contact with both the Cuban and Soviet Embassies then a higher significance was placed on his contact with them. He further explained why all of the information gathered by the Mexico City Station on Oswald was not sent to Washington:

Mr. Scelso: The telephone center envoy was manned by (Operational Details) an American, or Mexican-American. These people were just inundated with information and apparently did not extract this and transmit it back to Washington. The later contacts with the Cuban Embassy, and so on, which only were divulged after the assassination. It is an enormous problem. Mexico is one of the biggest and most active telephone intercept operations in the whole world and the job of processing this material is just impossible... I think there are about 30 lines being tapped altogether (from both the Soviet and Cuban embassies.)

Why all the material gathered on Oswald was not sent to CIA headquarters can be summed up in the bureaucratic maze that attacks all large companies, be it government or private; "a question of too much material to process and too many important

10 Scelso Report Pg. 150.

priorities. And possibly they would have gotten around to doing it, you see. They have a backlog. They would have gotten around to it."

Besides not being given access to information concerning Oswald's activities in Russia, Mr. Scelso was not informed by the Mexico City Station on any of Oswald's previous contacts with either the Soviet or Cuban Embassies prior to the assassination. When queried if he should have been advised of this activity, he responded in the negative by saying that since Oswald was just trying to get a Cuban visa to go to Cuba in order to get a Russian visa, there was nothing sinister about it and therefore he need not have been informed. He did however; say that all of this information was in the hands of the Mexico City Station within two weeks of Oswald's first contact on October 1.

"It was someplace in the pipeline in the station. You do not know whether the tapes were transcribed, you see. You don't know whether these Mexicans in the intercept stations had even listened to the tapes, let alone transcribed them. They may have just stacked them up – taken them off the recorders and stacked them up?"

While Scelso's opinion of Oswald's activities in Mexico City are not conspiratorial in nature, it is interesting to hear in his own words the significance of what he thought he was doing there:

Mr. Scelso: Certainly, even if J. Edgar Hoover had said, have the man arrested by the Americans and we will send a military plane down and have him put him on it and we will take him back. This was done with military defectors, but I do not think that the agency would have done it. They would not have had a shred of legal right to do it.

Mr. Goldsmith: Another possibility, aside from the fact that he may have been trying to redefect, another possibility was that Oswald, when he returned to the states, was actually a Soviet spy. Another possibility, that he was making contact.

Mr. Scelso: That makes it of interest that is correct. It still would not have warranted his arrest because there was no evidence that he was a Soviet spy, even today.

Mr. Goldsmith: Had the information concerning Oswald's visit to the Cuban embassy in addition to the Soviet one, that Oswald had been requesting a visa, if it had been sent to CIA headquarters, would his case prior to the assassination have been handled in any different manner?

Mr. Scelso: It would have been in the case of dissemination of information about him, but I do not think that any operational action would have been taken to apprehend him or to contact him or to try to force him back to the United States.[11]

At the time of the Kennedy assassination, the CIA had one of the most comprehensive intelligence gathering activities programs actively running in Mexico City. They were "absolutely enormous," according to Scelso. "We were trying to follow the Soviets and all the satellites and the Cubans. At the same time, the main thrust of the station's effort was to attempt to recruit Russians, Cubans and satellite people."

Another twist in the CIA covert espionage game in Mexico City also directly involves Lee Harvey Oswald. Recently discovered documents reveal that a CIA message dated September 16, 1963, informing the FBI that "the agency (CIA) is giving some consideration to countering the activities of the FPCC, Fair Play For Cuba Committee, in foreign countries. Oswald was the lone member of the FPCC in New Orleans during the summer of 1963 and was arrested in a scuffle with Carlos Bringuier, an anti-Castro Cuban. Oswald had previously approached Bringuier offering his services in anti-Castro operations, while he was handing out pro-Castro leaflets only a short time later. It is interesting to note that the day after this CIA memo dealing with a covert

11 Scelso Report. Pg. 1-63 & 1-64.

action against the FPCC, which had a direct Oswald connection, Oswald was applying for a Mexican tourist visa card. Is there any connection?

What is obvious is that the covert action arm of the CIA was very active in tracing developments of the Oswald case in Mexico City and placed much of its top personnel to that task.

Birch O'Neal worked for the CI (counterintelligence) staff and was in charge of the Special Investigation Section, CI/SIG that was reviewing all of the Oswald tapes sent by the Mexico City Station. The Special Investigation Section of the CI was only responsible for one type of work-special investigations. "That was CIA counterintelligence investigations which were so sensitive or of such a general super regional nature that they should be handled by one of the area divisions. And this, in particular, applied to investigations of CIA employees who were suspected for working for foreign intelligence organizations or where mixed up with this, too."[12] Mr. Scelso, inadvertently telling us that Lee Oswald was a CIA agent, and that the CI/SIG was investigating him?

One of the most interesting aspects of the Scelso interview is his impressions and working relationship with the head of the CIA's CI Division, James Angleton. Angleton was one of the most controversial members of the CIA and his legacy is still hotly debated almost twenty years after his death. By the time his long career at the CIA ended in the early 1970's, Angleton would launch a paranoid search for a suspected "mole" hidden deep in the bowels of the CIA. In the end though, no Soviet traitor was ever found (with the exception of Aldrich Ames and later, Harold Nicholson) and by the time he left in disgrace, some top level people at the CIA even thought that Angleton himself was the long buried Soviet mole. Angleton grew up in Idaho, went to Yale University where he distinguished himself as editor of a literary magazine called Furioso, and then attended Harvard Law School.

12 Scelso Report. Pg. 169.

After World War II broke out, Angleton was recruited by the OSS, and started his life one affair with American intelligence. After the war ended, he entered the CIA and quickly befriended the then fledgling security service of the newly created state of Israel. By 1948, Angleton was posted to "Staff C," as the counterintelligence staff was then called. It was in this capacity that he met and befriended Kim Philby, England's top liaison to the CIA, and also, unknown to Angleton and everyone else in US intelligence, Russia's top spy in the US. When two of Philby's counterparts in British intelligence, Guy Burgess and Donald Maclean defected to Moscow on Philby's orders, Angleton still refused to believe that his pal, Philby, was working for the Russians. Working as he did in the "wilderness of mirrors" at the CIA, Angleton became paranoid about the Soviet threat, even dismissing the Sino-Soviet split as a disinformation campaign by the Soviet's and the Chinese to weaken the west. He also distrusted any Soviet defector who came knocking at the CIA's door. Yet, by the early 1960's, Angleton would be up to his neck in "defectors;" he would now have to decide who was bogus and who was real.

The first defector to come knocking at his door was a Soviet KGB officer named Anatoly Golitsyn who came to the west in 1961. He told Angleton of a Soviet "master plan" to penetrate western intelligence and said that over the years many Soviet spies had wormed their way into the heart of the CIA. He even told of more disinformation agents to come in the years ahead. The next "defector" to appear was Yuri Nosenko (didn't Golitsyn say one was coining?) who went over to the west in 1964. But Nosenko came with much more than names and dates of Soviet agents and plans. He said that he was in charge of the file on President Kennedy's alleged assassin, Lee Harvey Oswald, when the young Marine "defected" to the Soviet Union in 1959. According to Nosenko, the KGB wanted nothing to do with Oswald (yet they let him stay in the Soviet Union for over two years, monitored his every move, allowed him to marry a Russian girl, and finally, authorized him to leave with his bride to the US). The Nosenko case and its aftermath sent the CIA into a tizzy, with Angleton seeing Nosenko as a Soviet agent, while others thought that he was a genuine defector. The Nosenko-Golitsyn cases set Angleton off on a decade's long "mole hunt" within the CIA, ruining many reputations of good men along the way. Under President Lyndon Johnson's orders, Angleton began a covert CIA domestic spying campaign, called OPERATION CHAOS in which the agency opened mail of ordinary American citizens. In 1974, the new DCI, William Colby, fired Angleton amid the ever-growing public scandals that rocked the CIA.

Scelso says that in his opinion, Angleton was not an easy person to get along with and ran his CI Branch with an iron fist. Often times during his CIA career, Mr. Scelso said that he was ordered by his superiors, either Richard Helms or Thomas Karamessines to investigate some of the operations that Angleton was running and "this always caused bitter feelings, the most bitter feelings."

Mr. Goldsmith: For what purpose would they ask you to look into Angleton's operations?

Mr. Scelso: Because Helms or Karamessinas suddenly found out about one of Angleton's operations and did not like the looks of it.

Mr. Goldsmith: How would you go about looking into that without Mr. Angleton's finding out about it?

Mr. Scelso: He knew it. They always told him. And then they said, now, you go tell Angleton you are going to do this. I used to go in fingering my insurance policy, notifying my next of kin. This happened many times over the years...

"You see, Angleton immediately went into action to do all of the investigating and Helms called a meeting which Angleton and a lot of others were present and told everybody that I was in charge and that everybody should report everything to me and that no one should have any conversations with anyone about the Kennedy case without my being present, which was violated from the word go by Angleton, who dealt with the Bureau and the Warren Commission and John Foster Dulles himself.

Mr. Goldsmith: Was there communication on a more or less ex parte basis between the CIA and Dulles?

Mr. Scelso: Yes, between Angleton and Dulles.

Mr. Goldsmith: How do you know that?

Mr. Scelso: From Angleton.

Mr. Goldsmith:. He told you that?

Mr. Scelso: Yes, on one or two occasions I went to talk to him about the case, or he called me in. It was a very strange situation.

Mr. Goldsmith: In what way?

Mr. Scelso: Well, Angleton ignored Helms' orders that no one was to discuss the case with anyone without my being present. He ignored that. I tried to get Helms to make him obey and Helms said, you go tell him.

Mr. Goldsmith: Why was not Angleton reprimanded, or even dismissed for failing to obey that order?

Mr. Scelso: None of the senior officials at the agency were ever able to cope with him. He had enormously influential contacts with J. Edgar Hoover. He had his own direct ties to the Director at various times he was – I believe he and his staff were intimately tied in with the House Subversive Affairs, or whatever it is, Committee. And Angleton was a very formidable person to deal with.

Mr. Goldsmith: Do you know of any improper action by Angleton?

Mr. Scelso: No, except that he violated Helms' instructions. In view of the fact that he got away with it, he probably figured it was condoned.[13]

As Chief of Division, Mr. Scelso had overall responsibility of all CIA activity that concerned Mexico and other parts of the Caribbean and Latin America. As part of his job he was fully aware of the CIA's covert plans to wage guerilla warfare against Cuba and of the agency's plans to topple Castro called Operation Mongoose. In his testimony, Mr. Scelso reveals bow his branch monitored the activities of not only the CIA's Western Hemisphere Branch in its anti-Castro activities, but also watched the activities of other nation's secret services, especially that of Nicaragua.

One of the United States' most trusted "allies" in the Caribbean was that of the dictatorship of President Samoza of Nicaragua. The Kennedy administration knew of Samoza's brutal regime, as it concerned the subjugation of his own people, and of his links to organized crime in the United States. But it was the period of the cold war and the US had to take whatever allies it could in order to battle Russian influence in the Caribbean and South America; and Samoza fit Uncle Sam's recipe just right. Nicaragua served as one of the jumping off points in the US-CIA sponsored Bay of Pigs invasion of Cuba in April 1961 and for that reason alone, the CIA would be forever grateful.

Scelso says that the CIA did not attempt to directly influence Nicaraguan covert operations as they unfolded. But he did say that the CIA did try to sway the Samoza government to improve the political conditions of their own people. While Samoza did try and help the CIA in the Bay of Pigs fiasco, Scelso says that the Nicaraguans did not support any anti-Castro Cubans in their covert war against Fidel. "What we were concerned about with Samoza were his activities inside of his home country, principally." The CIA says that if the Samoza regime did in fact give

13 Scelso Report. Pg. 1-74 & 1-75

any support, be it military or financial to the various anti-Castro groups then operating in the US, it would consider them as "trivial." But, he said, any information that came their way via Nicaraguan intelligence would be welcomed.

While the CIA knew of Samoza's illicit dealings with his own population as well as others in the region, they turned a blind eye. "You see, said Scelso, regarding the Nicaraguan dictator, "Samoza was active against Costa Rica. His diplomats were engaging in smuggling money for the U.S. Mafia. He was assassinating people, brutalizing the population, conducting guerrilla warfare. He was at odds with the government of Honduras, which harbored anti-Samoza groups and so on. If he was also in left field supporting anti-Castro groups, this was one facet of his operations and would not have been of any significance to us..."[14]

If Scelso and the CIA were not really interested in the goings on of President Samoza, they certainly were when it concerned the activities of one of its own; J.C. King, the head of the CIA's Western Hemisphere Division based in Miami, the site of the agency's secret war against Fidel Castro. King, it seems, supplied the anti-Castro groups with funds coming out of the CIA's secret bank accounts in Miami.

Mr. Scelso: The various stations had contact with anti-Castro groups at various stations in Latin America and may have financed them. Whether J.C. King may have done this—I would not have put it past him. He did all sorts of personal operations.

Mr. Goldsmith: Would that have been unauthorized?

Mr. Scelso: He could have authorized it himself as Division Chief. It seems-well, nothing is too farfetched for him to have done. He went personally into Columbia, or someplace, and went up into the hills and personally met the leader of some great guerrilla

14 Scelso Report. Pg. 1-99& 1-00

organization that had been murdering people right and left when he was Division Chief.[15]

The reader will now be familiar with the fact that Scelso was given the job of reviewing the circumstances surrounding the president's death for the CIA, and in his interview he gives the behind the scenes reasons for his appointment and a better understanding of how he carried out his duties.

On November 23, 1963, one day after JFK's death, a top-level meeting was held at CIA headquarters between Richard Helms, his deputy, Thomas Karramesiness, CI Chief Jim Angleton, and others. It was at this meeting that Scelso was given his job of writing a report on the assassination. Scelso says that he was picked primarily for the job because of his years as a top level CIA polygraph operator, whose job it was to successfully investigate very big security cases. One of the biggest jobs that Scelso performed during his CIA career was the investigation of the disappearance of the Chief of the West German Security Service in 1964.

Scelso says that when DDP Helms picked him for the job it was without prior constraints on his time or ability to do the job. When questioned by the Senate panel about the conditions of his work, Scelso said that Helms did not pressure him in any way towards finding or not finding a conspiracy in President Kennedy's death. Neither did Helms force a time limit on his study of the event. But once again, Scelso turned to Angleton and his part in the Kennedy assassination investigation.

Angleton, according to Scelso's testimony, kept on meeting clandestinely with the FBI and also certain members of the Warren Commission which were in direct violation of Helms' orders. But, continues Scelso, Helms refused to stop Angleton from conducting these secret meetings. Angleton did not invite Scelso to these affairs, since they were done under the table, without official CIA sanction.

15 Scelso. Pg. 1-99- 1-100

Handicapped as he was by not being given all the material that the CIA had on Oswald, Scelso wrote a summary report of the events in Mexico City and the information he was given regarding Oswald which, he says, was very sketchy indeed.

In late December 1964, Scelso and Birch O'Neil were allowed to read the preliminary FBI report on the assassination of the president. While the account laid the blame squarely on the shoulders of Lee Harvey Oswald, and Oswald alone, Scelso said that the FBI narrative had so much more information than the description he was writing. Some of the material that Scelso had no knowledge of in preparing his own study were details of Oswald's political activity in the United States, i.e., his New Orleans Fair Play for Cuba activities, the allegation that he took a shot at retired Army General Edwin Walker in Dallas in 1963, and other biographical material not given to the CIA.

Scelso would tell his Senate investigator about his report:

"It so happened that my report, my initial report – actually I wrote an initial report about two days after the assassination, which Mr. Helms took to President Johnson, the gist of which was, as far as we could see, Oswald was the assassin and there was no indication that we had that there were other participants in the assassination; and there was no indication, visible indication, that he was a Soviet or Cuban agent, even though the possibility could not be excluded. And my later report was more comprehensive, but was obviously, completely irrelevant in view of all of this Bureau information."[16]

Even though Scelso realized that he'd been short changed as far as the information not given to him by the FBI, he still reserved his choicest comments towards his boss, Jim Angleton. He tells the story of how, after he read the FBI's narrative on the assassination, a general meeting was held with the top brass of the CI Branch. Scelso relates what went on:

"I think that the day of the meeting, or the day before the

16 Scelso Report. Pg. 1-114.

meeting, I had read the Bureau's report in Katzenbach's office and made a few notes and came back and said my report is irrelevant; in view of all the added information, this thing now takes on an entirely different dimension. Whereupon, Helms – Angleton started to criticize my report terribly – without pointing out any inaccuracies, it was so full of wrong things we could not possibly send it to the Bureau and I just sat there and I did not say a word. This was a typical Angleton performance."[17]

While Scelso knew of his reports failings, he, i.e., that Oswald killed the president alone, there was no conspiracy, etc., and he still said that he believed in the story at that time. LBJ wanted something in writing that would put an end to the fears of an international conspiracy among some people in the country concerning Kennedy's death. "He (LBJ) wanted a rundown on what we had and thought. The thing was couched in such terms, we hedged." Scelso's memo was only a page or two and it was lost in the shuffle at CIA headquarters.

At the time of the assassination, there were rumors flying around that Oswald might have been either and agent for the FBI or the CIA, and in his testimony before the Senate Committee, Scelso addresses that very question. He said that the CIA traced and retraced Oswald's name in the Central Registry and also had a trace put forward to see it he had a 201 file on hand. "The next step," said Scelso, "was a full CIA computer trace to see if there were any references to him."

"Now, we knew right from the start that Oswald had never been an agent of the Agency, as far as the records show, and everybody concerned with it knew, or believed, that he had never been an agent of the agency."

Mr. Goldsmith: How did you know that?

Mr. Scelso: Because all agents of the agency are indicated in the Registry, you see, under a cryptonym or with reference to another

17 Scelso Report. P8. 1-115 & 1-116.

desk, with reference to a certain desk with an instruction, go to a certain desk and ask them. This is done with extremely sensitive cases and also done with security suspects of great importance. Oswald did not show up in any such contracts.[18]

While he is sure that Oswald was not an agent of either the CIA or FBI, he could not give a definitive answer when questioned on the possibility that Oswald worked for the Department of Defense Intelligence.

Mr. Goldsmith: If he had been would you have known about it?

Mr. Scelso: No, not necessarily. They could have concealed it from us. Technically, under Presidential order, they should have coordinated the operation with the CIA at some point, if Oswald was a source of theirs overseas. But compliance with that Presidential directive was spotty.

Any chance of Oswald's being an agent for US intelligence, according to Scelso, is put to bed in this exchange with counsel.

Mr. Scelso: Anything is possible, whether Oswald was a CIA agent, but it certainly was concealed from me if he were. I will say that Oswald was a person of a type who would never have been recruited by the agency to work behind the Iron Curtain, or anyplace else.

Mr. Goldsmith: Why not?

Mr. Scelso: Because his personality and background completely disqualified him for clandestine work or for work as an agent to carry out the instructions of the agency...Well, Oswald, by virtue of his background and so on, would miserably fail to meet our minimum qualifications. Oswald would have been debriefed had he walked in and volunteered information, you see. However, he would not have been given any mission to perform."

18 Scelso Report. Pg. 1-121

On the flip side, asked Mr. Goldsmith, could Oswald have been recruited by the Russian KGB?

Mr. Scelso: Indeed, he certainly must have been debriefed by the KGB. I would think they would have debriefed him on his military information. I do not think that the KGB would have recruited him to be their agent after he left Russia.

Mr. Goldsmith: Why not?

Mr. Scelso: Because they were intimately acquainted with his ways and his habits and his background and would not have regarded him as a reliable collaborator... However, the Russians are just as careful as we are and I just do not think Oswald's whole pattern of life was that of a very badly, emotionally unbalanced young man.

In his testimony, Mr. Scelso gives a full and detailed account of the depth of the CIA's investigation of the Kennedy assassination.

Scelso had about 30 staff members and 30 clerical people working full time on the case. In the early stages of their investigation, they were flooded with hundreds of reports, cable traffic from the various agency branches, allegations coming in from all over the globe, all of which had to be checked out. The main CIA Station that was directly involved in the headquarters investigation was the Mexico City Station due to Oswald's Mexican connection. After the CIA read the preliminary FBI report, then the CIA's Miami Station began to provide Scelso's people with information concerning Oswald's pro-Castro activities in the US, i.e., New Orleans. He also received information from CIA posts in Nicaragua, England, Australia and the Scandinavian countries due to the fact that Oswald was supposed to study at the Albert Schweitzer College in Switzerland (he never showed up).

Scelso says that the CIA was receiving huge amounts of bogus information from its worldwide informants in the weeks after the assassination, all of which had to be checked out in case one would pan out.

While he was in the middle of his investigation, Richard Helms suddenly turned the probe into the hands of Angleton's CI Staff. This was done because of the Soviet angle that had been discovered, i.e., Oswald's two-year sojourn in the Soviet Union, etc. Thus, the Soviet connection now took over from the almost as important Cuban connection that most likely would have lead to even more important clues as to why President Kennedy was killed.

In his testimony before the Senate Committee it is obvious that if Scelso knew about the CIA plots to kill Castro, (which he didn't), then his probe would have taken on an entirely different scope. He explained his reasoning in this exchange with Counsel Goldsmith.

Mr. Goldsmith: In what way would it have been different?

Mr. Scelso: We would have gone down to principally our Miami station and hand them kick off the full investigation. As it was, they were getting all kinds of leads, but we would have been putting much more emphasis in that direction, particularly in our analysis of the case. My present feeling about the case is that Oswald was a genuine pro-Castro nut and he was excited about what he read in the papers about our attempts to knock off Castro. I too, read these things in the paper and I thought, of course, that what Castro was referring to were the armed teams we were landing from time to time on the Cuban beaches. I did not know he might have been talking about general attempts to kill him personally as distinguished from overthrowing his government.

The anti-Castro plots then being carried out by the CIA were not the only aspect of the Cuban angle that Scelso did not know about. When questioned by the Senate panel he said that he was also kept in the dark on the AMLASH Operation to kill Castro. The CIA had a highly placed Cuban agent right in the middle of Fidel Castro's government named Rolando Cubela (more about AMLASH and Cubela later). Cubela was part of the CIA's assassination scheme to kill Castro but he was caught in the middle 1960's before he could take any action against Castro. The head of Cuban Operations at the time of the Castro plots was Desmond Fitzgerald and Fitzgerald never told Scelso about AMLASH because he did not need to know that particular piece of information.

As he testified concerning his knowledge, or lack thereof, of the anti-Castro CIA plots, Mr. Scelso had some very interesting comments to make on one of the most controversial men in the entire CIA-Mafia assassination effort; William King Harvey (more about Harvey later).

Mr. Goldsmith: What was Mr. Harvey like?

Mr. Scelso: Well, he is dead now. Harvey was really hard-boiled, unstable, ruthless guy who was, in my opinion, a very dangerous man. I had run-ins with him several times. I also had to investigate one of his big cases and although I was always on friendly terms with him – we never slugged it out with each other – he never liked me and I never liked him.

As the CIA-Mafia plots to kill Fidel Castro played out, there was increasing tension between the Kennedy administration and the CIA. Both John and Robert Kennedy wanted more "boom and bang" in the CIA's efforts to topple Castro. As the plots unfolded, Attorney General Robert Kennedy took on an increasing role in overseeing the covert efforts to kill Castro and one of the people whom he ran into was William King Harvey. Scelso had some revealing insights into Harvey and his relationships with the Kennedys.

Mr. Goldsmith: Do you know whether Mr. Harvey had any negative feelings towards the Kennedys?

Mr. Scelso: I only heard that he was sore at Bobby Kennedy. Bobby Kennedy fired him because Harvey was a three-martini lunch man – not because of the expense involved.

Mr. Goldsmith: Do you know whether Harvey was running any operations outside the ordinary course of business?

Mr. Scelso: I did not know at that time. I just heard about this assassin he had on the payroll and so on. To me, knowing nothing except that the man was a criminal, the assassin that he had on the payroll, and Harvey's nature... the thought of our engaging in assassinations as distinguished from guerrilla warfare or coup d'état, and so on, setting out by stealth or surprise to kill an important foreign person was abhorrent to the standards of the clandestine service and the fact that the way – you know, what the response was in the Lumumba case. They refused to carry out the order, but they were guilty of conspiracy to commit homicide.[19]

Scelso continued his thoughts on Harvey. "The very thought of Helms entrusting Harvey to hire a criminal to have the capacity to kill somebody violates every operational precept, every bit of operational experience, every ethical consideration. And the fact that he chose Harvey – Harvey could keep a secret, you see. This was one way to make sure that nobody ever found out about it."

"Later on, Desmond Fitzgerald came out on the TDY and heard some of these stones and relieved Harvey. Harvey went completely – which happens in the agency. The strain is tremendous...."

It is at this point that Scelso makes one of the most startling observations concerning Harvey, one that has not been considered in the long history of the Kennedy assassination case.

Mr. Scelso: Harvey was not the kind of personality who appeals to me and I certainly was not the kind of personality that appeals to him. I have wondered – wonder if the government has ever looked into the possibility that Harvey did not knock off Giancana. He lived in the same area, when he was retired. He was a great one with guns. I read it (the murder of Sam Giancana, the mob boss

19 Scelso Report. Pg. 1-145.

in Chicago whose name has been prominently mentioned as one the chief suspects in the Kennedy assassination) in the newspaper. I was overseas and I said to myself, I wondered if they look into Bill Harvey.

Mr. Goldsmith: This question may come to you out of right field, but do you have any reason to believe that Mr. Harvey himself may have been involved in the President's assassination?

Mr. Scelso: I do not have any reason to believe it.[20]

Mr. Goldsmith: Harvey instructed his wife that after his own death his wife should burn all his papers. Do you have any idea what would be in those papers that Mr. Harvey would be so interested to conceal?

Mr. Scelso. He was too young to have assassinated McKinley and Lincoln. It could have been anything.

Turning his attention to Richard Helms, Scelso said that he was shocked that he had appointed Harvey to create the secret assassination plots, later called "Executive Action/ZR RIFLE." "I think," continued Scelso, on the fact that Helms did not inform the Warren Commission on the Castro assassination plots, "that was a morally highly reprehensible act, which he cannot possibly justify under his oath of office, or any other standard of professional public service."

Asked why he thought Helms failed to tell the Warren Commission about the Castro plots he said that "I think that Helms withheld the information because he realized it would have cost him his job and would have precipitated a crisis for the agency, which could have had a very adverse effects on the agency."

In this narrative we have described Scelso's thoughts on James Angleton and his relationship to the JFK investigation being conducted by the CIA. In his testimony, he goes into greater detail on Angleton's views on the Russian defector, Yuri Nosenko, and on Angleton's possible ties to organized crime.

20 Scelso Report. Pg. 1-151.

Immediately after the assassination, Angleton, like the rest of the top brass in the CI Division, believed that there was no conspiracy in the president's death. Until Yuri Nosenko came along and told his incredible story of being the KGB agent who had overseen the Oswald file in the Soviet Union. Nosenko said that Oswald was not an agent of the KGB, and that the Soviet government wanted nothing to do with him. The problem that Angleton had with Nosenko is that he believed that the Russian might have been sent to the United States in order to infiltrate the CIA in order to protect some other KGB agent that was working inside the agency, or to sow disinformation inside the CIA.

Scelso said that while Angleton was an understanding man when it came to human nature, "his evaluation of people, was to be a very precarious thing."

Scelso now dropped another possible bombshell regarding Angleton's potential mob connections.

Mr. Goldsmith: Do you have any reason to believe that Angleton might have had ties to organized crime?

Mr. Scelso: Yes. Back when I was branch chief. The Department of Justice, Mr. Hunley, who was working against organized crime, asked people from the agency to come over and asked us if we could find out the true names of holders of numbered bank accounts in Panama because the Mafia was depositing money there, cash money skimmed off the top in Las Vegas. And we were, indeed, in an excellent position to do this and told them so, whereupon Angleton vetoed it and said that is the Bureau's business... Unless the Bureau requests us to do it, we are not going to do it, so we did not do it. And I told J.C. King this and he smiled a foxy smile and said well, that's Angleton's excuse. The real reason is that Angleton himself has ties to the Mafia and he would not want to double cross them, or something like that.[21]

21 Scelso Report. Pg. 1-168 & 1-169.

Mr. Goldsmith: Do you have more specific information linking Angleton to the Mafia, into organized crime?

Mr. Scelso: I do believe that I have heard that Angleton was one of those several people in the agency who were trying to use the Mafia in Cuban operations.

As head of the CI Branch, Angleton was aware of the covert relationship between the CIA and the American mob in the Castro assassination plots. After all, the plots were the brainchild of the CIA and Angleton, as chief of the one section that would have overall responsibility for the carrying out of the operation, must have had mob contacts, either personal or of a business relationship in order to see them through.

Another prominent name in the Kennedy assassination investigation is George de Mohrenschildt, a wealthy Russian exile who lived in Dallas at the same time that Lee Oswald was in that city in the months preceding the president's death. The two men were of vastly different backgrounds, yet the urbane and wealthy de Mohrenschildt, whose Nazi and intelligence past, earned him a huge file in J. Edgar Hoover's office, was a father figure to the lonely, Marxist, Lee Harvey Oswald. It has been alleged that de Mohrenschildt was working for the CIA during the time both men were in Dallas and that the cagey Russian was somehow involved in a CIA operation to monitor Oswald's daily activities. When counsel Goldsmith asked Scelso if he knew of any de Mohrenschildt connection with the CIA he replied, "Not to my knowledge, except for the allegation that I read in the book (*Legend: The Secret World of Lee Harvey Oswald,* Edward Epstein), that he was in contact with a man named Moore who worked for us. De Mohrenschildt was a puzzle to me, and after reading Epstein's book; it makes me wonder whether he was not a source of the FBI or one of the military intelligence services.

It is clear that the information contained in the Scelso interview is one of the most important documents to be released by the AARB since its inception. We now have a clearer picture as to the mechanics of the early CIA probe into President Kennedy's assassination, which people were assigned to perform certain tasks, the failure of the CIA to cooperate fully with the Warren Commission, and Scelso's revealing comments on the main people inside the agency, i.e., William Harvey, James Jesus Angleton, Richard Helms, among others, and how they conducted their own parts in the Kennedy assassination.[22]

In 2002, with the death of John Scelso, was his identity finally revealed. "Scelso" was John Whitten, the man whom the Agency tasked with the job of investigating their own mistakes in the aftermath of the president's death. At least one sleeping dog was now put to rest.

22 For those researchers interested in obtaining the Scelso Document, refer your queries to the National Archives for the following information. Record Number: 180-10131-10330. Agency File Number: 014728.

Chapter 4

The Warren Commission's Unanswered Questions

One of the major failures of the Warren Commission was its negligence in not calling to testify, those people who had a different version as to the events of November 22, 1963, who were in Dealey Plaza, but also individuals who had pertinent knowledge of a possible conspiracy in the assassination of President Kennedy before it occurred. As mentioned in the first chapter, the FBI had certain warnings about a possible conspiracy on the president's life but did not warn the Secret Service. It also turns out that other branches of the American intelligence community had their own warnings but failed to take these matters seriously.

The Warren Commission too had been apprised of certain information from the various intelligence agencies about a likely plot on President Kennedy's life but it too did not take them seriously when drawing up their report.

This chapter will describe some of the people and their information that the Warren Commission was aware of, along with certain tips linking Lee Harvey Oswald to American intelligence.

The Dinkin Allegation

One of the allegations brought to the attention of the Warren Commission (which was totally ignored) was a charge by a private in the US Army that there was a conspiracy pending on the life of President Kennedy, one week after it actually took place.

The man at the center of this story was Private first class Eugene Dinkin, then stationed in Metz, France. Before entering the army, Dinkin had studied psychology at the University of Illinois. He enlisted in the army in 1961, and took basic training at Fort Gordon, Ga. His job in the army was that of a cryptographic operator, which was actually run by the National Security Agency, the super secret department, which is responsible for communications, intercepts for the US intelligence community. By March 1962, Dinkin was sent to the 529 Ordinance Company in France as a "crypto operator." In the military intelligence pecking order, a person with a "crypto clearance" is considered a highly valued commodity.

Private Dinkin did his job well, and it was only in September 1963 that things seemed to go awry. One day during troop formation, Private Dinkin began a long, 25-minute speech on how the US government was stockpiling atomic bombs, a rather strange subject in which a Private First Class was to give. The subject of Dinkin's talk was forwarded to Lt. Colonel John Lippincott of the Pentagon's Legislative Liaison Office. Shortly thereafter, Private Dinkin was given a psychiatric evaluation after which, it was advised that his access to classified materials should be denied.

But Dinkin had other, more serious matters on his mind than the stockpiling of US atomic weapons; a plot on the life of the president that was being planned by elements of the right wing in the United States.

The Dinkin story is told in detail in Dick Russell's book on the Kennedy assassination, *The Man Who Knew Too Much,* (Caroll & Graf, 1992) and quoted here for this story.

According to CIA declassified documents released to the public in recent years, Private Dinkin's first allegation was sent to then Attorney General Robert Kennedy in an October 22, 1962 letter.

In his note, Private Dinkin told Robert Kennedy that his brother was going to be assassinated on November 28, 1963, and if it succeeded, it would be blamed on a "communist or a Negro." Furthermore, said Dinkin, the plot was to be engineered by certain elements in the American military establishment, and that a subsequent cover-up would ensue. He closed his letter by pleading with Robert Kennedy that a representative of the Attorney General be sent to Metz, France to talk to him concerning his allegations.

Dinkin had no illusions concerning what might or might now happen once his letter was sent to Robert Kennedy, and on October 25, he went AWOL and headed for Luxembourg in order to find a representative of the American government to tell his story to. At the American embassy he tried to get an appointment with the US Ambassador but he was out "playing tennis" and could not be reached. He did, however, have a hurried meeting with the U.S. Chargé d'affaires, Mr. Cunningham, who promised to relay his message.

On November 3, after briefly returning to his base in Metz, Dinkin again went AWOL, this time heading for Geneva, Switzerland where he told his tale to the editor of the *Geneva Diplomat.* What reaction the editor of the paper had is not known. But what is known, according to documents on the Dinkin case released recently by the CIA, and given to the Warren Commission, is this.

On May 19, 1964, Richard Helms sent a memo to the Warren Commission, which reads in part.

"Immediately after the assassination the CIA reported allegations concerning a plot to assassinate President Kennedy that were made by Pfc. Dinkin, U.S. Army, serial number (deleted) on 6 and 7 November 1963, in Geneva while absent without leave from his unit in Metz, France... Around 26 November, 1963, after President Kennedy had been assassinated, a Geneva journalist named Alex des Fontaines, stringer for Time-Life and correspondent for Radio Canada, was reported to be filing a story to the Paris office of Time-Life recounting Private (deleted) – Dinkin's, visit to Geneva and quoting (deleted) as having said that "they" were plotting against President Kennedy and that "something" would happen in Texas."[23]

The CIA documents concludes by saying, "All aspects of this story were known, as reported above, by US military authorities and have been reported by military attaché cable through military channels."

On November 6, Dinkin left Switzerland bound for Germany, stopping first in Frankfurt, and later in Bonn, where he went to the US Embassy, tried to tell his story, and given the brush-off by the employees there. Seeing that no one was interested in his tale, Dinkin decided to return to Metz and face the consequences. Upon his return he was interrogated by an officer in the Army's CIC (Counter Intelligence Corps), arrested, and put in the brig. On November 13, he was sent to the hospital ward at Landstuhl General Hospital for "examination."

Dinkin was still in the hospital psychiatric ward on November 22, 1963 when he heard the news of President Kennedy's death. The next day he was paid a visit by someone in civilian clothes who said he was with the Secret Service. The agent closely questioned Dinkin about who might have killed JFK, why the day was changed, and other matters relating to the president's death. Dinkin told his questioner that he would not talk further, as long as he was being kept under wraps.

The Warren Commission, in Commission Document 1107, reports "that Colonel W.L. Adams, Jr., of Army Intelligence, stated in 1964 that Dinkin was the subject of a closed investigation by the Office of the Assistant Chief of Staff; G-2, United

---

23 The Man Who Knew Too Much. Russell, Dick, Pgs. 554-555.

States Army Communications Zone, Europe." The file ends at the next page and its contents have yet to be released.

In early December, Dinkin was sent home to Walter Reed Hospital in Washington, D.C. for further treatment. In his therapy sessions, Dinkin was told that his warnings about the assassination of President Kennedy were really a projection on his part of hostility towards authority figures. Dinkin said that he was drugged and given a test by a doctor who told him to free associate to a list of words for a study he was conducting. Shortly after his hospitalization, Dinkin was given a medical discharge from the US Army.

The Dinkin story, like others, is still one of the many unexplained questions that the Warren Commission and the CIA failed to fully investigate.

The Tolstoy Foundation

In June of 1962, Lee Oswald, his new bride Marina, and their baby daughter, arrived in Texas after two years in the Soviet Union. They settled in Fort Worth, near Dallas and the ex-Marine got a job as a metalworker at the Leslie Welding Company.

On June 26, Oswald was visited by FBI agent John Fain who questioned him about his life in the Soviet Union. In these pre-assassination months, Oswald was not considered to be any threat by the FBI and the bureau just added papers to his mounting file. But what is interesting in this time period of Oswald's life is the circle of people whom he and Marina befriended upon their return to the United States.

In Forth Worth there was a small, but influential and wealthy group of White Russians who had immigrated to the United States in the years after World War II. Most of them were in the petroleum engineering business, the most important, as far as Lee Harvey Oswald was concerned, was George de Mohrenschildt.

As a Russian émigré Marina Oswald was taken in by this small group who attempted to help her get adjusted to American life. That cannot be said, however, about her husband. Lee Oswald was not liked nor trusted by these wealthy Russians whose anti-Communist ideas ran counter to those of the idealistic Oswald who saw in Russia a Marxist heaven that still eluded him.

Most of these Russian emigrants were brought to the US by a CIA backed and funded organization called the Tolstoy Foundation. As part of its investigation, the Warren Commission "would learn that the Tolstoy Foundation, while maintaining a European headquarters in Munich, received as much as $400,000 a year subsidy from the U.S. government."

During that time, the head man in Fort Worth of the Tolstoy Foundation was Paul Raigorodsky, a hard line anti-communist, and wealthy oil man who performed covert missions for the United States. One of the men whom the Oswald's met was George Bouhe who was heavily involved in both overt and covert assignments for the Tolstoy Foundation. Bouhe said that he and his friends tried to help both Lee and Marina get settled in Fort Worth and worked to get Oswald a job. While they had sympathy for Marina, that could not be said for Lee. He was not trusted by the group, not only for his lack of social or family skills, but for his pro-Marxist views. The bottom line is that he was not trusted by these well to do Russian-Americans who saw in Oswald all that they had fled from.

Another strike against Oswald (whether true or not) came from Igor Voshinin, an anti-Communist hard liner, and also a member of the wartime group known as NTS, the National Alliance of Solidarists, which was born after the Russian Revolution in 1917. During the World War II, thousands of its members worked with the Nazi's in joining the "Liberation" army of Andrei Vlassov, a Soviet General who had secretly joined forces with ànti-Bolshevist underground members who had worked their way into Stalin's headquarters. When the German army invaded the Ukraine, Vlassov's troops joined them. Their main political purpose was the restoration of the Czar who had been overthrown during the October Revolution.

Voshinin said that he personally distrusted Oswald because when he lived in Minsk, there was a KGB training academy in the city. According to Voshinin, a person attending the school took a two-year class, the same amount of time that Oswald lived in Minsk. "We felt very sorry for his wife, but after we heard this, Oswald was taboo." After the assassination, J. Edgar Hoover told the Warren Commission that he had no concrete intelligence that there was ever a KGB training facility in Minsk and if there was one, the Soviet's wouldn't tell us.

It seems odd indeed, that the one community in the United States that the Oswald's returned to was one ripe with CIA connections. The Tolstoy Foundation, George de Mohrenschildt's almost fatherly interest in the young Oswald couple, his attempts to find him work, and the network of old anti-Communist NTS members who distrusted Lee Oswald is ripe for the picking. Once again, the Warren Commission decided not to pursue this rather unusual intelligence connection.

Hints of Intelligence Training

At the end of 1958, Lee Oswald returned from overseas duty in Japan, took a month's leave in which he went back to Fort Worth to visit his family, and reported to his new duty assignment – the Marine Air Control Squadron 9 in Santa Ana, California. He was part of a ten-man unit that would study radar operations. Oswald's CO at El Toro, John F. Donovan, later testified to the Warren Commission that his unit's job was "basically to train both enlisted men and officers for later assignment overseas." All of the men in the unit had to have a "Secret" clearance, including Oswald. This seems rather strange considering that Oswald was charged with various crimes, including being court-martialed while stationed in Japan.

Oswald was considered a rather odd character by his fellow Marines, many of whom began calling him "Comrade Oswald-skovitch." In his spare time, Oswald learned Russian, and tended to keep to himself. Oswald's military record says nothing about his officially learning Russian but the Warren Commission had other ideas. In a Warren Commission executive session, which was declassified in 1974, chief counsel J. Lee Rankin said of Oswald's possible training in the Russian language, "We are trying to find out what he studied at the Monterey School of the Army in the way languages."

Over the years there have been constant rumors about whether or not Oswald attended the Monterey Language School. It is interesting to note that when Marina met Lee in Minsk she thought he was a Russian because of his fluency in the language. While the verdict is out as to Oswald's attendance at the Language School it is certain that he did more in Monterey than take the 17 Mile Drive.

Oswald and DeMohrenschildt

In its report on President Kennedy's assassination, the Warren Commission paid scant attention to the ever-present intelligence links of the alleged assassin's closets associates in Dallas, George de Mohrenschildt. The report said regarding the Baron, "The Commission's investigation has developed no signs of subversive or disloyal conduct on the part of either of the de Mohrenschildts. Neither the FBI, the CIA nor any witness contacted by the Commission, has provided any information linking the de Mohrenschildt to subversive or extremist organizations. Nor, has there been any evidence linking them in any way with the assassination of President Kennedy."[24]

24 Report of the Warren Commission: The Assassination of President Kennedy. The New York Time Edition. Pg. 262.

The de Mohrenschildt story has been told in various forms in the literature of the Kennedy assassination and the tale will not be repeated here, except to focus on the Commission's failure to conduct a full investigation of the Oswald-de Mohrenschildt relationship, and the Barron's obvious intelligence links.

George de Mohrenschildt was one of the most important people in the Dallas White Russian community at the time of the Oswald's arrival in Fort Worth. George de Mohrenschildt was the opposite of the young, inexperienced Lee Oswald. He was rich, well bred, came from a distinguished nobility in Russia, a member of the Dallas Petroleum Club and the World Affairs Council. He was a petroleum engineer, having worked around the globe, traveling extensively in all the hot spots of the cold war, and accumulating a rather extensive FBI and CIA file along the way. In Dallas he was friendly with the major players in that city; from LBJ, to construction tycoons George and Herman Brown, and a later American president, George Bush, among others.

Among the places that de Mohrenschildt and his wife traveled were Yugoslavia, Haiti, where they lived after the JFK assassination, Africa, and Latin and South America. In 1961, they took a seven thousand mile walking tour of Latin America; just happening to stumble upon the training site of the CIA backed rebels in Guatemala City just prior to the Bay of Pigs invasion. They stayed in the country until the furor over the invasion ended and then continued their "walking tour" of Honduras, Costa Rica, Panama and Haiti. In September 1962, they returned to Dallas and their fateful meeting with the young Oswald couple.

His links to various countries' intelligence services go back to the days prior to Pearl Harbor. In 1941, he worked as an agent of the French counter intelligence corps, helping to run an agent network in the US to monitor the shipment of oil to Europe. At the same time that he was working with the French, he was also covertly operating as a double agent for the German secret service. His activities were being watched by the FBI and when he was en-route to Mexico he was stopped by the FBI while sketching near a Texas Coast Guard base. He and his lady companion stayed in Mexico for nine months before being expelled for possible "subversive activities." Despite all this, in the summer of 1942, he applied for a job with the wartime OSS, the predecessor to the CIA. Naturally, his application was turned down because of the OSS's belief that he was a Nazi agent.

In his book, *The Man Who Knew Too Much,* author Dick Russell tells of an interview he had with Clare Petty, who worked with James Angleton in the CIA that concerned de Mohrenschildt. Petty said that in 1974, he had been looking at a potential Soviet intelligence link to de Mohrenschildt that dated back to World War II. The top secret information was gleamed from the VENONA project, a covert US code breaking enterprise that recorded intercepted messages from the Soviet Union to the United States. Some of the most important information coming out of the VENONA gold mine was material on the atomic spies, Klaus Fuchs, the Rosenberg's, David Greenglass, and a number of highly placed Soviet agents in the United States, Donald Maclean, among others. The VENONA archives were partially declassified last year and are available at the National Archives.

Petty told author Russell that in his opinion, he believed that at least some of the VENONA transcripts that were intercepted by the US Army Signal Corps, and more importantly, the code names used by the Soviets, might have referred to George de Mohrenschildt. "It was clear, said Petty, "that whoever was being described in the codes had been in the United States, went to Mexico during the war, and was a real wheeler-dealer. He also had another nationality; my recollection was that he was Polish."

That latter statement fits de Mohrenschildt perfectly as he was raised in Poland after his family left Russia during the Bolshevik Revolution that ousted the Czar While in Poland, de Mohrenschildt graduated from the Polish military academy and entered the army as a Captain in the reserves.

We now see that George de Mohrenschildt had extensive

ties to Russian intelligence and his activities (if proved correct) were monitored by the wartime OSS. But what is proven is his later links to US intelligence after the war ended, and during the height of the cold war with the Soviet Union.

As a geologist, de Mohrenschildt traveled the world seeking new fields of exploration. In 1957 he made a trip on behalf of the International Cooperation Administration, which wanted to develop new oil fields. When he returned to Dallas, he was met by a member of the CIA's domestic contact division stationed in that city. The agent questioned de Mohrenschildt on his travels and sent that news to various governmental agencies. These "informal contacts" between de Mohrenschildt and his CIA contact continued until the autumn of 1961. But now the intelligence story of de Mohrenschildt and the CIA, and its links to Lee Oswald get more interesting. Shortly before his death of March 29, 1977, de Mohrenschildt told author Edward Jay Epstein that he had met a CIA officer in Dallas named J. Walton Moore. Moore was with the agency's Domestic Contact Service and both he and Moore had a lunch in Dallas in which the name Lee Harvey Oswald came up. This was in 1961 and took place shortly after the Oswald's had returned from the Soviet Union. De Mohrenschildt told Epstein that Moore told him that Oswald had lived in Minsk, was an ex-Marine and that the CIA had an interest in him; could de Mohrenschildt "look after" Oswald, possibly meet him, and do the agency a big favor? In return, said Moore, the CIA would help him in his oil business. The rest is history.

In his massive study of the Kennedy assassination, Dick Russell, in *The Man Who Knew Too Much* tells of a conversation that he had with Richard Case Nagell that concerned George de Mohrenschildt and his Oswald-CIA connection. When Russell got Nagell's attention on de Mohrenschildt, the ex-spy said, "Now there's a relationship to pursue. I'm surprised Jim Garrison never really got into that." Later, Nagell said that, "there was enough of intermittent surveillance on Oswald by other people whose reports I read, that I have intimate knowledge who he was associating with. De Mohrenschildt's name popped up, not in connection with the CIA, though he might have been."

De Mohrenschildt's life had been associated with foreign intelligence, whether it was Soviet or American, and his death on March 29, 1977 had all the earmarks of a good writer of espionage fiction.

After a strange trip to Europe that he made in connection with an investigation into the Kennedy assassination by Dutch writer, Willem Oltmans, George de Mohrenschildt suddenly arrived at his daughter's home in Palm Beach, Florida. It was at this time that de Mohrenschildt contacted the staff of the House Select Committee on Assassinations in Washington that was conducting its investigation of the JFK murder. He said that he had information that might be useful in their probe and would someone like to come down and talk to him? The HSCA sent down Gaeton Fonzi who was stationed in Miami, and who was tasked with investigating the Cuban link to the assassination. When Fonzi arrived at de Mohrenschildt's daughter's home, she told him that her father was out and would be back later that day. Fonzi left his card and departed, never having a chance to hear what that baron had to say. Later that afternoon, in circumstances that have never been satisfactorily explained, George de Mohrenschildt was dead. The coroner said that the cause of death was suicide by putting a 20-gauge shotgun to his mouth.

Whatever information de Mohrenschildt was about to tell, went with him to his grave. But in a later interview with his wife Jeanne, author Russell said that she was certain that her husband did not kill himself, and furthermore, that Oswald did not kill the president. Russell also claims that Richard Case Nagell told him that he was certain that de Mohrenschildt was murdered before he could testify to the House panel.

Over the years, George de Mohrenschildt had become friends with Janet Auchincloss, who was the mother of Jacqueline Kennedy. In December 1963, shortly after the assassination, he wrote a letter of condolence to Mrs. Kennedy. At the end of the letter, de Mohrenschildt said that he still had lingering doubts about the guilt of Lee Harvey Oswald in President Kennedy's death.

JFK and the French Connection

One of the topics of investigation that the Warren Commission did not pursue is the so called "French Connection" to the Kennedy assassination. At the time of the assassination, a former French army officer named Jean Souetre, whose name was known to the Warren Commission, was expelled from Dallas shortly after the president's death. Souetre had a deadly background, and was linked to various underground French terrorist organizations whose purpose was the overthrow of the French government. But if the Warren Commission had the information that was to come to light twenty years later, would they have made a detailed study? I doubt it.

What is the French Connection, and how does it relate to the Kennedy assassination? And was the Warren Commission derelict in its duty in not pursuing the Jean Souetre matter to its ultimate end?

On November 22, 1963, while the United States and the world were still reeling from the shock of the assassination of President John Kennedy, a seemingly unrelated incident took place in Dallas. US authorities expelled a known deserter from the French army who also had connections to the outlawed OAS (Organisation del'Armie Secrete), which had been battling France over the status of Algeria. This mysterious figure was later identified as Jean Souetre who also went by the name of Michael Rioux and Michael Mertz.

Souetre was seen in Fort Worth on the morning of the president's murder and was placed in Dallas that afternoon. What this French soldier of fortune, ex-heroin smuggler, and gifted assassin was doing in Dallas at the same time that the President of the United States was being struck down is open to speculation.

The life of Jean Souetre and his possible links to the President's murder has come to life due in large part to the efforts of the late Bernard Fensterwald, the president of the Assassination Archives and Research Center in Washington, D.C. Mr. Fensterwald, a noted attorney and Kennedy assassination researcher, obtained 1,500 documents from the CIA under FOIA. Among the documents released was No. 632-796, which dug into the life of Jean Souetre and his troubled background. What this document revealed was a tangled web of intrigue concerning the French OAS, international drug smuggling, and assassination.

What part, if any, Jean Souetre played in the death of the president is still open to question. But what is known takes the life of this elusive Frenchman back to long forgotten CIA operations that have recently come to light.

In the 1960's, the CIA established a program called "Executive Action" which set up the criteria of the use of assassinations for political purposes. This plan was called ZR/RIFLE. Two of ZR/RIFLE's most important members were code named QJ/WIN and WI/ROGUE. It has been suggested by Kennedy assassination researchers that Souetre was QJ/WIN. Souetre's background and that of the mysterious QJ/WIN are tantalizing similar (new documents however, reveal the true identities of both QJ/WIN and WI/ROUGE).

Souetre served as a paratrooper in the French Air Force as a captain. He served in Algiers from 1955-59. It was at this time that he took up anti-De Gaulle positions on the freedom of Algeria and deserted from the Air Force. He and his like-minded compatriots formed an underground group of officers in the Oran province of France. It was at this time that he joined the OAS. He was arrested in 1961, charged with sedition, and served one year of a three-year prison term. It is believed that Souetre had a hand in various attempts on the life of French President Charles de Gaulle.

Released CIA documents say that QJ/WIN was under written contract as a principal agent with the primary task of spotting agents candidates. It goes on to say that he was contacted by someone in the government, "in connection with an illegal narcotics operation in the US..." Ex CIA Director Richard Helms said of QJ/WIN that he was the man to see if a murder sanction was ordered.

Souetre hotly denies any involvement in the Kennedy murder and says the only time he was in the United States was in 1974 or 1975. He says that he was in Spain at the time of the Kennedy assassination and that Michael Mertz might have been in Dallas using his name. But that might not hold up as Souetre used the alias of Michael Mertz, as well.

Souetre says that he was never contacted by American authorities until almost 20 years after November 22, 1963. Then living in France, he says he was contacted by a friend who lived in the US and who told him he was under investigation in connection with the president's death. The "friend" further stated that he had a note that would "surely interest him." Souetre won't say who his "friend" is, but shortly after getting the note he was visited by two reporters. He stated that they asked him the same questions sent to him by his "friend."

How did Souetre's "friend" know what queries the two visitors had in mind?

In talking about the Kennedy assassination, Souetre says... "but I believe that certainly there is a French connection to the assassination and that Mertz may well have been involved. Though if he was, I am sure he was not acting alone." Michael Mertz served in the German army in 1941, but soon joined the underground fighting the Germans. He adopted the name Major Baptiste and enlisted in the French army with the rank of captain (it is not known if the French military knew of Mertz's former Germany army connection). He was decorated by President Charles de Gaulle for bravery and sometime in the 1950's, joined the SDECE-French intelligence. Mertz married in 1947 and his father-in-law was linked to illegal activities including whorehouses in Montreal. Whether his father-in-law provided the push or he did it on his own, Mertz infiltrated the illegal OAS and became the eyes and ears of French intelligence. In 1961 he was arrested along with other OAS members for carrying out an attack against President De Gaulle. All of those who participated in the attempted assassination plot on De Gaulle were prosecuted except Mertz.

It was during this period of time that Mertz entered the gun running and drug smuggling market and fled to Canada to pursue his lucrative activities. American authorities suspected him of drug dealing and asked the French to curtail his activities. They refused.

In 1969, Mertz was turned in to U.S. authorities but posted bond one year later. He was found guilty of drug running, served a five-year prison term, and returned to France where he is now a rich man.

The similarities between Mertz and Souetre are very close. Could they be the same person? An intriguing sideline to the Mertz story concerns an FBI document that states that three people – John Mertz, Irma Mertz and Sara Mertz left from Texas on November 23, 1963 by Pan Am to Mexico. (Another good reference to the French Connection is "Triangle of Death" by Brad O'Leary and L.E. Seymour, WND Books, 2003).

The Steve Rivele Investigation

A second investigation into the French Connection to President Kennedy's assassination was carried out by a California writer, Steve Rivele. Rivele spent three years traveling the world, mingling with drug smugglers, soldiers of fortune, and other unsavory characters in his search for Kennedy's killers.

A few years ago Rivele published a book in Europe (but not in the US) called, *"The Men Who Killed Kennedy"* (a television documentary with the same name aired in the US on the Arts and Entertainment Network a number of years ago) in which he named three men who actually fired the shots that killed the president and those who gave the orders. Rivele got his first tip from a noted drug smuggler named Christian David who is currently serving a prison term in France. David was a member of the French Secret Service and worked against the outlawed OAS. He served in Algeria where he became a proficient marksman. In time, David turned into a professional killer, entered the Corsican Mafia, and racked up many "hits" in Africa.

In the early 1970's, David was arrested, tried, convicted, and was returned to the United States to serve out his term for bringing drugs into his country. But when the Senate Intelligence Committee began its investigation into the CIA's "Executive Action" program, David was urgently spirited out of the country, back to France. It has been rumored for years among people in the intelligence services that Christian David may be none other than the infamous WI/ROGUE (but that possibility has most likely been debunked over the years).

Through his underworld contacts, Rivele was put in touch with Christian David. After months of secret discussions, David told Rivele that he was offered the contract to kill President Kennedy by Meme Guerine, the head of the Marseilles Mafia in May-June, 1963. When David found out that the murder attempt was to take place in the United States he turned down the offer. David further told Rivele that there was a conspiracy by the American mob and the French Union Corse to kill the President in retaliation for Attorney General Robert Kennedy's war against organized crime in the U.S.

Two independent sources said that there was indeed a triangular conspiracy to assassinate President Kennedy. These sources confirm that the US Mafia made certain contacts with elements of far right wing extremist groups in this country. These groups were put in touch with a small, disgruntled band of renegade CIA agents whose hatred for President Kennedy ran deep.

In time, David revealed to Rivele the names of the men involved in President Kennedy's death: Sauver Pironit, Lucien Sarti and Roger Bocogononi. Bocogononi and Pironit are believed to be still alive, while Sarti is dead. David said the trio was fanned out in Dealey Plaza in Dallas in three locations; on the grassy knoll, in the Dal-Tex building, and the Dallas County Records Building. According to David, Oswald was in the Texas School Book Depository but was to be the fall guy in the assassination. After Kennedy's death, all three stayed in Dallas for a short period of time and were then flown to Canada.

A source close to the anti-Castro Cubans and a private researcher into the Kennedy assassination, told this writer that Jean Souetre was in Dallas at the time of the assassination. According to the source, Souetre's modus operandi was car bombings and that he was stationed past the triple underpass with a car bomb ready to explode if the assassins in Dealey Plaza failed.

Christian David's story is corroborated by an ex-con, a man now in the Federal Witness Protection Program named Michele Nicolli. Nicolli had known David for years but had not seen him since 1972. Yet, according to Rivele, Nicolli knew the exact information provided to him by Christian David. Rivele states that the three French assassins were picked because of their code of silence-if they were ever caught they wouldn't talk, and they couldn't be linked to the American Mafia, and would be unknown to U.S. law enforcement officials.

Before his death, the late Bernard Fensterwald told this writer that he believed there was a French back up team in Dallas on November 22, 1963 but that they played no part in the President's death. The possibility of a "French Connection" to the assassination was never taken seriously by the Warren Commission despite the fact that they were informed on the expulsion of Jean Souetre one day after the assassination.

Since the possibility of a French Connection angle to the JFK assassination has grown in popularity among the research community, new information by writers have been revealed in recent years. In the early 1960's, the French OAS had direct ties to the radical right in the United States, including members of the fascist John Birch Society, which were big in Texas. The Birchers believed that French President Charles de Gaulle was a communist sympathizer and men like Jean Souetre found a home away from home with them.

Dick Russell writes that Gilbert Le Cavelier, a friend of Bernard Fensterwald, and a politically well-connected French investigator, examined the Kennedy assassination for him a few years before he died. According to Le Cavelier, Souetre moved frequently in the years 1962-1971 in Latin America and the Caribbean, often settling down in Madrid, Spain. The Frenchman told Fensterwald that there were close political and military ties between the anti-Castro Cubans in Florida and members of the OAS in France. Le Cavelier also said that Souetre met with E. Howard Hunt in March or April 1963 in Madrid. Furthermore, Le Cavelier said that certain members of the French extremist's came to the United States in 1963, and made their way to New Orleans where they rendezvous with anti-Castro Cubans and Americans who were conducting guerilla warfare in the swamps in and around New Orleans, including Carlos Bringuier. It was Bringuier whom Oswald had his street encounter with in New Orleans in the summer of 1963. It has also been alleged that Souetre met with members of the Alpha 66 group in New Orleans and may have even met Guy Banister at his 544 Camp Street address. To add fuel to this already burning fire, Le Cavelier said that Howard Hunt was the CIA's contact with Jean Souetre, and that some of the renegade OAS guys were working for the US Defense Intelligence Agency. If all this is true, it directly ties in Souetre, Hunt, and the anti-Castro Cubans together in New Orleans in the months prior to JFK's murder.

The French Connection to the Kennedy assassination was never looked into by the Warren Commission, just another one of the hundred leads that were ignored or dismissed without a backward glance.

Oswald and the Japanese Connection

When one thinks of the many, varied people and events surrounding the JFK assassination, the obvious people and places come to mind; Dallas, Jack Ruby, Clay Shaw, David Ferrie, etc. But the casual reader would be hard pressed to know that there was a tenuous Japanese link not only to Lee Harvey Oswald but to the probe following the president's murder.

One of the most interesting puzzles to the story of Lee Harvey Oswald's service in the US Marines is the time he spent in Japan during the late 1950's. This period of time has been written about with considerable fascination as it is believed by many Kennedy assassination researchers that it was at this point that Oswald may have begun any possible intelligence duties for the US government. Oswald's Marine detachment arrived at Atsugi, Japan on September 12, 1957. Oswald was given a "confidential" clearance and was assigned as a radar operator overseeing the top secret American U-2 spy flights that overflew the Soviet Union and China (the U-2's also originated from bases other than in Japan). Oswald was thus, privy to the mechanics of America's most secret spy plane. Oswald was never one to get chummy with his Marine Corps buddies and he would often go alone to Tokyo on weekends and return in time for his duty on Monday mornings. What Oswald did during his covert sojourns into Tokyo got the attention of the Warren Commission, but, like other puzzles to any possible Oswald-intelligence connection, they went unnoticed. A possible answer to what Oswald was doing in Japan during this time was postulated by a controversial figure in the JFK case by the name of Richard Case Nagell. Nagell was a military intelligence officer in the 1950's, and a CIA contract agent from 1962-63 (for the most detailed information on Richard Case Nagell and his role in the Kennedy case see, *The Man Who Knew Too Much,* by Dick Russell). During his long relationship with author Russell, Nagel told him that Oswald was seen entering the Soviet embassy in Tokyo and that a photograph was taken of him. Nagell then was introduced to Oswald using an assumed name and both men began a covert relationship that would last until Oswald's death by Jack Ruby. Nagell said that Oswald had gone into the embassy to get some coins evaluated but he later learned that the real reason for his entering the embassy was to meet with a Colonel of the Soviet KGB, Nikolai Eroshkin. Eroshkin's cover was that of a military attaché. KGB officers who served in overseas posts were usually sent to coordinate military intelligence in the host country in which they served. According to Nagell's account, Colonel Eroshkin told him that the Soviet's believed Oswald to be on some "intelligence mission." We only have Richard Case Nagell's (Nagell died last year) word that he knew of the Oswald-Eroshkin meetings but this is not the first time that Oswald had been linked to some sort of foreign intelligence organization (KGB, Japanese).

Besides the Warren Commission and the HSCA's investigation into the Kennedy assassination, there was a third possible US military examination of the JFK case with possible Japanese connections.

When the HSCA began its probe of the Kennedy assassination, one of the topics they looked into was the military connection to Lee Harvey Oswald. One of the people whom the committee spoke to Mrs. Larry Huff, whose husband had played a role in the military's investigation (this is still a disputed fact) of Oswald in 1963. Mrs. Huff related the following story.

She said her husband left Hawaii on December 14, 1963 from Kaneohe Base on board a C-54-T aircraft, serial number. 50855 bound for Wake Island. The plane's commander was Chief Warrant Officer Robert Morgan. The man in overall charge of the mission was General Carson Roberts.

Larry Huff served as the navigator on the flight. On board were 10-12 C.I.D. investigators whose final destination was Atsgui, Japan. Huff said that C.I.D. men told him that the purpose of the flight was to investigate Lee Harvey Oswald's possible military connections. On the return flight, Huff said that he was given a 20-page typed report on the CID's findings. The report found Oswald was "incapable" of committing the assassination alone."

Huff reported that he believed that all army records concerning their trip to Japan might be stored in the Intelligence Division of the Marine Corps or with the Commandant of the Marines. When questioned by the committee, C.W.O. (Chief Warrant Officer) Robert Morgan said that he in fact had flown a plane, #50855 from Kaneohe Bay to Tachikawa AFB in Japan and that the names of the crew were available. But when the committee requested the list, they were missing.

The Department of Defense said on April 19, 1978, that it had no records of any investigation and that neither it nor the Air Force Office of Special Investigation had gone to California or Hawaii in 1963. They did say that the HSCA might have been mislead because they were doing an investigation of John Edward Pie, Oswald's half brother. The Pie records too, were destroyed.

The Japanese connection to the JFK case is reported once again in Dick Russell's, *The Man Who Knew Too Much.* Mr. Russell reports that in January 1964, a scant one-and-a-half months after the assassination, the Japanese government sent a representative from one of its intelligence services to the U.S. to look into the event. This incident was reported in the magazine, *US News and World Report,* in its June 8, 1964 edition.

The Japanese agent sent to the US was Atsuyuki Sassa, who met with FBI agents while he was in this country. According to the author of the *US News* article, it was the belief of the Tokyo government that Oswald was the lone assassin of President Kennedy. Asked why Sassa was involved in the JFK murder, he went on to explain, "You see, these things usually come in strings. We have had a number of assassination attempts in Japan over the past decade. We feared the next tries would be made with high-powered rifles. So I was sent to join the FBI's assassination investigation."

What makes this case worth noting is that in the next issue

of *US News & World Report,* the gist of the Sassa story is correct with the following major exception; agent Sassa did not work with the FBI but with "various security agencies in the US."

What other "agencies in the US" could they be thinking about? The various military intelligence groups, i.e., Army, Air Force, ONI? the DIA or the CIA? And if it was the CIA, what intelligence from Tokyo concerning Lee Harvey Oswald would interest the boys at Langley?

It is also worth noting that agent Sassa was in Dallas days after the assassination. What he did there and whom he saw, if anyone, are still not known.

The Wilcott Report

One particular incident, which the Warren Commission (and later, the HSCA) completely dismissed, concerned a possible CIA tie with the president's alleged assassin, Lee Oswald. The charge came from a rather unlikely source, whose allegations were reported, of all places, in the *New York Times,* a paper not known for its balanced coverage of the Kennedy assassination case.

The source of this startling information was a retired CIA officer by the name of James Wilcott who testified before the House assassinations panel looking into the president's death. Wilcott directly tied in Lee Harvey Oswald with the Central Intelligence Agency, of which he had been a part of for many years. James Wilcott had joined the CIA in 1957, working out of the agency's Tokyo branch as a financial officer. It was his job to distribute covert finds for ongoing, secret operations of which Lee Harvey Oswald was a part. Wilcott told the HSCA members that after the president's assassination, certain members of the CIA Tokyo station came up to him and said that Oswald was being handled by the CIA for a covert operation and that he, Wilcott, had directly dispersed finds for Oswald's assignment using a certain "cryptonym" or code name that he was not familiar with. According to the ex-CIA officer, the rumor that was going around after the events in Dallas was that Oswald was a deep cover operative for the CIA who was to be sent to Russia on an undercover mission. Without naming names, Wilcott said that Oswald was being run by certain CIA agents who knew the entire Oswald case file. When questioned by the HSCA members, Wilcott had forgotten all the names of these CIA bigwigs. He went on to say that he never saw a document with Oswald's name on it, and if any were written down, it would have been destroyed long ago. The CIA, according to the Wilcott testimony, had a special handle on Oswald because of something in his past. What that past is, is not clear but from the record it seems that Oswald might have been involved in a murder of a fellow Marine.

The Marine in question was Martin Schrand, who was stationed with Oswald's unit in the Philippines. The incident took place one night while Schrand was on guard duty. The circumstances are still cloudy but other guards found Schrand dead at his post with a bullet from his own gun located under the armpit. His gun was found lying on the ground a short distance from where his body was located. The Marines conducted a hurried investigation but found no foul play in Private Schrand's death. There has been speculation over the years that Oswald might have been somehow involved in the death of Private Schrand but no conclusive proof was found.

Did the special "handle" offered by James Wilcott that the CIA had on Oswald have anything to do with the death of Martin Schrand? And was he actually working as an undercover agent for either the Army or the CIA during his last days as an active duty Marine? Neither the Warren Commission nor the HSCA took much stock in James Wilcott's Oswald-as-CIA-agent and dismissed the allegation out of hand.

Angleton, the Soviet's & Department 13

As mentioned in the earlier part of this work, James Angleton, the Chief of the CIA's Counterintelligence Branch played an early, pivotal role in the Warren Commission's investigation. Angleton was good friends with Allan Dulles, who had previously served as the Director of the CIA until he was fired by President Kennedy after the failed Bay of Pigs invasion in April, 1961. As the Warren Commission's probe got under way, Angleton, on numerous occasions, would ask Dulles not to bring the investigation of JFK's death to a premature conclusion. As the spy chief saw it, the President's alleged assassin was dead, along with the assassin's assassin (Jack Ruby) and therefore, there were still unanswered questions to be gleamed.

But the reason that Angleton wanted to continue the inquiry was not to find a proper and truthful ending, but to look into the possibility of Cuban and Soviet involvement in the president's assassination. Immediately after Lee Harvey Oswald was arrested and his Soviet background was ascertained, the paranoid Angleton saw a Communist plot, either Cuban or Soviet, behind the tragedy in Dallas. Without even learning all the facts surrounding Oswald's background and political leanings, the fact that the ex-Marine had lived in the Soviet Union, had married a Russian woman whose family had Soviet military ties, was enough to convince Angleton that either Oswald was a Russian agent, or was somehow connected to them or their client state, Cuba.

Angleton was obsessed with the notion that the KGB's Department 13, which specializes in political assassinations, mostly on foreign soil, had a hand in Kennedy's demise. In some cases the KGB and Department 13 would use agents of other nations whom they were friendly with to carry out assassinations on the host country's soil. In other cases, they did the deed alone. Angleton believed that the Cuban's would not act alone in such an important matter as the murder of an American president, and as Oswald's Cuban connection grew in size, he regarded a Soviet Cuban alliance in the president's death to be a certainty.

Right after the assassination, Angleton said that he "discounted 1 million percent" that the event was a domestically carried out plot. And why did he come to this conclusion? Because the Soviet's said that the event was planned by certain right wing elements within the United States. Well, if the right wing, who truly hated President Kennedy carried out the assassination, than that automatically put the-blame not on any domestic conspiracy, but rather, directly upon the Soviet Union!

Newly released documents obtained by this writer on the Kennedy assassination under the *JFK Records Act,* provide additional information on Department 13 and the CIA's interest in any possible Soviet involvement in the Kennedy murder.

The formally "Top Secret" documents on Department 13 begin as follows:

"In 1936, Soviets wanted to assassinate opposition outside the USSR (e.g., Trotskyites and Czarist émigrés). In World War II, 13th Department sabotaged German army in Ukraine, and murdered collaborators even after the war. In the late 1950's, it de-emphasized assassinations but since then has continued to use assassination against Soviet defectors and intelligence agents.

In the event that war is likely, it is to use sabotage to weaken enemy's will to fight. It targets civilian facilities such as broadcast, communication and power facilities. In a war, Soviet military intelligence probably would have responsibility for sabotage of enemy military installations.

The Central Committee must approve any assassination. The KGB is tightly controlled by Central Committee. An attempt on Kennedy would have to have been approved by Khrushchev.

Normally, personnel are permanently assigned to 13th Department throughout their KGB career. Anytime KGB communicates information on its agent operations, it classifies information TOP SECRET and puts it in pouch rather than risk interception and decoding of an electronic signal.

In some cases, special, trained KGB personnel have actually performed the killing. In one case, the KGB recruited a Russian to do the killing but he was not technically KGB. In other cases, KGB recruited foreigners.

Basically, anyone who will kill. It often uses "hoods" or "thugs." It looks for someone who is pro-Soviet or someone who will kill for money. One common thread is that it looks for people who have a grudge against their country.[25]

The CIA document then goes on in detail to examine the possible Oswald-KGB Department 13 connection.

Question: Would KGB have screened Oswald when he was in Russia?

Answer: Yes. They would have close surveillance of him. KGB would have accessed his vulnerability to recruitment. KGB may not have had any interest in him but would know what his vulnerability was. May have gotten compromising photographs.

Question: Would 13th Department have interest?

Answer: Probably not. However, 13th Department dossiers are separate. Nosenko would not have had access to any 13th Department dossier on Oswald.

Question: Is it possible that Oswald was recruited after he left Russia?

Answer: It is possible. If KGB had no interest when he returned to the U.S., it could later have interest and could rely on its vulnerability assessment to use the right approach in recruiting him.

Question: Would Oswald be appealing to KGB since he was not stable and was pro Communist?

---

25 CIA Briefing on (Alleged) Soviet/Cuban Assassinations. Date. 1/15/76. Record No. 157-10011-10029.

Answer: Possibly. It would depend on the job the KGB wanted done. KGB has often used unstable, unreliable agents. KGB is not very adept at recruiting Americans. KGB is not concerned about an individual who is pro-Communist, but wouldn't like Oswald's getting publicity. However, KGB principally looks for men who need money and who are dissatisfied with their country or life.[26]

The same CIA document then goes into Oswald's trip to Mexico City in the fall of 1963 and any possible KGB connections.

Question: Could Oswald have met KGB in Mexico City under cover of visa application?

Answer: It is possible. In an unusual case, KGB will meet agents at Embassy or Consulate where there is a natural reason for meeting there. However, normally KGB meets agents and takes them, under heavy security, to a safe-house.

Question: What is your assessment of Oswald's telephone calls in Mexico City?

Answer: They seem to indicate only that he was applying for a visa. It does not seem plausible that if Oswald was meeting KGB, it would let him make these calls. There would have been no trace of contact with KGB. CIA knows a great deal about KGB Mexico City operations and Oswald's activities don't fit the normal pattern.

Question: Do Oswald's telephone conversations seem unusual?

Answer: Only with regard to the fact that he was asked to return to the Consulate to give them his address.

---

26 Ibid. CIA Briefing.

Question: There is an unusual conversation between Kostikov and Mirabil, the Cuban ambassador to Mexico, which takes place only twenty minutes after Kennedy has been shot. Mirabil calls for Yatskov, a KGB counterintelligence officer, but speaks instead to Kostikov. They talk about arrival of a "suitcase." Mirabil asks Kostikov to a picnic but Kostikov declines the invitation...

Answer: The conversation is strange. Perhaps this is some pre-arranged code, otherwise CIA doesn't understand the conversation.

Question: If Kostikov had been involved, would he have stayed in Mexico City?

Answer: No. He would have been flown out of the country. He stayed there until 1965 and was again assigned there from 1968-1971. It is unlikely he was involved in Kennedy's death.

Question: Were any of the employees of the Cuban Embassy who Oswald contacted or might have contacted members of the DGI-such as Duran, Calderon or Azque?

Answer: The CIA has no evidence that these individuals were DGI.

Question: If Oswald had any contact with a DGI agent, would the government of Cuba be aware of it?

Answer: Yes. However, there have been no reports from Cuba that Oswald contacted DGI.

While James Angleton's paranoia concerning the Soviet Union and its possible disinformation campaign concerning the Kennedy assassination is well known, he, in his own mind, may have had some semblance of maturity in his trying to associate Oswald with Department 13, no matter how flimsy the case.

Richard Case Nagell

One of the most controversial figures to come out of the JFK assassination case is Richard Case Nagell, whose life and association with the Kennedy assassination was narrated in Dick Russell's mammoth book, *The Man Who Knew Too Much.* While Nagell's story were debunked by certain members of the press and the assassination research community as being way out in left field, if only a certain amount of the information presented in the Russell tome is correct, than Richard Case Nagell was right on the mark.

As with many other witnesses or people who had a story other than that set forth by the Warren Commission or the federal government, the Warren panel did not even mention Nagell's name in their 26 volumes, nor did they ever investigate his charges of advance warnings of the impending assassination of President Kennedy in the months before Dallas. Who was Richard Case Nagell, and what did he have to say concerning the assassination of the president, as his association with Lee Harvey Oswald?

Richard Case Nagell was a military intelligence officer from 1955 to 1959, as well as a CIA contract agent from 1962-63. If one is to believe Nagell's story, his path crossed that of the alleged presidential assassin in Japan and elsewhere in the months before Dallas. To Nagell's believers, his tale is one of intrigue and military cover-up at the highest levels of government. To his detractors, his story is as fake as a winter snow in August.

I will not get heavily involved in the entire story of Richard Case Nagell (that has already been documented in the Russell book) but I will give the basic conspiracy story and the lack of Warren Commission interest in it.

On September 20, 1963, Richard Case Nagell walked into the State National Bank in El Paso, Texas, probably to get out of the shimmering heat. But that was not the only reason. He wanted to get arrested! No, he was not a hardened criminal. No, he was not fleeing from the sheriff after gunning down an innocent citizen. He wanted to inform the authorities of a plot to kill the president of the United States, John F. Kennedy, and what better way to do it than to commit a non-lethal crime, get caught, tell his story to the police, and be protected at the same time? As Nagell scrutinized the bank he saw one policeman standing guard in the lobby. What Nagell did next is hard to fathom. He went up to the counter and started to make out a banking transaction when suddenly, he took out a Colt .45 from his jacket pocket and fired two shots into the ceiling, then calmly walked out into the bright sun and sat on the steps of the bank, waiting to be arrested.

Minutes later the police were called and Nagell was arrested. Since a firearm had been discharged inside a federal building, the FBI was called and they took Nagell into their custody. The arresting officer was Jim Bunden who, after exchanging only a few words with his new prisoner, knew that he had a rather unusual prisoner on his hands. In their conversation at FBI headquarters in El Paso, Nagell said that he was glad he was caught, a rather peculiar statement for a person who had just fired a gun into a bank. But then he said something that was even stranger. He said that he was glad not to be in Dallas. Years later, Officer Bunden said that he had no idea what Nagell was talking about at the time, it was only after the Kennedy assassination that he had any idea. P.O. Bunden would also say that he believed Nagell's story about his pre-assassination knowledge of the assassination, and his belief that the government too knew more than it was letting on.

When the FBI began to investigate its new prisoner, they found a man with a quite a different background than their ordinary, run of the mill drunks, and perverts. Nagell was honorably discharged from the U.S. Army after serving 11 years, including a stint in Korea. He was discharged from the Army in 1959 with the rank of Captain where he received the Bronze Star. He also graduated from the Army's Military Intelligence School, and then served in the CIC, Counter Intelligence Corps where he was given a top security clearance.

As the FBI began its investigation into their new captive, they were intrigued with the personal possessions that they found in Nagell's hands. Among the treasure trove were notebooks containing references to meetings with FBI agents in the El Paso area, references to CIA operations, code books, code names, including notes of secret meeting places; all the paraphernalia of someone in the spy game. Interestingly, the FBI found notes written by Nagell on the as yet unheard of Fair Play For Cuba Committee of which Lee Harvey Oswald was a member, and communiqué concerning certain goings on in Mexico City. What could it all mean? But yet, wasn't Nagell in military intelligence during his Army years? Could he still be in the business, even after he left the service?

It seems obvious by his actions that Nagell was trying to send a message to the FBI concerning some secret operation. The FBI in turn, knew all the signs that Nagell was sending out but did not know what to make of them.

In the years following the assassination, records found in the National Archives tell a rather interesting story concerning Nagell's foreknowledge of the Kennedy assassination. One early document, dated December 20, 1963, concerning Nagell reads as follows:

Richard Case Nagell, incarcerated in the El Paso County Jail on a complaint charging him with bank robbery advised that "for the record he would like to say that his association with OSWALD (meaning Lee Harvey Oswald) was purely social and that he had met him in Mexico City and in Texas."

NAGELL stated that he decided to "clear the record up" since his fingerprints were taken on December 12, 1963 by Special Agents WHITE and BOYCE.

Although questioned as to where and when his contacts with OSWALD were made, he refused to comment further and said he had nothing more to say.

It also seems that Nagell had sent a written letter to the FBI before the assassination warning them of the events to come.

A document found in the National Archives addressed to Chief Counsel J. Lee Rankin of the Warren Commission dated March 20, 1964 written by Nagell reads as follows:

"Dear Mr. Rankin,

Has the commission been advised that I informed the Federal Bureau of Investigation in September 1963 that an attempt might be made to assassinate President Kennedy? Was the commission advised that the day before Mr. Kennedy visited Dallas, I initiated a request through jail to the FBI, asking them to contact the Secret Service Division in order to inform such agency of the same information, when it became apparent to me that the FBI believed my revelation to be mendacious?"

Richard Case Nagell
El Paso County Jail-El Paso, Texas

The Warren Commission did not take Nagell's letter seriously after the assassination, and as been mentioned above, his name was not even listed in their index.

A further 1967 letter written by Nagell to Senator Richard Russell, a member of the Warren Commission, tells of Nagell's association with Oswald and his prior knowledge of the events to come:

"Mr. Oswald and his activities came under my scrutiny during 1962 and 1963. My inquiries, coupled with data furnished me by reliable sources, ascertained the following:

Mr. Oswald had no significant connection with the Fair Play For Cuba Committee. He had no significant contact or relationship with so-called pro-Castro elements, though he was led to believe he had such. He maintained no significant association with any Marxist oriented group or movement. He was not affiliated with a racist group or movement. He was not an agent or informant, in the generally accepted sense of the words, for any investigative, police, or intelligence agency, domestic or foreign. He was involved in a conspiracy to murder the former Chief Executive during the latter part of September 1963. This conspiracy was neither Communist inspired nor was it instigated by any foreign government or organization or individual representative of any foreign government."[27]

Despite the letter sent to Senator Russell, and the lack of any response, Nagell continued to send letters to important Congressman and Senators in Washington with the hope of some response. In October 1975, Nagell sent another correspondence to Congressman Don Edwards (D. California) who was chairman of the House Judiciary Subcommittee on Civil and Constitutional Rights. Edwards' committee was beginning an investigation into certain aspects of the JFK case and Nagell thought Edwards would be receptive to his letter. In the letter to Congressman Edwards, Nagell said that the FBI should investigate his note to FBI Director J. Edgar Hoover that he had sent, telling of the circumstances surrounding the assassination. Nagell said that he had information that concerned Oswald and two Cuban's who were involved in the president's death. The Congressman wrote back saying that he would be very interested in meeting with Nagell.

On November 21, 1975, Nagell sent a letter back to Congressman Edwards with an enclosed affidavit concerning the information he said he wrote to J. Edgar Hoover in 1963. The summary of what Nagell sent to Hoover is as follows.

Nagell, using the pen name "Joseph Kramer," and using a return address in Mexico, sent his correspondence inside the U.S. He said that there would be a conspiracy directed against President Kennedy that would take place in late September, 1963, either on the 26th, 27, 28th or 29th of the month. He also sent a physical description of Lee Harvey Oswald, his aliases, and his current address. He also gave Hoover certain details of the planned assassination attempt (which he did not spell out in the

27 The Man Who Knew Too Much. Pg. 52.

affidavit). Nagell ended the letter by saying that once Hoover got the letter he, Nagell, would be out of the United States. Nagell also supplied the aliases he used when meeting with FBI agents previously.

But now it was 1975, and there was a new FBI Director, Clarence Kelley. Congressman Edwards gave Kelley the information supplied to him by Nagell. Kelley looked into the Nagell allegation and replied to Congressman Edwards that the Bureau did not have any such letter sent by Nagell to J. Edgar Hoover in its files. Whether or not the Bureau did indeed have Nagell's letter cannot be known. Nagell died last year as the result of a heart attack. But some skeptics, including author Dick Russell, in a telephone conversation with this writer, say that he might have died by other means.

Nagell said that he kept for safekeeping, a photograph of himself and Lee Harvey Oswald in a bank vault in Switzerland. The photo, according to Nagell, was taken in New Orleans. Also in the Swiss vault is a audio tape of Oswald and his two conspirators. Author Russell told the writer that the contents of the vault are still unknown.

If the Warren Commission really wanted a full and impartial investigation of the Kennedy assassination, they should have looked into Nagell's story, no matter how far fetched it might have seemed.

Chapter 5

"Executive Action," Project ZR/Rifle & JFK

During the last year of the Eisenhower administration (1960), and continuing into the Johnson administration (1966), the United States government conducted a secret plan to first topple the government of Fidel Castro and later, to kill him. This top-secret information was not known to either the Warren Commission in 1964 which was investigating the Kennedy assassination nor to the American public in general. It wasn't until the 1970s's when the Senate was conducting its probe into the Kennedy murder that the American people first learned of their government's secret covert plans to kill Castro. As the surviving members of the Warren Commission, and later the members of the HSCA learned of the Castro plots, they commented in the public press that if they had known of the CIA plots to kill Castro at the time of their (the Warren Commission) inquiry, they might have reached a different conclusion surrounding the assassination of the president.

The Cuban connection to the JFK assassination and more importantly, the CIA-Mafia plots to kill Fidel Castro, may lie at the heart of the Kennedy assassination. Could, as some writers and researchers believe, Castro, having learned of the US governments plans to kill him, have turned the tables and had President Kennedy murdered instead? That possible scenario was postulated in the 1970's by the late mobster, Johnny Rosselli, who told the

HSCA that Castro had "turned" a group of CIA-Mafia hit men who were sent to Cuba to kill Castro, but instead, returned to the US and got Kennedy in Dallas on November 22, 1963. All this will be covered in a later chapter but we will now focus our attention on the Kennedy administration's secret assassination plan called "Executive Action" and its CIA component, ZR/RIFLE, and two of its principal agents, ZR/RIFLE and two of its principal agents, QJ/WIN and WI/ROUGE.

One of the many important disclosures coming out of the 1975 Senate Intelligence Committee's investigation on the CIA's top-secret project to assassinate foreign leaders was Project ZR/RIFLE. This program, originally established to get rid of Castro turned into a nightmare, finally involving plots to kill Patrice Lumumba of the Congo, as well as other foreign heads of state whose policies ran counter to US interest.

Project ZR/RIFLE also has its domestic ramifications as well; involving militant anti-Castro Cuban's whose only goal was to reestablish their old business interests in Cuba. Besides the Cuban's, this top-secret project may have tenuous links to the assassination of President Kennedy. In its inception, Project ZR/RIFLE was operated by the CIA to facilitate the removal of Fidel Castro from Cuba. Castro was originally an ally of the U.S. until he surprised the Eisenhower administration in 1960 by declaring he was a Communist and turned to Moscow for help. ZR/RIFLE had another name, which became synonymous. "Executive Action," that was run out of the Technical Services Division of the CIA.

The "Executive Action" capability included "the development of a general, standby assassination capability." This program included research into the long-term possibilities and capabilities of killing foreign leaders. Despite all the intensive planning for Executive Action, in reality, the plan was never carried out.

The man put in charge of Executive Action/ZR/RIFLE was a tough, James Bond type CIA officer named William Harvey. Harvey was well equipped to deal with this new type of operation, having been one of the key players in the CIA's secret war against Castro, later called "Operation Mongoose." "Operation Mongoose" was run entirely by the CIA from its headquarters in Coral Gables, Florida, on land, which used to be the Richmond Naval Air Station south of Miami. On its south campus, hundreds of CIA agents set up shop, including dozens of "dummy" or "front" organizations. There was a tacit understanding between the CIA and the University of Miami not to interfere with each other's business. The CIA's corporate headquarters, if you will, was dubbed "Zenith Technical Enterprises Inc." To the untrained eye, Zenith Technical specialized in electronics research but in reality, it was the jumping off point on raids into Cuba.

As with all CIA operations, this one was given a code name-JM/WAVE. The man in charge of JM/WAVE was a CIA veteran named Theodore Shackley who had previously served as CIA station chief in both Laos and Vietnam. Both Shackley and Harvey knew each other when they were both stationed in Berlin.

JM/WAVE had over 3,000 people assigned to its base including American and Cuban agents and followers. In time, the JM/WAVE operation took on a life of its own, often competing with its mother at CIA headquarters. A fleet of high-powered boats berthed at the Homestead Marina and other small cays operating out of the Florida Keys, were used to smuggle raiders into Cuba where they would attack Castro's military installations. When any of these secret soldiers got into trouble with the local or federal law enforcement agencies, a single phone call was made and the offending party was set free.

The plans of Operation Mongoose and its son, JM/WAVE, were well known to the Kennedy administration. Attorney General Robert Kennedy was picked to oversee its operation and he rode rough shod over its developments. JFK said at one point, "a solution to the Cuba problem carried top priority in U.S. government. No time, money, effort or manpower is to be spared." To this date it is still not positively clear whether RFK or the president, knew of the CIA-Mafia plans to kill Castro.

What was not known by the public at that time was the fact that the CIA had hired certain members of organized crime to kill Fidel Castro. Men such as Johnny Rosselli, Sam Giancana and Santos Trafficante Jr., were brought in on the action and served as the go-between in the Castro assassination plots. Bill Harvey was furious when he learned of the mob connection arid refused to have anything to do with them.

Bill Harvey was head of the super-secret group called "Staff D" which was responsible for communications intercepts. All of the CIA's covert activities were given cover ids with letters for designation. Staff A was foreign intelligence, B, Operations, C, Counter-Intelligence. But Staff D was different, its doors physically guarded round the clock by armed Marines. To insure maximum security, Harvey brought in his own safe to supplement the other three already in the office.

At one point, Harvey called ZR/RIFLE, "the magic button" and "the last resort beyond the last resort and a confession of weakness." In the notes he left behind, Harvey never used the word "assassination," instead, when dealing with ZR/RIFLE his favorite expression was "maximum security" and "non-attributability."

In the world of lights and shadows at the CIA, the agency, when referring to ZR/RIFLE used the cryptonym KUBARK for its internal use. Nothing was to be written down, only "word of mouth and strictly person to person, singleton ops," no projects on paper. Those people involved would "require most professional, proven operationally competent, ruthless, stable, counter-espionage experienced ops officers."

As ZR/RIFLE-Executive Action began to take shape, Bill Harvey began an intensive investigation to find personnel to carry out their assassination plots. He used CIA Staff D, code named KUTUBE/D to recruit such individuals. *In Wilderness of Mirrors,* author David Martin writes, "no chain of connection permitting blackmail." The Executive-Action file directed… "no American citizen or residents or people who ever obtained US visas could serve as assassins. Corsicans recommended, but not Sicilians. Sicilians could lead to the Mafia."

He further writes, "As an added precaution, planning should include provisions for blaming Sovs or Czechs in case of blow. Should have phony 201 in RG (Central Registry) to backstop this, all documents therein should be forged and backdated."

But this directive by Harvey seems not to be the case. Under documents obtained by this writer under FOIA, a different tack was taken. A six-page memo written to Robert Blakey by S. D. Breckinridge dated September 27, 1978 reveals the following information:

"The ZR/ file, and the QJ/WIN file should speak for themselves. It was clear that Mr. Harvey and an associate initially contemplated trying to establish false files. It is equally clear to anyone willing to purse the question beyond its asking, that they did not do so. Why he did not cannot he recaptured as today Mr. Harvey is dead, but that he did not is clear. Perhaps he tried and simply could not. In any event, it was not necessary to do so anyway, if limited records were desired to enhance the security of the operation."[28]

But did the Kennedy administration know of the ZR/RIFLE program? In CIA document 126-JFK Exhibit F-527 dealing with the plots to kill Castro, it now seems clear that President Kennedy did in fact know of the plan as early as February 1961. William Harvey was briefed in February 1961 (by authority of Richard Bissell) on phase one of the gambling syndicate operation. That briefing was in connection with a sensitive operation that Bissell had assigned to Harvey. Harvey described it thus:

"Early in the Kennedy administration, Bissell called him to discuss what Harvey refers to as an Executive Action Capability, i.e., a general stand-by capability to carry out assassinations when required. Harvey's notes quote Bissell as saying, "The White House has twice urged me to create such a capability.

28 Exhibit-CIA #6114.

"Bissell recalls discussing the question of developing a general capability with Harvey. He mentioned the Edwards/gambling syndicate operation against Castro in that context, but he now thinks that the operation was over by then and that reference to it was in terms of a past operation as a case in point. It was on this basis that Harvey arranged to be briefed by Edwards. Harvey's fixing of the date as February was only after a review of events both preceding the briefings and following it. He says now that it might have been as early as late January or as late as March 1961."

These documents provide a further dimension to the Executive Action Program. Further stated in the IG's report is the following:

"Project/RIFLE was covered as an (   ) operation (ostensibly to develop a capability for entering safes and for kidnaping couriers). It continued on a course separate from the Edwards/gambling syndicate operation against Castro until 15 November 1961. Harvey has a note that on that dale he discussed with Bissell the application of the ZR/RIFLE program to Cuba. Harvey says that Bissell instructed him to take over Edward's contact with the criminal syndicate and thereafter to run operations against Castro."

Events began to move more quickly now as Bill Harvey hired his first "principal agent" code named QJ/WIN and such other principal agents and sub-agents as may be required. QJ/WIN was to be paid $7,200 per year ending on December 31, 1962. A further allocation of up to $16,200 was approved if necessary. QJ/WIN, according to newly released CIA documents, "is under contract as a principle agent, with the primary task of spotting agent candidates." It is now known that QJ/WIN worked for both the CIA and the Bureau of Narcotics.

While it is not known who QJ/WIN is, much can be told about him. "WIN is probably a European soldier-of-fortune, a man capable of anything." According to former CIA Director Richard Helms, QJ/WIN was a man who could carry out a murder at a moments notice. QJ/WIN's first assignment was to kill Patrice Lumumba of the Congo, however, he arrived on scene too late and Lumumba had already been murdered by his enemies. While in the Congo, QJ/WIN teamed up with another man, code named WI/ROGUE by the CIA and brought him into the ZR/RIFLE program. It is speculated that WI/ROGUE had ties to the French Corsica mob bases in Marseilles.

If this is not complicated enough, there is a possible WIN/ROGUE connection to the Kennedy assassination. When Jack Ruby went to trial he was asked by his attorney, Torn Howard, if there was anyone the state could produce who could do him serious harm. Ruby mentioned the name Thomas Eli Davis. Thomas Davis was a convicted bank robber, gun-runner and friend of Ruby's who frequently came to Ruby's nightclub. When JFK was killed, Davis was in North Africa probably setting up a deal to provide arms to the OAS. He was subsequently placed under arrest in a Tangiers, Morocco jail. The Moroccan police found a letter on Davis' person mentioning Oswald and the president's death. Author Seth Kantor in his book *Who Was Jack Ruby?* (Everest House, 1978) writes that Davis was released from his cell by QJ/WIN.

As mentioned before in this book, one of the areas that the Warren Commission failed to look into was the so-called "French Connection" to the president's assassination. While not repeating the entire French Connection story, another area in the saga deems mentioning in connection with QJ/WIN & WI/ROGUE.

Author Steve Rivele, an American journalist who was instrumental in focusing on the French Connection case may have learned the identity of QJ/WIN. While traveling throughout Europe and Africa, Rivele met many people who populated the mercenary world. During his investigation he pursued various leads, and in an article in which he wrote called, *"Trajectory of an Unguided Missile,"* he makes the case that Robert Blemant, a former police commissioner in Marseille turned gangster, may indeed by QJ/WIN.

Blemant served as a police inspector in the Marseille force after World War II. He had a reputation as a tough guy who put contracts out on those criminals he couldn't convict. In time, Blemant became heavily involved in gambling and prostitution not only in France but in England and Lebanon. Rivele says that Blemant worked with the CIA and was the liaison between the French mobster Antoine Guerini and the CIA.

Blemant entered the French Resistance in WW2 and later worked as an agent with the French DGER, counter-espionage in North Africa. After the war he bought a nightclub in Paris called the *Grand Circle* with mobster Jean-Baptist Andreani. In 1954, Blemant had a falling out with Antoine Guerini and had Joseph Leca, a friend of Guerini, killed. On May 4, 1965, Blemant and his wife were killed in a car shoot out. It is believed that the assassins were hired by Guerine and that four shooters were involved.

Rivele believes that Blemant was QJ/WIN for the following reasons. He had good connections in North Africa during World War II and the post war years including various police officials and members of the national government, including those of Morocco. He also had ties with the Luciano narcotics syndicate throughout the Middle East and North Africa and was a trained gunman. Rivele postulated that Blemant could have gotten Thomas Eli Davis out of jail in North Africa.

It now seems clear that President Kennedy and probably his brother Robert were aware of the ZR/RIFLE-Executive Action programs. Whether JFK ordered that Fidel Castro be "terminated" or knew of the Mahue-Rosselli-Trafficante-Giancana connection is another matter. It is very probable that the forces unleashed via Executive Action vis-a-vi the Cuban's, QJ/WIN and the Corsicans of Marseilles saw their ultimate plan being carried out when John Kennedy was murdered.

"Executive Action" and the Kennedy White House

This section in the "Executive Action" ZR/RIFLE story will concentrate on what the role was played by President John Kennedy, his brother, the Attorney General Robert Kennedy, and the various members of the president's national security team vis-a-vi the secret assassination plots, i.e., Castro, and the above mentioned ZR/RIFLE, Executive Action.

It is clear from the record that the first mention of Executive Action-ZR/RIFLE was discussed by McGeorge Bundy, the president's National Security Advisor with Richard Bissell of the CIA in early January or February 1961. According to the Church Committee's investigation of CIA involvement in the assassinations of foreign leaders, "Bissell did not recall any specific conversation with the "White House." However, his initial testimony assumed the correctness of Harvey's notes, and stated that, while he could have created the capability on his own, any urgings would have come from Bundy or Walt Rostow. In a later appearance, however, Bissell said he merely informed Bundy of the capability and that the context was a briefing by him and not urging by Bundy. Bundy said he received a briefing and gave no urging, though he raised no objections. Rostow said he never heard of the project."[29]

In early 1961, the Executive Action agenda was handed over to William Harvey to run and he did so on a strictly need to know, super-secret basis. The Senate report reflects Harvey's thinking on this matter as follows, "Harvey had also testified that, after receiving Bissell's initial instructions to establish an executive action capability, the first thing I did, was discuss in theoretical terms with a few officers whom I trusted quite implicitly the whole subject of assassination, our possible assets, our posture,

29 U.S. Senate Select Committee on Intelligence. Draft. "Assassination Report." 1975. Hereafter known as "Assassination Report."

going back, if you will, even to the fundamental question of A, is assassination a proper weapon of an American intelligence service, and B, even if you assume that it is, is it within our capability within the framework of this government to do it effectively and properly, securely and discreetly?"[30]

As one reads the Assassination Report it is clear that there are a lot of discrepancies in the testimony and recollections of the surviving participants of that era in this regard. By the time the Church Committee began its investigation of the Kennedy assassination and its related parts, many of the members of the late president's administration had either died, or had gone on to other jobs, forgetting the daily routine of state over a decade and a half ago. Others did not keep their notes or private papers and such, they could not accurately recall what transpired years ago.

Such is the case with William Harvey who took over the Executive Action-ZR/RIFLE program and Richard Bissell of the CIA who played such a prominent role in the affair.

The following excerpt regards the testimony between Bill Harvey and the White House regarding the Executive Action capability:

"Harvey testified that his missing notes indicated that Bissell mentioned White House urgings to develop an executive action capability. Harvey said that he "particularly remembered" that Bissell said that he received "more than one" urging from the White House. However, he had no direct evidence that Bissell actually had any such discussion with the "White House." No specific individual in the White House was named to Harvey. Moreover, he said that it would have been "improper" for him to have asked Bissell who he had talked to and "grossly improper" for Bissell to have volunteered that name."

It his testimony to the Church Committee, Richard Bissell said that he did indeed recall having assigned Harvey to take over

30 Assassination Report. Pg. 550.

the ZR/RIFLE Project but he too was not one hundred percent reliable when it came to exactly who gave him the go ahead to start up the enterprise. Bissell testified that he thought he had been given the go ahead by two top Kennedy administration officials; McGeorge Bundy and Walt Rostow, the Deputy Assistant of National Security Affairs. According to Bissell, both Bundy and Rostow were "the two members of the White House staff who were closer to CIA operations." But he later contradicted himself by saying that the creation of Executive Action may have originated within the CIA itself He also testified that "there is little doubt in my mind that Project ZR/RIFLE was discussed with Rostow and possibly Bundy."

According to the Assassination Report when Bissell testified before the committee on July 17 and 22 he said that he now recalled that there was no White House urging for the creation of the Executive Action project "although tacit approval for the "research" project was probably given by Bundy after it was established."

Bissell made this statement after reading the notes that Bill Harvey wrote and which were kept after his death. The notes, which did not mention any White House prodding, said that Harvey had been given his assignment on January 25, 26, 1961, only five days after John Kennedy had been sworn in as president. Now, that presents a major question in the entire ZR/RIFLE Executive Action scenario. Did President Kennedy and his brother Robert, consider such a plan of action in the time between his election in November and his inauguration on January 20, 1961? If so, then it can be assumed that the thought of getting rid of Castro, be it by assassination or the toppling of his government, was in the back of the brothers Kennedy's mind for some time.

Critics of this scenario will postulate that the Kennedy's had no time to consider such a complex scheme, relay their instructions to the CIA in the short, five days since he assumed office. After all, the critics will say, President Kennedy was just getting to know is job as President, he had other major crises to consider;

Laos, the Congo, that were much more important in the overall global scenario.

"Bissell went further and said that he informed Bundy of the program only after it had been created. But Bissell confirmed his original testimony that he did not brief Bundy on the actual assassination plans against Castro already undertaken by the CIA. Bissell was "quite certain" that he would not have expected Bundy to mention the executive action capability to the President."

Question: Would you think the development of a capability to kill foreign leaders was a matter of sufficient importance to bring to the attention of the President?

Bissell: In that context and at that time and given the limited scope of activities within that project, I would not.[31]

The arrogance of Bissell's statements is profound. If a trusted member of the CIA (Kennedy knew and trusted Bissell for many years) who had the confidence of the President of the United States knew about a secret plan to assassinate foreign leaders, with untold consequences if that policy went ahead, did not tell a sitting president about it, is dereliction of duty at its least. By all accounts, President Kennedy probably did not know about the CIA-Mafia plots to kill Castro at the outset of his administration and most likely did not know about the Executive Action/ZR/RIFLE program as well. But all that might have changed as time went on, as the Bay of Pigs invasion fizzled, and as the Mahue-Rosselli-Giancana-Trafficante plots got under way.

"Bissell said that he and Bundy spoke about an untargeted "capability" rather than the plan or approval for an assassination operation. Bissell said that although he does not have a specific recollection, he might have mentioned Castro, Lumumba, and Trujillo in the course of a discussion of executive action because

31 Assassination Report. Pg. 553. (Bissell testimony, 7/22/75. P. 35)

these were the sorts of individuals at that moment in history against whom such a capability might possibly have been employed."[32]

In order to get off the hook as to who gave Bissell the go ahead for executive action, his testimony further implicates Bundy.

Question... I think the testimony of this witness is going further in saying what you received from (Bundy) was, in your view, tantamount to approval?

Bissell: I, at least, interpreted it as you can call it approval, or you could say no objection. He (Bundy) was briefed on something that was being done, as I now believe, on the initiative of the Agency. His comment is that he made no objection to it. I suspect that his reaction was somewhat more favorable than that, but this is a matter that probably someone listening to the conversation on which such a person could have had differing interpretations.[33]

But in order to complicate the matter even further, the Assassination Report takes a new twist. Bissell now tries to turn the initiative over to William Harvey and the CIA. Bissell's statement implicates the agency in the start up of the project. Bissell said of the possible agency involvement:

"It was the normal practice in the agency and an important part of its mission to create various kinds of capability long before there was any reason to be certain whether those would be used or where or how or for what purpose. The whole ongoing job of a secret intelligence service of recruiting agents is of that character. So it would not be particularly surprising to me if the decision to create this capability had been taken without an outside request."[34]

---

32 Ibid. Pg. 553 (Bissell testimony 6/11/75, Pg. 50-51)

33 Assassination Report: Pg. 554. (Bissell testimony 7/22/75. Pg. 31)

34 Ibid. Pg. 554-555. (Bissell testimony, 6/9/75. Pg. 67-68)

The Assassination Report says that Bundy spoke with Bissell about creating an executive action capability but Bundy also includes the fact that they discussed the "capability included killing the individual. Bundy's impression was that the CIA was testing my reaction, not seeking authority." Bundy also says that he did not take steps to stop the proposed program because he believed that it would not come to fruition. But Bundy did support the time of his meeting with Bissell concerning the project saying that he first discussed it before January 25, 1961, a mere five days after JFK's swearing in.

Bundy was adamant that he never discussed the executive action agenda with President Kennedy. He said that Walt Rostow was not responsible for covert operations (and ZR/RIFLE sure was) and he would have had no knowledge of it.

In his statement before the Church Committee, Rostow said that he was "morally certain" that he never heard any mention of the executive action agenda while he served in the Kennedy White House. So, one can assume that if Rostow had no knowledge of executive action, he certainly did not inform the president. That leaves Richard Bissell as the prime candidate who had the foreknowledge of the creation of the program, whether it was initiated in the White House (with Bundy) or at the CIA.

With Bissell completely in the loop as far as the execution of Executive Action is concerned, we now turn our attention to whether or not DCI, Allan Dulles was involved or had knowledge of the project. Dulles was the DCI under the previous Eisenhower administration and was kept on under the new president. When John Kennedy won the Democratic presidential nomination in the summer of 1960, he was given a briefing by Allan Dulles and other top level members of his staff at the Florida home of the candidate's father, former ambassador, Joseph P. Kennedy. It was at this meeting that JFK was informed of the trouble spots around the world, including the American policy toward Cuba. If Dulles informed Kennedy about the agency's plans to topple Fidel Castro it is not known, but Cuba was mentioned in the briefing.

After Kennedy won the election, he was given a further, in depth summary of US policies, and was told of the impending Cuba invasion plot. Kennedy decided, despite his misgivings, to go ahead with the Bay of Pigs invasion and its terrible consequences for his new administration.

In its narrative, the Assassination Report describes Richard Bissell as being "quite certain" that Allan Dulles had complete knowledge of the Executive Action project for the following reasons. "1) it would have come to the DCI's attention at the time of the transfer of William Harvey between components of the agency to work on Cuban operations, and 2) Bissell would imagine it was mentioned to Dulles at the initiation of the project." The other top agency man to learn about the plan was Richard Helms who was DDP (Deputy Director for Plans). Bissell said that after Dulles was fired by President Kennedy after the Bay of Pigs failure, he did not inform the new DCI, Republican John McCone about the ZR/RIFLE-Executive Action program. In his testimony, McCone backed up Bissell's statement.

When Harvey spoke before the committee he said that he assumed that the project was approved by Dulles because of the high stakes involved in such a covert plan. "But Harvey testified that officially advising the DO of the existence of the project was a bridge we did not cross and would not have crossed until there was either specific targeting or a specific operation or a specific recruitment."

The reason for Allan Dulles' knowledge of the plan is obvious. He was the DCI, had overall control of the covert operations being run by the CIA, and thus, should have, and did know about this super-secret of all programs.

As far as the CIA not briefing John McCone, that is disgraceful. McCone was Harvey's and Bissell's boss, paid their salary and should have been told of all covert operations going on at the time. While it is true that McCone was the new boy in town, did not have the all-powerful position as Allan Dulles had, with all his years as the top man at the CIA. Dulles' time in office had spanned two president's, he presided over many top CIA covert operations to topple foreign governments, Iran, Guatemala, etc., and, along with his brother, Secretary of State John Foster Dulles, were two of the most powerful men in Washington in the 1950's. McCone was obviously not in Dulles' league, and it is assumed that those top level CIA men did not want to tell their new boss about the ZR/RIFLE program for obvious reasons: what McCone didn't know wouldn't hurt him and more importantly, what he didn't know could not be canceled.

In their many conversations, both Bissell and Bundy never mentioned any actual names of potential targets involved in the ZR/RIFLE plan; Lumumba, Castro, Trujillo. But Bissell did have knowledge of the ongoing CIA-Mafia plots to kill Castro and never told Bundy about them. And since Bundy was President Kennedy's man when it came to national security policy, and was in daily contact with Bissell at the CIA, it is inconceivable that Bissell did not mention the fact that the CIA was directly planning the murder of Castro. Another reason why Bissell did not tell Bundy was the notion of "Plausible Deniability." What the president did not know could not hurt him. Is it possible that Bissell, by not informing Bundy, was indirectly protecting the president?

If all this cloak and dagger, behind the scenes maneuvering were not enough, in November 1961, another added complication was brought into the equation. This was the so-called CIA-Mafia link to the Kennedy administrations effort to kill Castro. Like the ZR/RIFLE program, it is still not clear what direct knowledge both John and Robert Kennedy knew of the CIA-Mafia plots to kill Castro. New information on Robert Kennedy's possible role in these plots has recently come to light. While serving as Attorney General in his brother's administration, Robert F. Kennedy was put in charge of the attempts to kill Fidel Castro of Cuba. To that effect, the CIA made a secret pact with certain members of the American mob. Now, in a book concerning RFK's role on the war against organized crime in the United States, called

Perfect Villains, Imperfect Heroes, new information on Bobby Kennedy's role in the CIA-Mafia plots is brought to life. Author Ronald Goldfarb says that he was told by Samuel Halpern, a top CIA officer, that Robert Kennedy ordered the CIA to appoint an agency officer to meet with certain members of the Mafia to keep track of old mob contacts left over in Cuba. This unidentified CIA officer traveled to Canada as well as the US in his clandestine meetings (This man's identity came to light via the JFK Records Act. It is Charles Ford – there is more information on Ford in the Appendix of this book).

The origins of the CIA-Mafia plots to assassinate Castro will not be told here, only the facts as they relate to the ZR/RIFLE plot and its consequences. According to the Assassinations Report, both Bissell and William Harvey recalled a meeting in November 1961 at which time Harvey was ordered to make contact with John Rosselli, of the Los Angeles mob. Rosselli was a trusted member of the upper echelons of the mob, not a man with great power, but a man who was trusted by the dons of the mob, a man whom they could control, and who could keep his mouth shut.

It was at this meeting with Rosselli that the first CIA plan to kill Castro was set in motion; a poison pill would be slipped into Castro's food, which would cause an untraceable death. This was all part of the ZR/RIFLE program of which William Harvey would run. Harvey, at this time, gave up his other duties at the CIA and was put in charge of Task Force W, which was the focus of all CIA activity against the Castro regime. "According to Bissell and Harvey, the November meeting involved only the planning and research of a capability rather than a targeted operation against Castro. But Bissell acknowledged that the purpose of the Rosselli contact had been to assassinate Castro, and that it is a fair inference that there would have been no reason to maintain it (the contact) unless there was some possibility of reactivating that operation. Bissell stated that because the assassination plot against Castro involving the syndicate had been stood down after the Bay of Pigs... and there was no authorization to pursue it actively…the responsibility that was given to him (Harvey) was that of taking over an inactive contact."[35]

There has been an ongoing debate as to whether or not William Harvey took over an "on going" assassination plot against Castro or if it was stopped at an earlier date. The CIA's Inspector General's Report on the Castro assassination plots that was declassified a few years ago presents a different light on the matter. The IG's Report states, "After Harvey took over the Castro operation, he ran it as one aspect of ZR/RIFLE. Harvey recalled that during a discussion with Bissell of the creation of an executive action capability, Bissell advised him of "a then ongoing operation" involving the names of Mahue and possibly Rosselli and Giancana, which was part of the Agency's effort to develop... a capability for executive action." Harvey said that during this time period the operation against Castro was "in train" for almost two years or perhaps 18 months.

Not only did Bissell not tell anyone at the White House level (Bundy) about the ZR/RIFLE project, neither did he mention to those same White House officials of the CIA's clandestine link with the mob to kill Castro, the same mob that Attorney General Robert Kennedy was prosecuting at the same time.

In order to get down to who knew what at the White House and the CIA as far as the ZR/RIFLE program was concerned, the Church Committee called as a witness, former DCI, and DDP (Deputy Director for Plans) Richard Helms who was in power at the CIA during this time period. When questioned by the panel, Helms said that the ZR/RIFLE plan never considered the assassination of Castro as one of its main priorities. "In my mind," said Helms, "those lines never crossed."

But Helms' statement was partially contradicted by Bissell in later testimony. He said under questioning that "the contact with the syndicate which had Castro as its target… folded into the ZR/RIFLE project… and they became one. When asked by Senator

35 Ibid. Pg. 559-60. (Bissell testimony 7/17/75).

Howard Baker (R. Tenn.) about the executive action program as it related to the targeting of Castro, Bissell said, "that it was used in the later phase" (of the operation).

With the passage of the JFK Records Act we now have a better overall picture of the Kennedy administrations secret war against Castro's Cuba and of the entire Executive Action ZR/RIFLE plan as a whole. A May 1, 1975 document written by Mason Cargill to David Belin, the counsel for the Rockefeller Commission's investigation of illegal CIA activities in the US, concerns the Executive Action policy. This document concerns an examination by the committee of the files of John McCone, the DCI appointed by President Kennedy after the Bay of Pigs, as it relates to Operation Mongoose and the ZR/RIFLE plan. The pertinent parts of the file read as follows:

"All the documents in McCone's files relating to Cuba and the files relating to MONGOOSE certainly indicate a strong desire to bring about the downfall of the Castro government, along with extreme pressure from the President Attorney General to find a way to do so. However, in one of McCone's files there is an indication that the Agency was aware of plots by certain Cuban exiles to liquidate Castro and that these were reported to the Special Group .... Also, one document indicates that McCone once stated one ultimate objective of our policy toward Cuba should be to encourage dissident elements in the military and other power centers of the regime to bring about the *eventual liquidation of the Castro/communist entourage* and the elimination of the Soviet presence from Cuba."[36]

The same record also makes mention of the ZR/RIFLE plan. "Most documents in the ZR/RIFLE files indicate its primary purpose was to recruit foreigners. (Blank sentence). However, there are a few more incriminating papers which seem to indicate a second purpose of ZR/RIFLE, probably, the establishment an

36 Search of files for material relevant to Assassination Plans. Rockefeller Commission. 5/1/75. Agency: SSCIA. Record No. 157-10005-10201.

assassination capability, and perhaps, even a plan to use one agent (blank) (QJ/WIN), in an assassination attempt in the Congo."[37]

From the documentation in the public record it is obvious that there are different interpretations from the players involved in the Castro assassination plots via Executive Action ZR/RIFLE as to whether or not the original plan involved the murder of the Cuban leader. If it was indeed a cold, calculated plan to kill Castro, there would be nothing written down on paper.

And if the principal players, Bissell, Helms, Bundy, knew of such a CIA plan, they would be more than reluctant to confirm in any way that could compromise their position. And if they knew that there were no such plans afoot to kill Castro, they would have wanted that information to be included in any written documentation just to clear their names. So what have we learned? There are just too many discrepancies to come up with a clear answer as to whether or not the Kennedy White House knew for certain about the CIA-Mafia plans to kill Castro. It is also clear that many of the participants in the CIA, most notably DCI John McCone, did not know the entire story. That is to be expected in an agency whose primary job was secrecy and the dispensing of information on a need to know basis.

We will now turn our attention to what role or knowledge President Kennedy and his brother Robert knew concerning the Castro assassination plots.

What did Jack and Bobby know and when did they know it?

When one reads the historical record concerning the plots to kill Fidel Castro, the Church Committee and the CIA's Inspector General's (IG) Report, it is obvious from the testimony of the surviving members of the Kennedy administration that the

37 Ibid. Search of files for material relevant to Assassination Plans.

president did not know, and was not informed of the CIA-Mafia plots against Fidel Castro. But that same statement cannot be said about his brother, Attorney General Robert Kennedy. Bobby was the point man in the administrations covert activities against the Castro regime, running roughshod over the CIA in its plots against the "beard."

The Church Committee began its investigation into the Kennedy brothers' knowledge of the Castro plots by trying to link the president to the early CIA use of Sam Giancana and Johnny Rosselli. Both Giancana and Rosselli, two men who were then being investigated by Attorney General Robert Kennedy, were also working with the CIA in its early attempts to kill Castro. The cut-out in the early Rosselli-Giancana, CIA-Mafia plots was Robert Mahue, a former FBI and CIA agent who had close ties to both organizations even after his "retirement." The use of Mahue in the CIA-Mafia plots is a long, complicated story, and I will now attempt to tell the tale in its simplest form.

At the end of the Eisenhower administration (1960), Richard Bissell, then head of the agency's clandestine service (dirty tricks), ordered the CIA's head of Security, Colonel Sheffield Edwards to contact his friend, Robert Mahue who was then the owner of a private detective agency in Washington, D.C. Mahue had high profile clients, not only in Washington but throughout the country. One of his most valued clients was none other than the reclusive billionaire, Howard Hughes. It was Mahue's job to look after Hughes' political and business affairs. In his early days, Mahue worked for both the FBI and for the CIA, from 1954-1960. In his secret line of work, Mahue came in contact with both sides of the law; his buddies at the CIA and FBI, as well as certain members of organized crime, most notably, Johnny Rosselli. It was at this time (1960) that CIA officer, James O'Connell (Mahue's "project officer" at the agency) met with Mahue and asked him to recruit his mafia pal, Johnny Rosselli in a clandestine plot to kill Fidel Castro. Mahue told Rosselli that at the same time that Castro was to be killed, an American sponsored invasion of Cuba was to be initiated. This must have been great news to Johnny Rosselli whose mafia colleagues had lost millions of dollars when the former Cuban dictator Batista was overthrown by the young, brash, Fidel Castro. Castro in turn, closed down the lush gambling casinos that brought in millions of dollars into mafia coffers and also lined the pockets of Batista. Thus, the first American sponsored attempt to kill Castro took place in 1959-1960, filly one year before John F. Kennedy was elected President of the United States.

And who were the prime players and beneficiaries in the Cuba plots? Johnny Rosselli, Sam Giancana, Robert Mahue, Santo Trafficante Jr., Mafia boss Meyer Lansky who handled the mob's world-wide money and investments, James O'Connell, and to a lesser degree, Frank Sturgis, whose name would crop up numerous times in the Kennedy assassination investigation. Sturgis was a double agent working for both Castro and the CIA. He also had links to other mobsters like Norman Rothman, Jack Ruby and Louis McWillie, his best friend and mentor.

According to the Schweiker Report, in 1960, Bissell and Edwards briefed Allan Dulles, then DCI, along with his deputy, General Charles Cabell, on the Castro plots, including the assassination phase of the operation.

After Mahue's initial meeting with Rosselli, Rosselli contacted his friend Sam Giancana, the mob boss in Chicago. Giancana was quickly brought into the Castro plots. Another top mob figure to be brought into the plots was Tampa boss Santos Trafficante, Jr. In the summer of 1960, Mahue, Rosselli and Giancana met secretly in Miami Beach at the Fontainebleau Hotel to plan the Castro hit. It is not exactly clear if Santos Trafficante was brought into any of these covert meetings in Miami Beach at the time, but what is known is that he joined the conspiracy at a latter date. Other members of the CIA who made their way down to Miami Beach in the summer of 1960 to take part in the meetings with the mob were CIA officers, William Harvey and Jim O'Connell. In order to protect the identities of the Mafia dons, code names for them were created. Sam Giancana, became "Sam Gold," Santos Trafficante became "Joe," and was to be used as a courier to Cuba who would make all the arrangements with his contacts on the island. (It is believed that throughout his time in the Mafia-CIA plots to kill Castro, that Trafficante was a double agent working for Castro, informing him of every facet of the scheme). The CIA also had code names for the mafia guys when discussing the operation, "A" was Mahue, "B" was Rosselli and "C" was the principal in Cuba (Trafficante?). The code name for Jim O'Connell was "Big Jim." A total of $150,000 was appropriated for the operation, and when the agency brass discussed the plans to kill Castro, it was referred to as an "intelligence operation."

The CIA's first attempt to kill Castro came in the fall of 1960 when Castro, along with hundreds of other foreign heads of state, arrived in New York City to attend the annual General Assembly meeting of the United Nations. Along with Castro in the Big Apple was Russia's Nikita Khrushchev, Gamal Abdel Nasser of Egypt, among others. While the dignitaries were delivering their speeches at the UN, uptown, the CIA was planning Castro's demise. In the safety of the Plaza Hotel, near the vast expanse of Central Park, "Jim Olds" and his pals at the agency devised the first plan to eliminate Castro. Castro was fond of cigars and the CIA's Technical Services Division was ordered to place a poison in one of Fidel's cigars which, when smoked, would cause death. Another scheme concocted by the agency was the spraying of Castro's broadcasting studio with lethal-hallucinations.

If this weren't crazy-enough, the CIA had an even more bizarre scheme hatched while Castro was in town. Working covertly out of the Waldorf-Astoria hotel, the CIA tried to enlist the NYPD to kill Castro. The boys at the agency contacted New York Chief Inspector Michael Murphy (later to become New York City's Police Commissioner) with a special request. Would he place a doctored box of cigars in a suite where Castro was staying? As soon as Castro lit up, the cigar would explode, instantly killing him. Murphy was not amused and he sent the CIA man packing. After all, wasn't it his job to protect Castro, not kill him? Thanks to clearer heads, that plan was never carried out.

The beginnings of the "Cuba Project," which would end with the death or overthrow of the Castro regime, had its roots in the Eisenhower administration with Vice President Richard Nixon as the point man. Plausibility Deniability was the code word as far as the project was concerned; Nixon would be the point man, with Ike left out in the cold. But the Cuba Plan took on a life of its own, violating US laws ranging from the Neutrality Act, the Firearms Act, not to mention breaking the laws of several states. The CIA created its own army, navy, air force, all located in and around Miami Beach, with little or now intrusion from local authorities. The CIA's Special Operations Division ran the show with airlines, bogus businesses, arms depots, and covert training camps set up all along the Southern Florida coast from Miami to the Keys.

"The Cuba Project was the first time in the agency's history that these hired adventurers were extensively employed inside the United States. They were a splendidly checkered crew who accepted as a risk of doing business with the CIA the disagreeable fact that it would disavow them if they were caught. Other than that, the agency was not too sticky as an employer. Many CIA special ops found their intelligence covers gave them license to steal, usually with an official look the-other-way attitude; if smuggling guns or dope happened to be integral to their covers, they pocketed the profits."[38]

And what an adventurous group they were. Men like E. Howard Hunt, Frank Sturgis, Gerry Patrick Hemming, David Atlee Philips, William Pawley, Pedro Diaz Lanz, Gordon Novel, Howard Davis, among others, all soldiers of fortune, anti-Castro, and in time, anti-Kennedy, all volunteered to take on the Castro assignment. And after November 22, 1963, many of these same

38 The Fish Is Red. William Turner & Warren Hinckle. Pg. 16.

names were to be implicated in the Kennedy assassination. These same people who worked for the CIA in the Cuba plots were not mentioned in the Warren Commission's investigation of the assassination. It was as if the panel members did not want to know that these men might have had some knowledge of the events in Dallas, or if they did, they did not care to learn what they knew.

And if these adventurers made out good, so did the city of Miami. From a backwater, bug infested strip of land at the turn of the century, the Miami and Miami Beach of 1960 was now a thriving economic community. After the depression of the 1920's ruined many businessmen, the city turned around economically after the end of World War II. Hotels of every stripe and color were built to house the ever-growing number of tourists, many of them foreign, who flocked to the land of sunshine and bikinis. And who helped in the growing economic boom that landed in Miami? The American mob. The Mafia, whose lucrative casinos in Cuba were pumping millions of dollars into their hands in the pre-Castro days, sent a great deal of these profits to Miami. Living in Miami was a large number of super-patriotic Americans whose anti-Communism ranked among the most virulent in the country. Thus, the city was the perfect place for the CIA's secret war against Castro's Cuba.

It was in this atmosphere of covert activity and anti-Communism that led the CIA to the doorsteps of Johnny Rosselli. Johnny Rosselli was as well connected to the power elite (the mob) in Batista's Cuba as anyone else. He knew all the important people in the Havana casino gambling circuit, made deals with them, and carried their skimmed cash out of the country and into bank accounts in Miami. At their initial meeting in Miami between the CIA and Rosselli, a number of "hit" options were discussed as far as eliminating Castro was concerned. Jim O'Connell broached the subject of a clean, up-front murder to take care of Castro. But Rosselli, Giancana and Trafficante balked, telling the CIA man that their standard hit would not work in this case. Castro, they said, was too well guarded; another method was needed. Rosselli asked for something "nice and clean." He suggested a poison that would be placed in Castro's drink or food. A few days later, Castro would be dead and an autopsy would not be able to trace the cause.

The "how to" was given to the CIA's Joseph Schneider of the Technical Services Division who made up a batch of poison pills, which were tested on monkeys. After successful testing, the pills were given to O'Connell in February 1961. O'Connell in turn, gave the pills to Rosselli who turned them over to one of his agents in Cuba. The middleman in the poison pill delivery was "Joe the Courier," Santos Trafficante who gave the pills to the CIA's man in Havana, Juan Orta who was to be the one to actually plant the pills in Castro's food. Orta had served as the Office Chief and Director General of the Office of the Prime Minister (Castro). "The gangsters said that Orta had once been in a position to receive kickbacks from the gambling interests, had lost that source of income, and needed the money." Thus, the Orta channel was opened. After Orta received the pills he apparently got cold feet and soon returned them to the CIA. On January 26, 1961, Orta lost his job in Castro's office, and in April, took refuge in the Venezuelan embassy. Orta stayed under the protection of the Venezuelan's until October 1964, when he was given a pass to leave the country. In February 1965, he returned to Miami.

The CIA IG's Assassination Report has this to say concerning the Orta channel:

"It appears that Edwards and O'Connell did not know at that time of Orta's fall from favor. They have made no reference to it—ascribing Ortas's failure to cold feet. It would seem, though, that the gangsters did not know that Orta had already lost his access to Castro They described him as a man who once had a position that allowed him to rake-off on gambling profits, a position that he had since lost. The only job which we can associate Orta that might have allowed him a rake-off was the one he held in the Prime Minister's Office, which he lost on 26 January, 1961. It

seems likely that, while the Agency thought the gangsters had a man in Cuba with easy access to Castro, what they actually had was a man disgruntled at having lost access."[39]

The IG's account states further that when Orta ended his role as a CIA assassin he gave the agency the name of someone else who tried to kill Castro but failed. It is not mentioned in the report who this person was.

With the Orta channel collapsed, Johnny Rosselli gave the CIA another name who might be able to help in the Castro assassination plot. He was Tony Varona, an associate of Santos Trafficante, a man well connected to the anti-Castro cause. Varona was head of the Democratic Revolutionary Front, part of a larger umbrella group made up of anti-Castro sympathizers living in South Florida. In July 1960, after Senator John Kennedy won the Democratic Presidential nomination, four high ranking Cuban exiles meet secretly with Kennedy in his Senate office. They were Manuel Artime, Aureliano Sanchez Arango, Jose Miro Cardona and Tony Varona. All four would later play a large part in the overall Cuba Project; the Bay of Pigs invasion and the Castro plots. The meeting was arranged by the CIA who wanted to play ball with both Kennedy and Vice President Nixon, the eventual Republican nominee. The purpose of the meeting was to inform Kennedy of the CIA's plans to get rid of Castro. In this way, no matter who won the White House, its occupant would know of the CIA's plans to kill Castro and would be implicated up to his teeth.

The IG's narrative on Varona reads in part:

"Reports from the FBI suggest how Trafficante may have known of Varona. On 21 December 1960, the Bureau forwarded to the Agency a memorandum reporting that efforts were being made by U.S. racketeers to finance anti-Castro activities in hopes of securing the gambling, prostitution, and dope monopolies in Cuba in the event Castro was overthrown. A latter report on 18,

39 CIA Targets Fidel: The Secret Assassination Report. Ocean Press. Pg. 41.

January 1961 associates Varona with these schemes... Trafficante approached Varona and told him that he had clients who wanted to do away with Castro and that they would pay big money for the job... Varona is reported to have been very receptive, since it would mean that he would be able to buy his own ships, arms, and communications equipment."[40]

The agency once again enlisted the help of Rosselli and he got in contact with Varona. Rosselli passed along a certain amount of cash to Varona, (the amounts range from $25,000 to $50,000) for the necessary expenses. Authorization for the Varona channel was given by Robert Bannemian who was Sheffield Edwards deputy. Also involved in the Varona plan was Jake Esterline, who was high up in the Cuba Project. Esterline gave the go ahead for payment and he recalled it being only $10,000 plus expenses.

According to the IG report, when Esterline learned that Varona was part of the plan he called for its cancellation. This was because Varona, as head of the Revolutionary Front was heavily involved in the plans for the Bay of Pigs invasion and he feared for the safety of the operation. But Varona stayed in the loop, despite Esterline's attempts to end it.

Once again Rosselli gave the money and the poison pills to Varona. Varona in turn, handed over the pills to one of his contacts inside Cuba who had access to a restaurant where Castro frequently dined. This intrigue failed, as Castro did not come back to his one time favorite watering hole.

After the failure of the Bay of Pigs invasion of Cuba in April 1961, the CIA plots to kill Castro came to a temporary stop. Sheffield Edwards sent word to Rosselli via Jim O'Connell to stop all further attempts on Castro and cut off the finding. There were just too many complications in the wake of the fiasco to continue another, far ranging covert operation run by the CIA. But in the wake of the failed Bay of Pigs invasion the record becomes distorted about what exactly was the status of the plans

40 Ibid. Pg. 42-43

to kill Castro. In his testimony, Edwards's states that the operation was completely shut down after the Bay of Pigs and was not reactivated until the spring of 1962. O'Connell also states that the operation was shut down after April 1961 but he also says that it was only on a temporary basis. He said that there was some sort of activity going on in the intervening year but he wasn't sure what.

But William Harvey stated that when he took over the Castro plots, he was taking over an ongoing operation. Harvey was given the job as Cuba chief in a briefing by Richard Bissell in late 1961, early 1962. He met with Edwards in February 1962 and was briefed on the full aspects of the Castro operation. The Assassinations Report has this to say concerning Harvey's taking over the Castro function:

"After Harvey took over the Castro operation he ran it as one aspect of ZRRIFLE; however, he personally handled the Castro operation and did not use any of the assets being developed in ZRRIFLE. He says that he first came to think of the Castro operation and the ZRRIFLE as being synonymous. The overall Executive Action program came to be treated in his mind as being synonymous with QJWIN, the agent working on the overall program. He says that when he wrote of ZR/RIFLE, QJ/WIN the reference was to Executive Action capability; when he used the cryptonym ZRRIFLE alone, he was referring to Castro."[41]

In April 1962, Harvey contacted Edwards in order to set up a meeting with Rosselli. Edwards then contacted Richard Helms who gave his approval. Before and after his covert meetings with Rosselli, Harvey informed Helms on their discussions and plans.

"Edwards statement that he "verified Helms' approval" is the earliest indication we have that Mr. Helms had been made witting of the gambling syndicate operation against Castro. Harvey added that, when he briefed Helms on Rosselli, he obtained Helms' approval not to brief the Director.)"

41 CIA Targets Fidel. Pg. 50

While there is no dispute as to the turnover to Harvey of the Castro plots, there is some disagreement as to the circumstances concerning how it was done.

The IG's narrative goes as follows:

(A) *Edwards believes that the operation was called off completely after the Bay of Pigs and that there was no further operational activity in connection with it until Harvey met Rosselli and reactivated the operation in April 1962. O'Connell introduced Harvey to Rosselli and Edwards had nothing to do with the operation-with the exception of a meeting with Attorney General Robert Kennedy in connection with the Phyllis McGuire wiretapping incident. Edwards' records show that on 14 May 1962, Harvey called Edwards and "indicated that he was dropping any plans for the use of Rosselli for the future."*

(B) *Harvey's recollection of the turnover tends to support Edwards' summary, but he claims that he took over "a going operation." Some support for this claim in found in his description of just how it was planned to get the poison into Castro's food by employing someone with access to a restaurant frequented by Castro. The mechanics were identical with those described by Edwards and as reported in our earlier account of phase one of the operation.*

(C) *O'Connell's account of his own role in the operation in the early weeks following Harvey's supposed takeover makes it evident that there was not a clean break between the Office of Security's responsibility and that of Harvey. Further, O'Connell now believes that there must have been "something going on" between April 1961 (after the Bay of Pigs) and April*

> *1962, but he claims to be unable to remember any of the particulars.*[42]

What is of particular interest in the entire area was the fact that the CIA, in the persons of Edwards and Lawrence Houston, met with Attorney General Robert Kennedy on May 7, 1962 and informed him of the wiretapping case (see next section) that involved the mob, the CIA, and the initial plots to kill Castro. According to the IG'S report, Edwards "briefed (Kennedy) him all the way." This is the first incident that we know of that Robert Kennedy learned of the CIA-mob plans to kill Fidel. It is inconceivable that Robert Kennedy failed to tell his brother, the president, of this news. The men were so close, in all respects, both personally and on such an important policy position, that he could have kept such a secret from him.

But an incident involving the mob and some of Hollywood's most famous stars would now threaten to unravel the fledgling Castro plots and give the brothers Kennedy their first inkling of the CIA's deception.

The Las Vegas Wiretapping Case

At the center of the case was Sam Giancana, "Sam Gold," as the CIA called him. It seems that short, rather nondescript Giancana fell in love with Phyllis McGuire, one of the beautiful and successful singers in the then popular McGuire Sisters act. But it seems that Phyllis was also having an affair with comedian Dan Rowan, he of the also successful comedy act with his brother, Martin-Rowan and Martin's "Laugh In" would become a popular television show. Sam Giancana got terribly jealous and took measures to end the affair. All this took place in the fall of 1960, just as the secret CIA-Mob alliance to kill Castro was

42 Ibid. Pg. 52

taking shape. And who was directly involved in both of these secret capers? Sam 'Momo' Giancana.

It seems that Rowan and Phyllis McGuire were getting ready to open their respective acts in Las Vegas and Giancana decided to act. He asked Robert Mahue, the man who originated the covert CIA contacts with the mob, to put a bug in the signer's room. Mahue rejected Giancana's offer but the old mobster had Mahue and the CIA by the ropes. After all, said Sam, he wouldn't want to give the press the word that the agency was working with the bad guys, would they? Mahue reluctantly agreed to Giancana's blackmail and got a private detective friend, Edward DuBois who ran a private eye agency in Miami, to place the bug. DuBois sent one of his employees, Albert Belletti to Las Vegas to plant the bug in Rowan's room. When Rowan was out, Belletti placed a bug in the singer's phone but in his haste to leave, made a mess, leaving his tricks of the trade all over the place. The maid found Belletti's handiwork and called the local police. The material left over in Rowan's room was traced to Belletti and he was arrested. Belletti called Mahue, pleading that he clean up the mess. Mahue was able to use all his persuasion to get the charges dropped against Belletti, with the possible help along the way by Johnny Rosselli. But Belletti's call to Mahue alerted the FBI who decided to prosecute under the federal wiretapping code. When Mahue was approached by the G-men, he told them to see Sheffield Edwards.

Edwards told the Assassinations Committee that if Mahue got in trouble with the FBI during his work on the Castro plots he should tell them that he was working on an "intelligence operation" headed by him. Mahue told the FBI that he did not personally do the bugging of Rowan's room but that it grew out of an operation headed by Edwards. "The Bureau, in a memo from J. Edgar Hoover to the DCI, dated 23 March 1962, stated that: Mahue claimed that he ordered coverage of Rowan on behalf of the CIA's efforts to obtain intelligence information on Cuba through the hoodlum element, including Sam Giancana, which had interests there. Mahue said he was put in contact with Giancana in connection with these intelligence activities through John Rosselli, a Los Angeles hoodlum. Mahue authorized the wiring of Rowan's room and discussed this matter with John Rosselli."

There is also conflicting information on whether or not the CIA had given prior authorization to the tap being installed in the first place. In the Church Committee testimony, O'Connell testified that he had called Edwards and cleared the placement of an electronic bug in Rowan's room prior to the installation of the tap. Mahue asked O'Connell if the agency would handle the job but was told by Edwards it would not do it but would not object if a private agency could be found to take care of the problem. It also seems that the CIA paid for the tap anyway. "DuBois told FBI agents that Mahue had paid him a retainer of $1,000. O'Connell confirmed that CIA "indirectly" paid for the tap because "we paid Mahue a certain amount of money, and he just paid it out of what we were giving him."

But in a May 14, 1962 memorandum for Attorney General Robert Kennedy written by Edwards this is not the case. Edwards stated that "at the time of the incident neither the agency nor the undersigned knew of the proposed technical installation." (A memo by J. Edgar Hoover states that the Attorney General said he had been told by Edwards that the "CIA admitted that they had assisted Mahue in making the installation" – Memo, Hoover, 4/10/62).

"The Inspector General's Report accepted Edwards' assertion that the Agency was first unwitting and then a reluctant accessory after the fact, but offered no further evidence to support that contention."

But why was the tap put in place to begin with? Was it just to keep track of Giancana's girl friend, or was there some other motive involving the plots? The Church Committee wanted to know whether or not the CIA itself set up the tap in order to trace any possible leaks by Giancana about his involvement in the Castro plots. An October 18, 1960 memo from J. Edgar

Hoover stated that "a source whose reliability has not been tested" reported:

"During recent conversations with several friends, Giancana stated that Fidel Castro was to be done away with very shortly. When doubt was expressed regarding this statement, Giancana reportedly assured those present that Castro's assassination would occur in November. Moreover, he allegedly indicated that he had already met with the assassin-to-be on three occasions. Giancana claimed that everything has been perfected for the killing of Castro, and that the assassin had arranged with a girl, not further described, to drop a pill in some drink or food of Castro's."[43]

Rosselli testified to the committee that Mahue had given him two explanations as to why the bug was planted; first, that Giancana wanted to know about any possible affair between McGuire and Rowan and two, whether or not Giancana had told McGuire about the Castro plots. Mahue gave the second explanation to the Bureau, and Edwards, in his memo to RFK said, "Mahue stated that Sam Giancana thought that (Giancana's girlfriend) might know of the proposed operation and might pass on the information to one Dan Rowan, a friend of (Giancana's girlfriend)" – Memo, Edwards to Kennedy, 5/14/62).

When the FBI asked the CIA about the whole affair, the agency responded by saying that they would object to Mahue's prosecution because it "might reveal sensitive information relating to the abortive Bay of Pigs invasion." Herbert Miller, the Assistant Attorney General, Criminal Division, wrote in a memo dated April 24, 1962, advising RFK that the "national interest" would preclude any prosecutions based upon the tap. After a briefing by the CIA with Robert Kennedy, the case against Mahue was dropped.

Newly released documents obtained by the author describe the testimony of Joseph Shimon, a man well connected to the

43 Church Committee Report. Pg. 207

mob and the intelligence services in the 1960's, who gives his own account of the Vegas wiretap incident. According to Church Committee documents, Joe Shimon was in Miami in March of 1960 with Sam Giancana, Robert Mahue and Johnny Rosselli to see the heavy weight boxing fight between Igmar Johansen and Floyd Patterson. Shimon, Mahue and Rosselli all stayed at the plush Fontainebleau Hotel and it was there that Shimon was told by Rosselli about the Castro plots.

According to the documents, "Shimon stated that the wiretap in Phyllis McGuire's hotel room in Las Vegas, Nevada, did not involve the CIA. He stated that Mahue had the wiretap installed per agreement with Sam Giancana. Mahue was paid $5,000 by Sam Giancana to have a bug placed in the hotel room because he was concerned that his girlfriend was having an affair. Giancana could not have done it himself because he was a persona grata in Nevada. When the wiretap was discovered, Shimon stated that Bob Mahue went absolutely nuts. The FBI was on to Mahue soon after the wiretap was discovered and it was Mahue that put the FBI onto Johnny... Shimon stated that when the FBI came to Rosselli that they decided to go to the CIA in order to work something out... Shimon said that when the CIA involvement with the wiretap on Phyllis McGuire was revealed, Sam Giancana went nuts. Sam, it seems, was most irate at the idea that someone else had engineered that wiretap."[44]

The author of this memorandum, Andy Postal, had some very interesting comments at the end of the document. I think it is necessary for the reader to know some of what he wrote:

"Assuming that Joe Shimon is a credible witness, it would appear that our investigation into the Castro assassination question has been misled. With the passage of the pills first occurring in March of 1960, it appears that the original passage of pills may have been a project of W.H. (Western Hemisphere-CIA) four, under the direction of J.C. King. This raises the question of the

44 Chronology of Events as We Now Know Them. From Andy Postal. September 12, 1975. SSCI Box # 265-14.

nature, and extent of the involvement by the Office of Security personnel. It also raises a significant question as to the accuracy of the testimony of many of the witnesses involved in the Castro assassination plots, and the IG's report of 1967. Further, it is this writer's opinion that many of the people that I have interviewed who were top officials in the Department of Justice during the Kennedy administration have been less than candid in their accounts of what was or was not told to the Attorney General. It is conceivable that many of these officials knew something about the CIA underworld connection, and have acted to prevent further dissemination of the taint... In light of the change in the date of the initial passage of the pills, it is recommended that a reevaluation of the entire Castro assassination question be undertaken."[45]

What Mr. Postal is talking about is a possible earlier Mafia plot to kill Castro before officially getting involved with the CIA. If, as Joe Shimon says, the first poison pill transfer to Rosselli took place in Miami in March 1960, then the date of the *official* Mahue-Rosselli O'Connell meeting in September, 1960 is wrong. Could the mob have been working solo in their Castro assassination scheme before making its deadly alliance with the agency? It seems so.

By May of 1962, Attorney General Robert Kennedy was officially briefed on the Castro plots and the Las Vegas wiretapping incident. On May 7, 1962, Sheffield Edwards and Lawrence Houston met privately with him and as Edwards puts it, "briefed him all the way." Kennedy said that this presented a major problem for him as the Attorney General due to his ongoing federal investigation against Giancana and his fellow mobsters. He further said that he could not proceed with the wiretapping case against Mahue. Then Kennedy is quoted as having said, "I trust that if you ever have to do business with organized crime again – with gangsters – you will let the Attorney General know before you do it."

45 Ibid.

But what Bobby did not say to his CIA colleagues was NOT to have anything further to do with the mobsters. Instead, he only said that he wanted to be kept informed if they (the CIA) had any further meetings with his old enemies. But why would RFK, a man whose vendetta against Organized Crime in the United States that began in the 1950's when his brother, Senator John F. Kennedy was a member of a Senate panel investigating the mob, and he was the committee's chief counsel, not bang his fist on the table, scream at the top of his lungs, and say NO MORE? The CIA's alliance with the same members of organized crime whom his Justice Department was raking over the coals was now in league with these same people. Did it matter that much that the enemy of his enemy–the mob and Castro–were working toward the same end the murder of Fidel Castro? The enemy of my enemy is my friend. Did that ages old saying stop RFK from continuing on his years-on-end struggle against the bad guys? Or did Robert Kennedy see a plan to use his old foes to bring down his new one? And did it really matter when it came to the reality of power politics, circa 1962? This was the way the game was played and Robert Kennedy was the consummate player.

After briefing Kennedy, both Edwards and Houston wrote an internal memo about the meeting but did not inform the DCI, John McCone of what had transpired. They failed to tell McCone because he had previously been kept out of the loop as far as the CIA-Mafia plots were concerned and wanted to keep it that way. However, they did brief the DDCI (Deputy Director of the CIA) General Carter but did not tell him the complete truth.

After his meeting with Edwards and Houston, Robert Kennedy now assumed (incorrectly) that he would be given further briefings by the CIA if they did any more covert work with the mob. But right after RFK's May 7, 1962 summary of "Phase One" –that of the relationship with the gambling syndicate – "Phase 2" under Bill Harvey was already under way. On April 8, Harvey had been introduced to Rosselli and later that month Varona and his men had been given the lethal pills to kill Castro. But in reality,

Bobby Kennedy was not told that the plans to kill Castro were reactivated and that the agency continued to use the mob in its deadly business.

Back at the CIA, Richard Helms was told of the meeting with RFK and he agreed that was the proper thing to do. On May 14, Edwards wrote a memo for the record stating that Harvey had agreed to drop Rosselli in any further work. "Edwards' memo states that he cautioned him (Harvey), that I, (Edwards), felt that any further projects should have the tacit approval of the Director of Central Intelligence. Edwards informed us that he had no specific recollection of having told Harvey of Kennedy's warning that the Attorney General should be told in advance of any future CIA use of gangsters."

Robert Kennedy's knowledge of the Castro plots also came in a memo to the Attorney General on May 22, 1961 by FBI Director J. Edgar Hoover. This long memo described the agency's use of Robert Mahue as the "cut out" with the gambling syndicate and described how the mob could use their considerable resources still inside Cuba to keep track of Castro's comings and goings. It also told of Sam Giancana's agreement to work with the CIA in any way possible. The memo said in part, "Edwards added that none of Giancana's efforts have materialized to date and that, several of the plans still are working, and may eventually pay off." The summary went on to describe the major role played by Mahue and put Edwards' part as being untraceable to the mob. "Colonel Edwards said that since this is "dirty business" he could not afford to have knowledge of the actions of Mahue and Giancana in pursuit of any mission for CIA."

Robert Kennedy's knowledge of the gambling syndicate's role in the Castro plots is revealed in this passage from the Church Committee:

"Mr. Bissell, in his recent briefings of General Taylor and the Attorney General and in connection with their inquiries into CIA relating to the Cuban situation, the Taylor Board of Inquiry told the Attorney General that some of the associated planning

included the use of Giancana and the underworld against Castro."[46]

Hoover's memo to Robert Kennedy definitely caught his interest and the A.G. wrote on the margin a note saying, "Courtney, I hope this will be followed up vigorously." Courtney Evans was the FBI's liaison with the Attorney General and the President. In the Church Committee's Assassination Report, Evans says that he never saw the early FBI memos concerning the early stages of the Castro plots but that he did have discussions with RFK on the May 22 note.

Further interest by Robert Kennedy is seen in a short note from the Justice Department files dated October 6, 1961 which said, "Yesterday, P.M. told me that A.G. (Robert Kennedy) had inquired as to status of this case and think Harold (Shapiro) to it taken care of."

It is now evident that Robert Kennedy knew of the CIA-Mafia link in early 1961, a short, few months after his brother was inaugurated. Not only was he told of the plans to kill the "beard," but he acquiesced in them. He could have very easily told Edwards and Houston NOT to go any further; after all, wasn't he plotting to put Giancana, and Rosselli and the others behind bars? And it is inconceivable in this writer's mind that Robert Kennedy would not keep this very important information from his brother, the president. After all, Cuba was one of the highest priorities of the New Frontier, especially after the failed Bay of Pigs invasion. Their personal relationship was too strong for RFK not to keep this news from his brother Jack. After all, why had JFK put in brother in his official inner circle in the first place? So that he could have complete confidence in one man, above all others. And that man was Robert Kennedy.

Gus Russo, the author of the book *Live By The Sword: The Secret War Against Castro and the Death of JFK,* (Bancroft Press, 1998), confirms Robert Kennedy's active role. "Both JFK and RFK knew

46 Assassination Report. Pg. 174.

about the plans to kill Castro. This knowledge comes from the newly released files, and members of the Cuban Task Force who are still alive. Bobby was told by the CIA to do whatever they had to do to kill Castro. Robert Kennedy knew about the plots before the Hoover memo concerning the use of mob members." Russo told the author that the pressure to get rid of Castro came from the White House and abruptly stopped on November 22, 1963. "LBJ stopped the plans," continued Mr. Russo. "The CIA was very happy that the plans were ended."[47]

As we look at the historical record it becomes obvious that Robert Kennedy had early knowledge of the CIA-Mafia plots to kill Fidel Castro. It also seems obvious that Robert Kennedy most likely shared that information with his brother, the president of the United States, John Kennedy. But what is still in dispute is what knowledge did President Kennedy himself have of the Castro plots? The Assassination Report is replete with testimony of former Kennedy administration officials who officially deny that the president had any inkling of the plot to kill Castro. That is true in part as the top level CIA individuals involved in the plans, Edwards, O'Connell, Helms, failed to inform the president, let alone their own boss, John McCone. The term Plausible Deniability is ripe here, as the CIA team, for whatever reasons, did not want the president to become directly involved in the plans.

But the record is full of tidbits of information concerning members of the mafia, a girl friend of the president's who knew all sides in this puzzling tangle, and actions taken by the president himself that may put a damper on his aide's testimony.

What we have up to now is this: In early 1960, the CIA made a covert arrangement with the mob to kill Castro. Assorted covert plans were set in place, including the smuggling of exotic poisons into Cuba, along with a team of snipers to do the job. None of these plans worked. By May 1961, J. Edgar Hoover informed Robert Kennedy of the CIA's use of Sam Giancana in the

47 Phone interview with Gus Russo, 7/14/97.

CIA-mob plots, along with Johnny Rosselli and Santos Trafficante. JFK asked that he be "kept informed" of any future CIA dealings with the mob. It can be assumed that he told his brother, the president.

But now a new twist enters this already complicated picture. In the summer of 1960, right after winning the presidential nomination, Jack Kennedy was introduced to a lovely young woman by some of his show business friends, Frank Sinatra, named Judith Campbell. She was instantly taken by Kennedy's good looks and star quality and an affair shortly began. This love affair would last well into Kennedy's second year in office (1962) and would result in numerous phone calls by Campbell to JFK in the White House. (Campbell, now stricken with cancer, told the press that she was pregnant with Kennedy's child and that an abortion was arranged for her by Sam Giancana, the same man who was directly involved in the Castro plots). But while Campbell was getting it on with JFK at the White House and other hideaways, she also had a personal relationship with Sam Giancana and Johnny Rosselli. Over the years Miss Campbell has asserted that she carried secret messages to and from the White House to Sam Giancana, although she did not know what was in these missives.

The Campbell-JFK liaison was discovered early on by the FBI and J. Edgar Hoover took an immediate interest. Hoover hated the Kennedys and it was only the fact that the Attorney General happened to be the brother of the President of the United States that Hoover had to comply with Bobby's orders. But now Hoover had the dirt on the president and he effectively had JFK over a barrel. He had the fact that the president of the United States, a married man, was not only having an affair with another woman, but this same woman was also having an affair with a top mobster. This was powerful political dynamite and Hoover knew how to use it.

The Assassinations Report treats the Campbell-JFK affair as follows:

"Information has been developed in connection with the

investigation of John Rosselli one of the second group of forty hoodlums receiving concentrated attention, that he has been in contact with Judith Campbell. A review of the telephone toll calls from Campbell's residence discloses that on November 7 and 15, 1962; calls were made to Evelyn Lincoln, the President's secretary at the White House. The relationship between Campbell and Mrs. Lincoln or the purpose of these calls is not known. Information has also been developed that Campbell has associated with Sam Giancana, a prominent Chicago under world figure."[48]

The Assassinations Committee says that Evelyn Lincoln got a copy of the note and gave it to the president. Thus, President Kennedy was certainly aware of his girlfriend's association with two of the top mobsters that his brother was trying to prosecute; Sam Giancana and John Rosselli. What he did with this information, if anything, is not known.

Via the "JFK Act" we are now able to see the complete logs of phone conversations between President Kennedy and Judith Campbell from March 1961 until March 1962. In that time period, Miss Campbell called the President at the White House and other locations, a total of 81 times, the first call on March 29, 1961 to the Oval Office, and the last taking place on June 4, 1963.[49]

It was during this year long period, after the failure of the Bay of Pigs invasion, and the CIA's "Phase Two" of their covert war against Cuba, that directly corresponds to the time sequence of the JFK-Campbell phone conversations. No one knows what transpired between President Kennedy and Miss Campbell (despite the usual love talk) during their conversations and it would be silly to speculate as to any Campbell-Kennedy-Giancana link. But if one were a betting man it is not too difficult to postulate that the names of the mob and Castro came up. The time period of the Campbell-JFK calls also corresponds directly to the CIA's "Operation Mongoose," the agency's secret war to overthrow the

48 Assassination Report. Pg. 180.

49 Chronology of President's Activities. Record No. 157-10002-10027. SSCIA.

Castro regime. The logs of the president's phone conversations that were released by the National Archives begin on January 25, 1961 and end on June 4, 1963. The logs not only tell of the phone calls received by JFK from Miss Campbell but also, and more importantly to this story, of the hundreds of meetings, both on and off the record, between President Kennedy and his advisors concerning Cuba and other world hot spots.

The record is replete with conversations between President Kennedy, Robert Kennedy, John McCone, General Maxwell Taylor, Edward Lansdale, Desmond Fitzgerald, Sheffield Edwards, Dean Rusk, Robert McNamara, Richard Bissell, Allan Dulles, and many others. All of these men were deeply involved in the Cuba Project and the logs tell that the president met with them on a continuing basis. Among the subjects discussed in the presidential logs were the Balletti wiretapping case, the Hoover memo to JFK regarding the CIA's use of the mob, CIA briefings of Robert Kennedy on Cuban guerrilla warfare, the FBI's surveillance of Judy Campbell, meetings between RFK and his Organized Crime Section, RFK meetings with Richard Bissell & Landsdale, Helms, Fitzgerald (certainly Cuba came up somewhere in this meeting), a memo from Rosen to Belmont (FBI agents) requesting a re-interview of Sheffield Edwards concerning the Mahue prosecution, the Feb. 17 Hoover memo to RFK on Judith Campbell, a meeting between Bobby Kennedy and Taylor, Bundy, Lansdale, McCone and J.C. King (again Cuba?), a secret meeting between JFK and McCone, "and others from the intelligence community" at an unknown location a March 16, 55 minute meeting between JFK that is "off the record" at the White House, among others.

All this activity was not missed when the writers of the Assassinations Report were doing their work. "The President might have inquired further of the CIA. The Presidential calendar indicates that the President had meetings at which most CIA officials witting of the assassination plot were present during the period from February 27 through April 2, 1962. All of those persons have testified that the President never asked them about the assassination plot."

Over the years, in the few interviews she has given, Mrs. Campbell never revealed whether or not JFK discussed the Castro plots with her and even if she knew she probably wouldn't have said anything.

But the president's secret affair with Judith Campbell came to an abrupt end soon after a private meeting held between JFK and J. Edgar Hoover on March 22 in the White House. There is no public record of what transpired during that conference but the reader does not have to be a rocket scientist to figure it out. What probably happened was that Hoover told the president that he knew of his relationship with Miss Campbell, that if he did not end the relationship he would tell the press, thus, ending Kennedy's presidency, and holding him out for impeachment. After all, the President of the United States should not be having an affair, let alone with a woman who is also sleeping with a top mob figure. Directly after that closed door meeting, JFK ordered Evelyn Lincoln not to accept any more calls from his girlfriend and the affair was ended.

The Assassinations Report said of the JFK-Campbell-Hoover affair thus:

"The fact that the President and Hoover had a luncheon at which one topic was probably that the President's friend, Campbell, was also a friend of Giancana and Rosselli raises several questions. The first is, assuming that Hoover did in fact receive a summary of FBI information relating to Giancana prior to his luncheon with the President, whether that summary indicated that Giancana had both once been involved in an attempt to assassinate Castro and also in a CIA operation against Cuba that included "dirty business." If Hoover was made aware of those facts, he would have had both an opportunity and a duty to have brought them to the President's attention...."[50]

50 Assassination Report. Pg. 181-182.

The President's relationship with Judith Campbell, and Hoover's meeting with JFK is the first clue we have of Kennedy's knowledge of the plots to kill Castro. As we shall see, the record is clear that JFK had more than an inkling of what the CIA was secretly doing to "whack the beard."

On November 8, 1961, the Attorney General met with reporter Thad Szulc, to discuss the situation in Cuba. It was now seven months since the Bay of Pigs invasion, and Operation Mongoose was in full swing. The meeting was off the record, just a chat between two friends. RFK wanted to feel out Szulc to find out what the reporter thought of the administrations current policy towards Castro. At no time was the word assassination brought up. Before the meeting broke up, RFK asked Szulc if he would like to meet the president the next day. Szulc agreed and a meeting was set up. The next day, Szulc was escorted into the Oval Office by JFK's Special Assistant, Richard Goodwin (the husband of the historian, Doris Kearns Goodwin). Just before the meeting ended, JFK asked Szulc the following question: "What would you think if I ordered Castro to be assassinated?" The reporter told the president that if Castro was killed it would not necessarily change the political situation in Cuba, as someone else would take his place. He also said that the US should have no role in political assassinations. Szulc testified to Congress that President Kennedy then said, "I agree with you completely."

Szulc remarked further concerning his conference with the president:

"He (President Kennedy) then went on for a few minutes to make the point how strongly he and his brother felt that the United States for moral reasons should never be in a situation of having recourse to assassination. JFK then said he was testing me – that he felt the same way – he added, I'm glad you feel the same way – because indeed U.S. morally must not be part of assassinations. JFK said he raised question because he was under terrific pressure from advisers (think he said intelligence people, but not positive) to okay a Castro murder, and he was resisting pressure."

When Goodwin testified before the Committee he said that Szulc said that JFK told him in reference to a Castro assassination order, "well, that's the kind of thing I'm never going to do." Goodwin later said that in the days after the Kennedy-Szulc meeting, the president said in relation to Castro's death, "we can't get into that kind of thing, or we would all be targets."

The encounter between JFK and Szulc is important for two reasons. First, we have the President actually talking about assassinating Castro (he had to have gotten the idea from someone) and two, the fact that Kennedy suggested that some people in the intelligence community were putting pressure on him to act against Castro.

Another person whom JFK talked to in regard to assassinating Castro was then Senator George Smathers (D. Fla.). Smathers was not one of the president's Boston buddies but he was friendly enough with the Florida politician to invite him to the White House for a round of drinks and a walk in the Rose Garden. Smathers was well connected to the anti-Castro leaders who lived in his home state and was called "the Senator from Cuba" by friends and foes alike. One of his best friends was Carlos Prio, and a man who would walk the inner circle of Nixon pals, Charles "Bebe" Rebozo.

During one of Kennedy's and Smathers walks around the White House in 1961, the president broached the subject of assassinating Castro because that topic had come up in discussions among his advisors. Smathers said that if that took place, the US should also proceed with a staged invasion of the large American controlled Guantanamo naval base that would serve as a pretext for a full scale US invasion of the island. Eventually, Kennedy got so fed up with Smathers' war talk over Cuba that he stopped discussing the subject with the Florida Senator.

Smathers discussed his conversation with President Kennedy concerning Cuba and Castro in his Assassination Report testimony:

"...President Kennedy asked me what reaction I thought

there would be throughout South America were Fidel Castro to be assassinated... I told the president that even as much as I disliked Fidel Castro that I did not think it would be a good idea for there to be even considered an assassination of Fidel Castro, and the President of the United States completely agreed with me, that it would be a very unwise thing to do..."

Smathers further stated that he tried to talk to the president on other occasions about Cuba but that the president told him that he wasn't interested in discussing it again. "Senator Smathers concluded his testimony by indicating that on Cuban affairs in general, he felt he was "taking a tougher stance than was the President." But Smathers said that he disapproved of even thinking about assassinating Castro and said he was "positive" that Kennedy also opposed it."

Here we have conflicting accounts of President Kennedy's attitude toward Castro. First he asks Senator Smathers what the reaction would be to Castro's death, and then he turns around and says that he has no intention of carrying out that policy. It seems clear that the president was saying one thing to his colleagues in confidence, yet toying with a much tougher policy in private.

On the other hand are the numerous statements made by a host of President Kennedy's White House advisors whose testimony is covered in the Assassinations Report? To a man, they state that the president never discussed assassinating Castro with them.

Here is a sample of what JFK's most trusted advisors had to say:

"Secretary of State Dean Rusk, "I never had any reason to believe that anyone that I ever talked to knew about had any active planning of assassination underway."

Secretary of Defense Robert McNamara had this to say:

"I had no knowledge or information about....plans or preparations for a possible assassination attempt against Premier Castro." That statement belies the fact that while he was Secretary of Defense, Robert McNamara carried out detailed plans by his department to overthrow the Castro regime.

Another Kennedy administration official who was well versed in Operation Mongoose was General Maxwell Taylor, the military aide to the president, and later Chairman of the Joint Chiefs. General Taylor was chairman of a select group of men in the Kennedy White House that was called the Special Group that were overseeing the CIA's secret war against Castro called Operation Mongoose. Taylor said that he never discussed assassinating Castro with anyone in the White House, nor did he ever get a direct order from either the president or RFK to do so.

McGeorge Bundy, a top White House foreign policy advisor stated the following:

"No one in the Kennedy administration, in the White House, or in the Capitol, ever gave any authorization, approval, or instruction of any kind for any effort to assassinate anyone by the CIA." However, Bundy does say that he was briefed by Richard Bissell on the Executive Action ZR/RIFLE program.

Theodore Sorensen, a top aid to the president and his number one speechwriter, said that while his knowledge of Cuban matters was limited, he knew President Kennedy well enough to flatly state that assassinating a foreign leader was not in his make up:

"Such an act was totally foreign to his character and conscience, foreign to his fundamental reverence for human life and his respect for his adversaries, foreign to his insistence upon a moral dimension in U.S. foreign policy...."

Sorensen summed up his testimony regarding any possible Castro murder plots this way:

Question: Would you think it would be possible that the agency, the CIA could somehow have been under the impression that they had a tacit authorization for assassination due to a circumspect discussion that might have taken place in any of these meetings?

Sorensen: It is possible, indeed, I think the President on more than one occasion felt that Mr. Dulles, by making rather vague and sweeping references to particular countries was seeking tacit approval without ever asking for it, and the President was rather concerned that he was not being asked for explicit direction and was not being given explicit information, so it is possible. But on something of this kind, assassination, I would doubt it very much.[51]

Another high level Kennedy administration official with intimate ties to Operation Mongoose was Air Force Major General Edward Lansdale, a top military officer in the arts of clandestine warfare. Lansdale helped tame the Huk guerrillas in their fight to overthrow the government of the Philippines, and was influential in setting up the Diem government in South Vietnam. Lansdale was the character model in Eugene Burdick's popular novel of the time called *The Ugly American.* At the outset of Operation Mongoose, JFK called on General Lansdale to take charge of the US government's efforts to topple Castro. Lansdale came to the game quite willing to use any methods to do the job. He called for a lot of "boom and bang" on the island to get rid of Castro.

In his deposition to the committee, Lansdale said that he was certain that no discussion of assassinating Castro was ever broached to him by either the President or the Attorney General. "Lansdale further testified that the plausible deniability concept had no part in the fact that he never discussed a Castro assassination with President Kennedy or the Attorney General." Lansdale testified that he "had doubts" that assassination was a "useful action," and one which I had never employed in the past... When asked if he thought the President was not aware of efforts to depose Castro and his government by any means including assassination, Lansdale answered, "I am certain he was aware of efforts to dispose of the Castro regime. I am really not one to guess what he knew of assassinations, because I don't know."

But here Lansdale's statements get in trouble with the written record. He says that Bill Harvey never told him of the agency's efforts to kill Castro. But in a meeting of August 10, 1962 of the

51 Assassination Report. Pg. 298. Sorensen, 7/21/75

Special Group Augmented, Lansdale directed Harvey to prepare a plan for the "liquidation" of Cuban leaders. But no such plan was ever prepared. The word "liquidation" can be interpreted by the reader but what it comes down to is getting rid of the offending matter, and in this case the offending matter was Fidel Castro.

The last of JFK's advisors who had a detailed awareness of the Castro plots was former CIA Director, Richard Helms. In his testimony, Helms says that Robert Kennedy played a dominant part in Operation Mongoose planning and was always asking for progress reports concerning agency activity and results. RFK was constantly on the phone talking to either Helms, Fitzgerald or Harvey, even contacting their staffs at various times.

Helms said that, "although he did not know whether a Castro assassination would have been morally acceptable to Robert Kennedy, he believed that Robert Kennedy would not have been unhappy if Castro had disappeared off the scene by whatever means. And Helms stated that Robert Kennedy never told him that a Castro assassination was ruled out." However, Helms further testified that, "although Robert Kennedy was constantly in touch with Helms and their exchanges were marked by detailed, factual and highly specific discussions on anti-Castro operations, Robert Kennedy never raised the subject of a Castro assassination and never instructed Helms to assassinate Castro. Helms further stated that he had no knowledge that Robert Kennedy was ever asked to specifically approve an assassination plot."

What we have seen in this chapter is a secret CIA assassination capability called "Executive Action ZR/RIFLE that was initiated to target foreign leaders, including (at least in theory, Fidel Castro). While Executive Action wasn't used, it showed the lengths at which the CIA was willing to go in order to get rid of bothersome foreign leaders.

We have also seen documented proof that both President Kennedy and his brother, Attorney General Robert Kennedy knew, almost from the beginning, of the secret CIA-Mafia alliance to kill Castro. All this information was of course, not known by the

Warren Commission as it investigated the president's murder. But if they had that news, would their report have been any different?

In the next chapter we will tell the story of the massive, US government plot to topple the Castro regime.

Chapter 6

Cuba On My Mind

As we have seen in the last chapter, the Warren Commission (and the American people) where kept in the dark regarding two secret operations regarding the Castro regime in Cuba; 1) the CIA-Mafia plots to assassinate Fidel Castro and 2) the wide-spread, systematic, large scale US government efforts to topple Castro from power. The huge covert campaign was conducted by almost every Cabinet department, the CIA, and other, lesser governmental agencies with the approval and direction of President Kennedy and his brother, Attorney General Robert Kennedy. While this government wide plan had no formal name it brought under its umbrella, the CIA's "Operation Mongoose," the "boom and bang" effort to sabotage Cuba's military and economic infrastructure.

This chapter will detail the elaborate US government plans to topple the Castro regime and replace it with an American led, Castro free Cuba, led by a hand picked team of anti-Castro Cubans in league with the CIA and the US military. Most of the details herein are based on recently released documents obtained via the "JFK Record Act."

But in order to understand how the Kennedy administration got to the point where it began its secret plans to topple Castro, it is important to grasp the historical record and JFK's mind-set when it concerned Castro and Cuba.

The 1960 Presidential Campaign

The 1960 presidential campaign between Senator John Kennedy and Vice President Richard Nixon was one of the most bitterly fought in American history. While we didn't know it then, it also was a turning point in this country's affairs.

After winning the Democratic presidential nomination, Kennedy was given a briefing on world affairs by then Director of Central Intelligence, Allan Dulles. Clearly, Cuba, and the worsening diplomatic relations between Washington and Havana were discussed. It is clear that JFK was briefed on the still infant plots to get rid of Castro but to what extent is still not certain.

But more than anything, Kennedy was a rational politician and like Nixon, made Castro the enemy of the United States, at least for domestic political purposes. During the campaign, Kennedy made his most detailed remarks on Cuba in a speech in Cincinnati in October. He said that the State Department under John Foster Dulles had made a mistake in not taking to heart the fact that the Cuban revolution under Castro was going Communist instead of wishing it the other way.

As the campaign for president heated up, Cuba became more and more a very important topic. On the stump, JFK would speak of "strengthening the Cuban fighters for freedom." As mentioned before, CIA Director Dulles had given Kennedy only the briefest mention of events now going on in Cuba. But when Nixon heard that Kennedy was now talking tough on Castro, he became enraged. But Nixon was in a no win situation. As head of the Castro plots under President Eisenhower, he could not, under any circumstances, reveal his hand and tell the voters of the secret plans then underway to eliminate Castro. For Nixon, this must have been the most painful of moments. For here was this young, and inexperienced Senator, taking away from Nixon, the Vice President for eight years, the man who had "debated" Khrushchev, the world traveler, the very thunder which he knew could get him elected president. And he couldn't do anything about it.

During the fourth of the now famous television debates between Nixon and Kennedy, Nixon found himself attacking Kennedy on the very plan that he was secretly advocating. Nixon accused Kennedy of being reckless toward Cuba and said that JFK's plan was "probably the most dangerously irresponsible recommendation made in the campaign."

In July 1960, right before JFK was to be crowned with the Democratic presidential nomination in Los Angeles, he decided to cement his ties with a faction of the anti-Castro exiles then living in the U. S. In a secret meeting in Washington, Kennedy met with four of the leading Cuban exile leaders; Manuel Artime, Tony Varona, Aureliano Sanchez Arango, and Jose Mario Cardona. But this was no ordinary social chat. The meeting was set up by the CIA who were playing both sides of the political middle; they would either work with a President Kennedy or a President Nixon. Kennedy's most ardent supporter at CIA headquarters was an Ivy League spook named Richard Bissell. Bissell served as the deputy director of planning at the agency and was one of the men responsible for the planning and execution of the Bay of Pigs affair. In the 1950's, Bissell also ran the CIA's most sensitive covert operation of the time; the U-2 spy planes that flew secret reconnaissance missions over both Russia and China.

Kennedy was thus informed of the basic plans that the CIA had in preparation for action against Cuba. Limited though these discussions by Bissell and Dulles were, Kennedy was only given what they wanted him to know. Upon his election he would be given a thorough briefing on the Cuba Project. But by then events had progressed far too long to stop the imminent exile invasion.

The Nixon campaign was rooting for a Cuban invasion before the November election. If that happened, and it proved to be successful, Nixon and the Republicans would be given the credit for toppling Castro and might tip the election in their favor. As the campaign reached its final days, Kennedy went around the country accusing the Eisenhower administration of not doing enough to get rid of Castro. Nixon could only hold his breath and hope for an invasion that never came. In the end, Kennedy, the so called liberal whose party "lost China" in the 1940's, had bested Nixon on his own anti-Communist turf.

On Election Day, Kennedy won the presidency by little over 100,000 votes, one of the closest elections in modern American history. The problem of what to do about Cuba was his.

The Plot to Remove Fidel Castro

The Kennedy administrations efforts to topple Fidel Castro from power really took off after the failed Bay of Pigs invasion of April 1961. Kennedy had been humiliated in the eyes of the world, especially when viewed from the perspective of the Soviet Union. Russian Premier Nikita Khrushchev, looking from his balcony atop Red Square, saw, in his opinion, a weak, vacillating, young president who could not control his own administration, (in this case, the CIA). The Kennedys, who took failure personally, were out for revenge, against Castro and well as the top officers in the Agency who led them down the path to failure on the Cuban beaches. The first to go was DCI Allan Dulles and Richard Bissell, who had such an important hand in the Bay of Pigs planning, as well as the CIA-Mafia plots. The president replaced Dulles with Republican, John McCone in order to make the running of the CIA a bipartisan affair, and more importantly, to get control of the CIA under the wings of the administration. To facilitate the latter point, JFK appointed his brother, Robert Kennedy, to be the point man in the Cuba plots, which took on the name, Operation Mongoose.

A recently de-classified memo written by George McManus makes strikingly clear how the failure of the Bay of Pigs affected President Kennedy's judgment concerning Cuba:

"Looking back to the origins of MONGOOSE, one finds the

AG and Mr. McNamara seeking primarily to remove the political stain left on the President by the Bay of Pigs failure. Both the AG (Attorney General) and the Secretary of Defense felt it necessary for political reasons that some action is taken with respect to Cuba to ensure the President's future. In a nutshell, they were out to dump Castro or to make him cooperate."[52]

This is a striking memo as it lays out in stark detail why the Kennedy administration wanted to get back at Castro; to seek revenge for the Bay of Pigs and to ensure President Kennedy's re-election in 1964.

For the next two years, from the spring of 1961, to just after the Cuban Missile Crisis of October 1962, OPERATION MONGOOSE took root, blossoming into a full scale US government operation to get rid of Castro. In a March 5, 1962 memo for President Kennedy and his brother, the purpose of OPERATION MONGOOSE was put in writing:

"1) The U.S. will make maximum use of indigenous Cuban resources, internal and external to cause the overthrow of Castro, but recognizes the final success will require decisive US military intervention: 2) These resources will be used to prepare for and justify this intervention. The immediate U.S. objective will be in the coming months to acquire hard intelligence on the conditions inside Cuba. Lansdale will continue as Chief of Operations calling directly on the participating departments and agencies for support and implementation of agreed tasks. The heads of these departments and agencies are responsible for the performance through normal channels to the President."[53]

In the year between the April 1961 failure at the Bay of Pigs and the period beginning in early March 1962, the CIA and the US military began extensive plans for sabotage and both covert and overt operations against Cuba. A long chart prepared by the Special Group (Augmented), which consisted of RFK and

52 Source: 5 Nov. 1962 three-page memo signed by George McManus.

53 Source: Guidelines for Operation Mongoose, March 5, 1962.

a number of his close advisors from the White House and the departments, spell out just exactly how intelligence was to be collected on Cuba.

The following operations were to be conducted from 1-15 March 1962:

"1) *Dispatch one intelligence agent operation to key area selected by CIA. Purpose: Collect and report intelligence on anti-regime attitudes, on potential resistance, and on vulnerabilities and strengths of Communist security system. Considerations: There is a risk that his action will disclose this U.S. intelligence activity within Cuba. Selected personnel are being intensively trained. This first team has 2 agents. An area in which resistance has been reported has been selected. Agent operations must stay alive, make useful contacts, and report securely to CIA. Physical risk to personnel is substantial, due to lack of intelligence... "*

"Over time, says the memo, other agents will be infiltrated into Havana to "collect intelligence," agent handling, if future developments warrant."

During this time, the CIA began interrogations of newly arrived Cuban exiles in South Florida. They set up shop at the Opa-Locka Caribbean Admission Center, which was activated on March 15, 1962. The purpose of this function was "to collect intelligence required for the operations, to identify and earmark intelligence assets as refugees arrive, and to provide security against Communist agency operations."

The CIA, operating out of its JAM/WAVE center in Miami, contacted the British government for covert help. In a memo sub-titled "Other Operations," the CIA wanted to "continue negotiating for British help in contaminating locomotive lubricants to cripple Cuba's rail transportation. British assistance is required to undertake a successful sabotage of Cuban locomotives, through contaminating lubricants. It is expected that a minimum of 3 months is required before locomotives in Cuba start breaking down, once the contaminant is introduced."[54]

The goal, according to this memo is to get at least 105 agents selected and 50 agents trained by 31 March "to ready agent operations." An immediate goal was to develop intelligence potential of Cuban "colonies" in U.S. to exploit the intelligence possibilities of former residents of Cuba (now in the United States).

The CIA had other areas of interest in recruiting Cuban nationals besides the US. "As Opa-Locka becomes fully activated, CIA will activate other interrogation centers as promptly as feasible. A center is being activated in Spain, Negotiations with local authorities are being undertaken to activate centers is possible, in Mexico City, Caracas, and Aruba..."

By May, the Agency hoped to have additional teams of single and double agents inside Cuba, "the main factor of determining location of resident agents is to find a place where a trained agent can stay viable." The end of the month also called for a plan to counterfeit Cuban currency. By June the scenario called for up to 15 teams successfully infiltrated into Cuba for the collection of psychological material, surveillance of military installations and communications centers, and by the end of July, to infiltrate agents into Cuban government organizations or to get "agents in place."

The newly de-classified documents also describe a full-scale series of operations to destabilize the Cuban government:

"Operation Mobilize." Objective: Seek to maintain maximum mobilization of Cuban Armed Forces. Possible Courses of Action: Mislead Cuban authorities into believing preparations are being made for an invasion in the Cienfuegos-Trinidad area by: Interrogating Cuban refugees on the following items in the Cienfuegos-Trinidad area: Beaches, roads and trails, port facilities... Conducting survey to locate and recruit for future use, persons: as interpreters, capable of operating commercial radio stations...

54 Operation Mongoose Phase 1 (CIA).

Conducting amphibious exercises in Southeast US-Caribbean-Latin American areas and giving wide public dissemination to the exercises...

"2) Operation Dismount: Objective: Disruption of Cuban Economy…"

"3) Operation Discredit Sino-Soviet Bloc. Objective: to discredit Sino-Soviet Bloc assistance provided to Castro/Communist regime..."

"4) Operation Smasher: Objective: the objective is to disrupt/disable military and commercial communications facilities in Cuba..."

"5) Operation Hornswoggle. Objective: to crash or force down Cuban MIG aircraft with an all weather intercept capability by communications intrusion…"

Another US government agency that was involved in covert plans to disrupt the Cuban government was the US Information Agency. Donald Wilson was the USIA's Representative to Operation Mongoose and sat in on some of the important planning. USIA, along with the Special Group came up with a detailed plan for psychological operations against Castro. This was called 'Course B' and consisted of two plans:

"1) increase the flow of information to Cuba, exposing the weaknesses and perfidies of the Castro/Communist regime."

"2) Improve the informational capability throughout Latin America to 'isolate' Castro/Communism and build up support for pro-democratic Cuban elements."

One of the proposed elements in the USAID plan was the broadcasting of propaganda into Cuba from US locations. The agency proposed ten possible sites throughout the US that could transmit clear, loud signals into Cuba. "Our study also shows," says one declassified report, "however, that Castro has the ready capability to jam our effort with an extraordinarily high percentage of success..." The memo goes on to say… "However, if none of these contingencies occur, we will have an expensive operation on our hands with small listernship to show for it."

Other contingency plans proposed by USAID against the Cuban government were the following: a) balloon deliveries to drop propaganda, b) smuggling of printed materials, also for propaganda purposes, c) the playing of suitable musical themes "that might stir the resistance forces in Cuba," d) radio broadcasts, not only in Cuba, but in Latin America as well, e) cartoon books (yes, that's right) "the Agency has done six anti-Castro cartoon books (5 million copies what a waste of paper) having a widespread impact over the area. This program could be stepped up, Books - "Our book program has several good anti-Castro titles although the circulation is small."

A further study by USAID was an impact study on how a possible successful overthrow of the Castro government might effect other countries in the world .For example, in dealing with Latin America, "…There would not be widespread negative reaction if our campaign were closely identified with a Cuban liberation movement and directed solely at Cuba, not throughout the area generally." "Africa, like India, is particularly sensitive to any heating up of the Cold War. If Moscow's response is particularly vigorous, African political and opinion leaders are likely to become more skittish with a resulting slowdown in the pursuit of U.S. objectives in Africa."

Military Plans Under MONGOOSE

The newly de-classified documents paint a detailed military plan of attack proposed by the Department of Defense, the Department of State and the CIA. As previously mentioned in this work, the CIA, under its JM/WAVE station in South Florida, ran its covert war against Castro's Cuba out of this area. Using front companies, as well as legitimate businesses, the CIA had hundreds of agents, sub-agents, boats, planes, and personnel, all training and operating from Miami to the Florida Keys. It also seems that the CIA was using the facilities of the US military for training of its personnel. A March 12, 1962, memo from the Special Group (Augmented) paints a detailed picture of what US military resources were actually used.

"1. *Use of US military installations. CIA desires to train small groups of Cuban nationals on the US. Air Force Bombing Range, Avon Park, Florida, immediately. Defense reports that the proposed area is adequate for this training, but that such training of covert agents who will be introduced ultimately into Cuba represents a security problem and a departure from past security procedures, due to the fact that the US government sponsorship will be apparent to trainees..."*

"2. *Arming of Cuban guerrillas. CIA needs a policy determination on the supplying of arms and equipment to deserving Cuban guerrillas, as they are located, assessed and request help. Such requests are starting to surface, as the intelligence-collection effort is increased, and it is logical that the number of requests will increase as the operation proceeds..."*

"3. *Use of U.S. military personnel and equipment. CIA has requested Defense assistance in air and sea capabilities, including supplying equipment and supplying U.S. military crews to operate the equipment. Included in these requests are 2 LSD's to lie off the coast in support of CIA maritime operations, with U.S. Navy crews of 200-300 depending upon the mission, 3 USAF cargo aircraft with "sheep-dipped" USAF crews for air re-supply, 2 amphibious aircraft with "sheep-dipped" USAF crews,*

> *and 2 submarines for black operations... (Sheep dipping is an intelligence term that is used to hide the true identity of people, mostly active military personnel in sensitive missions)."*[55]

Once Operation Mongoose took shape, Attorney General Robert Kennedy practically ran the show, as seen in a November 11, 1961 "Eyes Only For the President and the Attorney General" report sent by presidential aide, Richard Goodwin.

"I believe that the operation should be organized with five staff components:

1. *Intelligence collection and evaluation.*
2. *Guerrilla and underground.*
3. *Propaganda.*
4. *Economic warfare (exclusive of covert activities within Cuba).*
5. *Diplomatic relations."*

Each of these divisions would be headed by someone directly responsible to you. In addition you would have a deputy who would do the actual contact work between this operation and the various governmental agencies involved... I would act as Staff Assistant to you... I have talked to McNamara and he has promised to supply a topflight guerilla and underground man, as well as whatever additional personnel we need. I think this is the best way to handle it... Both the diplomatic relations and economic warfare people can come from State...

"One of Bob Amory's brightest young men should be assigned to intelligence collection and evaluation. As for propaganda, I thought we might ask Tad Szulc to take a leave of absence from the Times and work on this one-although we should check with Ed Murrow and Dick Bissell.

55 "Policy Questions: Operation Mongoose." 3/12/62.

"These people should have a headquarters. It should probably be at the Pentagon because a) we might get better security; b) McNamara will be easier to work with in terms of getting whatever staff services, etc."[56]

While all these preparations were secretly under way, Edward Lansdale, the chief of the Cuba Project, wrote a detailed brief, outlining the military and political justifications for the entire operation and sent it along to both JFK and RFK. It reads in part:

1. As requested in reference memorandum, the position of the Department of Defense, with respect to the military stake and role in the removal of the Communist regime in Cuba, has been determined based upon the following factors:
   A. *National Security policy.*
   B. *Current intelligence.*
   C. *Operations against the Castro regime will be covert, at least initially.*
   D. *Time favors the Castro government.*

2. The basic military implications of Castro's Communist government are as follows:
   A. *It exposes the Western Hemisphere to an increasingly serious threat to its security. This increases our national vulnerability and defense costs as forces are developed or shifted to meet this threat.*

   B. *It provides the Soviet Union with the most effective base they have ever had for spreading Communism throughout the Western Hemisphere...*

56 Organization of the Cuban Operation. 11/2/61.

3. In view of the factors set forth above, the Department of Defense holds that the Communist regime is incompatible with the minimum-security requirements of the Western Hemisphere. The Department of Defense is prepared to overtly support any popular movement inside Cuba to the extent of ousting the Communist regime and installing a government acceptable to the United States. While the possibility of Communist Bloc reactions in areas other than Cuba is recognized, it is believed that this can be accomplished without precipitating war, and without serious effect on world public opinion.[57]

Not to be outdone, the CIA also wrote a detailed plan called "Guidelines for Operation Mongoose." Below are some of the important points:

1. Operation Mongoose will be developed on the following assumptions:

   A. *In undertaking to cause the overthrow of the target government, the U.S. will make maximum use of indigenous resources, internal and external, but recognizes that final success will require decisive U.S. military intervention.*

   B. *Such indigenous resources as are developed will be used to prepare for and justify this intervention, and thereafter to facilitate and support it.*

   C. *The immediate priority objective of U.S. efforts during the coming months will be the acquisition of hard intelligence on the target area... These actions, insofar as possible, will be consistent with overt policies of isolating the local leader (Castro) and of neutralizing his influence in the Western Hemisphere.*

57 Cuba Project. 6/17/62.

2. In order to get the covert phase of this program in motion, it will be necessary at the outset to use U.S. personnel, bases and equipment for the support of operations inside the target area. However, the CIA will concurrently expedite the development of non-attributable resources in order to reduce or eliminate this dependence should it become necessary after the initial phase.[58]

The large military role is also spelled out in another Mongoose memo:

"The Group agreed that it would have to accept the proposition that re-supply operations will probably require U.S. military personnel and equipment to include aircraft and sea craft... In connection with small boat operations, the Secretary of Defense undertook to provide anything that was available within Defense establishment for which a requirement might be established... At the Attorney General's suggestion, General Lansdale undertook to examine the possibility of sabotage or other means of destroying the Soviet boats which have been or will be delivered to Cuba."[59]

As military plans for MONGOOSE took shape, Robert Kennedy's role in the operation quickly became dominant. This is plainly seen in an October 4, 1962, "Memorandum For The Record of the Mongoose Task Force" in which RFK's views, along with others in the CIA are spelled forth:

1. *The Attorney General opened the meeting by saying that higher authority is concerned about progress on the MONGOOSE program and feels that more priority should be given to trying to mount sabotage operations... He urged that massive activity be mounted within the entire MONGOOSE framework... Mr. Johnson said that massive activity would have to appear to come from within...*

---

58 Comments on CIA's Recommended Changes For Operation Mongoose. 3/13/62.

59 Minutes of Special Group Meeting on Operation Mongoose 3/13/62.

2. *Mr. McCone (the CIA Director) then said that he gets the impression that high levels of the government want to get on with activity but still wish to retain a low noise level. He does not believe that this will be possible. Any sabotage will be blamed in the United States...*

3. *The result of this discussion was that it was agreed that DOD and CIA should get together on recommendations for targets within Cuba that require coverage and on recommendations as to how to achieve this coverage.*[60]

As the Special Group debated on how to avoid the "noise level" coming from the United States in its plans for possible military intervention against Cuba, it ran smack into proposals from other members of the intelligence community and the military that would seem to make this point mute.

"Secretary of State Rusk felt that he Guidelines should make it clear that, while MONGOOSE is concerned with covert operations, the U.S. is simultaneously pursuing an overt course which may contribute to the same end...," says a Memorandum for the Record, dated 5 March 1962. If the administration was really interested in separating itself from any traceable military, covert action inside Cuba, the next statement in the same memo makes light of that fact:

"In making the above point, Mr. Rusk pointed out that if it should be possible to prove Castro's involvement in efforts to subvert other Latin American countries then this might present an excuse to intervene either unilaterally or multilaterally. He said that Cuba should be viewed as the "East Germany" of the Western Hemisphere."

Not to be left out of the military plans for a takeover in Cuba, the Joint Chiefs of Staff also got into the act of planning ahead.

60 Minutes of the Mtg. Of the Special Group Re: Operation Mongoose. 10/4/62.

Their proposed action was spelled out in a memo of the Special Group dated 13 March, 1962.

Their proposed action was spelled out in a memo of the Special Group dated 13 March, 1962.

"Task 29 - Determine how to reduce CINCLANT's reaction time and yet provide adequate force to quickly take Cuba. CINCLANT and supporting commanders have received CINCLANT's contingency plans and made study of prepositioning steps required if reaction time is to be drastically reduced.

"Task 29 - (b) Be prepared to brief DOD's immediate capability to respond to a request from insurgent Cubans for military assistance...

"Task 32 - Defense to submit a plan for special operation use of Cubans enlisted in the US Armed forces...

"Task 33 (b) - Plan for Incapacitation of Sugar Workers-completed 2 February. Task as assigned was to develop a plan for incapacitating large segments of the sugar workers by the covert use of BW or CW agents. Study revealed the idea was infeasible and it was canceled."

To show just how far the Joint Chiefs of Staff and the Special Group were planning their Cuban overthrow plan, a contingency strategy for a new form of government in Havana was designed.

"E. Begin preparation of a Civil Affairs! Military Government Plan for implementation on order. Also, a communications plan, in support of the CA/MIG Plan, based on the assumption that existing communication facilities would be destroyed or inoperable. Target date for completion, 15 March 1962."

Operation 40

As the military plans for an invasion of Cuba took shape, an interesting memo from the desk of presidential advisor Arthur Schlesinger Jr., to White House aide, Richard Goodwin was received. The memo revolved around a little known group of Cuban exiles operating out of Miami with both CIA and mob ties, called "Operation 40." Before getting into the murky background of this terrorist group, I would like to quote from the document sent by Mr. Schlesinger:

"Sam Halper, who has been the *Time* correspondent in Havana and more recently in Miami, came to see me last week. He has excellent contacts among the Cuban exiles. One of Miro's comments this morning reminded me that I have been meaning to pass on the following story as told me by Halper.

Halper says that the CIA set up something called Operation 40 under the direction of a man named Captain Luis Sanjenis, who was also Chief of Intelligence. It was called Operation 40 because originally only 40 men were involved; later the group was enlarged to 70.

The ostensible purpose of Operation 40 was to administer liberated territories in Cuba. But the CIA agent in charge, a man known as Felix, trained the members of the group in methods of third-degree interrogation, torture and general terrorism. The liberal Cuban exiles believe that the real purpose of Operation 40 was to "kill Communists" – and, after eliminating hard-core Fidelistas, to go on to eliminate first the followers of Ray, then the followers of Varona and finally to set up a right-wing dictatorship, presumably under Artime..."[61]

The Joaquin Sanjenis mentioned in the Schlesinger synopsis died in 1974, leaving a murderous legacy throughout the Caribbean on behalf of the CIA. For ten years, he was head of Operation 40, one of the most sensitive and clandestine operations run out of Miami by the Agency. As the commanding general of this secret army, he sent hundreds of men and their ships and planes into Cuba, many of whom failed to return. Sanjenis, in his pre-Castro days, worked in the dreaded SIM, the secret police organization of the former Cuban dictator, Batista. Once Castro

61 Re: Operation 40. 6/9/61.

came to power, Sanjenis fled to Miami. Sanjenis was part of the Bay of Pigs invasion whose job it was to follow the first wave of troops and then kill any local town leaders who were opposed to the CIA backed forces. Another part of his job was to spy on his fellow members of Operation 40 and report on their activities back to CIA headquarters.

One of Operation 40's most important successes for the CIA was its hunting, and subsequent killing Fidel Castro's "Numero dos," the second on command of the Cuban Revolution, Che Guevara. Two Operation 40 commandos helped a specially trained group of Special Forces in Bolivia to hunt and eliminate Che on October 8, 1967 in the small town of La Higuera.

By 1970, Sanjenis was receiving over $2 million a year from the Agency, not only for clandestine raids into Cuba, but for illegal domestic spying operations, as well. Operation 40 members picketed the embassies of various countries that did business with Cuba, and tried to track down Castro's spies among the large Cuban-American population in Miami.

For the CIA, the cutthroat members of Sanjenis' Operation 40 were just the men the Agency was looking for in its no holes barred, secret war against Fidel Castro. Like the Agency's use of such renegade characters like QJ/WIN and WI/ROGUE, Sanjenis' soldiers would serve a common purpose in not only eliminating Castro from power, but ensuring that their own people, those who were allied with Sanjenis, would take part in the new Cuba run by the United States.

All of the months of planning by the United States government for the eventual elimination of the Castro regime took root between the end of the gay of Pigs and the aftermath of the Cuban Missile Crisis of October 1962. If there was any one document that summed up both Robert Kennedy's supervision of the CIA's secret war against Castro, and the reasons for our covert policy, it is reported in a "Memorandum For the President," dated November 1, 1961, again from Richard Goodwin to President Kennedy:

"I believe that the concept of a "command operation" for Cuba, as discussed with you by the Attorney General, is the only effective way to handle an all-out attack on the Cuban problem... The beauty of such an operation over the next few months is that we cannot lose. If the best happens we will unseat Castro. If not, then at least we will emerge with a stronger underground, better propaganda and a far clearer idea of the dimensions of the problems, which affect us. The question then is who should lead this operation. I know of no one currently in Cuban affairs at the State Department who can do it... I believe that the Attorney General would be the most effective commander of such an operation. Either I, or someone should be assigned to him as Deputy for this activity, since he obviously will not be able to devote full time to it. The one danger here is that he might become too closely identified with what might not be a successful operation. Indeed, chances of success are very speculative... His role should be told to only a few people at the very top with most of the contact work in carrying out his decisions left to his deputy... This still leaves a substantial danger of identifying the Attorney General as the fellow in charge. The danger must be weighed against the increased effectiveness of an operation under his command."[62]

Operation Mongoose and its parallel parts–those of the various cabinet posts, the U.S. military, the CIA, who were planning large scale operations against the Castro government, were withheld from the American people. While ostensibly at peace, the Kennedy administration was waging a secret war to unseat, and probably kill, another government's leader. Some theories of the Kennedy assassination believe that Castro, having learned of the United States covert plan to kill him, turned around and had the president murdered instead. One of the agents that CIA used in its assassination-overthrow plots against Castro was one the Prime Minister's most trusted aides, Rolando Cubela, aka, AM/LASH.

62 Re: All Out Attack on Cuba. 11/1/61.

The AM/LASH Scheme

One of the major faults of the Warren Commission's investigation was that it wasn't informed of the CIA-Underworld plots to kill Fidel Castro. But not all of the members of the Commission and its allies were unaware of these schemes. Allan Dulles, the former head of the CIA, a man who was fired by JFK after the Bay of Pigs invasion, knew of the Agency-Mob plans to kill Castro. Dulles never revealed that information to his fellow members but saw to it that his ally in power, J. Edgar Hoover, the FBI Director, knew of the plots. Hoover found out about the Rosselli-Giancana-Mahue plans from his Bureau informers and that information was confirmed by Dulles.

The plots to kill Castro went ahead full tilt until after the Cuban Missile Crisis of October 1962, when, at the instruction of President Kennedy, a halt in Operation Mongoose was ordered. The President saw that it was better in the long run for the US and the Soviet Union to lessen world tensions, rather than increase them.

But not all the members of the CIA thought that way and they went ahead, despite JFK's orders, to keep in contact with the anti-Castro underground in Cuba, while at the same time, giving encouragement to the Para-military, ring wing groups that were training in the swamps of Florida and outside of New Orleans. When President Kennedy learned of the continuing training camps, he sent in teams of FBI agents to dismantle them. The FBI did their job reluctantly, arresting the soldiers-of-fortune, and then letting them go after a short time in jail.

By the end of 1962, it was obvious that even Fidel Castro knew of the underworld plans to kill him but he probably did not link them to the CIA. But this was not the case with the CIA's association with Rolando Cubela, aka, AMLASH.

High-level CIA officers were in constant contact with Cubela, unlike the Harvey-Rosselli operation where no CIA men, except for a selected few like Harvey, etc., were meeting with the mob.

The AMLASH operation was also different from the CIA-Mafia plots in that they were going on at the time of the assassination of the president in November 1963. By then, the mob agency program had been disbanded, only to be taken over by the AMLASH program.

When one reads the CIA Inspector Generals Report on the Castro assassination history, this is the only part of the 120-page report that is still blacked out in certain parts. Why, after 35 years this is so, is not revealed (possibly to protect sources and methods, or to protect the identities of people who are still alive). But the IG Report, along with the Book V of the Church Committee Report published in 1976, give us as complete report on the AMLASH operation as possible.

The first meeting between the CIA and Rolando Cubela took place in Mexico City on March 9, 1961 in order to find out his views on the Cuban revolution. Cubela did not give the questioner any favor and the meeting ended.

In 1961, Cubela was the second ranking member of the Directorio Revolucionario (DR), a revolutionary group of students who worked for the overthrow of the former Batista regime. It is believed that Cubela was part of the team of men who killed Lt. Col. Antonio Blanco, then head of Batista's military intelligence unit in 1956. Cubela's DR group, while working for the same goals as that of Fidel Castro's 26th of July movement, did not see eye to eye, and kept each other at a distance. In the final days of the Cuban Revolution, Cubela's group took over the presidential palace, refusing to turn it over at first to Che Guevara, but finally, and reluctantly, to Castro. When Castro finally took power, Cubela held the rank of Major in the Cuban armed forces.

The IG's Report on the early days of Cubela and his relationship to Castro reads as follows:

"Prior to his appointment to the post of Cuban Military Attache to Spain and his subsequent departure for Madrid on 27 March, 1959, Rolando Cubela frankly expressed to Prime Minister Fidel Castro his dissatisfaction over the present situation in

Cuba. Cubela privately told intimates that he was so disgusted with Castro that if he, Cubela, did not get out of the country soon, he would kill Castro himself."

After the CIA learned of Cubela's anti-Castro remarks, new, covert dispatches were sent to him and further meetings were arranged. Thus, the AMLASH operation was born.

"Although the March 1961 meeting between (deleted) and Cubela in Mexico City was inconclusive, it led to other meetings out of which grew Project AMLASH. Cubela (AMLASH 1) repeatedly insisted that the essential first step in overthrowing the regime was the elimination of Castro himself, which Cubela claimed he was prepared to accomplish. He repeatedly requested that we furnish him the special equipment or material needed to do the job..."

Now that the CIA had established a relationship with Cubela, he informed his new handlers that he wanted to defect to the U.S. This news was given to the JMWAVE Miami Station in March 1961. Along with Cubela, another man deeply involved in the CIA-Mafia plots to kill Castro, Juan Orta, also wanted to defect. But the CIA nixed the idea because of possible awareness of Castro's security forces concerning Cubela's and Orta's ties to the United States.

The IG's report says this about the Orta-Cubela connection:

"This is one of three name-links we found in the AMLASH file between Rolando Cubela and persons involved in the gambling syndicate episodes. The other two links are even more nebulous than this. If Cubela was in fact one of the gangsters' assets inside Cuba, that fact was unknown to either the CIA officers running the gangster episodes or those handling Cubela."

By June 1962, Cubela had contacted the CIA once again and told them that he would be attending the World Youth Festival in Helsinki, Finland and that once again he wanted to defect. At this point, the FBI, through one of its informers, was advised of the Cubela defection plan and they in turn, asked the CIA for confirmation. That information was indeed given, and the two top US intelligence agencies were now monitoring Cubela's activities. The IG's Report goes on to say that the CIA was in touch with an unidentified asset who would be willing to aid in the defection of Cubela. This unnamed informant and a CIA agent met in New York City on July 13 & 14, 1962 at which time an official relationship was cemented.

From July 30 through August 6, 1962, this unidentified asset arrived in Helsinki to meet with Cubela. After hours of intensive discussions, Cubela changed his mind and decided to be an agent in place for the CIA, rather than defect to the United States.

The IG's Report says this concerning this part of the Cubela story:

"He said he was considering not going back to Cuba, but after talking to (deleted) he felt that if he could do something really significant for the creation of a new Cuba, he was interested in returning to carry on the fight there. He said he was not interested in risking his life for any small undertaking, but that if he could be given a really large part to play, he would use himself and several others in Cuba whom he could rely upon... Cubela stated that many times during the course of this and subsequent meetings that he was only interested in involving himself in a plan of significant action, and which was truly designed to achieve rapidly his desire to help Cuba."

In the middle of August, Cubela and his Agency contacts met once again, this time in Copenhagen and Stockholm, Sweden, but nothing of importance came out of these meetings. The IG Reports of these encounters say the following:

"At one time when we were discussing the various aspects of Cubela's future role in Cuba, we used the term "assassinate." The use of this term, we later learned from (deleted) and from Cubela himself was most objectionable to the later, and he was visibly upset. It was not the act he objected to, but rather merely the choice of the word used to describe it. "Eliminate" was acceptable."

By the middle of August (14-23), representatives of the CIA

and Cubela met in Paris for an intensive, two-week series of meetings and training sessions. A Spanish speaking case officer came to France and Cubela was given S/W training, was taken to the South of France where he was given demolition training and was taught other clandestine warfare methods. He was also asked to take a polygraph test but he refused. The CIA wrote this final comment after Cubela's Paris training session, "have no intention give Cubela physical elimination mission as requirement but recognize this something he could or might try to carry out on his own initiative."

CIA headquarters quickly responded to the field officers letter by saying, "Strongly concur that no physical elimination missions be given Cubela."

So it now seemed that the one man who the CIA wanted to use in a plot to either kill Castro or to use in some way to bring about the demise of his government was not trusted enough by the Agency to carry out this highly sensitive mission. But for lack of any other agent in place, the Agency pinned their hopes on Cubela, despite the many warning signs that trouble might be ahead.

In the early part of September 1963, AMLASH went to Porto Alegre, Brazil to attend the Collegiate Games as a representative of the Cuban government. He was met there by a number of CIA officers and by his friend from revolutionary days, now also working for the CIA, code named AMWHIP. He told his CIA colleagues that he wanted to approach a number of Cuban army officers who were anti-Communists but were pro-Fidel about his secret ties with the US but was reluctant to do so.

In documents released via the "JFK Act," this meeting had some significance. According to the documents, "AMLASH told AMWHIP he felt there were only two ways of getting rid of Castro. The first was an invasion by U.S. forces that AMLASH knew was out of the question and the second was an "inside job." AMLASH indicated he was awaiting a US plan of action. He referred to the explosives demonstration CIA gave him a year earlier as "too cumbersome" for his purposes.

"At the conclusion of the meeting with AMLASH, headquarters cabled on 9 September that, based on what little feel headquarters had, AMLASH appeared hopeless as an intelligence performer and should be approached as a chief conspirator allowed to recruit his own cohorts. He should be urged to recruit a few trusted friends to assist him, initially in "FI and Ops reporting" and then progress to sabotage and more serious matters on an orderly basis."[63]

Not only did the CIA know of Cubela's relationship with some of the anti-Castro elements on the island, but so did Castro himself. In a September 19, 1963, cable from the CIA's JM/WAVE Station in Miami to headquarters it states that AMLASH was part of an anti-communist group whose members are well known to the Castro government and that "Fidel is allegedly aware of the two groups and acts as moderator between them in order to maintain cohesion in the government of Cuba."

But true to his friend, AMWHIP traveled with Cubela to Europe in the fall of 1963 winding up in Paris in early October. There, they were met by case officer "O" who sat down and heard Cubela spill his guts. Cubela said that he was mad that he was given "low level espionage" tasks to perform, saying that he believed that he had a more important role to perform. Case officer "O" assured him that was not the case and said that his possible expanded role was being given consideration at the "highest levels" within the Agency. "With this problem, which had undoubtedly been bothering AMLASH considerably, off his chest, a much more relaxed AMLASH departed restating his desire return Cuba to undertake 'the big job.'"

Now, apparently feeling his oats, Cubela told his case officers that he wanted to meet a high-ranking American official. Cubela contacted his CIA contact, "O" who was unsuccessful in dissuading him in his request. "AMLASH convinced that if such

63 Connection Between AMLASH Operation and Investigation of JFK Assassination.. January 27, 1976.

meet does not take place at this time it will be almost impossible come out again and we will be in same situation as last year with no definite decision... The message notes the fact that AMLASH does have excellent entree to highest target level which believe we cannot afford overlook."

The high official that AMLASH wanted to meet was Attorney General Robert Kennedy but that was one request that he would not get.

Instead, Cubela met with Desmond Fitzgerald, a senior CIA officer who ran the Special Affairs Staff, which was the CIA branch that ran all Cuban affairs, including AMLASH. During World War II, Fitzgerald served with the OSS in the China-India-Burma Theater and was the liaison officer with the Chinese army in Burma and China. After the war was over, he returned to New York where he practiced law. But the call to duty was too much and in 1951 "Des Fitz," as he was called, joined the infant CIA. He went to work for the top secret Clandestine Service, serving in the Far Eastern Division. In the 1950's, Fitzgerald worked with General Edward Lansdale in the overthrow of the government of the Philippines and the installation of Ramon Magsaysay as president of that island nation. He later ran the CIA's Chinese operations in Japan, and in 1963, was put in charge of the Special Affairs Staff whose job it was to remove Fidel Castro from power in Cuba. In 1964, Fitzgerald was named Chief of the Western Hemisphere Division, and in June 1966, he succeeded Richard Helms as deputy director for plans at Langley headquarters.

Fitzgerald met Cubela in Paris on October 29, 1963, and told him that he was a personal representative of Robert Kennedy. He told Cubela that the U.S. was prepared to give him all necessary assistance and support any anti-Communist group of his choosing in Cuba, which would succeed in toppling Castro from power. He told him that American support would only come after a successful coup.

"Nothing of an operational nature was discussed at the Fitzgerald meeting. After the meeting, AMLASH stated that he was satisfied with the policy discussion but now desired to know what technical support we could provide him."

During their discussion, Cubela told Fitzgerald that without Fidel in control in Cuba, the military would break up into 4 or 5 groups and the regime would disintegrate. Cubela said that he requested from the CIA a high-powered rifle with a telescopic scope which he would use to assassinate Castro. Fitzgerald rejected that request, saying that the United States did not do such things.

Cubela's reaction to his meeting with Fitzgerald was spelled out in detail by his associate, AMWHIP a few weeks later. AMWHIP said that Cubela was not pleased with the support he was receiving from the US. "While AMLASH was satisfied on policy grounds, he was not at all happy with the fact that he still was not given the technical assistance for the operation plan as he saw it. AMLASH could not understand why he was denied certain small pieces of equipment which promised a final solution to the problem, while, on the other hand, the US gave much equipment and money to exile groups for their ineffective excursions against Cuban coastal targets. AMLASH accepted the fact that he had to work with the CIA, but CIA might loose him if it continued to procrastinate. AMLASH talked about going to the French terrorist organization, the OAS, but realized that was not feasible."[64]

Fitzgerald's talks with Cubela in Paris were sufficiently positive enough for him to recommend to his superiors at CIA headquarters to trust him. In a CIA memorandum of November 18, 1963, the CIA approved of Cubela's planned coup attempt. Headquarters also gave the go ahead to provide him with rifles and scopes which he previously requested. On November 20, 1963, the CIA sent a message to Cubela asking him to postpone his trip back to Cuba in order to see case officer "O." The purpose of the discussion was to inform him of the "technical support," i.e., guns, scopes, etc., that he had requested were approved. The next meeting would also be in Paris on November 22, 1963.

64 Connection Between AMLASH Operation and Investigation of JFK Assassination. January 27, 1976.

In what started out as just an ordinary day between the CIA Case Officer and his agent, Fitzgerald met AMLASH in a secret location in the late afternoon. Since Desmond Fitzgerald is now dead, and Cubela is not talking, we have to rely on the CIA IG's Report to reconstruct the events of that day.

Cubela stated that while he wanted to do away with Castro, he was not willing to lay his life on the line. He told Case Officer "O," who then went back to the technical support boys at CIA for a solution. Cubela was also a medical doctor and he gave his suggestions to Dr. Gunn who was the "O" of the CIA–the man who could come up with the exotic weapons to eliminate an enemy. What they came up with was a poison called Black Leaf 40, a common insecticide containing about 40% nicotine sulphate. Nicotine could be given to the victim either by injection or by absorption through the skin. By November 20, two days before the Fitzgerald-Cubela meeting in Paris, the device for administering the poison, a ballpoint pen rigged as a hypodermic syringe, was ready for shipment. After a number of tries, the pen was ready for shipment and it went out on the next plane to Paris, November 21. Case officer "O" then gave the poison pen to Cubela who, according to the Report, did not take it. He said that as a medical doctor, he was well aware of how Black Leaf 40 worked but would not take it to Cuba with him. He then said that the CIA should come up with something more sophisticated for him to use.

Cubela then said he was returning to Cuba and was determined to initiate a coup against Castro, with or without US support. He asked that certain other military equipment be sent to him inside Cuba, including 20 hand grenades, two high-powered rifles with telescopic sights, and about 20 lbs. of C-4 explosives and related equipment. This material would be placed on a friend's farm.

"As they were coming out of the meeting, (blank) and Cubela were informed that President Kennedy had been assassinated. Cubela was visibly moved over the news. He asked, "Why do such things happen to good people?" The contact report does not state the time nor the duration of the (blank) Cubela meeting, but *it is likely that at the very moment President Kennedy was shot, a CIA officer was meeting with a Cuban agent in Paris and giving him an assassination device for use against Castro."*

As Malcolm X, the Black revolutionary leader of the time said upon hearing about the assassination of the President, "the chickens had come home to roost."

In the wake of the president's death, most covert operations regarding Cuba were put on hold, including the AMLASH project. In the first week of December, a number of confusing cables were sent and received between CIA headquarters and the JM/WAVE station in Miami. At first, the top brass at the CIA gave their approval for a drop of arms to the resistance in Cuba. But on December 7, that order was countermanded when it was learned that a "major top level Cuban/Caribbean policy review" was going to be held the following week. JM/WAVE responded by saying that they were receiving contradictory instructions and they did not know what to do. The final word came from headquarters when it asked JM/WAVE to present its infiltration plans to "higher authority" "even though there is a reasonable chance operation may be postponed or delayed as was case with the scheduled operation...Believe by January, CIA should be in position better evaluate status of internal assets."

Cubela left Paris on November 27 and arrived in Cuba on December 1. It was now apparent that with Lyndon Johnson in the White House, and with LBJ's suspicions that the Cuban's might have been responsible for the assassination of the president, and may even have given aide to Lee Harvey Oswald, the president's alleged assassin, that the toppling of Castro would be put on the back burner.

According to the most recently declassified files on the AMLASH project, the last file on Cubela's activities came in December 1963. It reads in part:

"22 November 63, Mr. Fitzgerald assured subject that this

agency would give him everything he needed (telescopic sight, silencer, all the money he wanted). The situation changed when (blank) Mr. Fitzgerald left the meeting to discover that President Kennedy had been assassinated. Because of this fact, plans with subject changed and it was decided that this agency could have no part in the assassination of a government leader (including Castro) and it would not aid subject in his attempt. This included the following. We would not furnish the silencer, nor scope nor any money for direct assassination; furthermore, we would not lift a finger to help subject escape from Cuba should he assassinate Castro."[65]

This same document goes on to say that several independent reports obtained by the CIA reveal a possible awareness by the Castro government of Cubela's plotting against him. It seems that Cubela's one time mistress might have been working for Cuban intelligence and her brother was known to be working with Cuban intelligence. "And, one CIA informant reported in 1966 on one known double agent of Cuban intelligence working for the CIA and said the CIA's Cuban operations had been penetrated at a high level by Cuban intelligence. He identified this latter individual only as one of the Cuban exiles who was knowledgeable of a number of the most important operations..."

Despite the Kennedy assassination, and the continuing speculation that Oswald may have been working for the Cuban's, the CIA secretly kept up its ties with AMLASH. In December 1964, the CIA again met with him in Paris where he was told that the agency would no longer back plans to get rid of Castro. By now, the CIA was in contact with other dissident military officers in the Cuban armed forces that were working covertly with the agency in toppling the Castro regime. However, Cubela still kept up his covert activities, meeting secretly with Manuel Artime in Spain in 1964 to coordinate exile plans against Cuba. By February

65 Connection Between AMLASH Operation and Investigation of JFK Assassination. January 27, 1976.

1965, Cubela, probably through Artime, received one pistol, with silencer and one Belgian FAL rifle with silencer from Artime's secretary. Both weapons came from US stocks in Madrid. Once again, Cubela, Don Quixote like, set out to kill the "beard."

By June 1965, the CIA decided to cut off all of its relationships with the key members of the Cubela group, including AMLASH himself. The agency believed the operation was leaking like a sieve and that it would be too risky to continue.

On March 1, 1966, the CIA received a cable that Cuban security police had arrested two high ranking military officers for counterrevolutionary activity inside Cuba. The two men arrested were Major Ramon Guin and Rolando Cubela, a.k.a., AMLASH.

Was the AMLASH Operation Secure?

Was the CIA right in canceling any further operations with the Cubela group? From reading the literature, one would have to say yes.

The entire AMLASH project, would in later years, bring more controversy among those who participated in it. For example, former CIA Director Richard Helms, who was the highest-ranking member of the agency to work with the Warren Commission, told the Rockefeller Commission that he did not believe the AMLASH operation was relevant to the investigation of the assassination of President Kennedy. He also testified that he believed that the AMLASH project was not intended to be an assassination plot against Castro. All this flies in the face of the CIA's actions in giving Cubela a poison pen on November 22, 1963 for use against Castro, and for the years of encouragement in aiding him in the agency's plans to get rid of Castro.

A contrasting view of the AMLASH project comes from Joseph Langosch, who, in 1963, was the Chief of Counterintelligence for the CIA's Special Affairs Staff (headed by Desmond

Fitzgerald), which ran all Cuban matters. Langosch's job was to safeguard the SAS against penetration by foreign intelligence services (KGB, DRE), particularly the Cuban intelligence service. According to Langosch's testimony:

"...The AMLASH operation prior to the assassination of President Kennedy was characterized by the Special Affairs Staff, Desmond Fitzgerald and other senior CIA officers as an assassination operation initiated and supported by the CIA."

"Langosch further recollected that as of 1962 it was highly possible that the Cuban Intelligence Services were aware of AMLASH and his association with the CIA and that the information upon which he based his conclusion that the AMLASH operation was insecure was available to senior level CIA officials, including Desmond Fitzgerald."[66]

But to muddy the waters just a little further, testimony comes from another top level CIA officer who contradicts Langosch's findings.

The Committee received an affidavit from a man named Kent Pollock (a CIA pseudonym) who served as Executive Officer for Desmond Fitzgerald during the time he was SAS chief. Pollock knew about the AMLASH operation and said it was not characterized as an assassination operation.

"To the best of my knowledge, Mr. Fitzgerald considered the AMLASH operation to be a political action activity with the objective of organizing a group within Cuba to overthrow Castro and the Castro regime by means of a coup d'état. I heard Mr. Fitzgerald discuss the AMLASH operation frequently, and never heard him characterize it as an "assassination operation." Mr. Fitzgerald stated within my hearing on several occasions his awareness that coup d'état often involves loss of life.[67]

66 No title. No date. HSCA report. Record No. 180-10142-10050.

67 Ibid.

He further stated:

"Desmond Fitzgerald did not characterize the AMLASH operation as an "assassination operation;" the case officer did not; I, as Executive Officer, never discussed any aspect of the AMLASH operation with Joseph Langosch..."

While the trio of Fitzgerald, Langosch and "Pollock" may differ, when the Church Committee studied the ramifications of the AMLASH project, they came to one important conclusion.

"Based upon the presently available evidence it is the Committee's position that such information, if made available to the Warren Commission, might have stimulated the Commission's investigative concern for possible Cuban involvement or comply city in the assassination. As J. Lee Rankin commented before this Committee:

"...when I read the Church Committee's report–it was an ideal situation for them to just pick out any way they wanted to tell the story and fit it in with the facts that had to be met and then either blame the rest of it on somebody else or not tell any more or polish it off I don't think that could have happened in 1964. I think there would have been a much better chance of getting to the heart of it. It might have only revealed that we are involved in it and who approved it and all that. But I think that would have at least come out."[68]

The question of whether or not the AMLASH project was penetrated by Castro's intelligence forces is spelled out in a recently declassified CIA document consisting of hand written notes on the subject. While most of the 14-page memo is legible, some parts are not. I will highlight the most important (and readable) as follows:

"Action: In view of the foregoing, the allegation:

A. S*hould be put in proper perspective, i.e., not ignored because of the potential embarrassment but considered in*

68 Ibid.

the light of what we already know... concerned with the AMLASH group, whose members reliability reputation and good faith are questionable.

B. *Should be treated so as to protect us against any charge of laxity and so as to establish the facts but, at the same time, treated so as to avoid attributing to them more importance than they deserve.*

C. *Should be kept in mind as example of other charges which may be brandied about and reported by the AMLASH group to other governmental agencies or to other governments or to news media...*

D. *Preliminarily Analysis: As pointed out in a preliminary analysis of the AMLASH complex, made in March 1965 when I was preparing to travel to Madrid in connection with the (blank) case. There is no convincing evidence that the group is working either for or against the regime of Fidel Castro. Reports on their contacts with us and their discussions among themselves are at variance. In 1962 Fidel Castro reportedly knew about the plots against him related to AMLASH and other members of his group to enlist their support against Anibal Escalante Dellunde and the Communists in Cuba. Possibly they are playing both ends against the middle. They certainly have been and are in contact with the two ends...*

A. The AMLASH Conspiracy:

(Blank) on a meeting of the AMLASH group, including AMWHIP-1 mentioned the following significant points:

1) *Kubark (a code name for the CIA) was criticized for "fooling around for years" without helping and for jeopardizing the operation.*

2) *The group was to be prepared to denounce US government as responsible if the operation fails and believed that the resulting scandal would make the Bay of Pigs seem insignificant.*

"...as reported by (blank) on 4 June 65, based on meetings with Espinosa, the problem seem by (blank) is that the AMLASH circle is wide and each new friend of whom we learn seems to have knowledge of the plan. I believe that the problem is a more serious and basic one. As indicated in paragraph 3 of the present memorandum, Fidel Castro himself reportedly knew as far back as 1962, that the group was plotting against him and knowing it, enlisted its support. Hence, we cannot rule out the possibility of provocation. Assassination obviously is a dangerous game, not merely to the plotters in a physical sense, but to a sponsoring government which may suffer severe political repercussions at home and abroad if its involvement is made known.

"...Considering the individuals who are involved directly, their contacts with KUBARK officers, and their reported plan to expose USG (US government), persisting in the plan could be highly embarrassing to KUBARK."[69]

While the author of these notes is not named, it is certainly someone high up in the SAS staff that had a detailed, working knowledge of the entire AMLASH project on a regular basis. From reading these notes it is obvious that the author was highly suspicious of Cubela and the other plotters that he was bringing in. If only one person knows a secret it stays a secret. But if two or more people share a secret it no longer becomes a mystery. This is what happened in the AMLASH case. Cubela, not known for his reliability nor his loyalty to anyone but himself (not to mention his paymasters at the CIA), told anyone who would listen about his plans to kill Castro. If, as it seems possible, Castro knew of the plots to kill him using the Cubela group, the entire AMLASH operation was compromised right from the start.

---

69 No title. No date. Record No. #180-10146-10048 Agency: HSCA.

Cubela and the Mob

While it seems obvious that Cubela was not the CIA's ideal choice as a covert agent whose job it was to kill the leader of a foreign country, another strike against him may have been his links to organized crime.

The CIA first got in contact with Cubela through his close friend, Carlos Tepedino, a wealthy jeweler from Havana, who was also associated with Florida mob boss, Santos Trafficante. Despite Tepedino's mob ties, it seems that he was the middleman between the Agency and Cubela. On July 8, 1962, the JMWAVE station in Miami reported a conversation between Tepidino and the station chief concerning Cubela. It was at this time that Cubela was still in Cuba and was thinking of defecting. Tepedino told the case officer that the source of Cubela's defection plans was a man named Echavarris. Tepedino then went to the FBI in Miami telling the G men that Cubela was not happy at the way he was treated by the CIA in their meeting in Paris where he was persuaded not to defect.

So what we have here is a close tie by Cubela with one of the top mob bosses in the country, Santos Trafficante, who was also working secretly with the CIA to kill Castro. What is also interesting concerning the Cubela-Tepedino alliance is the fact that the two top intelligence agencies of the US, the CIA and FBI, were aware of who Cubela was, and what he was doing.

A second link by Cubela to the mob came in the person of Rafael Garcia Bongo, a Cuban lawyer whose brother held a top job in the Cuban Ministry of Sports. This incident took place in mid-March, 1965, two years after the Kennedy assassination, at a time when the Agency was still trying (still with little success) to topple Castro. Bongo made covert contact with the CIA saying that he was in contact with a group of Cuban military officers opposed to Castro (this was obviously the AMLASH group).

After their initial meeting with Bongo the CIA found out that he had worked for the Capri Hotel and Casino in Havana, and had been in jail for almost three months beginning in July 1962, for allegedly working for Santos Trafficante. Trafficante had been jailed by the Castro government in the months following the successful revolution that toppled Batista. But why did the Castro government wait three years (Trafficante was jailed in August, 1959) to extract revenge against Bongo? It has been postulated that Bongo approached the Cuban's for permission on Trafficante's behalf to reopen the Capri casino.

But now speculation becomes rife in the whole JFK assassination-Cuban scenario. One of the possible theories of the Kennedy case was reported by mobster Johnny Rosselli and summarized by columnist Jack Anderson. Anderson said that Rosselli told him that a CIA hit team sent to Cuba to kill Castro had been captured, and then "turned," sent back to the US, and were responsible for the murder of President Kennedy. Is it possible that Bongo's purpose in contacting the CIA was to act as a double agent for Castro, and report back to him on the CIA-AMLASH murder plots?

The HSCA report on this incident reads as follows:

"…If Castro had begun his suspicions of AMLASH's role with the CIA during late 1964 or early 1965, it is likely that he would have begun counterintelligence measures to confirm his fears that could have led to Castro sending Bongo on the trip to contact the Agency. Given the Trafficante-Bongo relationship, it can be postulated that Trafficante would have been aware of Bongo's true mission prior to his departure or at least become knowledgeable at some later date. Given the extent of Trafficante's high-level contacts within the exile community and the low-level security in the CIA exile operations, it is therefore logical that Trafficante and other members of the underworld knew, in some fashion, part or all of the AMLASH plot..."

The circumstantial evidence points to a cursory relationship between Cubela and certain members of organized crime, most notably in the form of Santos Trafficante.

AMTRUNK and the Exile Plans to Kill Castro

Besides the AMLASH project, the CIA, by late 1963 and beyond, turned its attention to ousting Castro from power by making an alliance with various Cuban exile groups based in Miami and elsewhere, along with a secret network of dissident Cuban military officers who were willing to do the Agency's work. The code name for this operation was AMTRUNK, whose primary purpose was to instigate a revolt inside the Cuban military. But this plan was not entirely run by the CIA; the State Department also had a hand in its inception.

Called "Operation Leonardo," one of its original parties was George Volsky (AMTRUNK-1) along with Cuban exile leader Nestor Moreno, and New York Times columnist Tad Szulc, who had a good working relationship with both Robert and President Kennedy. In early 1963, this plan was presented to the Kennedy White House in the form of a meeting with the State Department Cuban Coordinator, Robert Hurwitch. The administration then went to the CIA asking it to develop a program to divide the Castro regime from within. But unexpectedly, some members of the CIA, including the powerful chief of the JMWAVE Station, Theodore Shackley, did not like the idea at all. Shackley believed that the "AMTRUNKER's," as he called them, were not entirely loyal to the CIA, were using their relationship to them to further their own ends, and asked that the plan be dropped as soon as possible.

But the CIA's objections were overruled and the AMTRUNK operation went on as planned. The earliest phase of the operation was the assassination of Castro and infiltrating agents into Cuba, but after the Kennedy assassination, the new President, Lyndon Johnson, changed the modus operandi to that of sending rifles and other military hardware to agents who were working in place for the CIA.

It seems that the CIA went ahead with its own plans to aid the Cuban military officers and others by supplying cash to fund operations inside that country, approved sabotage operations by exile groups, etc. It was these same AMTRUNK groups that in 1964, would deliver assassination weapons and other material to Rolando Cubela in Cuba.

But as the AMTRUNK operation got under way, there was a fundamental disagreement between the CIA and those high up in the Kennedy administration who knew of the plans. The CIA wanted to fight an outside war against Castro, as opposed to the internal revolt hoped for by the President, the Attorney General and others. The CIA wanted to fight a World War II type of conflict (despite not learning its lesson at the Bay of Pigs) where men would land from ships waiting off shore and invade an island. The Kennedy plan was to ferment a revolution from within, using as many dissident elements of the Cuban military and civilian population as possible.

Another objection that the Agency did not care for was that it had to share responsibility with other government departments, the State Department, the Department of the Army, for example, in the carrying out the program. The high state of secrecy that the CIA wanted in an operation as sensitive as this one was beyond its control.

Once the AMTRUNK operation started, a man named Ramon Tomas Gum Diaz, along with his pals, Orlando Orozco Basulto and Carlos Pedraza Aguilar, were recruited in Cuba. Guin was arrested in February 1966 (at the same time as Cubela). Orozco was taken out of Cuba in March 1964 and stopped working for the CIA. He later returned to Cuba in December 1964 on another, independent mission. The files on the AMTRUNK project say that Orozco might have been working for the Cuban security service, G-2 and caused a number of planned infiltration missions to be scrubbed. Pedraza was arrested in December 1965 and given a 30-year prison term. "JMWAVE Station advised in March 1966 that four former AMTRUNK internal assets were arrested for counterrevolutionary activities during early 1966, in addition to CUBELA and GUIN, and that all of the principals of the AMTRUNK network active during 1963 and 1964 had been rolled up."

"Comment: It appears that the opposition might have succeeded in obtaining CIA financial and material support for an operation which was controlled by the planners. They succeeded, it seems, in identifying, neutralizing, and exposing on-island anti-Castro forces, and tying up CIA time, money and manpower for an operation of their own creation…"[70]

The internal documents give the following reasons for the failure of the project.

It seems that the three principal agents in the AMTRUNK affair, Tad Szulc, Jorge Volsky and Moreno, were not on the CIA's list of friends that they would want to take to dinner. All three men were anti-CIA, anti-USG and would accept assistance from anyone who would aid their cause. But the most striking objection was that the trio was not under any CIA control. Szulc got the most heat from the CIA, saying that while he was not directly involved in the operation, he was fully briefed by Moreno. Another strike against him was his close contact with the Kennedy White House, and the CIA's fears that he might pass along secret information to the opposition (who ever that might be).

Jorge Volsky (AMTRUNK-1), aka "Chico" was a Cuban citizen of Polish origin. He lived in Poland from 1921 until 1939. During World War 11 he served in the Royal Air Force Polish Group, spent some time in a Russian prison in the 1940's, and then enlisted in the Polish Air Force Service under the British Operational Command. After the war ended, Volsky established a pen pal relationship with a Cuban girl. He was able to get into Cuba without a valid passport and married his girl friend. Once in Cuba, he was the owner of a publicity company from 1947 until 1961 when he came to the US. He was a Castro supporter

70 AMTRUNK OPERATION. Interim Working Draft. 14 February 1977.

and was allegedly arrested shortly after the Bay of Pigs invasion and then released.

Once back in Miami, Volsky met Paul Bethel who was in charge of the Miami office of USIA (a department with long standing CIA ties) and immediately went to work for them. Bethel, it seems, was also working for the JMWAVE Station from October through December 1961.

Volsky also knew Tad Szulc, spoke Polish with him, and a strong friendship was born. Szulc, who had a close working relationship with many members of the Kennedy administration, arranged for a meeting with Volsky with Richard Goodwin, a close aide to President Kennedy in August 1962. During the Cuban Missile Crisis of October 1962, Volsky made covert contact with Major Manuel Pineior Losada, Chief of the DGI, the Cuban external service.[71]

In late 1962, Volsky devised a plan to split the Castro regime. He immediately told Tad Szulc who got in touch with his friends at the State Department and at the White House. "Because SZULC's opinions carried weight with the administration he sat in on State/CIA meetings concerning the plan. His influence is believed to be the primary reason the plan was so quickly adopted by the CIA. In 1963, a State Department official in Miami was a frequent visitor of VOLSKY and kept him informed of State Department affairs."

One of Volsky's contacts in Miami was Raul Chibas Rivas, a member of the anti-Castro exile group JURE (Cuban Revolutionary Junta).

"(blank) In March 1963 JURE created an intelligence group to infiltrate agencies of the US Government. A JURE official, named Jose Aguilar, was making a list of CIA agents and their assigned tasks for JURE and Volsky assisted him."

71 Information on Volsky can be obtained by asking for Jorge Volsky (AMTRUNK-1) 14. February 1977 report in National Archives.

On June 6, 1963, the head of JURE, Monolo Ray, arrived in Miami from Puerto Rico and ordered that no more attacks be made on the US government as he was going to have a talk with Robert Kennedy in Washington regarding the Cuban situation. "On June 27, 1963 Ray returned to Miami from Washington, went directly to JURE offices, held a meeting, and said that he had gained more from his Washington contacts in the last month than he had in the two previous years. He later had a conversation with Volsky that lasted over a half hour. On 18 July, 1963, Ray said that CIA agents are more dangerous than the Kennedy administration as the administration will end but CIA agents always stayed and their memory is longer than that of elephants; they never forget or forgive."

It was also reported by sources that Volsky told refugees with knowledge of Cuban affairs not to talk to the CIA as they were the enemy of the Cubans who wanted to fight Castro.

The following short excerpt comes from a document prepared by the HSCA in its investigation of the JFK case regarding Volsky:

"...The analyst speculated that Volsky's knowledge of clandestine methods of operations, together with his Russian prison background, and his ingenuity as a middleman in US Government/CIA activities, made him an excellent candidate for a Communist penetration agent, and that the possibility existed that he might be a singleton, sleeper, or stringer for the RIS."

Like Cubela-AMLASH, Volsky's bona fides were deeply questioned by the CIA.

The Cuban exiles were not the only ones interested in overthrowing the Castro regime. One of their most important patrons was President Luis Somoza of Nicaragua who came to the United States on a private trip in the summer of 1963 to meet with exile leaders. President Somoza's trip was first covered by the *Miami Herald* in its July 14, 1963 edition. The article said that Somoza was interested in helping the anti-Castro cause in the United States and that "something big" was going to happen. Somoza, while in

Miami, met with various groups including ex-Cuban politicians and the leaders of the American-Cuban community telling them that he was looking for a top-notch military man to lead them.

Another twist to this story was an article in the Miami News written by reporter Hal Hendrix, the Miami News Latin American Editor, called "Back Stage With Bobby." Hendrix said that Robert Kennedy was secretly backing a anti-Castro operation, had hand picked the leaders of this organization, and was in constant contact with anti-Castro leaders such as Manuel Artime, Enrique Ruiz Williams and Roberto and Jose San Roman, all of whom were highly placed members of the anti-Castro group Brigade 2506, which took part in the Bay of Pigs invasion. The article then went on to say that RFK, along with the above-mentioned men, had some sort of secret relationship with the ex-President, Luis Somoza, in which Somoza had given the exiles land in his country to train for an invasion of Cuba.

In hindsight of history, Robert Kennedy's participation in the plans to overthrow Castro was correct. But in 1963, the American public did not know about this information, and the articles in the Miami papers just added fuel to the already simmering fire of anti-Castroism.

FBI documents obtained by the writer tell of more foreign interest in getting rid of Castro. The information comes from an FBI informer called MM T-1 who had furnished reliable information in the past, and is associated with members of various anti-Castro action groups of Cuban exiles… MM T-1 said that Santiago Alvarez, a leading figure in "Commandos L" an anti-Castro organization in Miami, had secret meeting with Somoza, who offered training camps, military equipment, and bases from Nicaragua in which to mount raids into Cuba. He said that Laurenano Batista Falla, the military head of the "Movimiento Democracta Cristiana," an anti-Castro organization, had been meeting with the leaders of "Commandos L." Alvarez and Batista, said the informant, were ready to join their groups to topple Castro.

"Guillermo Belt, the representative in Washington, D.C., of

"Commandos L," has been contacting United States officials to obtain guarantees that exiles in Florida will be allowed to move their boats and arms out of Florida without confiscation. Alvarez and Batista prefer to operate from Florida and the Bahamas on raids against Cuba, but feel that this is impossible under present U.S. policy. They will move their operations to Nicaragua with some reluctance although they trust Somoza, and believe that he is acting in good faith."[72]

Another FBI informer, MM T-2, reported that he had met with Luis Somoza during the latter's visit to Florida and that the ex-leader told him that Somoza was ready to help the anti-Castro cause in the US as much as possible, that he would be someone whom the exiles could rally around, and that he would do all he could to talk the Kennedy administration into backing his clandestine plans.

A third FBI informer called "MM T-3, a member of the Movimiento Revolucinario de Pueblo," a group associated with the Second Front of the Escambray and the most militant of the anti-Castro groups, Alpha 66, said that Antonio Veciana, had met with Luis Somoza in Miami. Somoza offered a training base in Nicaragua and further told Veciana that in his opinion, the Kennedy administration was not handling the Cuban situation very well. "MM T-3 said that Veciana rejected Somoza's offer as being too little."

"MM T-6," another FBI informer passed along this important piece of information. He said that Somoza tried to have a meeting with President Kennedy to discuss the anti-Castro operations but was unsuccessful. However, he did meet with Secretary of State Dean Rusk. "MM T-6" said that President Kennedy then allegedly called Somoza "and indicated that although he did not believe that the Cubans in exile alone would be able to liquidate the internal problems in the various countries, this might be a step towards the unification of the Cuban exiles..."

72 Anti-Fidel Castro Activities, Internal Security-Cuba. 7/19/63.

In the July 16, 1963 edition of the Miami News in an article called "Top Exile Fighter Quits US for Base," Hal Hendrix said that Manuel Artime decided to leave the US to direct an anti-Castro army from a secret hideaway in Central America. One part of the Hendrix article says: "Almost all doors in the US have been closed to us, so we are going to a country from where we can fight against Castro's Communist regime." Did Artime make a deal with Somoza to use his base?

The article went on to say that Artime hotly denied any political relationship with Robert Kennedy. He quotes Artime as saying that if his exile groups decided to stay in the US and launch clandestine raids against Cuba, he would always be looking over his shoulder for the CIA and the Border Patrol who were on the lookout for any raids into Cuba from US territory. "It's impossible," said Artime, "to work against Castro from this country."

It was not only foreigners like Luis Somoza who were aiding the anti-Castro cause, but Cuban exiles in the United States who were willing to put up large amounts of money to kill Castro.

Newly released CIA documents obtained by the author tell of numerous plots, beginning in early 1964 among wealthy Cubans living in America to plot the demise of Castro. One CIA document tells of a March 2, 1964 meeting of a Cuban exile by an acquaintance who wanted to discuss a plan to assassinate Fidel Castro. The acquaintance was, the exile was told, a wealthy businessman who was a ship-owner and flew under the British flag. This man was also legally allowed to place slot machines in gambling houses, and thus, had good contacts with the American mob. An unnamed partner of this shipbuilder was an ex-police officer from St. Louis who had influence with the mob. The unnamed exile told his guest that certain members of the "Cosa Nostra" had offered up to $150,000 to kill Castro. "The Cuban exile commented that he believed he had been approached with this plan because of his family's wealth; he told his acquaintance that he was not interested and suggested that an approach might be made to someone who has much more money."

Another exile agent for the CIA reported that he met a man named Byron Cameron, the owner and operator of the M/V CAYMAN HOPE, who lived in Ft. Lauderdale, Florida. Also attending the meeting were Teofilo Babun Franco, co-owner of the Antillean Marine Shipping Co in Miami, and two of Babun's employees, Oscar Fernandez Viego and Eliseo Gomez Fernandez. In the course of the conversation, Cameron said that he was in contact with mob elements and that his group was willing to assassinate Castro, his brother Raul, and Ernesto "Che" Guevara. When the price for killing the trio, $150,000 was mentioned, those in the party said they weren't interested as "just another attempt to swindle patriotic Cuban exiles."

But Cameron did not close the door entirely and told his contacts that he would check with his paymasters concerning any Castro hit. On March 15, Cameron, Babun and others, had a meeting in which the following terms were agreed upon for the assassination of Cuban officials: "Fidel Castro, $100,000; Raul Castro, $20,000; Che Guevara, $20,00 and $2,500 for expenses, payable in advance. The time limit for the proposed mission would be 90 days from the date when Babun could verify, to the satisfaction of Cameron, that he had $100,000 at his disposal for the payment. The contract for payment would be honored only upon the presentation of evidence that the three Cuban officials died at the hands of the assassins connected with Cameron's contacts."[73]

In early April 1964, Eliseo Gomez Fernandez met with Jose "Pepin" Bosch. Bosch gave Babun and his men $100,000 for the Castro kill. Another wealthy Cuban exile who gave money was Julio Lobo Olavarria, who did not want his name to be publicly associated with the task. The documents say that on April 25, 1964, Cameron's team was already in Cuba and were waiting for another man to arrive. The final comment was "we hope to

73 Plans of Cuban Exiles to Assassinate. Sel. Cuban Govt. Leaders. 6/10/64. Record No. 157-10002-10182.

have some good news for you between 20 May and 25 May." Unfortunately, no such "good news" was heard.

What is important in this Castro assassination plot is that the Cameron group was closely associated with the mob in this particular incident. Cameron was so worried about the consequences of a failure was that he knew he could be charged with conspiracy "and that if there is any treachery on his part, Babun and his associates would not hesitate to sink his ship, the M/V CAYMAN HOPE.

The documents also reveal on July 9, 1964 Julio Lobo notified his CIA contacts that he had been approached in April and May by Teofilo Babun and asked to contribute $100,000 toward a Castro assassination. Lobo said that he would put the money in escrow until proof that the assassins were hired and that he wasn't being scammed. Lobo said the assassins would be three or four "Chicago-type Cosa Nostra" individuals who were in Europe, presumably in Italy, and who would be going to Havana, Cuba on legitimate business."

Lobo said that he was willing to go along with the plans if the CIA would give him the ok. Lobo was told that Langley wanted no part of the deal. When he was interviewed by the CIA in July, 1964, Babun said that he was never involved in any Castro murder plots, nor did he ever ask for any money towards such ends.

JFK's Carrot and the Stick

After the end of the Cuban Missile Crisis, the Kennedy administration conducted a two-track foreign policy as far as Cuba was concerned. On the one hand, the Kennedy led and run, Operation Mongoose was "officially" ended, but separate, exile raids against targets in Cuba continued. With Manuel Artime's commandos heading for the safety of Nicaragua where they could mount their clandestine raids against Cuba, the Kennedy administration, on March 30, 1963, announced that it was going to take whatever measures were necessary to stop exile raids from US territory against Cuba. Robert Kennedy's Justice Department quickly stepped up FBI undercover surveillance on the secret training camps run by the anti-Castro groups such as Alpha 66 in such places as the Florida Everglades and outside of New Orleans (where David Ferrie, Guy Banister and the New Orleans contingent to the JFK assassination were training).

It seems clear that at this point in time, President Kennedy and his brother Robert, who was the titular head of the administrations anti-Castro operations, were conducting what was to be called a "Separate Track" approach to Castro.

Another reason for the administrations new policy was also to reduce the tensions between the United States and the Soviet Union. In the Missile Crisis, Soviet Premier Khrushchev left Fidel Castro out of most of the important military policy, sending in his nuclear missiles, manning them with Russian technicians, and conducting the negotiations with the Kennedy administration to end the crisis without ever consulting Castro. Castro was mad, but Khrushchev still held the nuclear card and President Kennedy still had to respect Russian power and deal with it.

One of the Kennedy administrations first secret contacts with the Soviet Union took place on September 30, 1963, when JFK sent his Press Secretary Pierre Salinger, to meet covertly with a Russian named Colonel G.V. Karpovich. Karpovich was a KGB (Soviet intelligence) officer who was attached to the Soviet Embassy in Washington. Khrushchev himself had approved of this secret contact hoping to bypass the normal diplomatic channels that might stifle important contacts between the two countries. While it was hoped that this back channel negotiations would lead to increasing contact, it did not significantly materialize.

In another diplomatic move to lessen Soviet-American divisions, JFK sent US Ambassador Averill Harriman to Moscow on April 23, 1963 where he had several meetings with Prime Minister Khrushchev. Among the topics covered were Cuba and other important items. Another important American to visit

Khrushchev that spring was Norman Cousins, the editor of the *Saturday Review.* Upon his return to the US, Cousins met with JFK and told him that Khrushchev wanted to have a new start with the administration. Also in April, Fidel Castro arrived in Moscow and met the Soviet leader. Before leaving the Soviet Union, Castro had an interview with American journalist Lisa Howard. Castro told Howard that he was ready to reach a rapprochement with the United States.

But while this was going on, the Kennedy brothers were mounting a second, large-scale covert war against the Castro regime. Operation Mongoose had been revived in a smaller form, but was still run by the CIA. Why the Kennedy administration was using the carrot and the stick is open to speculation but one can assume that they wanted it both ways. The next year was an election year and Kennedy did not want to be accused of losing Cuba like Truman had been accused of "losing China" after World War II. But he also wanted to placate the doves that wanted to see an easing of the tensions with Cuba, especially after the Missile Crisis of 1962.

Information on the Kennedy's covert second war against Castro come from the newly declassified documents and shows this two-tier approach. A chronology of this two-tier track follows.

In two meetings dated October 19-20 and Nov. 14, 1962 between William Harvey, Richard Helms, John McCone the following is discussed:

Harvey states, "It should be noted that all action operations which could be put on ice by the CIA, in accordance with the instructions, were put in ice..."

November 14, 1962 conference regarding Operation Mongoose:

Lansdale states, "On October 30-31 for an 'Eyes Only' background memorandum requested by Roswell Gilpatrick, information was requested from CIA on the current status of all operations. CIA reported all militant operations have been ordered held at a stop, although the volatile Cubans were frustrated and not under complete control..."

November 5, 1962 notes by George McManus regarding Cuba, Mongoose and the Special Group:

"McManus states that if these agreements (i.e., Kennedy and Khrushchev) are carried out, it seems clear that Cuba will be dealt with as another denied area in a manner differing not really from that in which CIA handles other areas. If the agreements are not carried out, military action cannot long be delayed. In either event, the Mongoose structure as it has existed in government is through."

November 5, 1962 notes from a conference between President Kennedy, Robert Kennedy, Robert McNamara, General Taylor, William Bundy, Roswell Gilpatrick and others:

"McManus states, when the President, in his letter to Khrushchev of 27 October gave assurances against the invasion of Cuba in consideration of the Soviet removal of offensive weapons in Cuba under UN supervision, Operation MONGOOSE was on its death-bed. When the President stated in his letter of 28 October to Khrushchev, "I consider my letter to you of 27 October and your reply of today as a firm undertaking on the part of both our governments which should be promptly carried out, Operation MONGOOSE died."

At the same time that this was going on, a new course was being chartered within the administration. The record reads as follows:

October 4, 1962 meeting between JFK, RFK, McCone, Taylor, etc.:

McCone states, "The Attorney General reported on discussions with JFK on Cuba; dissatisfied with lack of action in the sabotage field and distressed that nothing was moving forward, commented that one effort attempted had failed, expressed general concern over developing situation."

October 4, 1962 meeting between RFK, John McCone and Thomas Parrott:

Parrott notes, "The Attorney General opened the meeting by saying that higher authorities concerned with the progress of the MONGOOSE Program and feels that more priority should be given to trying to mount sabotage operations. He urged that massive activity be mounted within the entire MONGOOSE framework. Kennedy questioned whether we are going down the right road or whether more direct action is not indicated... All efforts should be made to develop new and imaginative approaches to the possibility of getting rid of the Castro regime."

March 19, 1963 meeting of the SGA:

Fitzgerald states, "The consensus of observers is that a popular uprising will overthrow Castro. Current policy included the overt use of US military force to overthrow Castro. He suggests that economic strangulation program will follow in near future with a request for policy approval to mount sabotage operations against Cuban ships and cargo vessels. CIA proposes to devote main effort against key officers in the armed forces and militia who are disenchanted with Castro's management of Cuban affairs. Effort will be to identify these officers and convince them that their future lies only in disposing of Castro..."

November 12, 1963 encounter with JFK, RFK, Rusk, Helms, Bundy and McNamara.

"On Nov. 12, 1963, at a meeting with President Kennedy and others, Mr. Fitzgerald discussed covert collection in Cuban operations, pointing out that CIA had three kinds of agent's activities inside Cuba: (1) "Singleton" operations (2) Collection nets (3) agents involved in black net operations. Some 25 agents had been either captured or killed in the past year. There is increasing effectiveness of Castro's internal security forces, accounting for the loss of agents."

And while these covert activities were going on, Track Two was being developed.

June 6, 1963 meeting between McCone, Bundy, Johnson & Kilpatrick regarding Mongoose, Castro and the SGA:

"On June 6, 1963, the SGA discussed various possibilities

of establishing channels of communication with CASTRO. All members of the group agree that this is a useful endeavor. Mr. Bundy cautioned that of course CASTRO should not be made privy to any US positions, while Mr. McCone emphasized the necessity of keeping any such approach entirely secret."

November 6, 1963 meeting with Bundy, Johnson, Vance and McCone regarding Mongoose planning:

"On November 6, 1963, Bundy told the SG that "it has come to the attention of the White House that Castro would like to have a talk designed to bring about some arrangement with the US." To hear what Castro has to say and to know on what basis he might wish to negotiate would be of some use to the US. After discussion, it was decided by the SG members not to try to reach a firm decision at this time (as to an emissary to talk to Castro) but to study the problem for several days and to attack it again."

November 6, 1963:

"On November 6, 1963, higher authority (President Kennedy) disapproved all Cuban operations scheduled to be run before November 12. Two operations dated November 8 and 10 are therefore disapproved."

President Kennedy's interest in lessening the political and military tensions between not only Cuba and the Soviet Union as well, began to take shape in the summer of 1963. The resolution of the Cuban Missile Crisis the year before had left an indelible impression on the young president. The world had come ever so close to nuclear war and Kennedy never wanted to let that happen again.

In June, he made one of the most important speeches of his presidency at the commencement at the American University in Washington, D.C. This was President Kennedy's "peace speech" in which he offered the olive branch of cooperation to the Soviet Union. The president declared that he did not want a "Pax Americana," and American peace, dictated by American military might. "I am talking about genuine peace—the kind of peace that makes life on earth worth living, the kind that enables men and nations to grow and hope and to build a better life for their children—not merely peace in our time, but peace for all time... Therefore, let us reexamine our attitude toward the Soviet Union..." And in one of the most controversial parts of the address, the president said, "Let us reexamine our attitude toward the Cold War," and called for the swift passage by the United States, Britain, France and the Soviet Union of a ban on all-nuclear testing in the atmosphere. The president ended his speech with these words, "The most basic link was that we all inhabit this small planet, we all breathe the same air, we all cherish our children's future, and we are all mortal."

While the president's speech was hailed in the press and by our allies (and some of our not so allies) as forward looking, certain groups, such as the militant anti-Castro exiles, and even some disgruntled members of the CIA, thought differently. One world leader who saw some promise in the president's speech was Fidel Castro.

As mentioned before, Fidel Castro was not joined at the hip with Nikita Khrushchev, especially after the humiliating defeat (in Castro's eyes, anyway) after the Cuban Missile Crisis. Castro wanted some autonomy vis a vi the Soviet Union, but not enough that his actions would cause the loss of the billions of Russian rubles that propped up his economy.

In the summer of 1963, Robert Kennedy found himself at odds with the State Department as far as Cuban was concerned. The Attorney General worked for an ending of travel restrictions of Americans who wanted to go to Cuba. The State Department lobbied against any such change in policy. In quick succession, the Senate ratified the Nuclear Test Ban Treaty, and in late summer, President Kennedy went on a very successful swing across the American west discussing his plans to lessen tensions with the Soviet Union. He was greeted with large and cheerful crowds; a prelude to what he hoped would be a smashing re-election victory in 1964.

In September 1963, the administration received tentative

feelers from Fidel Castro wanting to know if the Kennedy administration would be willing to enter into secret talks with him. Both JFK and RFK were interested and privately asked William Atwood, a former editor of *Life* magazine to act on their behalf. At this time, Atwood was part of the US delegation to the United Nations, having formally been US Ambassador to Guinea for two years. In a September 18, memo to the State Department, Atwood argued that it would be wrong to permanently isolate Castro, and that might lead him further into the Soviet orbit. He also stated that his contacts told him that Castro was disillusioned with Khrushchev and wanted more freedom to run his own country. Atwood asked JFK if he could put out feelers to the Cuban Ambassador to the UN, Carlos Lechuga. He also asked the president if he could persuade Lechuga to gain an invitation for him to go to Cuba, could he do it. The president gave his permission and soon, a chance encounter was arranged. Journalist Lisa Howard, who had interviewed Castro in the spring, hosted a dinner party at her home. Among those attending the party were William Atwood and Carlos Lechuga.

The day after the Howard party, Atwood reported to the White House where he met with both JFK and RFK. While nothing of real substance took place, and the Attorney General thought Atwood's contacts with Castro were "worth pursuing." William Bundy told Atwood that the president himself was in favor of "pushing towards an opening toward Cuba to take Castro out of the Soviet fold and perhaps wiping out the Bay of Pigs and maybe getting back to normal."

Lisa Howard's covert contacts with top ranking Cuban's continued and she had a good discussion with Dr. Rene Vallejo, Castro's friend and private doctor. On October 31, Vallejo told Howard that Castro was ready for a meeting with a high-ranking American diplomat. JFK was informed and told Atwood to go to Cuba.

But the Atwood-Vallejo channel was not the only one burning. Another man to be used as an intermediary between the US and Havana was French journalist Jean Daniel of *L'Express*.

The president learned that Daniel was about to go to Cuba to meet Fidel Castro. On the day before his departure, October 24, 1963, Daniel found himself talking with JFK about Cuba. Kennedy asked Daniel if he would pass along a message from him to Castro. The gist of the note was that the US could live with a Socialist Cuba if certain conditions were met, among them, the ending of Cuban revolutionary activity in Latin America. Kennedy told Daniel to tell Castro that he had nothing against the Cuban people and that he would await Castro's reply.

Daniel waited in Havana for three, long weeks until he was finally granted an interview with Castro, November 20, 1963. For hours, Castro and Daniel discussed the world scene, including the remarks made by President Kennedy to the Cuban leader. After learning that Kennedy had denounced the former Cuban dictator Batista whom Castro had overthrown, Castro called Kennedy, "a capitalist whom we can talk." Castro further said of the American president, "I believe Kennedy is sincere... He still has the possibility of being, in the eyes of history, the greatest President of the United States." He also told Daniel that he would publicly say that Senator Barry Goldwater (the eventual Republican Presidential nominee in 1964) was his best friend in order to raise Kennedy's chances of re-election. Castro told Daniel that he was in no rush to start negotiations with the US but saw positive steps in their meeting. They would meet again in two days for further discussions; November 22, 1963.

Castro was with Daniel when they learned the news of Kennedy's assassination. "This is bad news," lamented Castro. "There is the end of your mission for peace."

Castro asked Daniel what he knew about the new president, Lyndon Johnson, and what control he had over the CIA.

While the Kennedy-Atwood-Daniel back channel negotiations were going on, Castro lashed out at the United States. On September 7, Castro had a meeting with reporter Daniel Harker of the *Associated Press* at the Brazilian embassy during a three-hour interview. In that interview, Castro issued the following warning to the United States: "We are prepared to fight them and answer in kind. United States leaders should think that if they are aiding terrorist plans to eliminate Cuban leaders, they themselves will not be safe."

Conspiracy theorists involving Cuba in the Kennedy assassination point to this statement as Castro's rationale for being behind the president's death. This statement has other, important implications as well. Did Castro know of the CIA-Mafia plots to kill him? Was he privy to the Kennedy administrations "Operation Mongoose" and ZR/RIFLE Programs? Did Castro have a double agent in the Cuban exile community feeding him this sensitive information? And could that double agent have been Santos Trafficante? It seems reasonable, from all the facts that the answer is yes. Except for the most critical fact? Did Castro order the assassination of President Kennedy? The answer to that query, based on the historical evidence, is NO. If it was probed beyond a reasonable doubt that Castro was behind the assassination, Cuba would have been invaded by US troops and the Castro government toppled. I believe that Castro truly wanted a political accommodation with the United States in November 1963 and was working toward that end.

What about Lee Harvey Oswald? Was he acting on behalf of Castro? That's another story entirely.

What about Rolando Cubela, A.K.A. AMLASH? He was given a long prison sentence, which was reduced by Castro because of their long-standing friendship. CIA documents on the AMLASH trial reveal that he did not reveal the actual names of those people inside the Cuban armed forces whom he worked with in the Castro plots. "Several careful readings of the entire proceedings of the trial appear to indicate that as soon as Cubela learned the extent of the regime's knowledge of the plot to assassinate the Premier he adopted an immediate line of defense his own 'weakness,' emotional instability, deterioration, liking for gay parties, the 'dolce vita.'"[74]

74 The Cubela Trial 14 April 1966.

An analysis of Cubela's reactions at his trial were monitored by the CIA's Technical Service Division (the same group who gave us the poison pen).

"...He has some skill in adjusting his style to that of the people he is talking to. While he can be rather eloquent, he is not likely to divulge anything which should be kept secret... He has his feelings and impulses under the strictest control. He is a role player who may appear more natural and spontaneous than he actually is... He can exercise various deceptive mechanisms in the most adroit fashion, and while demonstrating a smooth behavior."[75]

Just the kind of agent the CIA is always looking for!

75 Ibid.

Chapter 7

The Guns of Dallas

To the causal reader of the Kennedy assassination literature, the name of Frank Ellsworth may not ring any bells. But as the years went by, and new documents and information on the assassination were released, the name of Frank Ellsworth gained importance in the overall story. In November 1963, Frank Ellsworth was an agent for the Internal Revenue Services Division of Alcohol and Tobacco Tax (now called the Bureau of Alcohol, Tobacco and Firearms Division ATF–which gained such wide spread publicity during the standoff at the Branch Dividian compound in Waco, Texas). In the weeks prior to the president's trip to Dallas, Frank Ellsworth would play an unnoticed role that would lead to the arrest of a Dallas gun dealer who sold the same type of ammunition used by the president's alleged assassin, Lee Harvey Oswald, and whose sting operation would lead right back to the same anti-Castro Cubans and Americans who were in league with the CIA during the plots to kill Castro.

But Frank Ellsworth was just a player in the gunrunning operation in Dallas in the weeks prior to the assassination of the president, along with a number of bit performers, along with a man with high name recognition, Jack Ruby.

Frank Ellsworth's name is barely mentioned in the Warren Commission's Report, and nothing of the gunrunning episode that he was investigating. If the Warren Commissioners had been informed of the entire episode they would have been able to tie in the radical right in Dallas, CIA agents, anti-Castro Cubans, the FBI, Jack Ruby, and Lee Harvey Oswald. All these groups have been implicated in one way or another in the assassination of President Kennedy.

This new information was first brought to life in 1996 by journalists Ray and Mary La Fontaine, in their book, *Oswald Talked: The New Evidence In the JFK Assassination,* (Pelican Publishing Co., 1996). Previous articles by the La Fontaine's on the Kennedy case were printed in such mainstream newspapers as the *Houston Post* and the *Washington Post.* The jacket cover of the book says that the La Fontaine's do not have an "agenda" as far as coverage of the Kennedy assassination is concerned. Their book has received both praise and ridicule among the so called "research community" – a group of writers and those people deeply interested in all facets of the Kennedy case. In *Oswald Talked,* the authors tell the complete story of Frank Ellsworth and the gunrunning operations that took place in that city prior to November 22, 1963. They also make startling revelations concerning Sylvia Odio, and the theory that Lee Oswald was working for the FBI and gave the Bureau forewarning of the plot on JFK's life. They also reveal the name of a man who was arrested by the DPD in the hours after the assassination and the startling information he allegedly learned from Oswald during their time in the Dallas jail.

In the frantic first hours after the assassination of President Kennedy on November 22, 1963, Dallas Police were on the look-out for a man with a gun who was said to have shot DPD Officer J.D. Tippit. Shortly after the assassination, three "tramps" were arrested after they were taken off of a train that was about to pull out of the rail yards next to the now infamous grassy knoll. The three tramps have become part of the Kennedy assassination lore and some conspiracy theorists even said that they were really E. Howard Hunt, Frank Sturgis, and Charles Harrelson (the father of *Cheers* star, Woody Harrelson). Over the course of time the tramps were identified as Harold Doyle, John Foresrter Gedney and Gus Abrams. The three were never fingerprinted or had their statements taken but, were allowed to go free later on the day of the 22nd.

But not known to the public at large was the fact that another man was arrested that day, put in the same cell as the accused presidential assassin, Lee Oswald, and had quite a story to tell. Unfortunately, his story was not known by researchers over the years and his very presence in the Dallas Police Jail was refuted by the FBI ever since.

The man arrested on the afternoon of November 22, 1963 was John Elrod who happened to be walking near the railroad tracks on Harry Hines Blvd. While Elrod did not have a rifle on him, the mere fact that he was strolling near the tracks was enough to give the police a reason to arrest him. He was put in a cell on the fifth floor of the DPD jail on charges of "investigation to commit murder." Just as soon as Johnny Elrod was imprisoned, things began to happen. Almost an hour after he was arrested, he noticed a man with a battered face being brought into the jail. Elrod's cellmate too saw the bruised man being brought into the jail and he proceeded to tell Elrod a most amazing story. It seemed that Elrod's cellmate told him that he had been in a motel room a few days before with the very man that was now being brought into the jail. The man was there with a group of other men who were given a sum of money to do a contract. Later, the cellmate said that the man with the battered face also drove a late model Thunderbird with a trunk load of guns inside.

But the clincher, as far as Elrod was concerned, was what his roommate said next. One of the men in the hotel room was none other than Jack Ruby. And who was Elrod's cellmate? If one can believe the La Fontaine's-Lee Harvey Oswald!

After Jack Ruby killed Oswald on November 24, 1963, before an entire grief stricken nation on live TV, his entire background was investigated by the FBI; or so it seemed. The Warren Commission reported its findings that neither Ruby nor Oswald has any previous connections and further, that Ruby had no ties to organized crime. If they had looked deeper into Ruby's background they would have had a different perspective on "Sparky" as he was called in his days as a runner for Al Capone in Chicago.

The man with the broken face was identified as Lawrence Miller. Along with Miller, another man was incarcerated that day (he was a friend of Miller's), Donnel Darius Whitter. It seems that both Miller and Whitter had been the object of a local-state undercover operation involving the transportation of illegal weapons in Dallas-the Ellsworth connection. The two men were being investigated by units of the Dallas Police Department, as well as a member of the Alcohol, Tobacco and Firearms Division of the US Treasury Department. The Bureau of Narcotics officer, as mentioned before, was Frank Ellsworth, who was on a night stakeout assignment on November 18, 1963. He had made a purchase of illegal arms supplied by a local Dallas gun shop owner named John Thomas Masen. Masen told Ellsworth and his partner that if they waited at a particular location in Dallas, he would meet them and an exchange would be made. But Masen never showed up and Ellsworth's night of bitter coffee drinking was a bust.

But not far away the Dallas Police would have better luck. At nearby Trunk Street, FBI agent Joe Abernathy and his partner also sat in their undercover car along with another unit of the DPD. Suddenly they noticed a late model, 1963 Dodge come to a stop near their location. Earlier in the day the police had received a tip that a load of guns that had recently been stolen from a National Guard armory in Terrell, Texas was going to be unloaded at that location. However, the driver remained in his car. Soon though, a new model Thunderbird convertible showed up and the two men in the car began unloading a catch of automatic rifles, two air cooled .30 caliber. Browning machine guns, and one .45 caliber M-3 sub-machine gun. Agent Abernathy decided that he and his partner would follow the car with the guns and began a tail that would lead them across the city. When the police car spotted the

T-Bird making an illegal turn, they came after them, with their lights and flashers blaring. The driver of the T-bird led the police on a high-speed chase, finally cracking up at a light pole. The men in the car were Lawrence Miller and Donnel Darius Whitter.

After being taken to Parkland Hospital where they were patched up, both Miller and Whitter were taken to the Dallas City Jail where they had the brief encounter with John Elroy and he calmed that he instantly recognized them. On the afternoon of the assassination, Frank Ellsworth arrived at the jail and was one of the few non-Dallas police members to question Lee Harvey Oswald. When Ellsworth arrived to question the suspect, he had quite a shock. John Thomas Masen, the man who set up the buy with Ellsworth was a dead ringer for Lee Harvey Oswald. (In the weeks prior to the assassination, there were frequent reports of Oswald sightings in and around Dallas when the real Oswald was at other locations – could the fake Oswald have been Masen?). It seems that Whitter had worked for the gas station owned by V.E. Moralli in Dallas where Jack Ruby often times brought his car in for repairs. Soon, a social relationship began between Ruby and Miller.

As mentioned by Elroy's calmed, Jack Ruby was one of the people in the hotel room where a deal was to go down. It is conceivable that when both Whitter and Miller where caught, they were doing a gun running deal for Jack Ruby. Ruby had a background in running guns to Cuba starting in the late 1950's, so it is not inconceivable that he would stay in this most lucrative business.

Newly released Dallas police files on the assassination reveal that Miller and Whitter were placed in the same cellblock F as that of John Elroy. Another prisoner who was in the same cellblock as Elroy, Miller and Whitter, was a young man named Daniel Wayne Douglass who walked into the police station wanting to confess to car theft and instead, was charged with suspicion of murder. Oswald was placed in an adjoining cell near Douglass and the young car thief had a good view of him. Police logs showed that both Douglas and Oswald were allowed to make phone calls during their stay in jail. What is obvious is that all the early suspects in both the Kennedy and Tippit slayings were placed in Cell block F, that a lot of talking went on, and if the Elroy story is true, the alleged presidential assassin spilled his guts to him.

In the end, Elroy was let go and immediately left Dallas for good. But here the story gets even more interesting. There were NO records of Elroy's arrest on November 22, 1963 – they only came to light years later when they were found by a researcher.

But the story of what happened (or didn't happen) in cellblock F is only part of the story. For the gun running sting operation investigated by Frank Ellsworth, had ramifications far beyond Dallas, and involved another invasion of Cuba, with the guns heisted from a nearby army base.

The secret that neither the Warren Commission, nor the public in general knew was that a second invasion of Cuba was being prepared for the last week in November. This was not to be an armed strike by US Marines, but a large-scale invasion of the island led by certain elements of the Cuban exiles based in Florida. The group that was heading for Cuba was called the DRE, or Cuban Student Directorate. The DRE was closely monitored and watched by the CIA but did not have complete control over it as it had other exile groups. (In the summer of 1963, Lee Harvey Oswald was publicly associated with certain members of the DRE in New Orleans and his actions in that city were watched closely by the CIA–New information has come forth that reveals the name of a CIA agent named George Joannides who was also monitoring the DRE and at that same time-more about him later in the book).

The source of this powerful information was Agent Frank Ellsworth's contact at Fort Hood in Texas, U.S. Army Captain, George Nonte. Nonte was the commanding officer of D Company, 123rd Maintenance Battalion, 37 years old, and held a top-secret clearance. Ellsworth has been investigating a string of ordinance thefts originating from Fort Hood in which large amounts of military supplies, including heavy tanks and guns, were stolen from the base. These stolen military supplies were then funneled through John Thomas Masen to the various anti-Castro groups in Dallas like ALPHA 66, which was one of the most militant of them all. During his investigation of the Fort Hood thefts, Agent Ellsworth was in contact with Burt Griffin, the counsel to the Warren Commission. Ellsworth told Griffin that Masen was selling these illegal arms to a man named Manuel Rodriguez Orcaberro, one of the leaders of ALPHA 66. Griffin filed away this information but no further investigation was conducted.

Ellsworth and his partner, fellow agent William Fuller, had originally made contact with Masen when they came to his gun shop and told him that he, Ellsworth, was a cop on the take who was interested in making extra money in the gunrunning business. He told Masen that while he did not have the necessary cash to finance a gun deal, he did know a wealthy man from New Mexico who would back him up. In turn, Masen put Ellsworth in contact with George Nonte at Fort Hood.

During his first trip to Fort Hood, Ellsworth spoke to the two most important federal intelligence agencies that were housed at the base; the FBI and the army's Criminal Investigation Division (CD). The army spies told Ellsworth that "somebody was stealing them blind." A tank had been stolen from the base, as well as large quantities of ordinance. Ellsworth confided to them that he had been investigating the trail of stolen arms in Dallas and that the track led him right back to George Nonte. It was agreed that Ellsworth would return to Dallas to pursue the case against Nonte.

But Ellsworth failed to nab Nonte when Miller and Whitter were arrested by the FBI on the night of November 18 when Ellsworth's bust went bad. After the arrest of Miller and Whitter, Masen backed off any further contact with Ellsworth and his case against the Army officer went nowhere.

But it seems that Nonte had a double life of his own. While Ellsworth was investigating Nonte, Nonte was working with the

FBI as an informer in his own scheme to pilfer military supplies from Fort Hood. The FBI could not care less that Nonte was stealing military supplies; they just wanted to know where the guns were going. And they were going to the militant anti-Castro groups like ALPHA 66, the DRE and other groups in Dallas and elsewhere for the planned invasion of Cuba in the last week of November 1963.

Nonte told the FBI, after talking with Masen, that the guns were destined for an operation against Cuba, from an unknown base in the Caribbean, and that it involved a large force. Nonte said that his source was a man named Martinez, a Miami based weapons dealer who came to Dallas some months previous. Martinez' full name was Joaquin Martinez de Pinillos, a member of the DRE. Martinez' name had first come to the attention of the FBI from a Cuban exile named Fermin de Goicochea Sanchez. De Goicochea told the FBI that Martinez traveled from Miami to Dallas in the summer of 1963 along with the head of the DRE military wing, Juan Manuel Salvat. The primary reason for de Goicochea's trip to Dallas was to get money for medical supplies for the Cuban exiles. Funds were indeed raised during his trip, and the Cuban military man met General Edwin Walker who was interested in helping the anti-Castro cause. But the underlining cause of his trip was to acquire guns for the new invasion of Cuba. And here is where the Mason Nonte connection fit in perfectly. The guns siphoned from the stocks at Fort Hood went to Salvat's cause. Salvat came to Mason with his shopping list of military stocks that he needed. Masen contacted Nonte at Fort Hood and the ordinance officer made the deals with the anti-Castro Cubans.

Newly released documents obtained by the writer tell of the interest both the FBI and the CIA had in Juan Manuel Salvat.

One FBI memo on him reads as follows:

"On 3/7/67 Juan Manuel Salvat, principal officer of the DRE, which is called the Cuban Student Directorate in English, advised that he DRE has been inactive for approximately the past year inasmuch as it lacked funds to continue operation and also there appeared to be no logical action which the DRE organization could undertake in the exile movement against the Castro regime.

"Mr. Salvat, who is the owner of a bookstore called Libreria Universal in Miami, Fla., stated that during the several years that the DRE had been active subsequent to the Castro takeover in Cuba its delegations always acted pursuant to advice from the DRE headquarters at Miami. DRE delegations at present are inactive but in the case of Carlos Bringuier, who has been the DRE representative at New Orleans, there has been evidence of an independent attitude. Mr. Salvat explained that ever since Bringuier was developed as a witness in the investigation of the assassination of President Kennedy, due to Bringuier's contacts with Lee Harvey Oswald in New Orleans, the whole issue of the assassination has become for Bringuier, a cause célèbre."

"Salvat advised that about 3/1/67 he made a long distance call to Bringuier in New Orleans in view of statements made by Bringuier to the press relative to the current investigation of a conspiracy in the President's assassination which is being conducted by New Orleans DA Jim Garrison. Salvat said Bringuier was quoted as stating, in effect, that no Cuban exile was involved in the assassination but that perhaps there was some involvement on the part of Fidel Castro. Salvat stated that he admonished Bringuier that the entire matter of the assassination was very serious and that he should refrain from making any statements or expressing personal speculations."[76]

While this FBI memo was written in 1967, four years after the assassination of the president, it still shows how much interest there was in keeping track of the DRE and Salvat.

A CIA background memo on Salvat describes his early life in the DRE (19 October, 1960).

---

76 No Title. HSCA Record No. 180-10020-10157. Date 3/10/67

"Three univ. students escaped after hiding in Havana 2 months; Alberto Muller, Ernesto Fernandez Travieso & Manuel Salvat. Escape possible under protection of Brazilian Embassy. All three blamed Major Rolando Cubela (AMLASH), Castro's personal choice to head the University Student Federation. The three, on arrival in Miami, offered their services to Cuban Democratic Revolutionary Front–want to organize an anti-Communist student org. within the front…"

"3 Sept. 1960: DRE to be formed 5 September 1960. DRE Committee to travel to a Latin American country to make public announcement of formation of group. Propaganda head of DRE is Manuel Salvat."

"Nov. 4, 1960: MASH planning to infiltrate first DRE team Havana province by 10 Nov. 1960 in order to be present when student general strike occurs on 14 Nov. Long range objective of team is to organize anti-Castro student propaganda and harassment force within student circle. Salvat and Muller on this team."

"May 9, 1961: Salvat arrested in Cuba about 18 April. His true identity did not become known to authorities & following interrogation & investigation, he was released."

"Salvat's PM duties will be limited, but involves some sabotage & demolition as well as distribution & organization of clandestine guerrilla groups within Cuba. When DRE leader, Alberto Muller was in Sierra Maestra with 400 guerillas, CIA failed to support effort with material air drops. With their leader abandoned and in jeopardy, Salvat wrote to friends in US that he would kill CIA personnel involved if anything happened to Muller."

"8 March 1962: Salvat is action type, considered one of the bulwarks of the free Cuba student world. Has infiltrated Cuba & worked in underground, undergone arrest & interrogation, freed & returned to Miami, infiltrated again on three attempts that failed latter part of 1961. He is almost legendary among Cuban high school & university youth."

"13 March 1968: Request for cancellation. Salvat no longer of operational interest to CIA."[77]

So what do we have here? Manual Salvat was a powerful member of the DRE, was known for years by the CIA and FBI as one of the most important of the anti-Castro fighters. He was being supplied with guns for a water borne assault on Cuba in the last week of November, and that the assault was strictly a DRE affair; with the CIA's full knowledge (if not approval).

The CIA's JM/WAVE station in Miami kept a constant eye out on the DRE's activities and knew exactly what they were planning to do in November 1963. The chief of the JM/WAVE station was Theodore Shackley who was appointed to that post after the Bay of Pigs. It was Shackley's job to oversee the agency's clandestine efforts to topple Castro, and that meant working with the various anti-Castro exile groups in Florida. He would later serve in Southeast Asia, and in 1972 was head of the Western Hemisphere Division at CIA headquarters. His name was also mentioned in the scandal involving rouge CIA agent Edwin Wilson.

Shackley, in his cables to headquarters was less than happy with the planned exile invasion. He called the invasion "somewhat romantic," and said that it would be a logistical nightmare. He wrote of the plan:

"Supplying it (the proposed DRE base) "Martha" in a clandestine manner...would not be possible for any extended period of time. We cannot say how long this base could function without coming to the attention of the local authorities but probably no longer than six months. Discovery is a matter of eventual certainty. And when this occurs, (KUBARK, i.e., CIA) involvement is certain too. For it is a matter of general knowledge that AMSPELL, i.e. DRE, is dependent on KUBARK funds."[78]

Part of the DRE's plan was to relocate its base from the JM/WAVE location to camp "Martha," somewhere in the Caribbean.

77 No Title. HSCA. Record No. 180-10144-10129. 8/8/78.

78 Oswald Talked. Pg. 294.

Shackley objected to this in part because the CIA would have to come up with the funds. He was also upset that at the same time that the DRE invasion was about to go ahead, another one of the CIA backed exile groups (AMSPELL) was about to send in a large team into Cuba.

Shackley, growing ever more frustrated with the different anti-Castro groups, including the DRE and others, told them that he would only support legitimate college students who would not act like "generals" just because they were being financed by the CIA. Shackley cabled CIA headquarters asking that the agency not back the DRE's upcoming second invasion of Cuba, but also requested that the CIA reign in the various groups.

The top brass at Langley approved of Shackley's recommendation and on November 19, 1963, three days before the president's murder, that message was transmitted to the DRE leaders. The DRE's long awaited invasion of Cuba scheduled for the last week of November was canceled, and the exile leaders and their troops were left holding the bag. What the reaction among the exiles who were planning to invade Cuba and return to their old homes, must have been a terrible shock. Here they were, setting up an elaborate scheme that involved gun running with the help of the American military, the early tacit approval of the CIA, now abruptly ended. Surely someone had to pay for their second betrayal (the first one being the Bay of Pigs invasion). Would that someone be the President of the United States?

At the exact time that the CIA had canceled its support for the invasion of Cuba, the FBI received the first of many reports from its informers of a plot to assassinate President Kennedy. The first report came from an FBI clerk in New Orleans who said that his office had received a teletype message claiming that a "Cuban faction" was planning to kill the president in his upcoming visit to Dallas. In their book, *Oswald Talked,* the La Fontaine's postulate that after a November 16, 1963 meeting between Lee Harvey Oswald and the FBI, Oswald, acting as an informant for the Bureau, revealed his knowledge of the upcoming assassination plot. They also speculate that the reason Oswald walked into the Dallas FBI headquarters and left a note for Agent James Hosty, (the note was later destroyed) was to warn him of a plot against the president. They also speculate that Oswald may have also told the FBI about the Masen-Nonte gunrunning operation.

It is obvious that in the summer of 1963, Lee Harvey Oswald associated himself with various anti-Castro, anti-Communist groups, especially in New Orleans. It is believed that he acted as an agent provocateur in associating himself with the anti-Cuban Guy Bannister and used his address at 544 Camp Street as a base to *distribute* his literature on the street's of the city. But here is where the puzzle comes in. Why was Oswald giving out Fair Play For Cuba Committee literature while using the address of an anti-Cuban, anti-Communist address as that of Guy Bannister? Was Oswald, as many theorists believe, acting as an informant for some group in infiltrating the right wing, anti-Castroites during that time period?

One of the bit players in the Kennedy assassination, mob associate John Martino, who worked with the anti-Castro Cubans on raids into Cuba, told a reporter shortly before his death that:

"Oswald didn't know who he was working for—he was just ignorant of who was really putting him together. Oswald was to meet his contact at the Texas Theater. There was no way they could get to him. They had Ruby kill him."

Martino said that the anti-Castro Cuban's put Oswald together, probably the members of the DRE, the same DRE that was planning a second invasion of Cuba in the last week of November 1963.

But is it historically true, as the La Fontaine's say, that, the FBI, acting on Oswald's tip of a plot to kill JFK, as well as reporting on the gun running operation, arrested Whitter and Miller, thinking that at least one part of the conspiracy had been foiled?

It obvious that with the DRE's invasion of Cuba spoiled, any chance of regaining their homeland was gone. But one week later, the President of the United States was dead, killed allegedly by a loner with ties to pro-Castro groups. If that wasn't enough to summon an American retalitorary strike against Cuba, nothing would. It all sounds very reasonable. But the new president, Lyndon Johnson, fearing himself that Castro may have had a part in the plot, decided not to attack Cuba, thus, ending the dreams of the DRE and other anti-Castro cliques who would have to wait for another crack at Fidel.

This new information, the Nonte-Masen gunrunning plot, the second invasion of Cuban planned by the DRE, the abrupt cancellation of the strike, and a few days later, the assassination of the president of the United States in the city of Dallas by a pro-Castro "nut," seems to fit the bill for a conspiracy, and a retaliatory strike against Cuba by the United States.

But no one counted on Oswald, the "patsy" turning up alive after killing the president. Then it was up to Jack Ruby, the man who paid the bills at the secret meeting in Dallas, to finally silence Oswald. With Oswald dead there could be no trial, no leads that would implicate anyone else – Case Closed.

One very important sideline of the day President Kennedy was killed took place only a few hours before the bullets flew from Dealey Plaza and had an indirect bearing on the arrest of Miller and Whitter four days previously.

At the meeting were Frank Ellsworth, whose sting operation brought into focus the Masen-Nonte gun running ring, FBI Agent James Hosty, who had previous contacts with both Lee Harvey Oswald and his wife Marina, and Agent Ed Coyle of army counterintelligence (the 112th Military Intelligence Group operating out of San Antonio. The 112th's job was to give additional protection to the president's motorcade in Dallas and to augment the DPD. Two days before the early November 22 meeting, Ellsworth had arrested John Masen for the illegal selling of arms, and he called the meeting with his two federal colleagues to discuss the ongoing theft of military supplies from the army base. Another topic of conversation was the possible involvement of right wing groups in Dallas, headed by ex-Army General Edwin Walker and others. Ellsworth wanted to inform Hosty about the possible right wing ties that he had uncovered between Masen and certain members of the fanatic Minutemen in Dallas. Coyle was the Army's representative who would mostly be interested in the pilfering of army munitions.

The day before, both Hosty and Coyle, and another participant, Dallas police intelligence officer Jack Rivele, met to discuss the Fort Hood case. During their talk, according to Hosty, Rivele made a comment that he did not want to protect the "son of a bitch Kennedy" when the president arrived in Dallas. Hosty said he almost popped him for that remark.

The early morning conference between Ellsworth, Hosty and Coyle broke up about 45 minutes before the president was killed. The La Fontaine's report that immediately after the assassination, Agent Coyle was suddenly sent to another assignment; to Korea. Why Coyle was so abruptly posted to a combat zone is unknown, but conspiracy theorists will have a field day trying to dissect the reasons why.

Right after the assassination, Ellsworth and other ATF agents in the area around the Texas School Book Depository, were some of the first law enforcement officials to enter the building and reached the snipers perch on the sixth floor. It should be mentioned that the type of ammunition found in the snipers gun, rounds for the Italian made Mannlicher-Carcano, were the same type of ammunition that were bought in John Thomas Masen's gun shop in Dallas.

The information revealed in the *Oswald Talked* has been hotly debated in the Kennedy assassination "research community." Many people believe that their work is flawed, especially those critics who have a hard time believing their descriptions of Oswald and his fellow prisoners inside the Dallas jail, and to a larger extent, the story of John Elrod. Be that as it may, what they present, based on the new materials from the National Archives, give the reader a new, and most alarming theory on why President Kennedy was killed.

It is now clear that, based on the primary documents, a second invasion of Cuba by the DRE was planned for the last week in November, 1963, one week prior to President Kennedy's planned Texas trip. The ATF, in the person of Frank Ellsworth, was investigating a gun running operation based out of Fort Hood in the person of George Nonte, who was supplying guns to the DRE for that invasion. Two small time hoods, Miller and Whitter, were arrested for the illegal transportation of some of these guns in a wild car chase through the streets of Dallas. The CIA, ever mindful of what the DRE was up to, gave "meaningful glances" to their plans, pulled the plug on the invasion. Oswald, maybe an FBI informant, told agent Hosty and others in the Bureau of the plot to kill the president, after infiltrating the anti-Castro groups in Dallas, as well as the gunrunning operation. Oswald, after embracing the pro-Castro cause for whatever purpose, was the perfect "patsy" for the Kennedy assassination. Finally, feeling betrayed by the US government's (see CIA) second betrayal, found it necessary to kill the president, blame it on Oswald, the pro-Castro Marxist, and hoped for an all out US invasion of Cuba in retaliation for Castro's involvement in the assassination.

This theory is just as plausible, even more so than some of the others, involving the Soviet's, the Mafia, and other pet scenarios postulated by many writers over the years.

Chapter 8

The Whole Cast of Characters

If the Kennedy assassination were fiction, the bit players in the drama would be fine fodder for a spy novelist. Just think of what a writer like Robert Ludlum would do with such a cast. Among them were gun-toting soldiers of fortune, wading out of the swamps in the Everglades or outside of the New Orleans swamps, carrying out mock war games, while being pursued by the FBI. A number of ex-CIA and FBI agents, carrying out their own secret war against Fidel Castro, aligning themselves with anti-Castro Cubans who shared their views. Add to this mixture were any number of Mafia types who were in cahoots with the CIA, some of whom may also have been double agents for Fidel Castro, the homosexual underworld in New Orleans who mixed with all of the above, and you have a great plot. But unfortunately, this was just the mixture that filled the pot in the months before the president was killed.

This chapter will describe some of the supporting cast of players whose names dominate the behind the scenes story of the Kennedy assassination. It will fill in some of the blanks that the Warren Commission did not know of, or once again, failed to pursue. Once again, the new information will be based in materials found in the National Archives via the "JFK Record Act."

David Ferrie

As one pursues the thousands of newly released documents now available on the Kennedy assassination at the National Archives, the job can become just a bit tedious. Each piece of paper seems like the next, until one significant paper leaps out. One such document found by the writer is potentially explosive in its contents, or maybe just another "plant" to throw the Kennedy researcher off track.

Found among the newly released titles from the HSCA is a flight plan dated April 8, 1963, along with follow up documentation. The flight plan is an ordinary one, with the type of plane being operated, its destination and approximate flight time. But where this differs from one, say taking off from Newark Airport, is the "Captain" of the plane (a Cessna 37) by the name of **David Ferrie.**

David Ferrie was one of the most puzzling persons connected to the Kennedy assassination. He grew up in Cleveland, Ohio, attending Roman Catholic schools as a youth. He started attending classes in a Catholic seminary but eventually dropped out. One of his passions was flying, and he got his pilot's license and moved to New Orleans to purse his dream.

David Ferrie was a man of bizarre appearance, suffering from a rare skin disease called alopecia, a condition that left him hairless over his body. He wore a wig and false eyelashes, which made him look even stranger to passerbys. He was also heavily involved in cancer research, trying to concoct homemade remedies, which would cure the disease. He dabbled in a strange religious order called Orthodox Old Catholic Church of North America, was a closet member of the New Orleans gay community, and headed a squadron of the local Civil Air Patrol in the city. One of Ferrie's students turned out to be a young, Lee Oswald.

David Ferrie was a rabid anti-Communist, anti-Kennedy, anti-Fidel, private investigator and suspect contract agent for the CIA. It is believed that he flew a number of covert missions into

Cuba in the early 1960's, supplying guns and ammunition to the anti-Castro underground.

When he arrived in New Orleans, he got a job as a pilot with Eastern Airlines and served with distinction before the company learned of his blatant homosexual activities. Ferrie was subsequently fired from his job. Somehow he managed to connect himself with mob boss Carlos Marcello and did legal and illegal work for him. Another man whom Ferrie was well connected was an ex-FBI officer by the name of Guy Banister, whose connections to US intelligence and the anti-Castro Cuban community in New Orleans was legendary. Ferrie worked out of Banisters office at 544 Camp St. which was the unofficial home of various right-wing, anti-Castro, and US intelligence agents (as well as Lee Harvey Oswald).

On the day of Kennedy's murder, David Ferrie was accused of making a long distance car trip with a number of friends to Houston. Ferrie told New Orleans DA Jim Garrison that he went to Houston to go ice skating (I guess they didn't have a proper rink in New Orleans). It has been alleged that the reason Ferrie went to Houston was to act as the getaway pilot for the conspirators, including Oswald, who was to have been taken to Mexico and then eliminated. Another interesting fact concerning David Ferrie's activities, is that prior to the JFK murder, he deposited $7,000 into his bank account. Up to that point, Ferrie was living hand to mouth and it is still not clear where the money came from.

Upon his return to New Orleans, he was picked up in the investigation of the assassination of the president by DA Jim Garrison. Garrison was able to link Ferrie to Banister, Clay Shaw, a prominent businessman in the city (Shaw was later tried and was found innocent as a conspirator in the JFK assassination), and other anti-Castro Cubans in the city. Garrison turned Ferrie over to the FBI who found no hard evidence linking him to the Kennedy assassination. He was subsequently released.

But, let's get back to the Ferrie flight plan. What is most

intriguing on the flight plan are the names of the three passengers listed on the flight's manifest; Diaz, Lambert and Hidell. But there's more. According to the follow up material that goes along with the flight plan is an affidavit by a former prisoner in the US Penitentiary in Atlanta, Georgia (dated December 5, 1967) by the name of Edward Julius Grinus, that the "Lambert" listed on the plane's manifest is an alias used by **Clay Shaw.**

This in itself would be of considerable interest to the Kennedy assassination scholars, and particularly those interested in the Jim Garrison aspect of the case. According to Shaw at the time of his arrest, he used one alias, that of "Clay Bertrand." Now we have another name, "Lambert." But even more importantly is the name "Hidell" listed with "Lambert" and Diaz. If this document is authentic it definitely links both Lee Harvey Oswald and Clay Shaw together for the first time.

When Lee Oswald was arrested for allegedly killing JFK, he had on his person an identification card with the name A.J. Hidell. When the Dallas police asked him who he was (Oswald or Hidell), he said to them that they were the detectives and should figure it out themselves. After word had been received that a suspect had been arrested in connection with the president's death, word went out to the various intelligence agencies of the United States. The 112th Military Investigative unit searched its files and came up with a startling piece of news. They had a file on Oswald, along with the fact that he used an alias, A.J. Hidell. His name was listed because he was a "possible counter-intelligence threat." Oswald's file was listed under both his real name and his alias.

Oswald first used the alias in January 1963, when he sent away for a .38 Smith & Wesson revolver from a company called Seaport Traders, Inc. He also used that name when ordering through the mail, the infamous Italian made Mannlicher-Carcano rifle which he purchased from Kline's Sporting Goods in Chicago. Dick Russell, the author of *The Man Who Knew Too Much,* puts a more sinister spin on Oswald's choice of this name. The main character in Russell's book is Richard Case Nagell, a military intelligence officer and contract agent for the CIA. Russell writes that the name Hidell can be traced back to an intelligence mission in the Far East–in South Korea an operation in which Nagell had a role in.

The Grinus Allegation

In conjunction with the above-mentioned document is a three page memorandum dated December 7, 1967 from James Alcock, an Assistant District Attorney to his boss, the late New Orleans DA, Jim Garrison. In it, Alcock recounts his meeting with Grinus in the U.S. Penitentiary in Atlanta.

Edward Julius Grinus served a prison term for a violation of the Dyer Act (the interstate transportation of a stolen vehicle). He was released from jail at Leavenworth, Kansas on February 14, 1963 and moved to Pasadena, Texas near Houston. While living there, he used the alias, Edward Stark. In either February or March 1963, he made a short trip to New Orleans looking for old friends. When he failed to locate them he returned to Texas. In March 1963 he moved to Waco, Texas where he moved in with a woman.

Grinus and his companion then went to Dallas where he again got in trouble with the law and attended many of the strip clubs there, including the *Theatre Lounge* and the *Diamond Horseshoe*. It is believed that Jack Ruby may have been a partner in one of these clubs. Grinus made friends with many of the strippers and "Grinus met a friend of Jack Ruby's who was interested in buying guns. This man, who Grinus would not identify, was associated with a rabid right-wing group who had access to large amounts of money. Grinus also meet a man from New Orleans through this group who was interested in purchasing guns. As a result of a conversation with the man from New Orleans, Grinus moved to Leesville, Louisiana. Grinus would not identify this man from New Orleans." While in Leesville, he used the name "Ritter."

At this time (April, 1963), Grinus moved into a place called Marie's Hideaway with another woman companion. He began to buy and sell guns and made several trips to New Orleans. In May or June, on a trip to New Orleans, Grinus said he met Clay Shaw. "Grinus met Shaw in the Alpine Restaurant and bar. He was introduced to Shaw by a man who owns an apartment house on Exchange Alley or Place." Grinus then says that Shaw invited him to his home, located in Hammond, La. "Grinus felt that everyone in the group knew of his gun running activities."

A few days later Grinus again met with Shaw and the topic of conversation turned to guns. "Shaw was in the office and they started talking about guns. Shaw allegedly knew some people who wanted to buy some guns. Shaw made a telephone call, and some time thereafter two men came to the office. One of them was Lee Harvey Oswald. Oswald was introduced by Shaw to Grinus as Lee. Grinus cannot remember the name of the man who came in with Oswald."

Alcock ends his report with the following: "The last time Grinus saw Oswald was when he drove him to Catulla, Texas. This trip took place sometime in September 1963. While in Catulla, Grinus introduced Oswald to a friend of his who was an ex-Mexican army man. Oswald and Grinus' friend went into Mexico through Laredo, Texas. Their trip had something to do with getting Oswald a passport.

"Grinus attended several parties where Shaw was present. At least one of these took place in Hammond, La. Grinus thought it was Shaw's house, but was not sure of this. Oswald was at his particular party which took place in a large colonial, brick home which had a big yard all around it."[79]

Grinus' account of Oswald's going to Mexico via Laredo doesn't jibe with the known facts. According to the Warren Commission version, Oswald left New Orleans by bus on September

---

79 This is a 15-page document released as part of the HSCA's files Researchers interested in obtaining this release should refer to No. 006795 "Kennedy" or "HSCA RG 233" at the National Archives.

25, 1963 for Mexico City. Among the passengers who identified Oswald (or his double) on the bus were two Australian girls who struck up a conversation with Oswald, a British couple from Liverpool named Bryan and Meryl McFarland. Another person who met Oswald on the bus was a missionary with less than a credible past named Albert Bowen-Osborne.

What is one to make of this significant document? If it is true, this places both Clay Shaw and David Ferrie in direct contact with Lee Oswald prior to the president's murder. In light of this, all of Shaw's and Ferrie's disclaimers of never having known Oswald are false. (Let us not forget to mention the *PBS FRONTLINE* show of a number of years ago that showed a picture of a young Lee Harvey Oswald and David Ferrie together).

As far as the Hidell name on the flight plan, it too answers many questions. Either the real Lee Harvey Oswald was on the plane from Hammond to Garland, Texas or someone using his alias, and those knowing that Oswald used that particular name, was substituted for him. Researchers looking into the life of Clay Shaw now have another alias he used–Lambert–to delve into. What about of David Ferrie? If the flight plan is indeed genuine, it places this strange looking man in direct contact with Lee Oswald, and all that might entail, months before the assassination.

Gerry Patrick Hemming

One of the most interesting characters of the Kennedy assassination drama is a huge, bearded, ex-soldier of fortune, named Gerry Patrick Hemming. For those persons who have followed the Kennedy assassination case, the name of Gerry Patrick Hemming is well known. Hemming has given countless interviews to the mass media, has been a witness at the Senate panel investigating the Kennedy assassination and, like others who had some behind the scenes information regarding the events leading up to the president's death, was never questioned by the Warren

Commission. And if the Warren panel had questioned Hemming, what a story they would have heard.

This writer first met Gerry Hemming by chance in the summer of 1991 while at the Assassinations Archives and Research Center in Washington, D.C. Gerry and ex-pilot Howard Davis, were en-route back to Florida and decided to drop in to see Jim Lazar, the director of the AARC. I quickly introduced myself and for the next few hours, Gerry regaled me with tales of his adventurous life, including his take on the Kennedy assassination of which he has had personal experience.

Over the years, many different publications have interviewed Gerry Hemming, and his views on the Kennedy case are well known. Now, with the addition of hundreds of CIA files on Hemming just released by the National Archives, a fuller picture of this ex-Marine, can be glimpsed.

In the late 1950's, Gerry Hemming was part of an anti-Castro group in Florida called the Intercontinental Penetration Force, a.k.a., Interpen. Their unofficial headquarters was a rooming house operated by a spry, elderly lady named Neli Hamilton. It was from here that they planned their secret war against Castro.

As a young man, Gerry joined the Marines in 1954, after enlisting while still under age. He took basic training at Jacksonville, Florida and later was selected to work as an air traffic controller. He served in duty stations in Kansas, El Toro, California and Hawaii. While never actually serving with ONI (Office of Naval Intelligence), Hemming was approached by them shortly before his discharge. "They were interested in what I was doing with Castro's Cuba, supplying them with weapons. They wanted to get some information about security violations at Guantanamo where some time previously some naval and marine personnel were captured by Raoul Castro." Hemming said that at this time some of the Americans at the base were supplying guns and ammunition to the rebels.

While in the Marines, Hemming wanted to join the NROTC

program because he wanted to engage in the Special Forces training program but he was not successful. He left the Marines in 1958 and enrolled in the officer candidate preparatory school for the Naval Academy where he stayed for only a short period of time. "I decided that the Cuban thing was more in line with my warfare goals."

Hemming returned to California in October 1958 and worked at odd jobs like heavy labor. He left for Cuba via Miami around the latter part of February 1958 and immediately took up the Castro cause. CIA documents on Hemming give the following reasons for his joining the rebel army:

> "A) *A strong desire to experience the excitement and glamour of warfare, and particularly guerilla warfare, and the opportunity to gain experience in the field.*
>
> "B) *The opportunity to combine the above mentioned desire with identification with a "just" cause.*
>
> "C) *A desire to see for himself what was going on in Cuba, and possibly to carve a niche for himself from which he might be able to influence later developments."*

Once in Cuba, Hemming, according to the CIA papers, met with Captain Johnny Mitchell, a US national who was serving in the Headquarters, General Staff, Camp Columbia. It seems that Mitchell got along so well with Hemming that Mitchell gave him a pass for the base. There, Hemming talked to a number of Cuban military officers and told them that he had previously been in contact with the Cuban Counsel's office in Los Angeles before coming to Cuba. It was here, at the new Cuban mission in Monterey Park, that Hemming was to have his first encounter with Lee Harvey Oswald (more about that later).

A Cuban army officer named Camilo Cienfuegos took a liking to Hemming and appointed him to a new paratroop group that he was forming. Hemming went into the unit as a Sergeant, having been turned down as an officer by another Cuban officer named Enrico Borbonet. Hemming stayed with this unit until December 1959, helping to train paratroopers at the San Antonio de los Banos Air Force base and later near San Jose de los Lajoas.

In December 1959, Hemming transferred to the Cuban Air Force and was stationed at the San Julian Air Force Base where he flew patrols and helped train the militia. He was discharged from the Cuban Air Force in mid June 1960, flew to Mexico City and stayed there until the end of August. One month later he returned to the US via San Antonio, Texas.

Hemming had a long history of gun running (like that of Jack Ruby) and it was in this business and its related parts, that he met Lee Harvey Oswald. One day, as Hemming was working at the Cuban Consulate in Los Angeles, he was told by a Cuban "that there was an American looking for me. I went out and there was Oswald standing there." Oswald said he wanted to join the group. Hemming "was abrupt with him and ran him off."[80]

"The next morning over at the consulate," continued Hemming, "Oswald was seated inside the ante-room." Hemming asked the Cuban what Oswald was doing there. They (the Cuban's) thought Oswald was a friend of Hemming's because Oswald had asked to speak to "the American." According to Hemming, Oswald was still on active duty with the Marines and was livid that the Cuban's would invite an American military man into the building. Hemming feared an "international incident" should Oswald be discovered. At that point, Hemming took Oswald aside. "What is it you want?" he asked, thinking that the young Marine was some sort of a plant. Oswald replied, "I want to go to Cuba and join the revolution…"

According to Hemming, Oswald who had never met him before, began using military code words describing where he

---

80 The quotes from this section come from an interview with Hemming in the Winter 1992, issue of Back Channels.

was stationed (LTA Base), what kind of work he did, and knew of Hemming's military background. "Marines don't talk to civilians and use that slang. They would only say it to someone who they knew was a Marine. He's a snitch, or somebody's sending me somebody and now he's going to tell me about me," said an incredulous Hemming.

As they departed, Oswald said to Hemming, "I'll find you there (in Cuba). I know how to find people."

While he was in Cuba working for the revolution, a very curious thing happened to Hemming. In an unusual move, Hemming was allowed entrance to the presidential palace, a place where most Americans were not allowed to go. While at the palace, Hemming was taken aside by one of the men he knew at the Cuban mission in Monterey Park. The man said, "Do you remember your gringo buddy, the rabbit? He was here at the palace." That man was Lee Harvey Oswald. (There have been no other confirmations over the years to verify this story of Oswald being in Cuba).

A day or so later, Gerry was at his base at San Antonio de los Banos on the flight line when he was told that there were two Americans anxious to see him. A man called Johnny Monaco out of Key West said his friend he knew from the Marines and California wanted to speak to him. While not actually seeing Monaco's "friend," Hemming was sure it was Oswald.

By 1961, Hemming's activities via his INTERPEN activities were being closely watched by both the FBI and the CIA. This early, 1961 CIA memo on Hemming shows Agency interest:

"Hemming was approved for an ad hoc contact on 6 March 1961. He was the source of 15 contact reports on Cuba. His group, INTERPEN, had no Agency connection. Although Hemming is not accepted by leading Cuban organizations, he is well known to them."

"Subject's (Hemming) file reflects an ad hoc contact clearance was granted on 6 March 1961 for debriefing on military, economic and political developments in various Latin American countries. At the time, Hemming was engaged in revolutionary activities in Nicaragua. On 2 June 1961, the Contact Office (CIA) was advised that National Agency Name Checks on Hemming disclosed no pertinent derogatory information."

While Hemming had no actual connection to the CIA, that of being an active or contract agent, he, often times led people to believe that he was indeed working for the Company.

"In February 1962, Hemming was the subject of a (blank) investigation. The Los Angeles Sheriff's office had recovered a US pistol from a car in the area on 30 January 1962. Hemming appeared at the Sheriff's office to claim the pistol stating that he was a CIA agent on a training mission in connection with a Cuban assignment. Hemming was interviewed by the LA Contact Office concerning the incident, and according to the interviewer, Subject never claimed to have worked for the CIA. He had furnished certain information concerning activities in Cuba in the form of reports to the LA Contact Office since approximately October 1960."[81]

In early 1962, Hemming went to New Orleans to help the anti-Castro cause there. CIA documents state:

"It (an article in the *New Orleans States/Item*) concerned subject (Hemming) who showed up in New Orleans in February 1962 apparently at the invitation of local Cuban Revolutionary Council leaders and other Cubans who wanted to take direct action against Castro. With the help of anonymous US patrons, the Cubans began supplying PATRICK with machine guns, explosives and other military supplies. PATRICK made regular trips here (New Orleans), slipping in and out of the port secretly in a modern, well equipped P.T. boat."

"Last spring, 1962, another anonymous US patron offered the Cubans a large tract of land-complete with air strip on the north shore of Lake Pontcharatrain. PATRICK agreed to set up a training base, handling classes of 50 or so Cuban recruits at a

81 Subject, Gerald Patrick Hemming, a.k.a., Jerry Patrick. CIA document. 28 December 1967.

time. After completion of the training, the guerrillas would be like their Everglades counterparts, transported to Cuba secretly to work with the anti-Castro underground."[82]

In December 1962, Hemming and his group of mercenaries were arrested by US Customs officers at Sombrero Cay after an abortive mission into Cuba to verify the withdrawal of the nuclear weapons after the missile crisis. After being released by their lawyer, the party was taken to a Miami hotel only to be met by a throng of reporters. Standing alone, among the newsman, was Oswald. (Again, there is no other confirmation to this story).

Hemming recalled another, bizarre incident that took place one week before the president was killed. He was approached by two men in civilian clothes who wanted to know if Hemming and some of his friends would serve as extra guards when JFK came to Miami on November 18, 1963. The man, whom Hemming believed to be a military intelligence officer, told them to come unarmed. He told Hemming that a possible Cuban hit team might be in the area and since Hemming knew many of the Cubans, he might be of some assistance.

Hemming, smelling a set up, reluctantly agreed to go along. He said that despite the warning not to come unarmed, one of his men came with a .45 pistol. At the Miami airport, Hemming and his men stood within 20 feet of the president. To this day he still can't fully understand why they were there.

In 1967, New Orleans DA Jim Garrison began his secret investigation into the death of President Kennedy, focusing on Lee Harvey Oswald's actions in the summer of 1963. One of the many people who were interviewed by Garrison was Gerry Hemming.

On May 2, 1968, Stephen Jaffe, an investigator in Garrison's office, held a meeting following a talk by a right wing individual who was connected to the mob, and was mentioned as someone who might have known something about the assassination of the

82 Ibid.

president; Loran Hall. Seated at the table with Jaffe were three men, Art Kevin, Gerry Hemming and Roy Hargraves, who was a member of Hemming's anti-Castro group. Neither Hemming nor Hargraves knew that Jaffe worked for Garrison. Hemming stated that he had given Hall all his contacts when it came to soliciting funds for their cause.

"Hemming, according to Jaffe's memorandum following the meeting, said that he had been present at numerous meetings in which the assassination of the president was discussed. He said that Hall would not have been allowed to take part in the assassination of the president because he was "unreliable, unstable, over talked person." Patrick stated that if discussion of possible assassination was made during any kind of a meeting it was dismissed as "wishful thinking" unless, if the people were serious, there was money placed on the table. That's when PATRICK would take the "contract" seriously, and he added that he'd attended a few meetings where this occurred."

"Patrick further stated that in St. Louis, Chicago, Miami, Dallas, and elsewhere there were a lot of powerful elements who desired to get rid of President Kennedy. Patrick said that he'd given most of his information to Garrison and that he thought that Mr. Garrison was on the "wrong track." He later repeated this thought in stronger language. He stated that he knew Oswald did not do it alone and he knew that the assassination of President Kennedy had been a highly planned professional execution performed by experts."[83]

Hemming told Jaffe of a man named Edward Anderson Collins who had been involved in his soldier of fortune company. Collins told Hemming that he was a member of a group, which had organized a hit on the president. Collins was supposed to be in Dallas in September, 1963 and that his group was ready to take on the hit. In December of 1963, Collins died by drowning in 8 inches of water in a boating accident in Key Biscayne.

83 No title. HSCA Record No. 180-10085-10340. 5/4/68.

Later that year, Hemming was notified that Jaffe was working for Garrison but he didn't seem to mind.

Soon, Hemming began publicly to be associated with Garrison's investigation, and dropped in to the DA's office on a regular basis. He told Garrison that as soon as he heard of the assassination, he called Lester Logue in Dallas to find out if Hall was there. "Patrick said he did this because he believed at that time that Hall very well could have assassinated the President. Patrick said that he still does not reject the possibility that Hall was involved." According to Hemming, Lester Logue was the person who bailed out Hall and Seymour in October 1963 after they were arrested for narcotics possession. He also said that the people who showed up at Sylvia Odio's home were Hall, Howard and Seymour. He also said that a fourth man called Enrique Molina Rivera, who was a Castro agent, also was with them.

Hemming told Garrison that there were numerous teams of adventurers who were trying to get Kennedy and that he had no solid proof of any involvement by Hall, Howard and Seymour.

"...Patrick said that many of these groups had been approached by wealthy backers or sponsors who wanted to see Kennedy dead and had even been given money to do the job. Then, on November 22, Kennedy is killed – maybe Oswald got there ahead of them... and there the story temporarily rests. However, the mounting controversy of the last 12 months has resulted in a curious new development, according to Patrick. Some of the members of the original teams, taking advantage of public uncertainty as to who was responsible for Kennedy's death, have been returning to their backers and saying, in effect, "we did it," and adding that for a large financial consideration they wouldn't say anything about the original involvement of the backers. The backers have retaliated to this blackmail by hiring the mafia to rid themselves of the blackmailers. (This may be the true story behind the Del Valle murder, reported earlier this year in the *National Enquirer*.) [84]

84 No title. HSCA. Record No. 180-10085-10377. 9/18/67.

After the acquittal of Clay Shaw in the assassination of President Kennedy the case went into limbo, not only for Hemming but also for the many interested parties around the country. It wasn't until the late 1970's that the Kennedy assassination case was re-opened at the Congressional level. Hemming's name had been known among the staffers of the newly created House Select Committee on Assassinations (HSCA) and in 1977, Hemming was called to testify before the inquiry. For a total of 13 1/2 hours, the ex-soldier of fortune told the panel members his account of the Oswald meeting in LA and Cuba. Hemming told the author that following his testimony the members said to him, "this opens new doors," concerning Oswald's activities But alas, nothing was done to look into Hemming's information. "The problem with you people is that you never ask the right questions," said Hemming to the HSCA members. "You never mention the right names."

Newly released CIA files on Hemming summarize the Agency's evaluation of him:

"While it is difficult to assess Hemming's true motive for his past activities and possibly still more difficult to ascertain where his true loyalties lie, it does appear that he might be useful either now or in the near future..."

"Hemming maintains that he is "first and foremost" an American and that his true loyalty remains to this country. This may well be true, but it should be noted that his reasoning appears to be based primarily on his respect for the superior ability exhibited by the US military personnel he has served with in the past. He appears to be little influenced by deep beliefs in democratic principles."[85] Note-Gerry Hemming is now deceased.

---

85 Jerry Hemming, Jr. Ex-US Marine who served in Cuban Army and Air Force, February, 1959-June 1960. 1 Nov. 1960.

E. Howard Hunt

Of all the possible players in any Kennedy assassination conspiracy, the name of E. Howard Hunt always keeps coming up. Hunt has had a successful career both as a spy novelist and of a member of the covert intelligence branch of the CIA for over 20 years. Since the seasoned Kennedy assassination researcher knows most of the details about Hunt's career, it is not necessary to go into the details once again. But a document obtained by the author seems to indicate that Howard Hunt wrote a detailed, and secret account of the Kennedy assassination for the Nixon White House, one, that has never seen the light of day. But before we delve into that aspect of the case, a little background is in order.

On June 23, 1972, shortly after the buglers were arrested at the Watergate complex, a meeting was held at the White House between President Nixon and his chief of staff HR. "Bob" Haldeman. This seemingly innocent meeting would later prove to be one of the bombshells that would drive Nixon from office. And the only way that anyone would have known about this conference was that President Nixon secretly taped all conversations that went on in the Oval Office.

The meeting concerned the aftermath of the Watergate break-in, would focus on the activities of the CIA, the men involved in the burglary, the 1961 Bay of Pigs invasion, and its possible connection to the Watergate affair.

Nixon began by saying that, "Well, we protected Helms (CIA Director) from one hell of a lot of things." Then the president mused about how to control the CIA. He said, "Hunt... will uncover a lot of things. You open that scab there's a hell of a lot of things...tell them we just feel that it would be very detrimental to have this thing go any further. This involves these Cubans, Hunt, and a lot of hanky-panky that we have nothing to do with ourselves."

Nixon continued his statement concerning Hunt:

"…just say (unintelligible) very bad to have this fellow Hunt, he knows too damned much, if he was involved – you happen to know that? If it gets out that this is all involved, the Cuba thing, it would be a fiasco. It would make the CIA look bad, it's going to make Hunt look bad, and it is likely to blow the whole Bay of Pigs thing which we think would be very unfortunate both for the CIA and for the country..."

It was obvious that Nixon was paranoid about getting the CIA off the case and later that day Haldeman and John Ehrlicman met with both Helms and Walters – the CIA deputy director. Helms told Nixon's men that the CIA was not connected to the break-in in any way and that none of the suspects had worked for the CIA in the last two years. That statement was false. Martinez, one of those arrested, was a current CIA contract officer.

Eventually, Richard Helms agreed to Nixon's demand that the CIA intervene with the FBI's probe but not after Helm's violent reaction by saying to Haldeman, "The Bay of Pigs had nothing to do with this. I have no concern about the Bay of Pigs."

But what was so dreadful that Nixon would reopen the "whole Bay of Pigs thing?"

The possibilities are endless. The one that immediately comes to mind is the CIA-Mafia plots to kill Fidel Castro. As previously mentioned, Nixon was the point man for the covert deals to assassinate Fidel Castro and overthrow his government. Surely Nixon realized the possible consequences of this action if Castro found out (which, eventually he did). It was also at the early stages of the Bay of Pigs planning that the original Mafia-CIA contacts began. The larger question to be answered is this; did President Kennedy order the CIA to contract the mob to kill Castro? If so, did Nixon know about it after the fact? And why was the Nixon White House so worried about what Howard Hunt knew or would tell if cornered? Did Hunt know more about the Bay of Pigs-Castro assassination plot than he says he did?

In his book, *The Ends of Power*, H.R. Haldeman, the late chief of staff to Nixon, writes about his interest in the Kennedy murder. He says that he had always been intrigued into the various theories concerning JFK's death and that he had asked Nixon if it would be possible to get all the facts out. Nixon, not surprisingly, said no.

Haldeman also writes that what President Nixon was really referring to when he talked about the "whole Bay of Pigs thing" was in reality, an open reference to the Kennedy assassination. Haldeman says that President Kennedy's murder could have been the result of the CIA's failed attempts on Castro's life and a possible Castro retaliation against the president.

The Cuban connection to the Watergate affair is given new insight in a newly released document originating from the records of the Rockefeller Commission. The memo is from David Belin to William Schwarzer entitled, "Cuba and the Politicization of Police Power." In part it reads:

"A Cuban explained how the Cubans got into Watergate. They were used to us. When Bay of Pigs operatives like Hunt moved over to Watergate they sent for their old Cubanos. They work a little like the "Mafia" he continued. "When they want to issue an anti-Communist contract or what looks like an anti-Communist contract, they contact us. We're reliable, intelligent, and professional. And we're learning to keep our mouths shut. We're learning to live with this. And we fear the Company. We know the Company. The Company can drop a word and change your life. You don't get a job or a loan for your business, or you're in trouble with police or immigration. To such people the bizarre requirements of Watergate seemed not unnatural but SOP."[86]

When the Watergate affair first broke, and after Hunt was arrested along with the other burglars, columnist Dick Russell, then working for *the Village Voice,* interviewed White House advisor, Chuck Colson concerning the Nixon/Haldeman June 23 tape. Russell asked Colson if he thought that Hunt knew anything

86 Re: Cuba and the Politicization of Police Power. Rockefeller Commission. 2/12/75. Record No. 157-10011-10071.

about the Kennedy assassination. Colson responded, "I doubt it. I really do. I don't think Hunt had anything to do with that."

"E. Howard Hunt may not have had anything to do with that," as Colson said, but information which has only recently become available indicates that Hunt was, at the very least, quite interested in – and concerned about – the assassination of President Kennedy. This new information further indicates that a secret report about certain aspects of the Kennedy assassination (aspects particularly related to Cuba and Fidel Castro) was prepared by Hunt and his future Watergate burglar associates – and was in fact circulated to Charles Colson and the Nixon circle as well as officials within the CIA. As will be seen from this information, and other long obscure Watergate data, a picture seems to be emerging which places the secret Hunt report on the Kennedy assassination at the heart of the feverish cover-up activities of the Nixon circle in the immediate days following the Watergate break-in of June 17."[87]

If Hunt has no information to give on the Kennedy assassination, his silence on the topic is suspect. Hunt served as Acting Chief of Station for the CIA in Mexico City in August and September 1963, the exact time that Lee Harvey Oswald is supposed to have been in Mexico City trying to get a passport back to Russia. The CIA took a photograph of a man it said was Oswald coming out of one of the Communist embassies but this mysterious man certainly was not Oswald. It is inconceivable that Hunt, if he was working in the Mexico City CIA station, did not know about the mysterious comings and goings at the Cuban Consulate and the Soviet Embassy concerning either Oswald or an impostor.

87 Title: E. Howard Hunt's Missing Report on the Kennedy Assassination/ Sturgis. From Mike Ewing. HSCA. Agency File No. #015106. The material in this section is based on the above-mentioned document and is available at the National Archives.

Hunt alludes to certain CIA activities relating to Dallas and Mexico City that went on during that time. In his 1974 autobiography *Undercover,* Hunt's says "that the CIA did in fact use Dallas as a "backstop" location for changing the identities of CIA agents operating in Mexico City. Hunt told of a CIA break-in at a Communist Embassy which he had coordinated during one of his tours of duty in Mexico City. Before dawn the entry team had flown from Mexico to Dallas, where they changed identities and flew to Washington."[88]

Hunt has denied that he was in Mexico City at the time that Oswald was there. Hunt's record at the CIA has been a closely kept secret and prompted this observation. A Justice Department official who once was denied access to a partial set of requested Hunt CIA records, has remarked, "They treat those Hunt files like they were the Hope Diamond. It's just incredible."

As the Watergate affair began to break in earnest, Charles Colson, the White House counsel, and the man who had brought Hunt into the White House, confirmed to John Dean of Hunt's links to the Nixon White House. It seems that Hunt had kept a secret safe in his office at the Old Executive Office Building-Room 338. Hunt's safe was drilled open on June 19th by the Secret Service and its contents removed. What was found in the safe were a clip of live ammunition, a gun, holster, secret files on the Plumbers operation on Daniel Ellsberg, files concerning Ted Kennedy's Chappaquiddick incident, and forged State Department cables concerning the death of President Diem in 1963. But what was missing, and now reported in the document called "E. Howard Hunt's Missing Report on the Kennedy Assassination/Sturgis," is information on another Plumbers probe into the Kennedy assassination – information that was not found in Hunt's safe.

The story begins in an April 1974 NBC interview with Watergate burglar Bernard Barker by newsmen Robert Rogers and Edwin Newman. "Barker told of a secret assignment that he and

88 Ibid. Pg. 6.

fellow Watergate burglar Frank Sturgis had conducted for their important White House friend and patron, Mr. Hunt. Unfortunately, Barker garbled a key point in the interview, mistakenly referring to "the death of Bobby Kennedy" rather than the death of John Kennedy, which was the actual subject of this Baker/Sturgis assignment for Hunt."[89]

This is a partial account of the interview:

"Rogers (NBC): And in Miami we learned that Hunt and Barker conducted at least one interview – the results of which supposedly went to the CIA."

"Barker: Mr. Sturgis said to me that he had some information about some lady that had been at the home of the Castro family at the time of the death of Bobby Kennedy and that she was telling some very strange stories or very interesting stories, as he put it. I spoke to the lady in Spanish and brought her – took her – to Mr. Hunt. Mr. Hunt personally examined her, in the sense that he questioned her, and he took it down on tapes. Mr. Hunt told me that he would be turning this information over to the old agency."

This information was never given to the Ervin Committee then looking into the Watergate affair and stayed buried until found in the newly releases coming out via the "JFK Record Act."

The report speculates that Hunt was trying to tie the Cubans to the Kennedy assassination or "perhaps a more likely explanation behind Hunt's decision to probe the Cuban woman's information about Castro and the Kennedy assassination, is that he was ordered to do so by superiors."

The next part of the story is an interview that Hunt gave in November 1975 with two reporters from the *Providence Journal,* Jack White and Randall Richard. The two reporters questioned Hunt on his possible involvement in the Kennedy assassination,

89 Ibid. Pg. 11.

and while Hunt hotly denied that he had anything to do with the Dallas tragedy, he added more information on the then secret probe of the assassination. Hunt said that one of the burglars of the Watergate complex, Eugenio Martinez, was also involved in the secret Kennedy murder probe in addition to Frank Sturgis and Bernard Barker. While this was going on, Martinez was still working for the CIA on a retainer basis. Hunt told the newsmen that the interview of the Cuban woman took place in the Ambassador Hotel in Miami, sometime between July 1971 and June 1972, and that Martinez helped translate the woman's story.

Hunt said that this lady was in the Castro household when the news of JFK's death reached him. Castro was shocked and saddened of Kennedy's loss.

Further on in the interview, Hunt told the reporters that he sent this secret report to the CIA, and also a copy to Charles Colson. While Hunt did not say who he sent the report to at the Agency, it most likely, according to the document, was CIA Director Richard Helms, who was a good friend of Hunt's.

Hunt said that he kept one copy of the JFK probe for himself and put it in his safe at the White House.

But twenty-five years after the Watergate affair, none of the three most important people in the story, other than Hunt, Colson, Dean and Ehrlichman, have refused to speak up on what happened to Hunt's secret Plumber's investigation of JFK's death.

Before leaving the White House after being fired, Hunt told Colson that his safe contained sensitive material. "Before I left the White House for the last time, I stopped by Mr. Colson's office, not to see him but to inform Mrs. Hall, whom I knew held the combination to my safe, that it contained sensitive material. I simply said to her, "I just want you to know that the safe is loaded." It seems obvious that Colson knew of the "sensitive" materials in Hunt's safe. So why isn't he telling?

The Ewing story goes on to say, "As scrambled as the testimony is at this point, a couple of things are clear. The Hunt report relating to the Kennedy assassination is missing. No copy of it has ever surfaced, nor have the tapes that Hunt, Barker, Martinez, and Sturgis made during the probe ever been found."

"The possibility that this secret Hunt report was either hidden or destroyed following the opening of his safe on June 19 is obviously strong. Not only did Gray burn "politically sensitive" Hunt documents that he received from Ehrlichman and Dean, Ehrlichman and Dean themselves had discussed much the same "game plan" shortly after Hunt's safe was drilled open..."

John Dean told the Ervin Committee of an Ehrlichman plan for handling the secret papers in Hunt's safe:

"He told me to shred the documents and "deep six" the briefcase. I asked him what he meant by "deep six." He leaned back in his chair and said: "You drive across the river on your way home at night don't you?" I said yes. He said, "Well, when you cross over the bridge on your way home, just toss the briefcase into the river."[90]

For the record, Ehrlichman denied Dean's story.

"The last thing in the world," says the Senate narrative, "the Nixon men needed at that point was a secret report about the Kennedy assassination coming out of Hunt's safe-written and produced by Hunt and his burglar friends-Barker, Martinez, and Sturgis."

But this is exactly what happened, if we are to believe the Senate report and the evidence they gathered.

But now the story gets even more involved. It concerns one of the Watergate burglars, Frank Sturgis, and any possible links he may have had to Lee Harvey Oswald.

By June 19, the FBI had sent over a large amount of material they had gathered on the initial Watergate investigation and background material on those men arrested. A large amount of information concerned Frank Sturgis. The FBI report said that Sturgis was a gunrunner to Cuba, a soldier of fortune, and was tied to organized crime. Part of this report was an article on Sturgis

90 Ibid.

that appeared in the Pompano Beach, Florida, *Sun Sentinel,* dated November 25-26, 1963. Part of the article read:

"Frank Fiorini (Sturgis), Head of an anti-Communist Brigade, said that Lee Oswald had telephone conversations with the Cuban Government G-2 during November, 1962."

The article was written by a friend of Sturgis,' Jim Buchanan, who, at one time, was a member of Sturgis' Anti-Communist Brigade. The FBI report said that upon reading the article, Sturgis said that Buchanan had "misquoted him."

"With his background, perhaps it was inevitable that Frank Sturgis would be the one who triggered the secret Hunt probe into the Kennedy assassination, and the "very strange stories" he had heard about Castro's reaction to it."

In the Bureau's files was another article written by Buchanan concerning Sturgis and Oswald.

"Oswald also tried to infiltrate several other major organizations in Miami, including the Anti-Communist International Brigade, which is headed by Major. Frank Fiorini. Fiorini said his outfit turned down Oswald's application because they could not find out anything about his background."

This article concerning Sturgis' possible meeting with Oswald in Miami corresponds to pervious statements by Gerry Hemming in which he alleges that he had seen Oswald in the Miami area.

On August 22, 1973, during a news conference, President Nixon himself made a curious statement on the Kennedy assassination that left the reporters in the room wondering what he was talking about. While commenting on a reporters question concerning the disclosure that Nixon had approved a domestic spying operation called the Houston Plan, President Nixon said the following:

"...I understand the heights of the wiretaps was when Robert Kennedy was Attorney General in 1963. I don't criticize him, however. But if he had 10 more and as a result of wiretaps had been able to discover the Oswald plan it would have been worth it."

Nixon continued to speculate on the Oswald matter:

"...I said if 10 more wiretaps could have found the conspiracy, if it was a conspiracy, or the individual, then it would have been worth it. As far as I'm concerned, I'm no more of an expert on that assassination than anybody else, but my point is that wiretaps in the national security area were very high in the Kennedy administration for a very good reason."[91]

What did President Nixon really mean by his comments on Robert Kennedy's wiretaps and any Oswald connection? But it is obvious that the president had an ongoing interest in the background of the Kennedy assassination, knew about the plots to kill Fidel Castro (actually ran it in the Eisenhower administration) and was paranoid about facing Senator Edward Kennedy for the presidential nomination in 1972.

The Ewing report reveals information on one of President Nixon's Plumbers unit, New York police detective John Caulfield, and his investigation of the Kennedy assassination. As a member of the NYPD's Bureau of Special Services, Caulfield, in late 1963, investigated the activities of the DRE, the militant anti-Castro group that was planning the second invasion of Cuba in the last week of November 1963. Caulfield reported that several members of the DRE were arrested in New York for protesting against the Kennedy administration actions taken against anti-Castro exile groups. This Caulfield information was given to the Warren Commission, who found it interesting to say the least. Also, at the same time that Caulfield was looking into the actions of the DRE, the FBI was investigating Frank Sturgis and his apparent knowledge of Lee Oswald's possible Cuban activities. The Senate report fails to clarify what role, if any, Caulfield played in the Hunt-JFK probe.

So, what do we make of all this? Howard Hunt's safe was drilled open on June 19, 1972 and its contents removed, minus the Kennedy report. The next day, President Nixon met with

91 Ibid

H.R. Haldeman, presumably to discuss the Watergate affairs and possibly the contents of Hunt's safe. Nixon aide Gordon Strachan, said that the same day, Haldeman ordered that various confidential files belonging to him be destroyed. Nixon then phoned John Mitchell to talk about Watergate but this call was never recorded (this is the famous 18 minute gap). Did the conversation that was never recorded have anything to do with the Hunt investigation?

If, as this most interesting document turns out to be correct, then Howard Hunt truly knows more than he has been saying over the years. And if the Hunt-JFK investigation is ever unearthed, what bombshells would it contain?

Jack Ruby

"The Commission has found no evidence that either Lee Harvey Oswald or Jack Ruby was part of any conspiracy, domestic or foreign, to assassinate President Kennedy."

One of the prime players in the Kennedy assassination drama, Jack Ruby, WAS closely examined by the Warren Commission, knew all the inconsistencies in Ruby's background, yet once again failed to check out all the leads that were brought to their attention regarding the slayer of Lee Harvey Oswald. Ruby's background as a bit player in the realm of organized crime in the decades following World War II was indeed checked out by the Warren Committee members, but if they had any doubts they decided not to probe further. Ruby's role in the assassination was examined more closely by the HSCA, and while they too found that Ruby had no direct connection to Lee Harvey Oswald, or that he was a major player in the Mafia, they knew of Ruby's close ties to certain American Mafia figures who were directly involved in anti-Castro Cuban operations, and Ruby's own trips to Cuba. The HSCA said of Ruby:

"The Committee, as did the Warren Commission, recognized that a primary reason to suspect organized crime of possible involvement in the assassination was Ruby's killing of Oswald. For this reason, the committee undertook an extensive investigation of Ruby and his relatives, friends and associates to determine if there was evidence that Ruby was involved in crime, organized or otherwise, such as gambling and vice, and if such involvement might have been related to the murder of Oswald. The evidence available to the committee indicated that Ruby was not a "member" of organized crime in Dallas or elsewhere, although it showed that he had a significant number of associations and direct and indirect contacts with underworld figures, a number of who were connected to the most powerful La Cosa Nostra leaders. Additionally, Ruby had numerous associations with the Dallas criminal element."

This was more than the Warren Commission ever went in linking Ruby to the Mafia, and with Robert Blakey at the helm of the HSCA, whose main candidate for the Kennedy assassination was the American mob, Ruby's ties fit neatly into the hole.

Before going into the new evidence concerning Ruby and the Kennedy assassination, a little background information on "Sparky" as he was called, is necessary.

Jack Ruby, born Jacob Rubenstein, was the fifth of eight children, on March 19, 1911. His father, Joseph, immigrated to the United States from Poland, as well as his mother Fannie. Jack's early childhood was in Chicago were the young Ruby children learned quickly to survive on the means streets. Both parents argued frequently and finally separated. At age 11, Jack was sent to the Institute for Juvenile Research by the Jewish Social Service Bureau because of his unruly behavior. The doctors called young Jack, "quick tempered" and "disobedient," and in 1924, he and two other siblings were sent to foster homes. He attended the Chicago public school system, while getting into his first scrape with the law. Jack quickly learned to take care of himself in fist fights with other kids but did not pick fights with those he came in contact with.

In 1933, he and a few friends went to Los Angeles and San Francisco, looking for work, but soon found themselves back in Chicago. In 1937, Ruby became active in Local 20467 of the Scrap Iron and Junk Handlers Union. For three years, Ruby worked as a union organizer. On December 8, 1939, Leon Cook, the local's financial secretary, was shot by John Cook, the union's president. He was acquitted by a jury on the grounds of self-defense. Ruby's name is mentioned in the minutes of a union meeting on February 2, 1940, in which Ruby is quoted as saying that he wanted to take over the union following Cook's demise. Following Cook's death, Ruby left the union.

In 1941, Ruby and associate Harry Epstein started a novelty business, which sold candy and gambling devices. While he was not a success in any of his business ventures, he did make friends with heavyweight boxer Barney Ross and attended many of his bouts.

In September 1941, Ruby joined the Army Air Force and besides his routine training, continued to sell merchandise shipped to him from Chicago to his service buddies. After his discharge from the Army, Ruby came back home and went into business with his three brothers but this venture too, went nowhere. It was in this time that Jack Ruby made a decision that was to change his life forever. He moved to Dallas, Texas in 1947, where, almost twenty years later, his name would go down in history.

Jack went to Dallas to help his sister Eva run a nightclub called the Singapore. Upon coming to Dallas, Eva met and befriended a man named Paul Roland Jones. Jones was in hot water with the law for the attempted bribery of the new sheriff of Dallas, Steve Guthrie. Jones was associated with the Chicago mob that wanted to take over mob activities in Dallas. Jones offered Sheriff Guthrie a percentage of the illegal gambling profits if he would look the other way. Guthrie said that Ruby's name came up in his bribery investigation of Jones but nothing that would stick. Ruby's first establishment in Dallas was the Silver Spur Club, which was the home away from home of various Chicago mobsters including Paul Roland Jones. Later, Ruby would take over the Vegas Club. He later took control of the Carousel Club, which he managed with Ralph Paul. It was at the Carousel Club that many people say Ruby and Oswald secretly met.

While in Dallas, Jack made friends with both the Dallas police and certain members of the Mafia, mostly from Chicago. Dallas Police Officers would frequently come into the Carousel Club, watch the strip teasers do their thing, have a few drinks, and schmooze with Ruby. Ruby also met a man who was closely associated with the mob, and its ties to Cuba, Lewis McWillie. McWillie would later become Ruby's best friend and introduce him to the illegal gun running activities in Cuba. Ruby's reputation in Dallas had also been observed by the Federal Bureau of Narcotics, and in 1956, Ruby became an undercover informer for them as "a contact for a large narcotics set-up operating between Mexico, Texas and the East." He also served briefly as an informer for the FBI, but supplied little significant information.

It was Ruby's pal, Lewis McWillie who would introduce him to the world of Cuban intrigue, gun running and an association with some of the mobsters who were to be allied with the CIA in its plots to kill Castro. McWillie had run a number of illegal gambling operations before heading south for Cuba. It wasn't the warm, tropical climate that brought him there; it was the huge profits that could be gained from the casinos. Once in Cuba, McWillie got a job at the Sans Souci casino as a pit boss. The Sans Souci was owned by Florida crime boss Santos Trafficante. He later moved over to the Tropicana casino in September 1958. While in Cuba, McWillie was intimate with some of the most important crime bosses in the US; Santos Trafficante, Meyer Lansky, among others.

Ruby went to visit McWillie in Cuba in late summer or early fall of 1959. The Warren Commission said that Ruby made only one trip to Cuba but the evidence seems to contradict their findings. Ruby, according to the HSCA, made a least three trips to Cuba, not one. And what did he do while in Cuba? It seems that

Ruby may have been in contact with Santos Trafficante when the crime boss was arrested by the newly formed government of Fidel Castro who dared to close down the mob controlled casinos.

Before heading to Cuba to see Trafficante, Ruby contacted an exporter in Florida named Robert McKeown who had contacts in Havana. McKeown testified that Ruby offered in 1959 to purchase a letter of introduction to Fidel Castro in the hopes of freeing three people from a Cuban jail. McKeown also said that Ruby talked to him about selling jeeps in Cuba. McKeown said that Ruby offered him a large sum of money, maybe $25,000 for an introduction to Castro. McKeown turned him down, but Ruby somehow managed to get into Cuba by himself.

Ruby's visit to the jailed Santos Trafficante was reported to the Warren Commission by a British journalist named John Wilson-Hudson, that "an American gangster type named Ruby" visited Cuba in 1959. Wilson was in jail with Trafficante and said that he saw Ruby visit the mob boss during that time. Trafficante was released from Trescornia jail on August 18, 1959 and deported to the United States. This corresponds to Ruby's official presence in Cuba as noted by Cuban travel documents. While this alleged incident took place before John Kennedy was elected president, and had no bearing on his death, if it is true, then a positive Ruby-Trafficante link is established, with far reaching consequences on November 22, 1963.

It has also been reported that Ruby was running guns to Cuba for Norman Rothman to Castro before his overthrow of the Batista government. After the assassination it was reported that Ruby was in the Florida Keys in June 1958 with a stash of guns hidden in the marshes, ready to be shipped to Castro's forces. Another report of Ruby's Cuban gun running connections comes from an FBI informant named Blaney Mack Johnson. Johnson says that Ruby worked with Edward Browder, a big time gunrunner for Norman Rothman.

Another important Ruby link to the top men in the crime syndicate who were also involved with the CIA in the Castro assassination plots supposedly took place in late 1963. According to reports, a federal investigator looking into the activities of Johnny Rosselli, said that Ruby met with Rosselli in Miami two months before the Kennedy assassination. Rosselli was said to have told columnist Jack Anderson that Ruby was "one of our boys," and referred to him as "the crazy Jew."[92]

Shortly before he was killed, Johnny Rosselli gave all of his information concerning the Kennedy assassination to Jack Anderson, the syndicated columnist. Rosselli told Anderson that when Oswald was arrested, those members of the mob who were involved in the assassination feared that Oswald would talk and lead federal officials straight to them. Consequently, Oswald had to be eliminated and that Ruby was ordered to kill Oswald. While in jail, Ruby told his psychiatrist that he was involved in a conspiracy to kill the president, which involved high government officials. He also told the doctor that he was blackmailed into killing Oswald because of his gun running activities.

The other prominent mob godfather who came across Jack Ruby's path was New Orleans crime boss Carlos Marcello. From his headquarters in New Orleans, Marcello ran mob-controlled drugs, prostitution rings, gambling across the southwest, including Dallas. Ruby frequently came to New Orleans to recruit girls for his strip clubs and had to have had close ties with Marcello's henchmen who told their boss everything that went on. Three weeks before the president's assassination, Ruby called Nofia Pecora, one of Marcello's most influential aides. He also made a series of phone calls to various mobsters across the country, including associates of Teamster boss Jimmy Hoffa, Marcello and Trafficante. Another mobster whom Ruby was associated with who also had a close relationship with Carlos Marcello was Joe Campisi, who ran the Texas rackets for Marcello.

---

92 Information on this section was reported in *The Secret Life of Jack Ruby, New Times* 1/25/78.

The Nancy Perrin Rich Story

New information concerning Ruby and the second invasion of Cuba is found in *"Oswald Talked: New Evidence in the JFK Assassination"* by Ray and Mary LaFontaine. Unlike other material concerning the assassination, the Perrin story was known to the Warren Commission but they decided that it wasn't (again) worth going any further.

In 1962, Nancy Perrin Rich traveled to Dallas to look for her husband Robert, who came to that city without explaining the circumstances behind his visit. Upon arriving in Dallas, she got a job as a bartender in Jack Ruby's Carousel Club. She didn't stay long and left after Ruby slapped her. She finally located Robert and was looking for new work when the most interesting job offer came their way. Nancy and Robert were introduced to a man named Dave Cherry who asked them if they would be interested in getting some people out of Cuba. They agreed and were taken to meet another couple named Jack and Nancy Starr. With them was a US Army Colonel. The unnamed officer offered the Nancy and Robert $10,000 if they would pilot a boat to bring some refugees out of Cuba. A few days later, they met again with the Colonel in Oak Lawn and this time the deal had changed. In addition to getting people out of Cuba, the Colonel asked them to bring guns into Cuba, mostly Enfield rifles. These guns were stolen from his military fort and were currently stored in Mexico. Nancy was allowed to see the weapons and she testified that the arsenal included Browning automatic weapons, hand grenades, land mines, and boxes of ammunition. The Colonel told the Riche's that the deal was not done as they were still waiting for the necessary finances to kick in. Then, according to Rich, a man walked into the apartment, someone she knew from before; Jack Ruby. Ruby and the Colonel met privately in the back room and when they returned a few minutes, all was smiles across the room. "All of a sudden just before Ruby came in they couldn't go, and right after Ruby left they were on the plane the next morning, so to speak."

At yet a third meeting, Nancy and Robert asked that they be given $25,000 for their participation in the scheme. The Colonel said that he'd have to take the matter up with his unnamed bosses. Nancy told Warren Commission attorney Leon Hubert in 1964 that she believed that the son of crime boss Vito Genovese was at their meeting. She also said that she and Robert left the gathering, refusing to have anything more to do with either the boat trip or the gun running scheme.

Shortly after the gathering, Nancy was arrested for vagrancy and prostitution, was released and left Dallas with her husband, bound for New Orleans. Later that year, Robert died at his own hands.

If the Nancy Perrin Rich story is true, we now have a direct connection between Jack Ruby and the second invasion of Cuba slated for the last week of November 1963. But who was the mysterious "Colonel?" Was it George Nonte, the officer who was responsible for the theft of supplies of weapons at Fort Hood bound for the invasion of Cuba? And if Oswald was indeed an informer for the FBI or the ATF knew about the gun running operation and the second invasion of Cuba, we now have a perfect reason for "Sparky" to kill Oswald in the Dallas Police Department parking garage.

In his new book, *"Taking Charge: The Johnson White House Tapes,"* historian Michael Beschloss, writes of a conversation between LBJ and FBI Director Hoover directly after the assassination. In the tape, Hoover tells Johnson that the FBI was looking into the Ruby-Oswald connection and went on to say that the Dallas Policemen who were guarding Oswald as he was being transferred to the waiting van, never moved out of the way of the oncoming Ruby. They only reacted *after* Oswald was slumped on the floor, the life ebbing out of him.

This study has brought to life certain information not known to the Warren Commission in 1964, and has highlighted the new data that has been released by both private researchers and government documents. Among the most important is the CIA-Mafia plots to kill Fidel Castro, President Kennedy's two track policy in dealing with the Castro government, the Executive Action/ ZR Rifle project, the DRE's planned second invasion of Cuba in November 1963, Jack Ruby's gunrunning operation and its possible ramifications in the Oswald rub out, The Scelso Documents which show that even the major players in the CIA knew little about the secret agency plots to kill Castro, the Ferrie flight plan which linked both Clay Shaw, David Ferrie and Lee Harvey Oswald together, long before the assassination, and the still secret Howard Hunt investigation of the Kennedy assassination.

The Warren Commission was flawed from the start and influenced heavily by the actions of Allan Dulles and J. Edgar Hoover. The Commissioners were hampered by both a time constraint and the political considerations at play in the United States and the world. President Johnson had strong reservations about Oswald's acting alone but he dared not publicly tell the country of his doubts for fear of an all out nuclear war. Better to let sleeping dogs lie than confront the awful truth in the murder of President John Kennedy. But history has a way of changing impressions, bringing new information to a new generation, looking for answers that need to be solved. Hopefully, that will continue to be the case.

Appendix 1

The FBI's Dirty Little Secret

One week after the eternal flame was lit at the grave of John F. Kennedy at Arlington National Cemetery, the new president, Lyndon Johnson, under severe pressure from both the congress and an anxious public, looking for answers to the nation's tragedy, signed an executive order creating a blue-ribbon panel of distinguished Americans to investigate the circumstances surrounding the assassination of President Kennedy.

LBJ did not want to create such a panel, hoping that in the natural course of time, the terrible events of the past week would begin to fade away. But that was not to be the case. In Texas, the scene of the crime, state and local officials were beginning to make noise about conducing their own, wide-ranging investigation into the events in Dealey Plaza. If the Texas crowd began their own inquiry, there would be no telling where that would lead.

The two prime suspects in the assassination, the alleged assassin, Lee Harvey Oswald and his killer, night club owner Jack Ruby, a man with ties to both the mob and the FBI, both lived in Texas. Even though one was dead, the local press, who saw the story of a life time in front to their eyes, might uncover facts that the White House might rather not see the light of day.

In the weeks since the assassination, persistent rumors began to swirl of a possible conspiracy in the president's assassination. Both the FBI and the CIA had information that Oswald was possibly involved with both the Soviet Union and Cuba. They knew that Oswald had defected to the Soviet Union under rather shady circumstances and lived in that county for over two years. They also knew that he was in Mexico City in the months prior to the assassination and that while he was in the Mexican capital, he met with a high ranking KGB official named Valery Kostikov, who was a member of an assassination squad set up by the Russian government.

They also knew that Oswald had been a member of the Fair Play For Cuba Committee, a pro-Castro group that advocated a lessening of tensions between Havana and Washington. In time, both spy agencies found out that Oswald was conducting his own Fair Play For Cuba activities in New Orleans in the summer of 1963, while, at the same time, associating with certain individuals (David Ferrie, Guy Banister, etc) would were once associated with US intelligence.

In both the White House and at CIA headquarters in Langley, Va., gossip was going around that Oswald was either in the employ of Castro or the KGB and that the president's assassination was either sanctioned by Moscow or Havana. Could Oswald have been an agent of either power?

At the FBI, J. Edgar Hoover, decided early on that Oswald was the lone assassin and that he had no confederates, either domestic or foreign. Hoover did so in order to hide the fact that his agency had failed to alert the Secret Service of Oswald's presence in Dallas prior to November 22, 1963. He also didn't want the public to know that his agency had met with Oswald many times since his return from Russia the year before. Hoover also wanted to hide the fact that Oswald had an encounter with FBI agent James Hosty who interviewed Marina Oswald, his wife. Furious at the FBI, Oswald entered the Dallas office of the FBI and in what is still open to debate, either told the FBI to stop talking to his wife without this permission or, as some people think, gave the FBI information on the upcoming assassination attempt on the president's life.

Back in Washington, President Johnson was worried abut all the conspiracy talk swirling around the nation and he took steps to stop it before it got out of control.

Acceding to popular demand, the president called in Chief Justice of the Supreme Court Earl Warren for a meeting at the White House. In an impassioned talk, the president laid out in stark detail that rumors about possible Russian or Cuban involvement in the assassination and said that if it could be proved, that war was inevitable and that millions of American lives were at risk. He pleaded with Warren to head the investigation that he was planning and did so as a matter of the highest priority imaginable. Reluctantly, Chief Justice Warren agreed, despite his reluctance to take on another high-profile job.

Warren proceeded to pick his fellow commissioners and by mid December 1963, they began their preliminary sessions, setting priorities, hiring staff and getting down to business.

As the Chief Justice began his work, he had no idea that the task they were about to begin would turn into a nightmare, one whose findings would still be debated almost fifty years later.

As their work began, the Warren Commission began to rely heavily on the tepid investigation undertaken by the FBI. Despite the currents of doubt relating to Oswald's guilt or innocence, Hoover decided that he was the lone assassin and shut the case down. Official dissent was out of the question and anyone who shared that opinion was swiftly headed out to pasture.

One of the thorniest issues that raised its ugly head was the nagging rumor that Oswald was a paid informant of the FBI. This issue would come to dominate the panels Executive sessions as time went on.

The possibility of Oswald being an FBI informer came up on January 1, 1964 during the Commission's Executive Session. The Commission's legal counsel, J. Lee Rankin started the conversation by telling his fellow commissioners the following story. He said that he had a telephone conversation with Wagner Carr, the Attorney General of Texas that Oswald was an FBI informant and was given the designation of Number 179. Oswald was supposed to have been paid two hundred a month from September 1962 to the time of the assassination. When asked by Rankin how Carr had gotten the information, he said that the news had been given to the defense team for Jack Ruby. Rankin said that he immediately told Chief Justice Warren and that Warren broached the possibility of bringing Carr up to Washington for further testimony.

Rankin later said that Carr had called him back and reported that the source had been a newspaper reporter. Rankin further said that he was worried that the press would get hold of the story and blow it out of proportion.

During their session, the commissioners talked among themselves as to the possible ramifications of such a fact being true. Rankin said that "Now it is something that would be very difficult to prove out. There are events in connection with this that are curious, in that they might make it possible to check some of it out in time. I assume the FBI records would never show it, and if it is true, and of course we don't know, but we thought you should have the information."

Commission member John Sherman Cooper asked Rankin if it would be possible to absolutely prove that Oswald was or was not an FBI informer. Rankin responded by saying. "It is going to be very difficult for us to be able to establish the fact in it. I am confident that the FBI would never admit it, and I presume their records will never show it, or if their records do show anything, I think their records would show some kind of a number that could be assigned to a dozen different people according to how they wanted to describe them. So that it seemed to me if it truly happened, he (Oswald) did use postal boxes practically every place that he went, and that would be an ideal way to get money to anyone that you wanted as an undercover agent, or anybody else that you wanted to do business with without having any particular transaction."[93]

Commissioner Allan Dulles, the former head of the CIA whom Kennedy had fired after the botched invasion at the Bay of Pigs in April 1961 which was overseen by Dulles, took up the next question. He asked rhetorically concerning Oswald by saying, "What was the ostensible mission? I mean when they hire somebody they hire somebody for a purpose. It is either…Was it to penetrate the Fair Play for Cuba Committee? That is the only thing I can think of where they might have used this man. It would be quite ordinary for me because they are very careful about the agents they use. You wouldn't pick up a fellow like this to do an agent's job. You have got to watch out for your agents. You really got to know. Sometimes you make a mistake."

Commission member Gerald Ford (later president of the United States) said, "He was playing ball, writing letters to both the elements of the Communist parties. I mean he was playing ball with the Trotskyites and with the others. This was a strange circumstance to me."

Dulles: "But the FBI get people right inside you know. They don't need a person like this on the outside. The only place where he did any at all was with the Fair Play for Cuba Committee."

Commissioner Hale Boggs had many lingering questions about Oswald being the killer of the president and he posed this question.

"Of course it is conceivable that he may have been brought back from Russia you know."

Dulles, who knew a lot about the inner workings of the tradecraft of espionage said, "they (the FBI) have no facilities, they haven't any people in Russia. They may have some people in Russia but they haven't any organization of their own in Russia. They might have their agents their. They have some people, sometimes American Communists who go to Russia under their guidance and so forth and so on under their control."

93 Warren Commission Executive Session 1/22/64, 5:30 - 7:00 PM.

It is evident from this conversation that the members of the panel were concerned enough about Oswald's stay in Russia and the possibility that he might have been sent under the auspices of the FBI in some undercover capacity. If Dulles knew about any relationship Oswald might have had with the CIA in Russia (or anywhere else), he never would have mentioned it in open session.

A few days later, during another Warren Commission session, Rankin posed the possibility to the other members that he ask Director Hoover about the rumors of Oswald being in the employ if the FBI. "In light of that, I suggested the possibility for the Commission to consider that I should go over and see Edgar Hoover myself, and tell him this problem and that he should have as much interest as the Commission in trying to put an end to any such speculations, not only by his statement, which I would be frank to tell him I would think would not be sufficient, but also if it was possible to demonstrate by whatever records and materials is they have that it just couldn't be true, and see if we couldn't get his cooperation to present that with the understanding that the Commission, and stated understanding, at the time, the Commission would have to feel free to make such other investigations and take testimony if it found it necessary. In order to satisfy the American people what that question of the undercover agent was out of the picture."[94]

The informer that Rankin was talking about was a Houston, Texas newspaperman named Alonzo Hudkins. The Secret Service interviewed Hudkins and he told them that his source was Allen Sweatt, the chief of the criminal division of the Dallas sheriff's office. Hudkins said that Sweatt told him that, "Oswald was being paid two hundred dollars per month by the FBI in connection with their subversive investigation (and) that Oswald had informant number S-172."[95]

94 Warren Commission Executive Session January 27, 1964
95 Act of Treason. Mark North. Carroll & Graf Publishers, New York, 1991. Page 512.

Allen Sweatt was never questioned by the Warren Commission, although the commission members did have some discussions about bringing him to testify before them.

During the commissions executive sessions relating to the Oswald-as-an-FBI-informer allegation, FBI Assistant Director Alan Belmont was questioned often by the members in sometimes heated fashion. One of his questioners was Samuel Stern, a Warren Commission staff assistant counsel. Stern wanted answers from Belmont about an April 6, 1964 FBI letter written by Belmont which was sent to J. Lee Rankin. The letter consisted of material consisting of 69 items contained in the FBI's file on Oswald. Previously, the commission staff wrote thirty questions it wanted answered on what material the FBI had on Oswald prior to the assassination. Belmont said that he was responsible for handling the Oswald file and the Bureau's investigation of him.[96]

On a number of occasions during his testimony regarding a possible Oswald-FBI link, Stern asked Belmont pointed questions on the topic but often times was stopped in his tracks by Chief Justice Warren. Stern proceeded anyway in asking Belmont to comment on any FBI-Oswald link, his defection to the Soviet Union, the matter of Oswald's fingerprints, and his attempt to enroll in Albert Schweitzer College (which Oswald never attended). Belmont did say that "the FBI had set up certain connections with the State Department passport file on Oswald dealing with the US Embassy in Moscow." He further said that Oswald was "not known to be connected to FBI sources in New Orleans."

That flies in the face of certain events that took place there. During the time he was in New Orleans, Oswald established his own one man Fair Play for Cuba Committee, a pro-Castro organization. He was seen handing out leaflets in the city and was once arrested by police during a fight with an anti-Castro person.

96 "This Dirty Rumor." George Michael Evica. June 1995 Vol. 1. Issue 2. The Assassination Chronicles.

Oswald was associated with numerous people in New Orleans who had US intelligence connections including an ex-FBI agent named Guy Banister. Oswald was reported seen in Banister's company at the latter's office at 544 Camp Street. Another person with intelligence links whom Oswald was seen with was a strange looking man, an ex-Pan Am pilot and CIA mercenary named David Ferrie.

The topic of Oswald's security file came up again and Stern asked Belmont about certain materials on that file "you would prefer not to disclose." Belmont said that the file contained names of FBI informants in subversive movements and no further questions were asked.

Commissioner John J. McCloy tried to elicit Belmont to answer more questions about the Bureau's Oswald file but once again Warren nipped that in the bud. Belmont did say that the FBI file on Oswald was "available to the Commission."

Counsel Rankin asked Belmont if the panel members could see the entire Oswald FBI file but Chief Justice Warren raised objections saying that Belmont's appearance and testimony before the commission was sufficient.

If Warren was satisfied with Belmont's answers, John J. McCloy wasn't. McCloy was given access to a copy of the FBI file said that Belmont's summary was "disturbing, not a complete description of the file's content as McCloy examined it."[97]

An angry McCloy further said that the commission "might miss the full impact of all the narrative in the FBI's reports on Oswald."

Allan Dulles took up Warren's defense, supporting the Chief Justice's attempts to limit what the commission could see regarding the entire FBI file on Oswald. Dulles had his own dirty little secret-the fact that the Mafia had made a pact with the CIA (of which he was head) to murder Fidel Castro. Dulles failed to inform the Warren Commission of that very important fact

97 Ibid.

and it wasn't until the middle of the 1970's that a congressional investigation into both the Kennedy and King assassinations as appraised of that fact.

Belmont told the panel members that Oswald was not, nor had never been an agent of the FBI. However, persistent rumors about a possible Oswald-US intelligence connection failed to go away, even to this day.

On the same day that President Johnson set up the Warren Commission, he had a meeting with FBI Director Hoover regarding the events of the past week. Kennedy had been buried and, as far as Hoover was concerned, the investigation was all but over. However, the president wanted to hear from Hoover just what evidence the FBI had on Oswald and a meeting was arranged. They discussed who might be appointed to the commission that the president had just authorized, with the president giving his opinion on the men he was about to appoint.

Once the meeting got under way, the president asked Hoover what information he had on Oswald's trip to Mexico City the previous September. Hoover gave LBJ what he had, talking in generalities regarding Oswald's mysterious southern sojourn. Hoover got right to the point saying, "This angle in Mexico is giving us a great deal of trouble because the story is they have this man. Oswald, getting $6500 from the Cuban Embassy and then coming back to this country with it. We're not able to prove that fact but the information was that he was there on the 18th of September in Mexico City and we are able to prove conclusively that he was in New Orleans that day. Now then they're changing the dates – the story came in changing the dates to the 28th of September – and he was in Mexico on the 28th. Mexican police have again arrested this woman Duran who is a member of the Cuban Embassy – and will hold her for two or three more days – and we're going to confront her with the original informant – who saw the money pass, or he says, and we're also going to put lie detector test on him."[98]

98 Phone conversation between President Johnson and J. Edgar Hoover Nov. 29, 1963 1:40 PM.

The allegation of Oswald receiving $6,500 that Hoover was referring to, revolves around a man named Gilberto Alvarado, an informant from Nicaragua. Alvarado told members of the staff of the American embassy in Mexico City on November 24, 1963, that he had seen Oswald being paid that sum of money by unidentified Cubans on September 17. During his alleged incident, Alvarado also said he overheard Oswald and these people talking about a plot to kill Kennedy. This story proved to be a false lead.

The mention of Duran pertains to Sylvia Duran, a secretary who worked at the Mexican Consulate in Mexico City. Duran worked at the consulate at the time that Oswald paid a visit to the consulate seeking travel papers to Cuba with his final destination being a return to Russia. Duran was arrested twice (at the behest of the CIA) and her relationship with Oswald has come to be part of the untold story of Oswald's trip to Mexico City and the unusual events that took place there.

Johnson then asked Hoover what information the FBI had on Jack Ruby. Here, Hoover also spoke in generalities, telling the president only what little information the Bureau had learned from its sources in Dallas. The president wanted to know if there was any relationship between Oswald and Ruby. Hoover said he didn't know but portrayed Ruby in a not so flattering light.

"Now, this fellow Rubenstein is a very shady character – has a bad record, street brawler, fighter and that sort of thing – and is the place in Dallas if a fellow came in there and couldn't pay his bill completely, Rubenstein would beat the very devil out of him, and throw him out of the place." Hoover described Ruby as being an "ego-maniac."

Johnson pressed Hoover to give him any information as to whether or not Oswald was connected in any way with the Castro government.

Hoover said the FBI was still investigating that allegation, told the president of Oswald's relationship with the Fair Play for Cuba Committee, and about his correspondence with the Soviet Embassy in Washington.

Johnson asked Hoover if the Bureau had any evidence of why Oswald might have killed the president and Hoover replied by saying, "None of these letters, however, tells of any indications of violence or contemplated assassination. They were dealing with the matter of a visa for his wife to go back to Russia..." [99]

The day that LBJ set up the Warren Commission was a very busy one indeed, especially for J. Edgar Hoover. As soon as Hoover learned of the establishment of the panel he ordered the FBI to start a file on each member of the commission in order to monitor their progress and have leverage over them in case the need arose. As mentioned before, Hoover's main objective was to brand Oswald as the lone assassin of the president and more importantly, to hide the fact from the public that FBI agents had met with Oswald and his wife in Dallas in the months prior to the assassination.

Hoover had a friend on the commission, Congressman Gerald Ford of Michigan. As the commission delved into the assassination, Ford would be the secret conduit with Hoover, providing him with detailed information on the commission's progress. William Sullivan, the Assistant FBI Director, would have a telling comment to make on Ford's relationship with Hoover. "Hoover was delighted when Ford was named to the Warren Commission. The Director wrote in one of his internal memos that the bureau could expect Ford to look after FBI interests, and he did, keeping us fully advised on what was going on behind closed doors. He was our informant on the Warren Commission."[100]

A number of commissioners were skeptical of the FBI's lack of response to its inquires regarding what information they had on Oswald, Ruby and whether or not Oswald had a prior relationship with the FBI. On May 24, 1964, Hoover reluctantly appeared before the commission for questioning. Chief Justice Warren asked Hoover if Oswald was or was not an informer of the FBI.

---

99 Ibid.

100 Act of Treason. Pages 448-449.

Hoover categorically denied any relationship between Oswald and the FBI by saying, "I can most emphatically say that at no time was he ever an employee of the Bureau in any capacity, either as an agent or as a special employee, or as an informant."

Counsel Rankin asked Hoover if the FBI found any information regarding either a foreign or domestic conspiracy to kill the president. Once again Hoover denied the allegations.

Allan Dulles asked Hoover if their was any connection between Ruby and Oswald. Again he denied the charges.

Commissioner Hale Boggs asked Hoover why Oswald had killed the president and Hoover said that he believed Oswald was a Communist. "I personally believe it was...the twisted mentality the man had."

Senator John Sherman Cooper pressed Hover further on the allegations of Oswald being in the employ of the Bureau. Hoover again denied any relationship but he did say that the FBI was concerned about Oswald's participation with the Fair Play for Cuba Committee in New Orleans, wondering if his actions were financed or supported by the Castro government. Hoover's reference to Oswald and the FPCC wasn't the first time he made that statement and the record is clear that Oswald's FPCC activities troubled him.

On May 8, 1964, President Johnson honored his long time friend and neighbor, J. Edgar Hoover in a White House ceremony. Hoover was to reach the mandatory retirement age of 70 on January 1st but Johnson had no intention of relieving him from his duties. Hoover died on May 2, 1972, still the keeper of all the secrets he'd accumulated in his decades long reign as the only head of the FBI.

Appendix 2

Jane Roman and the CIA's Oswald Investigation

One of the many failures of the Warren Commission's investigation into the assassination of the president was that it wasn't made privy to a large amount of intelligence gathered on Lee Oswald before the events of November 22, 1963 coming from both the FBI and CIA. Hoover admittedly denied to the WC that Oswald was ever an employee of the Bureau. The CIA also said that they had no official relationship with the ex-Marine. But that wasn't all true. It seems from the new documents, and from interviews conducted by researchers over the past few years of a long standing CIA knowledge of Oswald before the assassination.

One CIA analyst who had prior knowledge of Oswald was Jane Roman who was the senior liaison officer on the Counterintelligence Staff of the CIA at headquarters in Langley, Va. The story of Jane Roman and her role in the pre-assassination doings of Oswald, came from the dogged work of Dr. John Newman, a retired intelligence agent and author, and Jefferson Morley, then a writer for the *Washington Post.*

Morley got interested in Oswald's pre-assassination story in 1994 when he was working for the *Post.* In 1994, Jane Roman was living in Washington, D.C. and Morley, who had an abiding interest in the Kennedy assassination (he later wrote a book on the subject called "Our Man in Mexico: Winston Scott and the Hidden History of the CIA"), asked his editors for permission to do a story on her. Morley believed that Jane Roman could provide information on her work at the CIA at the time of the assassination and he wanted to track her down. It seems that Jane Roman's name had been listed on routing slips attached to certain CIA documents about Lee Harvey Oswald before November 22, 1963 and Morley wanted to see if she could provide any useful information on Oswald that might be of interest. Digging through records at the National Archives in College Park, Maryland, Morley found Roman's initials on a routing slip attached to an FBI report about Oswald that was dated September 10, 1963.[101]

It was that one reference that sent both Morley and Newman on their hunt for Jane Roman.

Morley and Newman showed up at Jane Roman's door on November 2, 1994 at her invitation. After a few minutes of small talk, their discussion got down to business. Their first question to Roman was, "When was the first time that you recall having heard about Lee Harvey Oswald and saying something about him, or hearing somebody saying something to you about him?"

Roman replies by saying, "I don't think I ever heard about him before the assassination."

Jane Roman might not have personally heard about Lee Oswald before, but the CIA surely did. The agency knew that Oswald was a defector to the Soviet Union and opened up a 201 file on him. A 201 file was opened on people who had special interest by the CIA for whatever reasons. They knew he married a Russian woman, worked in a radio factory in Minsk and had returned to the United States with his wife in May 1962. They knew all about his Marine background, including the fact that he was stationed at Atsqui Air Base in Japan, the base from where

101 "What Jane Roman Said: A Retired CIA Officer Speaks Candidly About Lee Harvey Oswald." By Jefferson Morley. www.History-matters.com.

the U-2 spy planes flew over Russia and China. Oswald was a radar operator at the base and was well versed on the U-2's tactical capabilities.

The Oswald file was handled by James Angleton's Counterintelligence Staff, one of the most secretive parts of the agency. The Counterintelligence Staff was the mole hunting group at CIA headquarters and when Oswald returned home the agency did not know if he was an agent of the Soviet Union or just a disgruntled American who had seen the light. Another secret group at CIA HQ who had possession of the Oswald file was the SIG-Special Investigations Group-whose mandate was to hunt potential moles inside the CIA. At this point, no one inside the CIA knew who Oswald was and they needed to find out. Jane Roman read the early files that passed her desk, signed them, and passed them on to her superiors.

Morley and Newman showed Roman a sheaf of files that the FBI had on Oswald, including some material on his stay in New Orleans in the summer of 1963. Some of these files came from the Directorate of Plans, then the covert division at the CIA.

"Is this the mark of a person's file who's dull and uninteresting?" asked Newman.

"No, we're really trying to zero in on somebody here," said Roman.

As the interview continued, Roman said that the CIA first got interested in Oswald in late 1963 when Oswald was in New Orleans handing out FPCC (Fair Play for Cuba) literature. The FPCC was then financed by the Castro regime and the counterintelligence staff wanted to know if Oswald was somehow involved with the Cubans.

The FBI also had documents on Oswald's arrest by the police on August 9, 1963 during a scuffle with certain members of an anti-Castro group called the DRE (the Cuban Student Directorate). After his arrest, Oswald asked that an FBI agent come in to take his statement, a curious fact indeed. Later, Oswald would go on a radio show in New Orleans debating the merits of Marxism and communism. The CIA knew all about the DRE and it went by the code name AMSPELL.

DRE members at the time were based in the United States and were part of that group's military wing which were under the direct sponsorship of the CIA. One of the secrets that the Warren Commission did not learn about was that second invasion of Cuba was being prepared for the last week of November 1963. The group that was heading for Cuba was the above mentioned DRE. They were closely watched and monitored by the CIA but did not have complete control over it as it had other exile groups.

By February 1966, due to the changing political situation vis a vi Cuba, the CIA decided to reduce its funding and control over the DRE and decided only to expend the amount of $1 million beginning in that month because, "the AMSPELL organization has been affected by the loss of many of its most capable members who have outlived the youth/student category and have resigned to seek employment outside of the JMWAVE (CIA-Miami station) area...It is expected that the Station will be able to maintain a productive contact with the AMSPELL organization, which will continue to function but with reduced financial support, and that AMSPELL members will be available for whatever specific operations the Station may wish to pursue in the student field."[102]

But that was not the case in the fall of 1963.

Only a few weeks after he left New Orleans, Oswald traveled to Mexico City where one of the most highly debated facets of the pre-assassination months comes into play. During his brief stay in Mexico City, Oswald visited both the Cuban and Russian embassies, seeking a visa permit to Cuba, with his final destination, the Soviet Union. The Oswald Mexico City paper trail grew bigger by the day and soon reports of his activities in the city would up on the desk of Winston Scott, who was head of all Cuban operations in Mexico City for the CIA. On October 8, 1963, Scott sent a cable regarding Oswald's mysterious Mexican sojourn to CIA HQ.

102 RIF No. 104-10170-10101.

This three page cable dated October 10, 1963 was written by Charlotte Bustos who worked for the CIA's Mexico desk. She worked on the cable and then sent it on its way up the ladder. One of the people who saw Charlotte Bustos's cable was Jane Roman. But now, it seems, the people in the CIA pecking order who saw the October 10th cable gets more interesting. Also reading it were J. C. King, the head of the CIA's Western Hemisphere Division, Thomas Karamessines, who was deputy to Richard Helms, the head of the CIA's covert operations branch. That night, the cable was sent back to Mexico City.

When asked to comment on the Oswald paper trail which was current, and all the people who read it, Roman said, "The only interpretation I could put on this would that this SAS group would have held all the information on Oswald under tight control."

What Roman and most Americans did not know was that right after the failure of the Bay of Pigs invasion, the Kennedy administration began a secret war to oust Castro dubbed Operation Mongoose. Mongoose was run the by the CIA, and also involved other branches of the government, including the Department of Defense. Its base of operations was Miami Florida at a CIA base named JMWAVE. From there, military assets, including air, sea and land were utilized to mount hit-and-run raids into Cuba in order to disrupt the Cuban economy and attack its military installations. The SAS was run by Desmond Fitzgerald, an old OSS officer and a veteran of the CIA's operations in the Philippines in the late 1950's. He was also the case officer who debriefed the CIA's top assassin in its plots to kill Castro, Rolando Cubela, a.k.a. AMLASH.

At one point during their interview, Roman said regarding the dozens of files that she had been shown that, "All these things that you have shown me so far before the assassination would have been very dull and very routine."

She also said that, "I wasn't in on any particular goings-on or hanky panky as far as the Cuban situation."

When Newman pressed her on the obvious fact that she

signed off on information that she read regarding the Oswald cables which were not really true, she said, "Yeah, I mean I'm signing off on something that I know isn't true." [103]

Roman said that the person ultimately responsible for the Oswald cable was Thomas Karamessines.

As their interview was coming to and end, Jane Roman said this regarding the cable on Oswald that had been reviewed by the CIA, "To me its indicative of a keen interest in Oswald held very closely on the need to know basis. There wouldn't be any point in withholding it (the recent information about Oswald). There has to be a point for withholding information from Mexico City."

Speaking about who knew what about Oswald, Miss Roman said, "Well, the obvious position which I really can't contemplate would be that they thought that somehow…they could make some use of Oswald."

"I would think that there was definitely some operational reason to withhold it, if it was not sheer administrative error, when you see all the people who signed off on it."

As we can see, Jane Roman had seen and signed off on very interesting cables on Oswald which the CIA had in its possession months before the assassination. Her answers to just why the CIA had operational interest in Oswald, she cannot say for certain. But they knew enough to figure out that something rotten in Denmark was going on in Mexico when Oswald was there. But what, and in what way was he involved?

Oswald's brief trip to Mexico in September 1963 has been studied by both the HSCA and private researchers and it is one of the prime mysteries surrounding the pre-assassination story. Government documents, as well as private research have given us a good clue of what was going on at the time of Oswald's visit but the story is far from complete and will probably remain incomplete as long as all the remaining files on the Kennedy assassination continue to be kept secret.

---

103 What Jane Roman Said, 3. "A Keen Interest in Oswald."

As early as October 9, 1963, the CIA knew that Oswald had phoned the Soviet Embassy in Mexico City and realized he was the same person who defected to the Soviet Union in 1959 and returned in 1962. The CIA then sent this report to the FBI, the State Department and the Navy Department for their perusal. The CIA then sent a long cable about Oswald's background to its Mexico City station, asking for more information on him.

In its cable of October 9, 1963, the CIA Mexico City Station said it had a photograph of an American looking person leaving the Soviet Embassy on October 1, 1963 the very day that Oswald phoned the embassy. In a report written by the Agency called "CIA's Investigation of Oswald's Activities in Mexico City," they wrote at one point that, "A very sensitive operation in Mexico City provides us with secretly taken photographs of many but not all visitors to the Soviet Embassy there, taken with telephoto lenses. Accordingly, we cabled the Navy Department on 24 October 1963 asking for a photograph of Lee Oswald from his Marine Corps days so we could compare photos. We had not received this photograph by 22 November 1963, but in any event, it turned out that the man photographed outside the Soviet Embassy was not Oswald anyway. As chance would have it, none of our several photo observations points in Mexico City had ever taken an identifiable picture of Oswald."

Just what this "very sensitive operation in Mexico City" was is still open to debate. It may involve a secret CIA or FBI investigation of the FPCC or maybe something to do with trying to turn certain KGB operatives assigned to the Soviet Embassy.

In the days immediately after the assassination, the CIA was busy collating as much information on Oswald as possible for dissemination to the rest of the government. An FBI report saying that Oswald was the assassin of the president was sent to CI Chief James Angleton and then to Birch O'Neal of his Special Investigation's Unit. The CIA's report on Oswald in Mexico City states that in the week after the assassination, a dozen people were working feverishly collating as much information on Oswald as possible. In one week, 27 cabled reports were sent to the White House, the State Department, and the FBI. It is most likely that Lyndon Johnson was privy to these cables and he got a glimpse of the mysteries of Oswald's trip during that time.

The CIA also said that they looked into their telephone taps in Mexico City "and came up with several more conversations probably involving OSWALD, but not actually mentioning this name; these connected him also to the Cuban Consulate in Mexico City."

At the CIA and the White House, persistent reports came in linking Oswald to either the Soviet's or the Cubans while he was in Mexico City. The CIA's Report tries to answer these questions but only in a cursory manner.

"To date," the narrative says, "there is no credible information in CIA files which would appear to link Lee Oswald with the Cuban government or the Cuban intelligence service."

"The whole question of whether Lee Oswald had any secret connection with the Soviets or Cubans cannot yet be answered, but certain parts of the evidence indicate to the contrary. Silvia Duran and the Soviet Consular officials spoke of him as a man with no friends in Cuba on the one hand, and as a man not known in the Soviet Embassy, on the other. The very openness of his visits and the phone calls speak against any secret role. His trip to Mexico was not itself a secret act; he traveled under his real name or a close variant of it, lived openly in Mexican hotels, and corresponded with the Soviets through the open mails about it when he got back to the US. His trip to Mexico was apparently made necessary because it was the nearest Cuban diplomatic installation where he could apply for a visa."

What made the CIA anxious about Oswald's Mexico City trip was his association with Valery Kostikov, a KGB officer assigned to the Soviet Embassy. The report says, "A particular sinister aspect of Oswald's dealings with the Soviets in Mexico City arises from the likelihood that he met with Soviet Counsel Valery Kostikov...Kostikov is accredited as a Consular Attache and does actually a lot of consular work, but he is believed to be a Soviet KGB officer, and it is believed that he works for Department 13 of the KGB, the Department charged with sabotage and assassinations. The suspicion that Kostikov is a KGB officer arose from his work habits, and his association with other KGB officers."

The narrative goes on to say that, "But unless some direct evidence of Soviet complicity is discovered, it is most likely that Oswald's dealings with KGB men Obyedkov (an embassy guard) and Kostikov was nothing more than a grim coincidence, a coincidence due in part to the Soviet habit of placing intelligence men in the Embassies in positions where they receive a large portion of the visitors and phone calls. All of the five consular officers in the Soviet Embassy are known or suspected intelligence officers. Certainly if Oswald had been a Soviet agent in training for an assassination assignment or even for sabotage work, the Soviets would have stopped him from making visits and phone calls to the Soviet Embassy in Mexico after he tried it a couple of times. Our experience in Mexico, studying the Soviet intelligence service at close range, indicates that they do make some mistakes and are sometimes insecure in their methods, but that they do not persist in such glaring errors."

CI Chief James Angleton was a proponent of some sort of Cuban-Soviet involvement in the assassination of the president and said he didn't believe Oswald was an American agent. During the Warren Commission's investigation, he urged Allen Dulles not to drop the case but to pursue that particular angle. He believed that Department 13, the one that Valery Kostikov was possibly linked with, might have been involved in the assassination. He told researcher and writer Dick Russell that he discounted any possibility of a domestic conspiracy, pointing to the fact that the Soviet's made noises after the assassination linking the right wing in the US with the affair.

Angleton also told Russell that he briefly looked over the material provided by the Soviets to the US after the assassination and he basically said it was worthless. "Its faceless information," he replied, "not the kind of dossiers they keep on foreigners, especially Americans. He'd had special training in the Marines. It would be a matter of intense interest to them as to why he would defect."

Roman's statement that the CIA had a "keen interest in Oswald" was shown dramatically in the interest taken by James Angleton about the latter's trip to Mexico City and whatever association with Valery Kostikov he might have had.

When the CIA took over the investigation of the president's assassination in 1964, Angleton's CIA Staff took on the major responsibility for finding out as much about Oswald. as they could. The CIA and the FBI needed to get their positions straight as far as the Warren Commission was concerned, and they reluctantly put aside their mutual distrust, at least for a while. In order to do that, Angleton contacted William Sullivan, the FBI's Assistant Director to coordinate their answers. Angleton told Sullivan that if the Warren Commission began asking each other the same questions about Oswald, they better get their answers straight. He suggested that they have a session whereby they would rehearse their answers, particularly ones relating to the possibility of Oswald was either working for the CIA or FBI, or if their was any evidence of a conspiracy. In each case, the answer would be no.

Right after the assassination, a dispute between the CIA and FBI came to the fold as far as who might have pulled the trigger in Dallas. Angleton and his CI Staff believed that Oswald was part of a communist conspiracy and was somehow linked with KGB assassin, Valery Kostikov. On the other hand, Hoover's FBI pined the blame squarely on the shoulders of Oswald, discounting any possibility of a conspiracy, either foreign or domestic.

Tempers flared again between the FBI and CIA when a news story ran nationally that said that the FBI was convinced that Oswald was the lone killer of the president. That assertion was disputed by nationally known columnist Drew Pearson. Hoover decided that CIA Director John McCone was the leaker and in a memo written for the Pearson file, Hoover wrote, "Information developed by Mr. De Loach has indicated that John McCone, Director, CIA, has attacked the Bureau in a vicious and underhanded manner characterized with sheer dishonesty." Hoover wanted to publically call out McCone, but soon, cooler heads prevailed.

Angleton did his best to appraise the FBI on his beliefs about a Soviet link with Oswald. In due course, he asked Sam Papich, an FBI agent who was the intermediary between Hoover and Angleton, to come to Langley headquarters where Angleton would give Papich the information on a possible KGB-Oswald link. Angleton told Papich about certain "sinister implications" revolving the Russians and Oswald. He told Papich about a Soviet defector named Anatoliy Golitsyn who had defected to the United States in December 1961 (the FBI already knew about Golitsyn). Among the intelligence that Golitsyn told the CIA was that a fake defector from Russia would one day come knocking on its doors with disinformation that would rock the CIA. Angleton believed that Yuri Nosenko, a KGB officer who ultimately defected to the United States, was that fake defector. To make matters more interesting, Nosenko told the CIA that he had seen the KGB-Oswald file and had read it right after the assassination. Nosenko said that Oswald was not a KGB recruit and the Soviet's never had any interest in him (wrong on the second count). Over time, Nosenko would become the CIA's secret prisoner before finally given his bona fides, many years later. One of the things that Angleton told Papich was that Golitsyn said that in 1961 that the KGB had a plot to kill a "western political leader." Was that leader JFK?[104]

Sam Papich would later say regarding Angleton's beliefs about Oswald and the Russians. "He and I had a lot of discussions on that. As far as we knew, Oswald acted alone. But Jim felt

---

104 Wedge: The Secret War Between the FBI and CIA. Mark Riebling, Alfred Knopf, New York, 1994. Page. 205.

that we couldn't be sure until we had the full story on Oswald's possible links to the KGB. That meant getting the full story on his stay in Russia."

When Jane Roman said that the CIA had a "keen interest in Oswald," she wasn't kidding.

Appendix 3

The Chicago Assassination Plot

The Warren Commission could only deal with the information that it received by the FBI and other governmental agencies and they did a poor job in what they had. But with the passage of time, new leads that could have altered their conclusion, if they had known about them, have come to light. One of the most startling is a plot that was hatched by certain unnamed individuals that was to have to taken place on November 2, 1963. The plot was discovered by local police and reported up the chain of command. In light of the plot, the presidents's motorcade to Chicago was cancelled at the last possible moment.

Two people who had knowledge of the plot to kill JFK in Chicago played a prominent part in the story, one, a CIA affiliated mobster, ex-Chicago policeman named Richard Cain, and the first African-American Secret Service Agent, Abraham Bolden.

The city of Chicago played two important roles in the life of President Kennedy, one when he was a candidate for president, the other, after he was elected.

As a candidate, Kennedy had to placate the boss of Chicago politics, its powerful Mayor, Richard Daley. In 1960, the political boss still held sway in American politics and any candidate for national office, especially the presidency, had to play nice with these powerful leaders. Kennedy was vying for the democratic nomination against a slew of other notable contenders, including

Lyndon Johnson, the Senate Majority Leader, Senator Stuart Symington, and lurking in the shadows, Adlai Stevenson, the son of Illinois, and a two-time democratic presidential nominee. Kennedy had to play nice with Mayor Daley who controlled three quarters of the sixty-nine convention delegates in the Illinois delegation. Mayor Daley decided to withhold his support to see how the political winds would blow and make his announcement at the most opportune time. In the end, the Illinois delegation, under the control of Mayor Daley, voted fifty-nine and a half for Kennedy and two for Stevenson. It is very probable that Kennedy's powerfully connected father, the former ambassador to Great Britain during World War 2, Joseph Kennedy, who owned a number of real estate holdings in Chicago, coaxed Mayor Daley into giving his son the necessary votes to lead him on his way to the nomination.

On election day, the Daley political organization provided enough votes in Chicago to swing Illinois to Kennedy (despite the charges of voter fraud).

In 1962, during the build up to the Cuban Missile Crisis, Kennedy was in Chicago to make a political trip and shmooze with Daley. Kennedy knew not to antagonize the Mayor and he needed him in his good graces for his 1964 re-election bid. During his stay in Chicago, events in Cuba took on an ominous turn, and Kennedy asked press secretary Pierre Salinger to draft a message to the press informing them that the president had come down with a cold and had to cancel the rest of his trip and return to Washington.

As 1964 approached, Kennedy decided to make a trip to Chicago and have discussions with the mayor and other Democratic leaders. The last thing Kennedy needed was to cancel again on Mayor Daley but as events would unfold, he had no choice.

The plot to kill Kennedy in Chicago has been brought to life by two researchers Lamar Waldron and Thomas Hartman in their huge, and well researched 2005 book, *Ultimate Sacrifice: John and Robert Kennedy, the Plan for a Coup in Cuba and the Murder of JFK* (Carroll and Graf Publishers). As described by the authors, the plot involved an assassin lurking in a high rise building overlooking the parade route through the city, with the presidential motorcade making a round-about route, sneaking its way across the city. This scenario was the same one used by the assassins in Dallas on November 22, only three weeks later.

JFK was supposed to arrive in Chicago on November 2 and, along with Mayor Daley and other Chicago civic leaders, attend the Army-Air Force football game to be held at Solder Field.

According to the testimony of Abraham Bolden, who a few years later, would break FBI protocol and try to contact the Warren Commission regarding the lax behavior of a number of Secret Service agents guarding JFK, that the CIA had known before hand that an attempt to kill the president was in works. Bolden said that on October 30, 1963, the FBI sent a teletype to the Chicago Secret Service Office saying that an attempt to kill the president would take place in Chicago on November 2 by a four man hit team using a high-powered rifle. He said the message was given to Maurice Martineau, the Special Agent in Charge. On the morning of November 2, SAC Martineau told his fellow agents the details of the plot, saying that the attack would take place as the motorcade traveled from O'Hare airport across the Northwest Expressway and down the famous Loop.

The shooters were supposed to be a group of "right-wing para-military fanatics." The source on these men was an informant named "Lee." No one knows who this Lee person was.[105]

It is interesting to note that when Lee Oswald bought the rifle he alleged used to kill the president, he purchased it my mail order through a company called Klein's Sporting Goods in Chicago. Why Oswald would purchase a gun in such an open way if he was going to use it in a crime is uncomprehensible.

Abraham Bolden would later be arrested for trying to sell a file to a man indicated for counterfeiting. He spent time as a

---

105 "JFK And the Unspeakable: Why He Died and Why It Matters." James Douglas, Orbis Books, Maryknoll, New York, 2008. Pg. 200.

prisoner at the Federal Medical Center in Springfield, Missouri. Bolden always said that he was arrested and framed because he tried to tell the Warren Commission about the "general laxity among Secret Service agents assigned to President Kennedy."

According to a CIA Memo dated 12/11/76 regarding an article in the *New York Times* called "Plot on Kennedy in Chicago Told," Bolden "told three lawyers about the plot to kill Kennedy in Chicago. The three lawyers were Mark Lane, who wrote a number of best-selling books on the Kennedy assassination, including "*Rush To Judgement,*" Richard Burnes, an Assistant District Attorney in the office of then New Orleans DA Jim Garrison, and John Hosmer, a former judge and prosecutor from Marshfield, Missouri. The lawyers said that they got the information from Bolden during a three day period while he was serving his prison sentence."[106]

The same memo cites other newspapers reporting on the possible Chicago plot, including the New York Times for May 23, 1964 in which the Warren Commission asked the FBI to look into allegations made by Bolden of heavy drinking among Kennedy's secret service detail.

It also mentions an article in the "Chicago American" of May 26, 1964 saying that Bolden refused to discuss his charges of laxity against fellow agents in an interview with the Warren Commission. The article also said that Bolden's attorney, George Howard, said he would not allow his client to testify if he was subpoenaed before the Warren Commission and that Bolden accepted his advice.

The memo also cites an article in the "Chicago American" of November 26, 1963, in a column "Daly Diary" by Maggie Daly, which said that a rumor had been going around that the assassination of the president was planned "at a meeting on Chicago's west side in the early part of February 1963 by a dissident Cuban group and that the FBI was investigating this group."

106 CIA Memo on New York Times Article Entitled "Plot on Kennedy in Chicago." RIF No. 1993.08.04.11.27.57.250064.

This same detailed memo concerns the actions of Richard Cain, a name not known to the Warren Commission in its 1964 investigation. Cain, who went by the alias "Richard Scalzetti," was once a member of the Chicago Police Department, as well as a close associate of Chicago mob boss Sam Giancana.

Richard Cain was an enigma, a man with little formal education, yet he became a high ranking Chicago police official, as well as a hit man for the Chicago mob. During his life, he aided the anti-Castro cause in Chicago, meeting with a number of high-ranking anti-Castro Cubans, making several trips to Cuba on behalf of these people, and at the same time, offering his services to the CIA, who read his reports, yet did not want to formalize their relationship with him. Cain, in the company of an unidentified woman, was sent to Cuba to kill Castro. According to Cain's account, he made it into the office of Fidel Castro but was not able to hid the poison that he was going use (his woman partner was caught and executed).

From May 16, 1956 until May 16, 1960, Cain worked for the Chicago Police Department and rose to the rank of detective in February 1958. He resigned from the police force in May 1960 because of an investigation that was started against him by the police. At the time of his arrest he was working for the Police Sex Bureau Squad. He was accused of spying on City Commissioner Irwin Cohen, and was alleged to have been paid $1,700 by the State's Attorney's Office. (There are numerous files on Richard Cain that can be found on the Mary Ferrell Foundation website, as well as detailed book on him by his half-brother, Michael Cain called *The Tangled Web: The Life and Death of Richard Cain-Chicago Cop and Mafia Hitman*).

The CIA began its interest in Cain when an article on Sam Giancana was published in the *Chicago Tribune* dated December 28, 1973. In the fall of 1960, Cain made contact with the Domestic Contact Division of the CIA and gave them information on the activities of anti-Castro organizations in Chicago. In June 1961, Cain contacted a Mr. Lohmann of the CIA's Chicago Field

Office. He said that he had been contacted by a man named Mr. Kroupansky "who reportedly was negotiating with the President of Panama to investigate communism in Panama. Cain was to assist Kroupansky in this endeavor." In the summer of 1961, Cain and an unidentified CIA staffer met in Mexico City for "purpose unknown." In October 1961, Cain again contacted Mr. Lohmann and reported on his meeting with his contacts in Panama. At that meeting he offered his services to the CIA.

On September 12, 1963, Cain gave the CIA information on members of the DRE, the anti-Castro group which was sponsored by the CIA, who were planning to buy weapons for their organization. Cain said that he was going to meet at a later date with these people but the CIA told him to "get out of the picture" as soon as possible and to make no commitments. During this time period, Cain gave the CIA eight reports concerning exile Cuban activities in the Chicago area.

It was in the article by Maggie Daly that the connection of Richard Cain to the Chicago assassination operation comes into play.

On November 29, 1963, the Chicago office of the CIA wrote a lengthily memo on the allegations made by Secret Service Agent Abraham Bolden, as well as information concerning Cain and the president's death. The memo said that Cain, "then employed by the Cook County Sheriff's Office, said that his department had received information, "that early in 1963 the Chicoms (Chinese Communists), took over the operations of the U.S. for the Fair Play for Cuba Committee. In February 1963, a secret meeting of the Committee was held at 907 South Spaulding, Chicago, under the direction of Richard Criley Secretary of the Chicago Chapter. At the meeting, the assassination of the President of the U.S. was discussed...Cain then added that the information that Lee Oswald purchased the rifle that was used in the assassination of President Kennedy in March 1963. Cain then said that the Cook County Sheriff's Office had not established that OSWALD was at the February meeting. However, they had strong suspicions that OSWALD was in Chicago in April."

Cain alleged that he was instructed by Sheriff Olgilvie to look into the matter himself, and to ask the FBI "officially" for information on the Fair Play For Cuba Committee. The local FBI office bluntly told Sheriff Olgilvie that the FBI had jurisdiction into the Kennedy case and that Cain should defer to them, not go it alone."

In 1967, the CIA's Office of Security began its own investigation of Cain for his ties to organized crime in Chicago, and the Bureau pushed the CIA to discontinue its relationship with Cain. The Bureau was right in its claims that Cain was a member of the Chicago mob, or Outfit as it was called. Cain was in deep with the members of the mob in the Windy City, and was especially close to Sam Giancana, the top mob boss in Chicago. Cain's goal was to be a top member of the Outfit in Chicago, while at the same time, making clandestine relationships with both the CIA and FBI. Unfortunately, he couldn't have it both ways.

Richard Cain's violent end came on December 20, 1973 when he was having a meal at Rose's Sandwich Shop in Chicago with mobster Marshall Caifano. Dick Cain unexpectedly left the restaurant at around 12:30 p.m. He returned one hour later and found Caifano gone. Suddenly, two men wearing ski masks burst into the diner, and lined Cain up against the wall. He was shot point blank with a shot gun and died instantly.

Besides looking for these so called "right wing para-military fanatics," another interesting character was in Chicago at the time that Kennedy was supposed to make his trip, a Cuban by the name of Miguel Casas Saez, a.k.a., "Angel Dominguez Martinez" It seems that the CIA and the Immigration and Naturalization Service were looking for Saez but they failed to notify the Secret Service.

The CIA generated a number of reports on Saez and knew that he was in fact, a Cuban espionage agent. Just what was he doing in Chicago at the time of Kennedy's trip and how, if anything, does it tie in with the attempt on his life in the city?

On CIA report contained the following information on Saez. "He was a resident of Remedios, Las Villas in Cuba and left Cuba on September 26, 1963 by small boat. Before arriving in the US, he was caught up in hurricane Flora and wound up in Puerto Rico. The source said that Saez was a member of the Militias in Remedios and Caibarien, Las Villas Province, and speaks Russian well. Once he arrived in the US he tried to buy a boat for "unknown purposes." The source said that he entered the US under alias Angel Dominguez Martinez, and believes that CASAS is up to no good in the U.S."

Another source called AMOT-28 said that Saez "went to the United States as in infiltration to sabotage and report on your plans there. Casas belonged to the G-2 and the D.T.I and was one of the mean militiamen."[107]

Another memo from the CIA's JMWAVE Station in Miami wrote this memo on Saez's activities in the United States. "Age 22-23, 5'10 Dark, Strong Build, Dark Brown Hair, Brown Eyes." An unnamed source said that "AMLAME-4 reports CASAS Aunt Lucia told her dentist that nephew Miguelito (Saez's nickname) in Dallas Texas day of Kennedy assassination, managed leave through Laredo. Boarded Far plane Mexico for Cuba. Dentist informed AMLAME-4 Casas had firing practice in militias and capable of doing anything."

Why was Miguel Casas Saez, a Cuban agent with such a high pedigree in Chicago at the time of Kennedy's trip and why wasn't the Secret Service, whose main responsibility was to protect he president not informed of his presence in the city? This was another glaring fact that was not brought to the attention of the Warren Commission.

Another person who was interviewed by the police in the wake of the president's canceled trip to Chicago was Thomas Arthur Vallee. On October 30, 1963, the Secret Service was told that Vallee, an outspoken opponent of JFK, owned a number of

107 RIF No. 104-34-10283 Subject: Miguel Casas Saez-Cuban in Dallas, Texas.

weapons and might pose a threat to the president. The FBI went to his residence and found that he had in his apartment two M-1 rifles, a 22 caliber revolver, and almost 1,000 rounds of ammunition. Vallee also worked in a building overlooking the Jackson Street ramp where Kennedy's motorcade would travel. The Secret Service told the Chicago P.D. about Vallee and they decided to put a surveillance team on to him to monitor his activities. Two members of the Chicago police department, Daniel Groth and Peter Schurla followed Vallee around the city and took him into custody on the morning of November 2, the day of Kennedy's trip. Both officers stopped Vallee in his car for making an improper turn signal. They found a hunting knife in the car, as well as ammunition stored in the trunk. If Vallee had planned to harm the president, he did not now pose a threat.

Thomas Arthur Vallee had a similar background to that of Lee Oswald, and if one were to be of a certain persuasion, might believe that both men were posed to take the fall in the event of a successful assassination attempt on the president, either in Chicago or in Dallas. Like Oswald, Vallee was an ex-Marine and had seen action in the Korean War where he suffered severe wounds. According to Waldron and Hartman in *Ultimate Sacrifice,* Thomas Vallee said that in 1963, he had been recruited to train certain anti-Castro individuals in an attempt to kill the Cuban leader. Vallee said that the training took place around Long Island, New York, not in the south where other documented training facilities for anti-Castro Cubans were located (New Orleans, the Florida Keys).

Vallee served in the Marines from 1949 to 1952 and had two years of college. Unlike Oswald, he was honorably discharged from the Marines and re-enlisted in the Marines on November 28, 1955. He was later discharged and was said to have suffered paranoid schizophrenic tendencies.

Vallee had ties to the ultra right wing John Birth Society, an anti-governmental organization that was popular during that time. Like Vallee, Oswald was portrayed, (by the FBI particularly), as a right wing sympathizer, even though he was never a member of an organized group of that political persuasion.

In the wake of Vallee's arrest, the local NBC TV affiliate in Chicago made inquires about Vallee. He was driving a 1962 Ford Falcon with the New York license plate number 31-10RF. A background check made at the behest of an employee of the Chicago TV station, Luke Hester, asked his father-in-law, Hugh Larkin, a retired New York City policeman, to check on Vallee's car. It turned out that any information on the license plate was "frozen," meaning, that only the FBI was able to find out such information.[108]

Vallee also had other similarities to Oswald. While in the Marines, he was stationed in Japan at Camp Otsu, which, like Oswald's posting, was also the site of the U-2 spy plane. Vallee told a reporter that while he was at Camp Otsu, he was under CIA control.

Like Oswald, Vallee got a job in a warehouse on the route of JFK's Chicago trip. He worked as a printer in a company called IPP Litho-Plate which was located at 625 West Jackson Boulevard. Vallee worked on the third floor and if he was slated to be the fall guy assassin, would have had a good location on which to shoot a rifle on the approaching motorcade.

The story from a retired Chicago police Lt. by the name of Berkeley Moyland adds more to the story of Thomas Arthur Vallee and his possible role in the assassination attempt in Chicago. Lt. Moyland frequently ate a his favorite restaurant in Chicago and got to know the manager well. According to Moyland's account, one day a customer came into the diner and made disparaging comments about JFK. The manager told Lt. Moyland who was at the restaurant the next time Vallee showed up. Moyland had a personal talk with Vallee and from his brief discussion, determined that Vallee had mental problems and possibly posed a threat to the president. Lt. Moyland then phoned the Secret Service and told

108 JFK And the Unspeakable. James Douglas, Page. 203.

them about his talk with Vallee. The Secret Service investigated Vallee and due to the dogged work by the FBI, he was not on the street when Kennedy's trip to Chicago was planned. Lt. Moyland also told the U.S. Treasury Department of his encounter with Vallee and he was told in no uncertain terms not to talk with anyone about the incident and just forget it. In an ironic twist to the story, sometime later, Lt. Moyland and Thomas Vallee met for one last time at the diner, like two old friends, getting together after some time.[109]

It seems that Vallee had no connection to the four man sniper team that the Secret Service was following. The Secret Service picked up the trail of two of the four men and traced their location to a rooming house where they were staying. While following them in an unmarked car, two of the suspects suddenly reversed their direction and passed the approaching agents who saw them drive by. The agents were able to catch up with the fleeing men and they were taken back to the office of the Chicago Secret Service. The agents did not find any weapons in their car nor at their place of residence.

Abraham Bolden would later say that the men who were taken into custody at the Secret Service headquarters at that time did not look like Thomas Vallee. Bolden testified years later that the men taken in for questing gave their names as being "Gonzales and Rodriguez." While "Gonzales and Rodriguez" were being questioned, the other two shooters quietly slipped out of town. Soon, both men were also released and the feds were never able to determine just who these two suspicious men were or what, if anything they were planning, vis-a-vi JFK's trip to Chicago.

To add to the mystery of what happened in Chicago, Bolden said that all the notes taken by the Secret Service regarding the investigation into the possible assassination attempt on the president were flown out of Chicago en-route to Washington. The Chicago SS agents were told "to discuss no aspect of the

109 Ibid. Page 206-207.

assassination and investigation with anyone from any other federal agency now or in any time in the future."

Thomas Vallee was never called before the Warren Commission and the files on him remain sealed to this day.

There are more than a number of unanswered questions regarding the circumstances of the attempted assassination plot against Kennedy in Chicago on November 2, 1963. Were their any ties between Thomas Arthur Vallee and the CIA (remember, he said he was training anti-Castro people in New York for an attempt on Castro's life), and what were the real names of the two men taken into custody by the Secret Service and why were they released? Who were the other two suspected hit men who fled Chicago at the time their compatriots were arrested and was their any complicity between state or federal officials with them? Why were the Chicago SS agents told not to discuss the case with any other federal agency? Why are the files on Thomas Vallee still classified, fifty years later?

Appendix 4

The Tides of Change: 2000-2011

The material in this section describes the most recent research on the Kennedy assassination that has been divulged by writers and historians in the past few years. They give the reader a new perspective on a wide ranging tableau of issues on the Kennedy case that were not known to the Warren Commission back in 1964. A lot of material in this section concentrates on the wide spread US government efforts to topple the Castro regime, as well as information on the CIA's effort to spy on the anti-Castro groups in 1963, and its tangential links to the alleged assassin, Lee Oswald. Information on various people who played a key role in the anti-Castro plots and other, relevant matters, are also described in the following pages.

1) Robert Kennedy's Secret CIA Probe.

When the Congress passed the *1992 JFK Records Act,* historians and writers were able to take a birds eye view of the thousand days of the administration of John F. Kennedy. The primary focus of the act was to open to an eager public, all relevant documents concerning the assassination of President Kennedy. While this story does not concentrate on the assassination, the declassified record has brought to light a hither to secret investigation conducted by the CIA in Mexico City after the events in Dallas, and the role that Attorney General Robert Kennedy played in its eventual outcome.

The first person to report on the covert visit of Robert Kennedy to Mexico was author and former military intelligence officer John Newman in his book *Oswald and the CIA.* Robert Kennedy's visit to Mexico City is full of intrigue as his trip coincided with the ongoing CIA internal investigation of the alleged assassin, Lee Harvey Oswald's time spent in that city. According to released CIA files, the person who brought to light RFK's trip to Mexico was a CIA officer named June Cobb.

In 1960, Cobb worked at the Ministry Office of Fidel Castro in Havana, Cuba and was one of Castro's closets aids. Her name was brought to the attention of the CIA who was monitoring Castro after the overthrow of the Batista government in 1959. When Miss Cobb came to New York she was approached by CIA officer Henry Hermsdorf. In time, Hermsdorf was able to "turn" Miss Cobb into an American agent, reporting on Castro and his inner circle. According to Cobb's account, Attorney General Robert Kennedy made a secret trip to the Mexican capital in either September or October 1964, in conjunction with the CIA's investigation of his brother's death. The CIA's own files confirm that RFK was in Mexico City at the time.

One of the most important CIA officers to handle the agency's investigation of Lee Oswald in Mexico City was Winston Scott. Scott was the CIA's Mexico City Station Chief at that time. Scott wrote a long manuscript on the CIA's investigation of Oswald under the pen name "Willard Curtis." In his "memo for the file," Scott wrote of Bobby Kennedy's journey. "She (Elana Garro, who met Oswald in Mexico City in September 1963) ,wanted to tell him (RFK) she had personally met Lee Harvey Oswald when he was here in Mexico City. She said she had met him and two friends at the home of Horacio and Silvia Duran."

In doing the research for his book, Newman conducted an interview with former FBI agent James Hosty who was keeping tabs on Oswald and his wife Marina in Dallas, Texas in the months preceding the assassination. Hosty said that Thomas Karamessines, then the CIA's deputy director for plans, was also in Mexico City to "call off the investigation."

After leaving the city, the U.S. Ambassador to Mexico, Thomas Mann, called off the inquiry into Oswald's alleged southern sojourns. Hosty went further and said that his CIA contacts inside the US embassy in Mexico City heard Robert Kennedy ordering that any future probes to be stopped; they weren't.

Why Robert Kennedy went to Mexico City is still not known, but his visit might have been a reaction to his war against organized crime and its then secret collaboration with the CIA in their plots to kill Castro.

After the assassination of his brother, RFK was nagged by the thought that if he hadn't gone after the mob so ruthlessly (the HSCA said that organized crime had the "means, motive, and opportunity" to kill JFK), his brother might still be alive.

Maybe RFK wanted to stop the inquiry before any more damaging information concerning his brother, and any other elements connected to either the CIA or the mob in the aftermath of the assassination would be exposed. RFK's trip to Mexico City needs further clarification in the files still classified by the government.

2) Howard Hunt's JFK Confession.

The name of E. Howard Hunt is well known to those people interested in the Kennedy assassination as someone who probably knew more about the event than he ever revealed. Howard Hunt is also known for his role as a member of the Watergate burglars who were arrested trying to break into the headquarters of the Democratic National Headquarters in the Watergate Hotel. The Watergate affair led to the resignation of Richard Nixon in August 1974. However, new information has come to the fold in recent years that shed new light on Hunt's role in the assassination of the president, and the men who, according to Hunt, participated in the plot.

Shortly before his death in 2007, Howard Hunt wrote his memoir called *An American Spy: My Secret History in the CIA.* If anyone really believed that Hunt would reveal something earth shattering about the Kennedy assassination, they were wrong. That task would fall on the shoulders of his son, St. John Hunt who had a rather adversarial, so to speak, relationship with his father.

St. John Hunt took an active interest in the Kennedy assassination years after the event and was shocked to see a photo of the so called Three Tramps who were arrested in Dallas shortly after the president's death. St. John said that one of the tramps looked strikingly like his father. E. Howard Hunt always maintained that he was in Washington D.C. on November 22, 1963. St. John says that based on his recollections, his father was NOT at home when he returned from school that day. He also said that he never was really there for him when he most needed a father figure and that Hunt only had (the elder Hunt's) best interest in mind. St. John did reveal that he aided his father in destroying a suitcase that contained the electronic equipment that was used in the Watergate burglary. Both son and father went to the banks of the C& O Canal in Hunt's Pontiac Firebird and dropped the suitcase into the muddy water, never to be seen again.

In the months before Hunt's death, he called St. John to his bedside to tell him what he knew of his life in the CIA and more importantly, his knowledge of the Kennedy assassination. St. John Hunt took notes, as well as recording the conversation. The elder Hunt mailed the tape to his son in January 2007, and in a radio interview which was given wide spread publicity on the web, Hunt revealed the names of the men whom he alleged took part in the planning of JFK's murder. Most of these men had pivotal roles in the Kennedy administration's secret war against Castro. The names Hunt revealed were: Frank Sturgis, David Morales, David Atlee Phillips, Antonio Veciana, William

Harvey, Cord Meyer, a French Gunman Grassy Knoll and Lyndon Johnson.[110]

Hunt said he played no active role in the assassination planning but was just a "bench warmer" in their discussions. During his confession, Hunt wrote down the names of the people who were involved in the plot like a flow chart, connecting each dot as it went along its natural path. He wrote down "LBJ (Lyndon Johnson) first, followed by lines for each of the other players; Cord Meyer, who became the second highest ranking member of the CIA's Clandestine Staff, (also, JFK was having an affair with Cord Meyer's wife, Mary), Bill Harvey, who ran the Cuban plots and nurtured a bitter hatreds towards both Kennedy brothers, David Morales, a tough, CIA agent who worked in Havana and later in the CIA's JM/WAVE station in Miami, and had numerous connections with the top bosses in organized crime in the US, Frank Sturgis of Watergate fame, and a member of Gerry Hemming's IPF (intercontinental Penetration Force), David Phillips, a CIA propaganda officer who was stationed in Mexico City at the same time that Oswald was supposed to have been in that city, Antonio Veciana, the leader of the militant, anti-Castro organization ALPHA 66, and finally, the so called French gunman on the Grassy Knoll, possibly Lucien Sarti."

The scenario that Hunt laid out was that LBJ ordered the assassination of the president and passed on his instructions to the rest of the group. By implying that Lucien Sarti, a member of the Corsican underworld was on the grassy knoll, firing at the president, disproves the Oswald as the lone gunman theory into a conspiracy involving at least two people, possibly more. St. John Hunt states that his father gave him a document that spelled out how the conspiracy unfolded. Cord Meyer discussed the plot with David Atlee Phillips, who then met with William Harvey and Antonio Veciana. Oswald had a meeting with the

110 The Last Confession of Howard Hunt. RollingStone.com. Posted March 21, 2007.

above mentioned men in Mexico City. Veciana then meets with Frank Sturgis in Miami who brings David Morales into the plot. There is a change in the location of the assassination plot and it is finally agreed that Dallas is the place where the event will take place.

Hunt goes on to describe his involvement in the assassination planning. In 1963 he met with Morales and Sturgis in a Miami hotel room. Morales takes his leave and in comes Frank Sturgis who talks about a "Big Event" and wants to know if Hunt is willing to go along with their plans. Hunt asked Sturgis what the plan is and Sturgis replies, "Killing JFK." Hunt then asks Sturgis why he needs him. Hunt tells them that he wants no part of the deal.

St. John writes that he was shocked to hear of his father's confession, believing that he had been lied to over the decades by him and his constant denials that he had anything to do with the assassination.

Can Howard Hunt's death bed confession be true? If it is, then Hunt was a participant after the fact, knowing just what was going to happen, and did nothing to stop it. Or was it just a made up story that could be used to sell more books? (It should be noted that these allegations were not part of Hunt's memoire). St. John said that prior to his father's death, the elder Hunt was "deeply conflicted and deeply remorseful" that he didn't tell authorities about his foreknowledge of the assassination plot. But, once again, can we believe him? The Hunt allegation just adds fuel to the fire revolving around his probable links to the president's death

3). John Whitten. A.K.A. "John Scelso."

Until recently, the name of John Whitten, was not known to Kennedy assassination researchers. He went by the code name "John Scelso," as was written in the CIA's early investigation of the assassination. Whitten's role in the CIA's investigation of Oswald's activities are paramount in our knowledge of how the agency fudged its conclusions and decided to let Whitten and his staff of thirty analysts learn all they could about what transpired on November 22, 1963. If Whitten had been provided with all the detailed information available at the time, it is possible that the Warren Commission may have come to a different conclusion about Oswald and his possible association (if any) with the Castro government.

Less than twelve hours after the president was killed, the CIA was alive with activity as analysts were called in to learn all they could about the man they had in custody in Dallas. Whitten, at 43-years old, was the chief of the covert operations branch for Mexico City and Central America. Whitten had been on the phone with CIA Mexico City Chief Winston Scott when Scott told him that the CIA had on file a photograph of Lee Oswald entering the Cuban consulate that October. Whitten asked Scott to send the picture to him as soon as possible. What the picture showed was that Oswald had visited both the Cuban consulate and Russian Embassy. What was Oswald, a former Marine, doing at the embassies of America's enemies?

As Whitten began his investigation, it soon became apparent that he was being stymied in his search by none other than Richard Helms who stopped him from looking into Oswald's Cuba related activities in New Orleans in the summer of 1963, information that the FBI had on hand for months. In the end, Helms's decision to withhold vital information from John Whitten forced him to end his investigation and stop an avenue of intelligence that may have altered what the public knew about the activities of Lee Oswald, and have clouded the investigation of the JFK case for decades to come.

The name "John Scelso" was hidden from the public for as long as John Whitten was alive. However, when he died in January 2000 in a Pottstown, Pennsylvania nursing home, his identity was finally unveiled. In an interview shortly before his own death in Washington, D.C. on October 22, 2002, Richard Helms, when asked who John Scelso was said, "I don't recall the name."

John Whitten was born in 1920 in Annapolis, Maryland. He graduated from the University of Maryland and entered the US Army where he was posted to an intelligence unit interrogating German POW's. After the war ended, he returned to school and graduated from the University of Virginia's Law School. In 1947, he joined the CIA and for many years served in both Washington and Vienna (he would later retire to Vienna at the end of his life). By March 1962, he was promoted to the agency's Western Hemisphere Division. In March 1963, he was promoted to be chief of all CIA covert operations in Mexico City and Central America. So, it was to John Whitten's purview that the CIA turned to in order to look into the activities of Lee Oswald in the early hours of November 23, 1963.

In a frantic search for whatever tidbits of information he could find, Whitten, using only the information provided to him by the CIA, was able to report to Helms that Oswald was the sole assassin of the president and that he had no confederates at large. Whitten's preliminary findings were sent to the new president, Lyndon Johnson. Whitten thought his probe was over. However, that was not the case, as he would soon learn to his chagrin.

On December 6, 1963, Whitten was sent to the White House to look at the FBI report that had been prepared on Lee Oswald. To his shock, he found out that Helms had not been forthcoming with him about all of Oswald's activities. The most important information that Helm's withheld from Whitten dealt with Oswald's associations with anti-Castro people in New Orleans, as well as his membership in the FPCC. Whitten was shocked to learn of Oswald's Cuban connections and he voiced his objections to Helms in a no nonsense manner. To his amazement, Helms relieved Whitten of his duties and the investigation was turned over to the office of James Angleton, the head of the Counter-Intelligence division. Years later, when his almost 200 page deposition was released, Whitten said that his opinion of Oswald's guilt or innocence was subject to change. He said that he changed his mind about Oswald guilt by saying, "it was obviously, completely irrelevant in view of all this Bureau information." He also said, "Oswald's involvement with the pro-Castro movement in the United States was not all surfaced to us in the first weeks of the investigation."[111]

Angleton, it seems, had his own hidden agenda when it came to informing the Warren Commission on Oswald's links to both the Soviets and the Cubans. Angleton worked closely with commission member Allen Dulles who had been fired by JFK after the abortive Bay of Pigs invasion. The ace up Angleton's sleeve was a Russian defector named Yuri Nosenko who had come out of the cold and was taken in by the CIA. During his debriefing, Nosenko told his CIA handlers a rather intriguing story. He said that he was the KGB's controlling officer who handled the Oswald case when the ex-Marine defected to the Soviet Union. Nosenko said that the KGB had no operational interest in Oswald in the 2 ½ years that the lived in the Soviet Union. Angleton believed that Nosenko was a disinformation agent sent by the Russians to fool the CIA into believing his tale was true. Nosenko also said that the Soviet's had no role in the president's assassination.

Angleton worked with Dulles, feeding him all the information that came out of the debriefing sessions with Nosenko. In their deliberations, Dulles never once told the other commission members of the ties between the Mafia and the CIA to kill Castro.

A cryptic remark made by Angleton years after the assassination left many people wondering what he really meant to say. Angleton said regarding the Kennedy assassination, "A mansion has many rooms and there were many things going on. I a not privy to who struck John."

As Whitten began his investigation, he was immediately stymied on two fronts, one, from Angleton, and two, the FBI. The Bureau sent his team thousands of documents that they

---

111 The Good Spy, Jefferson Morley www. Washingtonmonthly.com December 2003.

knew Whitten and his staff could never read. Whitten called the information given to him by the FBI as "Weirdo stuff." Among the information that Whitten was not told by the FBI on Oswald's association with both pro and anti-Castro people in New Orleans, his alleged attack on right-wing general, Edwin Walker in Dallas in 1963, and the contents of Oswald's "historic diary" which he supposedly penned while he lived in Russia. Even more surprising was the fact that Whitten, who was supposed to have been knowledgeable of all CIA activities in Latin America and Mexico, had never been made aware of Oswald before November 22, 1963, even though the various U.S. intelligence agencies had a file on him since his defection in 1959.

When he later testified before the HSCA in 1979, Whitten said that if he had been informed of Oswald's Cuban ties he would have focused his investigation of the "possible involvement of the (CIA's) Miami Station." He told the HSCA that he did not believe that Oswald was in any way connected to the CIA, but after he learned of the Executive Action operation, he remarked that he could not rule out any agency ties to Oswald.

In his testimony before the HSCA, Whitten pulled no punches in his condemnation of the actions of Richard Helms and William Harvey. He called Harvey, the head of ZR/RIFLE-Executive Action "a thug." He had hard words for his old boss, Helms, saying that Helms violated "every operational precept, every bit of operational experience, every ethical consideration." (It is no wonder that Helms denied ever knowing a "John Scelso").

When asked by the commission if he thought William Harvey was involved in the president's assassination he said probably not. When he was told that immediately after Harvey's death, his wife destroyed his personal papers, believing Harvey may have had a "smoking gun," he said of Harvey, "He was too young to have assassinated McKinley and Lincoln. It could have been anything."

More important to his investigation, Whitten was not told of the identity of George Joannides who took over as the CIA's liaison with the DRE in Miami in 1963. Joannides was the paymaster to the anti-Castro group and followed closely Oswald's activities in New Orleans, including his meeting with Carlos Bringuier and other DRE members in the Crescent City. It was Helms who deliberately withheld the Joannides file from Whitten so the latter could not delve into Oswald's anti-Castro activities. Both Angleton and Helms desperately wanted to keep any mention of the Castro-Oswald connection secret, and put the blame on the assassination of the president squarely on the shoulders of the men in Moscow.

The "Scelso Report," is ripe with how far the CIA went in its internal investigation of Oswald, a fact that was deliberately withheld from the Warren Commission. When questioned about the Oswald file at CIA, Whitten's remarks were more than interesting. He told how the CIA did not have a substantional file on Oswald (not true) before the assassination (he called it a "scan file), made up mostly of information given to the CIA by the Navy, the Marine Corps, and information provided by the agency in Mexico City. He said that he had previously dealt with many other defector cases in the past and that Oswald incident was just "a typical case."

According to Whitten, the CIA first learned of Lee Oswald on the day of the assassination when his name was broadcast on TV and radio and "an officer of my branch came running in and said, with telegrams on Lee Harvey Oswald which we had sent, those telegrams which had gone out before the assassination. About a half hour after the assassination or fifteen minutes later, than we were all listening to this. I do not know how long after the actual shooting it was that Oswald's name became known, perhaps an hour and a half. Within minutes after that, they were out with the cables in their hands."

Whitten further stated that there was a fair amount of intelligence sharing cooperation between the CIA and the Bureau and other US intelligence agencies in Mexico City in the months preceding the assassination. The CIA passed along all information to J. Edgar Hoover's G-Men on leads on any American citizen in Mexico City who appeared around the Soviet and Cuban Embassies, and anybody who was possibly trying to defect. A similar arrangement was formalized with military intelligence.

Whitten had some very interesting comments to make on a number of the principle actors in the US intelligence community whose names played a prominent role in the investigation of the Kennedy assassination; James Angleton, David Atlee Phillips, William Harvey and Mr. Helms.

According to Whitten, who was related to David Atlee Phillips through marriage, Phillips was "one of the most brilliant, capable officers I have ever known, and nothing has happened since then that has changed my judgement."

When asked if it were possible that David Phillips ever sent out disinformation concerning the JFK assassination, Whitten said, "No, but I can conceive that it might have happened in the Mexico station. Perhaps they did, in their propaganda efforts which were going full-blast all the time, put in newspaper articles and so on to discredit somebody, some foreign power, in connection with the operation. I do not believe it was ever a policy to do so, but they were pretty much independent in formulating their propaganda."

Whitten also commented on the famous "mystery man" photograph that the CIA took in Mexico City that proved not to have been Oswald. He told his interviewer that the CIA had not received this photograph prior to the assassination, and when it was received, he did not know of the picture was the real Lee Oswald. While it seems that Whitten was kept out of the loop of information concerning who the mystery man was, he did say that he was certain that the CIA surveillance team did not photograph everyone who entered the Soviet Embassy. He said that the case officers whom he personalty spoke to regarding the mystery man photo were Win Scott and David Phillips, but cannot recall if Phillips was physically in Mexico City at the time of the assassination. The only clue to this man's identity, according to

Whitten, was that the CIA "conjectured that it (he) was a Mexican seaman."

According to Whitten's testimony before the HSCA, "Angleton ignored Helms' orders that no one was to discuss the (Kennedy assassination) without my being present. He ignored that. I tried to get Helms to make him obey and Helms said, 'You go tell him.'"

Angleton, according to Whitten's testimony, kept on meeting clandestinely with the FBI and also certain members of the Warren Commission which were in direct violation of Helms' orders. But, continues Whitten, Helms refused to stop Angleton from conducting these secret meetings. Angleton did not invite Whitten to these affairs, since they were done under the table, without official CIA sanction.

While he was in the middle of his investigation, Helms suddenly turned the probe into the hands of Angleton's CI Staff. This was done because of the Soviet angle that had been discovered, i.e., Oswald's two year stint in the Soviet Union, etc. Thus, the Soviet connection now took over from the almost as important Cuban connection that most likely would have lead to even more important clues as to why President Kennedy was killed.

It's obvious that Whitten did not like Richard Helms and his deposition is as ripe as a fruit on the vine. Speaking again about Helm's and his relationship with Bill Harvey, Whitten said that he was shocked that he had appointed Harvey to create the secret assassination plots called "Executive Action." "I think," continued Whitten, "on the fact that Helms did not inform the Warren Commission on the Castro assassination plots, that was a morally highly reprehensible act, which he cannot possibly justify under his oath of office, or any other standard of professional service."

Asked why he thought Helms failed to tell the WC about the Castro plots he said that, "I think that Helms withheld the information because he realized it would have cost him his job and would have precipitated a crisis for the agency, which could have a very adverse effects on the agency."

After departing the CIA, Whitten and his family left the United States and moved to Vienna, Austria. There, he took up opera and joined the Vienna Men's Choral Society. In Vienna, he never revealed his secret past.

It is clear that the information contained in the "Scelso Report" is one of the most important documents to be released by the AARB before it went out of business. We now have a clearer picture as to the mechanics of the early CIA probe into JFK's assassination, which people were assigned to perform certain tasks, the failure of the CIA to cooperate fully with the WC, and Whitten's revealing comments on the main people inside the agency, i.e., William Harvey, James Angleton, Richard Helms, among others, and how they conducted themselves in the assassination investigation.

Judge John Tunheim, who was the chairman of the JFK Records Review Board said of the "Scelso deposition," that it was "perhaps the single most important documents we uncovered." With the release of "Scelso's" real name, (John Whitten), at last one sleeping dog has now been put to rest.

4). Victor Espinosa Hernandez.

The name of Victor Espinosa Hernandez has recently come to the attention of JFK researchers from documents by the HSCA. He was a young man who had ties with many people, as well as groups, both in the United States and Europe who were actively planning an assassination plot against Castro and his top aids. He was also well connected with Rolando Cubela a.k.a. AMLASH, a CIA sponsored Cuban doctor who was preparing his own plot to kill Castro.

Victor Espinosa Hernandez was born in Cuba and came from a wealthy family whose business included farming and the petroleum industry. He went to the University of Havana for only one year before dropping out, and worked for the anti-Batista cadre inside Cuba. In 1955 he left Cuba for the United States where he enrolled in LSU-Louisiana State University. The Louisiana connection to the Kennedy assassination is well documented before, and there is no need to repeat the entire story here. Suffice it to say that a number of people connected with the plots to kill Castro and Kennedy began their operations in New Orleans, including such people as David Ferrie, Clay Shaw, Guy Banister, and others, including Lee Oswald who was born in New Orleans, and spent the summer of 1963 in the city, plying his trade as a possible double agent.

Upon the death of his grandfather, Victor returned to Cuba to manage the family business. He came into contact with many of the mob figures who were then encased in the lucrative casino business in Havana including, Mike McLaney and Norman "Roughhouse" Rothman.

He joined a group that took part in an assassination attempt against members of the Batista government. One of his co-conspirators was Rolando Cubela, who would later play a prominent role in the Castro plots.

After Castro took power, he took refuge in the United States, living both in Miami and New York. He was recruited to become a member of the team of exiles who were plotting the invasion at the Bay of Pigs and took military training in Guatemala and at a camp outside of New Orleans. He participated in several, covert missions inside Cuba but did not specify what these missions were.

In August 1963, the FBI interviewed two men named Rich Lauchli and Ralph Folkers who gave them information regarding the activities of Victor Hernandez. Folkers identified a picture of Hernandez as the person who "rented a U-Haul Trailer at Collinsville, Illinois on 7-11-63 destined for New Orleans, Louisiana. Lauchli orally admitted selling 2,400 pounds of dynamite in July 1963 to one VICTOR, who resembles VICTOR ESPINOSA HERNANDEZ. Lauchli claims VICTOR did not say why he wanted dynamite or where he obtained money to buy the same. Lauchli suspected dynamite was to be used against CASTRO."

In documents available via the HSCA investigation, both he FBI and CIA had interviews with Espinosa on an on-going basis.

An FBI document dated July 2, 1965, tells of a debriefing session by Bureau agents with Espinosa. William Doyle of the CIA informed the FBI on June 4, 1965, that Harold Swenson had come from Washington, D.C. to interview Espinosa. Also in attendance at the meeting was Special Agent Francis J. O'Brien.

"After ESPINOSA departed the NYO, Swenson advised that 98 per cent of the information furnished regarding the alleged assassination plots by ESPINOSA was accurate, and that the only reservation CIA has was that they disliked the two individuals who had contacted ESPINOSA concerning the plot and considered the contacts ESPINOSA, ALBERTO BLANCO, a.k.a. "El Loco" and JORGE ROBENO a.k.a, "Mago," to be individuals of questionable reputation."

Shortly after that meeting, both Blanco and Robeno left for Europe, with Robeno heading for Madrid, Spain, while Blanco was in Paris, France. A few days later, Espinosa contacted the New York Office of the CIA, telling them that he heard from Robeno and Blanco regarding any possible CIA assistance in their plots against Castro. On June 25, 1965, CIA agent William Doyle contracted Harold Swenson asking for assistance in this matter. Swenson told Doyle should inform Espinosa that, "This is a very difficult and far reaching question in which CIA could not definitely commit itself. Espinosa was to be advised that all the information furnished by him regarding the alleged plot to assassinate leading Cuban Government figures had been passed on in Washington, D.C. to the proper authorities, and that for the time being, CIA could not give any definite answer to Espinosa and his friends who were involved in this plot."

Despite his association with the CIA, Espinosa had bitter feelings toward them, as are evident in some of the released documents on him. In a report written by John Hart to Hal Swenson regarding Espinosa, he writes, "Paraphrase of the source's story;

I do not have a high regard for the CIA or for most of the exiled Cubans but I am against the Castro regime for which reason I have become involved in these matter about which I must be sure the CIA is informed."

"After Castro took over, I left Cuba and engaged in anti-Castro activities. I got shot in the process, I was betrayed by some of the Cuban exiles when I was going to bomb Cuba. I saw how the CIA bungled and I became bitter. I was bitter about Rolando (Cubela) too. I thought that he had turned communist. I sent him a message a long time ago, telling him that he was a traitor and no friend of mine."

"Some of the CIA people are not trustworthy. This is what bothers Rolando Cubela and El Lobo and El Mago and me too. This is why Rolando wants me to get his message through. He wants answers fast. The message is that Cubela and the others with him are able to kill Fidel and the others in the regime, but they need some help and they need to know whether the CIA and the U.S. Government are with them and willing to support them or not."[112]

In 1965, Espinosa traveled to France and Spain to meet clandestinely with members of the anti-Castro cause. While in Paris, "he was in contact with individuals involved in plot to assassinate Fidel Castro and leading Cuban Government Personalities." One of the men whom he met while in Paris was Rolando Cubela. He also met with Albert Blanco for a ten day period. Blanco worked for the Cuban Foreign Ministry and was in Paris to make a tour of the Cuban Embassy in France. Espinosa expressed the opinion that "He (Blanco) had no prior knowledge of this plot and went to Paris on the urging of Cubela, who has been a life-long friend of his. He also stated that involved in the plot was Major Juan Almeida Bosque." (More about him later in this chapter). According to the declassified files, Bosque was then serving as the First Deputy Minister of the Cuban Revolutionary Armed Forces.

---

112 RIF No. 104-10169-10253. "CIA Ops and Plot to kill Fidel Castro, Raul Castro and Other Key Figures of the Present Regime in Cuba."

"Espinosa advised that the plot calls for the assassination of Fidel Castro, Raul Castro, Ernesto "Che" Guevara and Ramiro Valdes. The assassination of these individuals is to take place in public so that everyone can see that the leaders have been killed. The plotters hope to seize the radio station and call for American help." The targeted date for the murder was July 26, 1965 which was to coincide with the July 26th celebration in Havana.

The information that Espinosa gave to the CIA regarding the plots to kill the leaders of the Cuban government were so sensitive that they were "restricted to the White House and the Attorney General."

5). Gilberto Lopez.

In the aftermath of the Kennedy assassination, the HSCA came across the name of an American citizen named Gilberto Lopez whose actions, before and after the assassination, paralleled those of Lee Oswald.

Gilberto Lopez was a resident of Florida, was 22-years-old, and spent time in both Key West and Tampa in 1962 and 1963. He was born on January 26, 1940. Lopez married an American woman named Andrea Leon Blanch and there is a record of their marriage licence application dated August 10-11, 1962. Like Lee Oswald, Gilberto Lopez entered Mexico on November 23, 1963, one day after the assassination, after obtaining a tourist card in Tampa, Florida, three days previously. Lopez left the United States at Nuevo Laredo on Nov. 23 on Cubana Airlines flight 465. He used his valid American passport, as well as a valid Cuban visa. It has also been stated that he attended a meeting of the Tampa branch of the FPCC on November 1, 1963. To add to the mystery, he was in Texas (bound for Mexico) on the day of the president's death.

While in Mexico, Lopez stayed at the Roosevelt Hotel until November 27, 1963. On that day, he left for Cuba as the only passenger on a Cubana airlines flight to Havana. Why was he the only one on board? Was there some special arrangement by the Cuban government that allowed Gilberto Lopez to travel to Cuba in such unusual circumstances?

Lee Oswald arrived in Mexico in late September 1963 en-route to Havana. It is also alleged that he tried to infiltrate the Tampa branch of the FPCC.

The CIA first got wind of the actions of Gilberto Lopez in December 1963 when they received a message that requested "urgent traces on U.S. citizen Gilberto Lopez." This information on Lopez was also in the hands of the F.B.I., who also wanted to learn as much about the activities of Lopez as the CIA did.

The CIA's interest in Lopez was on going in its earliest stages as per a photograph of Lopez that was given to the HSCA in 1978. The committee was given a picture of Lopez dated November 27, 1963, wearing sunglasses. That is the same date that Lopez left Mexico for Cuba. It stands to reason that the CIA Station in Mexico was aware of Lopez and was indeed taking pictures of him for future reference.

In August 1964, Lopez's cousin, Guillermo Serpa Rodriguez, was interviewed by the FBI at his home in Key West, Florida. Rodriguez said that Gilberto came to the United States after Castro came to power, resided in this country for about one year, and then returned to Cuba to see his family. He then returned to the U.S. by the end of 1961, fearing that he was about to be drafted into the Cuban army.

The FBI also spoke to Gilberto Lopez's wife, who stated that her husband had suffered epileptic attacks and was briefly hospitalized in Miami in 1963. He also was treated by doctors in both Key West and Coral Gables. She further said that she received a letter from her husband sometime in November 1963, saying that he had returned to Cuba. (Of which she was surprised). She also said that her husband attended a meeting in early November of the Tampa chapter of the FPCC and that some one in that organization probably gave him the money to get back to Cuba. Later, his wife said that she had learned via a person in the Tampa FPCC that indeed, her husband had safely arrived in Cuba.

As the Warren Commission was investigating the Kennedy murder, the CIA, in March 1964, received via a secure source, information on Lopez that he was involved in the Kennedy assassination. The source said that while in Mexico, Lopez visited the Cuban Embassy on November 27. Despite these tantalizing clues, the CIA failed to take the Lopez information seriously, prompting the HSCA in 1978 to question, "why the CIA had not taken more aggressive investigative steps to determine whether there had been a connection between Lopez and the assassination."

When Lopez lived in Key West, he worked for a construction company. In the article by Tim Gratz and Mark Howell in the November 20, 2003 edition of the *Key West Citizen*, the reporters wrote that the construction industry in Tampa during that time period was heavily influenced with the mob and that if Lopez' travels to Texas and Mexico might have some connection with the activities of the Tampa mob boss, Santo Trafficante.

The CIA began its own file on Gilberto Lopez on December 16, 1963, labeling it as a "counterintelligence case," meaning that it had to do with a foreign intelligence organization (possibly Cuban intelligence).

Both the CIA and FBI failed to provide sufficient information to the Warren Commission on the activities of Lopez prior to the assassination. American intelligence reports on Lopez' activities immediately after the assassination were labeled "suspicious," yet, a thorough investigation was not conducted.

Lamar Waldron and Tom Hartman, in their book *Ultimate Sacrifice,* add further interesting information on Gilberto Lopez. Lopez' brother lived in the Soviet Union at the time of Gilberto's Cuban adventures (Oswald too lived in the Soviet Union). The authors say that one of their law enforcement sources in Florida said that Lopez was an intelligence informer for some, unknown agency. They also point out that in one of the memo's written by the Warren Commission, they refer to Lopez' trip to Cuba as a "mission." They also note that Lopez was in Tampa at the same that a possible assassination attempt on JFK's life was to take place.

This previously unreported JFK assassination attempt was scheduled to take place on November 18, 1962, when the president arrived for a trip in that city. The attempted assassination was revealed by then Chief of Police J. P. Mullins. He said that the Secret Service had warned the Tampa police department that a credible threat by a person described as "white, male, 20, slender build," was planning to shoot the president from a tall building from a window. Added security was provided to the president's motorcade and nothing untoward happened that day.

In 1977, when the HSCA was looking into the Kennedy assassination, the CIA told them that they did not have enough solid leads to pursue any further investigation of Lopez, due to the lack of reliable sources. Had they known then of the attempted assassination plot against JFK in Tampa, and the fact that Gilberto Lopez matched the description of "white male, 20, slender build," who had some attachments to the pro-Castro FPCC, maybe they would have investigated further. This is only conjecture, but if the Tampa assassination attempt had succeeded, then it is possible that Gilberto Lopez, with his mob-Cuban ties, could possibly have been accused of the president's death, and maybe put in the position as a "fall guy."

The HSCA summed up their investigation of Gilberto Lopez by saying, "Lopez' association with the Fair Play for Cuban Committee, however, coupled with the act that the dates of his travel to Mexico via Texas coincided with the assassination, plus the reports in Mexico that Lopez' activities were "suspicious," all amount to a troublesome circumstance that the committee was unable to resolve with confidence."

6). Charles Ford.

The name of Charles Ford, CIA operative who worked in Bill Harvey's Task Force W, came to light with the publication of Seymour Hersh's book, *The Dark Side of Camelot.* Kennedy assassination researchers had not known about Ford and his alleged secret relationship with Robert Kennedy previously before the release of the Hersh book. The story that Hersh spun was that Robert Kennedy enlisted Charles Ford to be his personal representative to the Mafia in the Kennedy's secret war against Castro. With the release of Charles Ford's testimony by the HSCA, it seems that author Hersh got the story wrong. It now seems likely that the connection between Ford and RFK might have been a deliberate disinformation campaign arranged by Richard Helms and Morton Halpern, both of whom had an adversarial relationship with RFK.

Robert Kennedy had a years long feud with organized crime, dating back to his tenure as the chief counsel of the Senate Committee on Improper Activities in the Labor and Management Field. At 29, RFK was working for this powerful committee, better known as the McClellan Committee, headed by Sen. John McClellan. Among the members of the committee was JFK, who, along with the other members of the panel, grilled mobsters, assorted con-men and corrupt union officials about their links to organized crime in America. The American public now saw first hand the dark side of how the mob worked, with vivid tales of killings, and bribery coming out in the open.

Among RFK's top targets was the powerful and corrupt Teamster leader, James Hoffa. The Kennedy-Hoffa feud would last until the day Robert Kennedy died and would become the stuff of legend in American politics. Other targets of RFK's wrath, were Santos Trafficante Jr., and Carlos Marcello, both of whom would later be accused of playing a role in the president's death.

Both Kennedy brothers performance in front of a national TV audience via the McClellan Committee made them instant stars in official Washington circles, as men who would protect the public against the intrigues of the mob.

Robert Kennedy's anti-corruption crusade came upon a hard rock when his brother's administration began its secret war against Castro, and enlisted the help of some of the same men whom he had been prosecuting for so long; Johnny Rosselli, Carlos Marcello, Santos Trafficante, and Jimmy Hoffa. Another part of this intrigue was the hands off role that RFK took when it came to the CIA's role in plotting to kill Castro.

RFK did not entirely trust the CIA in its efforts to oust Castro and he took it upon himself to use individuals whom he could trust to carry out the administrations's anti-Castro plans. One of these men whom RFK looked toward was a Cuban revolutionary named Ernesto Betancourt. Betancourt was involved with the anti-Castro group ELC. He met with the Attorney General in September 1962 and plied him with a wild tale of a large scale revolt inside Cuba at the end of the month. He tried to convince Bobby that this operation could be undertaken without the help of the CIA. Betancourt told the eager Attorney General that his men could deal militarily with Castro's forces and launch attacks across the island.

RFK told Helms and William Harvey of the plan which they dismissed out of hand. In order to keep track of what RFK was doing, they instructed Charles Ford, who worked in the Office of Training/Deputy Directorate for Administration, to look into RFK's plan. Ford reported to his bosses that one of the men closely associated with Betancourt was actually a Cuban spy whose job it was to assassinate various ELC leaders.

The name of Charles Ford would come up years later when both Helms and Sam Halpern testified before the HSCA. They spun a fascinating tale concerning Ford and Robert Kennedy. According to the two CIA bigwigs, RFK asked the CIA to supply him with a trusted agent who would be his, RFK's, secret liaison with the mob to see if their old networks that had been closed down when Castro took over, could be resurrected. Charles Ford was chosen to serve as RFK's secret intermediary with certain mob figures. [113]

---

113 The Dark Side of Camelot. Seymour Hersh. Little Brown & Co, New York, 1997. Page 286.

As told in Hersh's book, Charles Ford was supposed to have traveled to cities in both the United States and Canada where he met clandestinely with mob figures to discuss their Cuban plans in a post Castro Havana. In an interview with Seymour Hersh, Sam Halpern said of the RFK-Ford relationship, "Charlie saw Kennedy in his office and of course talked with him on the phone quite regularly. Charlie was a good officer, and Bobby was his case officer. Charlie never reported that kind of information to me. He may have reported it to anybody. He was Bobby's man. Nobody's going to touch him." Hersh said that Ford made at least two trips to undisclosed destinations on behalf of RFK per month to such places as San Francisco, Chicago, and Canada. Upon his return from these trips, Ford never turned over any of his information to Task Force W which was running the Cuban Ops.

The accounts described by Hersh are one thing, but we now have a much deeper understanding of just what Charles Ford did via his testimony to the HSCA and their reports on his activities.

In his work for the CIA, Ford went by the alias of "Rocky Siscalini," as well as "Charles Fiscalini." He worked for the Office of Training/Deputy Directorate of Administration, joined the CIA in 1952 and later was assigned to Task Force W. The documents in the Ford file state, "That Mr. Ford was later assigned to Task Force W, and was to travel to New York on 31 March 1961 to meet with an unidentified attorney who had contacted Mr. Robert Kennedy, the Attorney General, concerning assistance for Cuban prisoners." In February 1963, he was still using the alias and was "utilized in the Continental U.S. for operational purposes in pursuit of the mission of the Special Affairs Staff." By July 1963, Ford's use of his alias was no longer necessary and he had been reassigned to Headquarters.

In a rebuttal to the Hersh allegation that Ford was used by RFK as his special agent with the mob, a memo from the Senate Select Committee on Charles Ford reads in part, "Charles Ford has been an Agency staff employee since 1962. The Office of

Security files relating to Mr. Ford do not contain any information which would indicate he had been used to contact underworld figures for possible use against Fidel Castro. However, in November 1961, Mr. Ford was assigned to the Deputy Directorate for Operations, Western Hemisphere Division as an Operations officer. A memorandum contained in the files, dated 30 March 1962, indicates that Mr. Ford was issued alias documentation under the name of 'Charles D. Fiscalini.'"

More information on Ford's Cuban work came from his testimony complied in a memorandum by the HSCA staff. Here are the pertinent parts.

His first job at the Cuban desk was to handle one particular Cuban agent who was going to build a cadre of men for eventual operations inside Cuba. Using the alias "Charles Fiscalini," Ford went to New York City in March 1962 to contact a New York lawyer whose name was supplied to him by the Justice Department, "concerning a client who had access to Cuba and wanted to visit Castro to put in a special plea on behalf of the Bay of Pigs prisoners." The unnamed person was the manager of the Toresa Hotel in New York. The name of the second man whom Ford met on the trip was "Bubbles" Abdallah. "Bubbles" was supposed to go with the lawyer to Cuba. Ford later found out that "Bubbles" Abdallah was wanted by Texas police for smuggling drugs from Mexico. No further contact was ever made between Ford and these two men. [114]

During his testimony at the HSCA, Ford was interviewed by investigators Andy Postal and Gordon Rhea who quizzed him on the assassination plots against Castro. Ford told them that he never heard any of his CIA colleagues in Task Force W ever discussing the assassination of Castro. He did however, say that in his discussions with his Cuban agents, there was always talks about killing Castro in revenge for what had happened to these men and their families.

114 RIF No. 104-10303-10001, "File on Ford, Charles/ RFK-Mafia."

Ford revealed that he traveled to New Orleans on CIA business "to attempt to find ways of establishing channels of communications between the exiled Cubans in New Orleans and their friends in Cuba." In New Orleans, Ford recruited an named Cuban who was willing to work with the CIA. This person was turned over to the CIA's FI (Foreign Intelligence) unit.

Ford said that at one time he met with General Edward Lansdale in the Pentagon, along with CIA officer Cornelius Roosevelt to discuss Ford's cadre of agents inside Cuba whom Ford ran. He also said that he had no direct knowledge of Operation Mongoose.

During his work at Task Force W, Ford was Special Assistant to Bill Harvey who had overall control of the operation. He also said that he often times got assignments from Sam Halpern, and also from another top Task Force W agent, Bruce Cheever.

Both Mr. Postal and Mr. Rhea quizzed Ford on any relationship he might have had with Robert Kennedy or knew of any connection between him and the anti-Castro leadership in the United States in the summer of 1962. He said that he did not have any direct knowledge of such a meeting and said, "I pointed out that it was common practice among many Cuban leaders to try to acquire support, or at least the appearance of support, of US agencies and prominent US political figures. I further stated that I had had one meeting in Washington with a Cuban leader who was constantly attempting to get us to support him as head of such an arrangement. I identified this man as Mario Garcia Kohly and added that he was sentenced to prison years later for counterfeiting Cuban pesos."

In his concluding testimony before the HSCA, Mr. Ford put to rest the allegations made by Seymour Hersh regarding his being the point man between RFK and the mob.

"This is probably the appropriate point to underline my conviction that the main, if not the only point of concern to the investigators is whether I was directed to sally forth and initiate contact with members of the underworld in the US and who had

directed me to do so. Their interest is even more pointedly forced on whether I had anything to do with the Rosselli, Giancana, et al, "operations." Once again, I explained that my job was broader than this by a long shot, and that I never directed to take the initiative in establishing contacts with the underworld. I said that several, probably no more than five or six, of the people with whom I dealt were somewhat "shady" characters, in some cases with recorded run-ins with law enforcement agencies." [115]

Charles Ford is deceased, but his story that he had no secret relationship with RFK and the mob, sets the record straight, and leaves out any preconception that RFK used Ford as his secret representative with the mob.

7). John Martino.

John Martino was born in Atlantic City, N.J. on August 3, 1911 and lived in that city for many years. Martino's name has been linked to the CIA-Mafia plots to kill Castro and was reported to have given a reporter information linking Oswald to the Cuban government in the murder of JFK.

Martino once worked in Cuba for mob boss Meyer Lanksy as an electronics expert and surveillance agent. He was responsible for the operation of electronically controlled gambling machines in the casinos, whereby the floor manager could watch the players via a small television camera and oversee the entire gambling operation. In 1959, Martino arrived in Cuba where he took over the race track called Oriental Park where he upgraded the tracks electronic operations. He was the author of a book on Cuba called "*I was Castro's Prisoner,*" which was an account of his three year imprisonment in Cuban jails, prior to the Bay of Pigs invasion. Martino's co-author was Nathaniel Weyl and he was released in November 1963.

When he arrived in Cuba with his 13-year-old son, Martino was stopped by Cuban immigration authorities and charged with

115 Ibid.

having flown in his own plane which they said he had hidden in a remote airfield near Havana. The Cuban police said that he was being charged with "counter-revolutionary" activities such as gunrunning, burning of sugar fields, and taking people out of the country. His son was let go but Martino was put in solitary confinement for three months before being put on trial. He was found guilty and put in prison. He was given a 30 year sentence but served only 30 months. He was released on October 2, 1962 "in exchange for some spies from a South American country." After his release, according to government documents, Martino was "closely associated with people from Guatemala and worked for the CIA." After returning to the U.S., he worked for H.L. Hunt and other Texas oilmen who were anti-Castro and funded the various anti-Castro organizations that were so prominent in various parts of the country.

After the assassination of JFK, the FBI received information that Martino may have had some knowledge of Lee Harvey Oswald and his possible ties with Cuba. He was interviewed by the Bureau on November 29, 1963. According to FBI documents on Martino, he told them that a source in the Miami area whom he would not disclose, told him that Oswald had traveled to Mexico City and from there to Cuba. Oswald was supposed to have come back to the US via the same route. Martino could not verify this information other than saying that his alleged source was a refugee from Cuba.

In an FBI report dated May 8, 1964, Special Agent James J. O'Connor, said that on April 4, 1964, he was told in Miami, Florida that Martino gave him information regarding Oswald's possible activities in Miami and Mexico to a Cuban source whom he would not name. Martino said that his source "included the allegation that Oswald had made a telephone call to the Cuban Intelligence Service from a private residence in Miami, and that Oswald had pamphlets of a pro-Fidel Castro character printed in Miami, Florida, paying the printer by check drawn on the Fair Play for Cuba Committee." Martino later said his source was in

California but might be coming back to Florida to join an anti-Castro group called MRR. The agent told Martino that his allegations about Oswald had to be checked out and that he might be called to appear before Warren Commission. "Mr. Martino said he could not be forced to reveal the identify of his source."[116]

The FBI report said that Martino's inference that Oswald was financed by the Cubans was his own, and that no genuine proof was available. He also said that Oswald was financed by the FPCC which had close ties to the Cuban government. The documents goes on to say that Martino was being sponsored in his travels across the country denouncing the Castro regime by the ultra right-wing John Birch Society. At the end of this document, the writer says that, "it is not deemed feasible to re-interview Martino at this time."

In a March 5, 1964 Department of Justice memo on Martino, a contact named "New York T-1" gave more information on Martino's Cuban-Oswald story. Martino was a guest of his friend, Nathaniel Weyl at his home in Delray Beach, Florida from December 30, 1963 to January 8, 1964. "During the evening Martino and the Weyl's discussed Lee Harvey Oswald and his wife, Marina. Nathaniel made the statement that he has no basis for his beliefs but thinks that Margarete Oswald, Oswald's mother, is probably an old line Communist. He added that he could not prove his belief."

Weyl said this about Oswald. "When you see Vic Lasky you can tell him the Cubans have been quite restrained about Oswald. They know the circumstances under which Oswald contracted the Cuban G-2 (military intelligence) by telephone from a private house in Miami, but they told the man who had the facts to give it to the FBI and then forget about it. It seems fairly definite that Ruby (Jack) went to Havana to make some shady deal with a creature called Praskin who works with the Communists and is also tied up with call girls..." [117]

116 Commission Document 961. May 8, 1964.

117 Commission Document 662. March 5, 1964.

The memo goes on to say that the source believes that Martino was the source of the Oswald-Cuban phone call story. The source also said that he was in residence when Martino and Weyl "discussed rumors that Oswald had been refused a visa to the Soviet Union and he made a quick trip from Mississippi to Cuba. Oswald returned from this trip with a sum of money, amount not mentioned, and purchased a car. The circumstances surrounding the purchase of the car was not disclosed. According to Nathaniel, the information of Oswald's trip to Cuba was reported by a girl in Miami whom Oswald "shacked up with." This girl is reportedly from Mexico or Miami but any additional information in this matter would have to be obtained form Nathaniel."[118]

The source said that in his opinion, the talks he heard with both Martino and Weyl "does not know if the statements are true or just gossip on the part of the above individuals."

In the JFK files, there is a memo dated August 29, 1977 from Ken Klein and Cliff Fenton of the HSCA staff regarding Martino's allegations regarding Oswald and his possible Cuban connections. Martino revealed the following information concerning the president's death. "JFK was killed because he betrayed Cubans by giving the Free Havana speech at Miami Stadium withdrawing support from the Bay of Pigs invasion. RFK was killed for the same reason as the go-between who negotiated with the Cubans for JFK."

On January 30, 1964, Martino gave an interview with reporter Kay Pittman of the *Press Simitar,* a daily newspaper in Memphis, Tennessee. In the article, Pittman said that Martino told her that Oswald had been paid by Castro to kill President Kennedy and that Oswald had been in Mexico and had left from as secret airport in Yucatan for Cuba, and was their in the week of October 4, 1963. Miss Pitman said that Martino said that he did not have first hand information regarding these Oswald allegations, but that he got this story from his sources in the "Cuban underground."

118 Ibid.

In reaction to this story, Martino said that he was "grossly misquoted" by Miss Pittman regarding his Oswald-Cuban story. In a Department of Justice memo dated February 13, 1964, Miss Pitman was interviewed by the Bureau and she elaborated on her interview with John Martino. She said that her interview with Martino was "somewhat misleading in that Martino did not actually say that he possessed any first-hand or direct information concerning a connection with Fidel Castro by Lee Harvey Oswald and did not possess any direct information that Oswald was paid by Castro to assassinate the late President John F. Kennedy in Dallas, Texas, November 22, 1963."

In now seems obvious that Martino's Oswald-as-a-Cuban associate story was certainly disinformation on his (or others) behalf to shift the blame on Castro for the assassination of JFK.

In the spring of 1963, Martino was part of a mad-cap exile raid into Cuba that was dubbed the "Bayo-Pawley Affair." It seems that Eddie Bayo, an anti-Castro soldier of fortune, had learned from his sources in Cuba that the Russians had missiles left in Cuba after the ending of the Missile Crisis of 1962. He said that his contacts on the island were holding two Soviet army officers who had defected and would provide the proof of these missiles. Martino was the conduit between William Pawley who went along with the raid, the CIA, which oversaw the goings on from a distance, and the editors of *Life* magazine who went along to document the whole thing. It was Martino who organized the exiles for the mission, and with Pawley, waited offshore for their successful return with the two Soviet officers. But the plan failed and none of the raiders returned.

After the assassination, Martino was questioned by the FBI regarding any information he might have on the assassination. He told the agents that his source was a man named Oscar Ortiz, a member of an unnamed anti-Castro group. The Bureau never found out who this "Ortiz" man was.

On November 29, 1963, Martino was interviewed by federal authorities and he told them that he had information that Lee

Oswald distributed pro-Castro literature in Miami. When asked whom he got the information from, Martino said that he got it from one of his Cuban sources in Miami, whom he would not name. He further stated that he did not know how reliable the report was, but he tended to believe its authenticity.

In the December, 1994 issued of *Vanity Fair,* author and reporter Anthony Summers wrote a long piece on the Kennedy assassination, including revealing information regarding John Martino. Summers wrote that Martino was a close friend of mob boss Santos Trafficante, the same man who was hired by the CIA to kill Castro. Summers found John Martino's wife Florence, then 80, living in Miami Beach. She told Summers that prior to the assassination, her husband told her that "they're going to kill him (Kennedy) when he gets to Texas." She said that after the news of JFK's death, her husband went white in the face, and was constantly on the phone that day. Mrs. Martino also said that John told her that there was another Cuban man in the Texas Theater and was allowed to escape, while Oswald was arrested by DPD officers.[119]

John also told her that one of the men came to their home two months prior to the Kennedy killing with another man who was involved in the crime. Florence Martino died shortly thereafter.

Further information on Martino's possible links to the Kennedy assassination came from reporter John Cummings who worked in the 1970's for the New York newspaper *Newsday.* After the assassination, Cummings contacted his sources in the anti-Castro exile community, including Martino. Martino spilled his guts to Cummings and told him the following story. He told Cummings that there had been "two guns (in the assassination), two people involved."

Shortly before his death in 1975, Martino again met with Cummings and talked further about the assassination. He said

119 "The Ghosts Of November" Anthony and Robbyn Summers. Vanity Fair, December 1994.

that he was part of the assassination but did not pull the trigger. He was used for "delivering money, facilitating things."

He further told Cummings a most revealing story. He said that several weeks before the assassination, he met with Oswald in Miami. He said that an FBI agent named Connors asked him to come to a boat dock on Biscayne Bay where he was introduced by Connors to Oswald. Martino said that Oswald looked like he didn't know what was going on and the real reason he wanted to introduce him to Oswald was because they were both anti-Castro. Martino said that he was under the impression that Oswald was an agent Connors was running. Author Summers said that he was able to trace down an ex-FBI agent by the name of James O'Connor who said that Martino's name rang a bell but that he did not met Lee Oswald.

That same year, Martino talked with his friend and business partner Fred Classen regarding the assassination. He said that Oswald was not the hit man and that the Cuban's "put him together."

John Martino died in 1975.

8). David Sanchez Morales.

David Morales could have been cast right out of a Hollywood script. He was a tough guy at the CIA, one of their top notch assassins, a man who took part in the anti-Castro operations that were run out of the JM/WAVE station in Florida, and some would say, made tantalizing remarks about the assassination of JFK.

David Morales grew up in Phoenix where he played four sports in high school; football, baseball, track, and basketball. He came from a broken home, and lived most of the time at the home of a good friend. He was called "Didi" by his school pals and was popular among his peers. After high school, he attended various colleges like Arizona State, the University of Southern California and UCA. In 1946, one year after the end of World War II, Morales joined the Army and was sent to intelligence training. His first posting was in Munich, Germany where he honed his intelligence skills in the now, intense cold war atmosphere that was brewing between the United States and the Soviet Union. By 1953, he was for all intents and purposes, working covertly for the CIA.

In 1953, he was attending the University of Maryland and was listed by the State Department as a "purchasing agent" for a lumber company, a classic cover story given by the CIA to its undercover agents. By 1964, Morales was working as a political officer for the State Department in Caracas, Venezuela. While in Caracas in the early to mid 1950's, Morales worked secretly with two other men whose names would be prominent in the Castro plots of the decade; David Atlee Phillips and Antonia Veciana. It was from his posting in Caracas that the three men worked on a plan to kill Castro when the latter made a trip to Chile (He was given a nickname by his CIA pals called "El Inido" which stuck with him throughout his career in the Agency).

In the late 1950's, Morales was sent to the American embassy in Havana where he and David Phillips worked on the agency's plans for the Bay of Pigs invasion of Cuba, and later was assigned to the CIA's JMWAVE operation in Miami. In between his Cuba digs, he was sent to such international hot spots as Vietnam and Laos where the CIA had numerous covert operations going at the same time. According to friends of Morales', it was on these secret assignments to Southeast Asia that Morales took on "Executive Action" assignments-assassination jobs for the CIA.

According to Morales' attorney Robert Walton, Morales took him to Miami for a trip in which he used a black card, like a credit card that enabled them to travel on a moments notice, without reservations, which was automatically accepted by the airlines One can only speculate what kind of access that card rendered the bearer (Morales).

Morales' handiwork as far as assassinations for the Agency was concerned, grew as did his reputation. It is reported that he carried out his assignments in such places as Uruguay, Venezuela, among others.

It has also been ascertained that one of Morales' jobs was working in South Vietnam for the agency's infamous assassination operation called the Phoenix Program. This covert operation was run by the CIA in order to eliminate any Viet Cong who were living in South Vietnam and were working for the North Vietnamese. The Phoenix Program turned out to be one of the CIA's most tortured secrets, leading to the murder of thousands of people in local hamlets, many civilians, who were suspected (wrongly or rightly) for aiding he enemy. A number of military officers from that era say that Morales was part of the Phoenix assassination operation.

Morales liked to drink and at times, had a hard time keeping down his liquor. In one very bad moment, he blabbed to a reporter that he was then working as the deputy director for Operations Counter-Insurgency and Special Activities in Washington. It was also reported that Morales had a private office in the Pentagon where he would hole up amid the top- brass and decision makers. What Morales did in the Pentagon is open to speculation.

When the CIA set up its secret JMWAVE station in Miami in the early 1960's, in its secret war against Castro, Morales worked under the direction of the Station Chief, Ted Shackley. He was given the title of branch chef and knew all of the secrets coming out of the agency's massive anti-Castro operation. In later years, when confirmation of Morales' role as Chief of Operations for the JMWAVE station came to light, it came as a surprise to the investigators who worked for the Church Committee studying the Kennedy assassination and the CIA's covert Cuban operations.

At the same time that David Morales was working with Ted Shackley at the JM/WAVE station in Miami, he came across another man who was hired by the CIA in its plots to kill Castro, Johnny Rosselli. Rosselli was one of the three mobsters whom the agency hired, and it seems that Rosselli and Morales got on famously. Rosselli came and went freely in the vast JMWAVE operation, giving advice and taking orders from Morales. What a weird combination that must have made. The debonair Rosselli, his mane of white hair and two hundred dollar suits, mixing with the CIA's top assassin must have been a sight to see.

Another person in the anti-Castro opposition whom Morales was associated with was John Martino. Martino said that when Morales worked in the US Embassy in Havana he was a CIA officer operating undercover and said that Morales was vocal in his opposition to Castro, and tried to get Washington to take stronger action against Fidel. Martino also said that he understood that Morales used an import-export business as a cover for his CIA work, especially after his retirement from the agency.

Another CIA associated person whom Morales was in contact with during the hectic, anti-Castro days was Rip Robertson. Robertson worked in the plot to overthrow the government of Guatemala in 1964. As the preparations for the Bay of Pigs invasion got under way, Robertson was given the job of infiltrating his teams of agents into Cuba for hit and run attacks. He was told not to set foot on Cuban soil but did so anyway, saying that he was only "training." He worked for Grayston Lynch, one of the CIA officers who was responsible for the training and recruitment of the landing force. Right before the exile invasion, Rip was given his assignment; he was to ferry a team of frogmen onto shore (two teams) and prepare the landing area. His boat, the "Barbara J." was to ferry five hundred pounds of supplies, and was supposed to offload his cargo and head back home. He, among many other CIA officers on the front line at the Bay of Pigs, took personally the disaster that ensued and held the president responsible for the fiasco.

The CIA gave Morales great leeway when it came to the training and supervision of the men who would eventually be part of the invasion force. He was given permission by the agency to operate three different groups of exiles whose job it would be to support the invasion, as well as to select certain individuals who would serve as the intelligence cadre, if and when the invasion to topple Castro was successful. A total of 39 top echelon exiles were trained by Morales as Case Officers and once their training was over, they were sent to Miami to spy on both pro-and anti-Castro groups in the city. Castro had his own, large number of spies infiltrating the exile groups in Miami, and he heard about the impending invasion, long before the American people did.

Morales was also responsible for the training of another group of exiles, this time, one hundred top men whose jobs would be to infiltrate the Castro regime, 61 of these men were sent for training in the CIA supported camp in Guatemala where the Bay of Pigs invaders were being trained. During the invasion, two of these men were killed. [120]

In his book, author Hancock writes that David Morales was in Mexico City sometime in 1963, taking time off from his duties at the JMWAVE station in Miami. It is not known what Morales as doing in Mexico at the time but he was associated with another top CIA officer who worked there, David Atlee Phillips. Hancock writes that Morales and Phillips worked on a seaborne operation to bring out a "Headquarters asset" out of Cuba.

Another CIA asset by the code name of "Sloman," who had something to do with this operation was coming via Mexico City Hancock writes that "Sloman" was really Tony Sforza, who was friends with David Morales.

Whether Johnny Rosselli had any long term influence on Morales is still debatable, it seems that "El Indio" began to cultivate private relationships with a number of top mafia figures in the United States. One of the men whom Morales worked with was Joe Fischetti, a cousin of the famous crime figure, Al Capone. Morales traveled frequently to Las Vegas where his mob connections would stand him in good steed with the high rollers. All the available evidence however, points to Rosselli as Morales' key mafia contact, whether in Las Vegas or working for the CIA in the Castro plots.

---

120 "Someone Would Have Talked." Larry Hancok, JFK Lancer Productions, 2006. Page 130-131.

Between 1971 and 1975, Morales was assigned to Latin America by the CIA and aided the governments of Panama, Argentina, Paraguay, and Uruguay. According to Morales' good friend, Rueben Carbajal (whose family virtually raised Morales), Morales took up station with the CIA's Western Hemisphere Division at the same time that the Nixon administration was seeking to oust the democratically elected government of Salvador Allende in Chile. During the CIA plots to kill Allende, General Rene Schneider of Chile, was killed. Is it a coincidence or not that at the same time that General Schneider was killed, coincided with the time that David Morales arrived in Chile? During his time in Chile, Morales wrote on his resume that he was working as a "consultant for the Joint Chiefs of Staff."[121]

Morales was deeply outraged against the failure of the Bay of Pigs operation and was very vocal in his criticism of President Kennedy's handling of the event. In later years, after his death on May 8, 1978, (it was rumored by the CIA that Morales had "died" a number of times), his attorney, Robert Walton, told a bombshell of a story concerning his client and friend, David Morales, and a reference to the Kennedy assassination. In a night of heavy drinking and anti-Kennedy bashing, Walton heard Morales say this about the death of JFK. "Well, we took care of that son of a bitch, didn't we." Morales' statements were overheard by another CIA veteran of the Castro plots, Morales' good pal, Ruben Carbajal. When asked for his comments regarding Morales' boast concerning the Kennedy assassination, he just nodded his head.

9). George Joannides.

It has only been in recent years that any information on the life of this previously unknown CIA officer has come to light, due to the diligent research of many in the JFK research community. As far as official reaction by the CIA is concerned regarding George Joannides, they have denied his role in conjunction with

121 Ibid. Page 135-136.

the D.R.E. (The Revolutionary Cuban Student Directorate), and that organizations relations with Lee Harvey Oswald in the summer of 1963. But more about that later. Just who was George Joannides, and how does he fit into the story that lead up to the assassination of JFK?

George Joannides was born in Athens, Greece on July 5, 1922. His family came to the United States and settled in New York City. George graduated from the City College of New York and then got his law degree from St .John's University. He worked as a journalist for a Greek-American newspaper in New York called the *National Herald* and became proficient in foreign languages like Greek and French. After a stint at the *Herald,* he moved to Washington, D.C. where he got a job in 1949 with the Greek Information Service.

In 1951, he entered the CIA whom he would serve the rest of his professional life. His first foreign posting was to Greece where he worked in the Athens station. For the next eleven years he shifted between postings in Libya and Greece and became proficient in psychological warfare operations.

He was posted back to the States where he and his family lived in Miami. As time went on, he was to become an integral player in the Kennedy administrations's secret war to topple the regime of Fidel Castro in Cuba. Unknown to Joannides at that time was that his role as the liaison between the D.R.E, the militant anti-Castro organization, would put his Cuban beneficiaries in touch with an ex-Marine named Lee Harvey Oswald prior to the assassination of the president.

The organization that George Joannides was assigned to watch was the D.R.E., one of the most militant, and one of the largest anti-Castro groups in the United States. By the early 1960's, D.R.E. membership totaled 2,200. It was founded in Havana only a few years before and immediately became the beneficiaries of CIA largess, in the form of money, training, and other assistance. The CIA sent one of its top officers, David Atlee Phillips, to work closely with the Cuban students.

The men who founded the D.R.E. were all Cubans; Alberto Muller, Ernesto Travieso, and Manuel Salvat. These men were originally pro-Castro but changed direction when Castro made a military pact with the Soviet Union and changed the Cuban Revolution into a Marxist run ideology.

The D.R.E. was to take a hit in the aftermath of the failed Bay of Pigs invasion. After the fiasco, Castro ordered the arrest of many of the top D.R.E. leaders, including Alberto Muller. Others managed to flee the island and take refuge in the United States and other friendly countries. In time, the D.R.E. was resurrected with CIA help and new leadership, including men like Salvat, Luis Fernandez-Rocha, and Isidro Borja took up the cause.

By 1962, Fernandez-Rocha had managed to slip back into Cuba to take charge of the continuing movement to oust Castro. The group also started a newspaper in English called *The Cuban Report,* as well as a Spanish publication called *Trinchera.* As the CIA cemented its relations with the D.R.E., they named George Joannides as their representative to that group. Joannides cover name was "Howard," as he was known to many in the group. Joannides was the intermediary between the CIA and the D.R.E., getting them guns, money, and any other assistance they needed. He earned their trust and the young Cubans liked him immensely.

Joannides worked out of the secret CIA base in Miami called JMWAVE. JMWAVE was the largest CIA base operating inside the Unite States and was located in Miami on swamp land that was then used by the University of Miami. The cover name for the JMWAVE group was called Zenith Technical Services. This cover organization had its own military in the form of ships, planes, and assets (CIA and anti-Castro mercenaries) at their disposal. They ran hit-and-run raids into Cuba, attacking both Cuban and Russian ships and installations. At one point, the Kennedy administration had to put a stop to these continuing raids for fear that they might provoke a Russian response against the United States.

Joannides' assignment at JM/WAVE was to be in charge of

psychological and disinformation operations on behalf of the D.R.E. He was assigned to the job by Richard Helms, who was DDP (Deputy Director, Plans) at the CIA. When the Warren Commission began its investigation of the assassination of JFK in 1964, Helms failed (on purpose) to inform the commission of George Joannides' role as liaison with the D.R.E.

Joannides served for 17 months as the contact officer between the D.R.E. and the CIA. According to the few records that the public was allowed to see on Joannides ties with the D.R.E., his job was to pay for "intelligence and propaganda" for the Cuban group. He instructed the D.R.E. to clear any public announcements that they made with him. Along with giving money to the Miami members of the D.R.E., Joannides also dispensed funds to its members located in New Orleans. The CIA's relationship with the members of the D.R.E., in New Orleans during the summer of 1963, let them have a unique perspective when Oswald tried to make contact with certain members of the D.R.E. that summer. When the Warren Commission was investigating the Kennedy assassination, the CIA failed to inform them of Joannides's relationship with the D.R.E., nor the fact that he was aware (or should have been aware) that Oswald had been in touch with people in the New Orleans group.

When Oswald arrived in New Orleans during the summer of 1963, he began handing out pro-Castro leaflets on the streets of the city on behalf of the FPCC. He subsequently got into an altercation with an anti-Castro shopkeeper named Carlos Bringuier whom Oswald previously had met and offered his services as an ex-Marine who wanted to help the anti-Castro cause. Bringuier said that Oswald had tried to worm his way into the D.R.E. in New Orleans in August 1963 but that he gave him no reason to believe that he would take up his offer.

Oswald was later arrested for the so called altercation and was bailed out of jail a few days later. While in jail, he had an interview with an F.B.I. agent. Oswald then went on a local radio station and had a debate with Carlos Bringuier regarding the

Cuban cause. During the debate, Oswald was stunned when his adversary confronted him about the time he spent in the Soviet Union.

It is unclear whether or not the leadership of the D.R.E. told their CIA bosses (as well as George Joannides), about their confrontation with Oswald in New Orleans. Fernandez-Rocha said he had "no specific recollection" about informing George Joannides about his organizations encounter with Oswald that summer. Isidro Borja said that, "The CIA officer was definitely informed." But was that CIA officer George Joannides? It seems logical that if Joannides was the action officer with the D.R.E., the paymaster, the babysitter for their organization, then he would have been privy to all the information coming from the D.R.E. And wouldn't the fact that Bringuier had a public debate with Oswald on the radio, and the fact that he (Oswald) was playing a double game in New Orleans (both pro and anti-Castro), was something that Joannides should have been appraised of?

Due to the "JFK Records Act," the CIA released a huge amount of information on its relations with the D.R.E. Its records for the period 1960 to 1966 are in the public domain. However, the records during the 17 month period of which Joannides was working with the D.R.E., from December 1962 to April 1964 are missing.

Imminently after the assassination of JFK, a one time leader of the D.R.E, Tony Lanusa, said that he called "Howard" and told him that Oswald had been arrested. Lanusa said that his group wanted to put out a press item right away, telling the world of their relationship with Oswald that summer. According to Lanusa, "Howard" said to wait until he got in touch with the CIA. However, the D.R.E. decided to release the news anyway and they contacted Clare Booth Luce, whose husband owned Time Inc. They also contacted Paul Bethel, who had formally worked for the State Department in anti-Castro efforts. They also contacted the *New York Times,* all linking Oswald to the anti-Castro cause and trying to link the government of Fidel Castro to the president's assassination. On November 23, 1963, the D.R.E. published a special edition of their newspaper, giving an eager public all the information they had on Oswald and his so called relationship with Castro's Cuba. The D.R.E.'s article was the first so called conspiracy theory (linking Oswald as a tool of the Cuban regime), and trying to pin the blame for the assassination on Castro's doorstep.

But the story of George Joannides does not end there. His name was to come up when the Congress opened up its own investigation of the assassination of JFK during the 1970's.

After his stint in Miami, Joannides went to Athens and later Vietnam. He subsequently retired from the CIA in 1976, and stayed in Washington as a private lawyer. He returned to the CIA in the general counsel's office at Langley headquarters. However, he would soon be thrust back into the aftermath of the Kennedy assassination in the 1970's, when the congress re-opened the case.

Due to public pressure, the House of Representatives in 1978, re-opened both the King and Kennedy assassination cases. The House panel demanded that the CIA supply them with as much of their secret information held in their vaults on Lee Oswald and any other pertinent information they had. In a move that he did not expect, Joannides was recalled by the CIA to act as their liaison with the House Select Committee. The House committee especially wanted to see what information the CIA had on Oswald's possible connection with the Cuban's, one area that the Warren Commission did not even look into.

Joannides was in a unique position, if he truly wanted, to enlighten the HSCA on his relationship with the D.R.E. in Miami during the summer of 1963, and his knowledge (if any), on the CIA's relationship with Oswald in New Orleans. Instead, he kept quiet, never revealing what he knew about those tumultuous days.

Joannides filtered the HSCA's request for documents, only giving the committee what he thought would not hurt the

Company's reputation. He also did not tell Robert Blakey, the HSCA's chief counsel, about his secret relationship with the D.R.E. Blakey, a former Notre Dame law professor, had gone into his job with the perception that the mob was responsible for the president's assassination. Years later, when he learned of Joannides's secret relationship with the anti-Castro group he said, "I was not told of Joannides background with the DRE, a focal point of the investigation. Had I known who he was, he would have been a witness who would have been interrogated under oath by the staff or by the committee. He would never have been acceptable as point of contact with us to retrieve documents. In fact, I have now learned, as I note above, that Joannides was the point of contact between the Agency and the DRE during the period Oswald was in contact with DRE."

Blakey went on to say that, "For these reasons, I no longer believe that we were able to conduct an appropriate investigation of the Agency and its relationship to Oswald."

After Joannides's relationship with the D.R.E. was made public, the CIA went into its protective shield. They stated in no uncertain terms that Joannides had no relationship with the D.R.E. whatsoever. Journalist Jefferson Morley, who took an avid interest in the Joannides story, said that when he asked J. Barry Harrelson, who worked in the CIA's Office of Historic Review, if the CIA had any relationship with the D.R.E. in 1963, he gave this answer, " We think the record speaks for themselves."

What is not in question is that the CIA had an important asset, George Joannides, inside the D.R.E. in 1963. By all accounts, the D.R.E. had information on the activities of Lee Oswald in New Orleans that summer, information that was withheld from the Warren Commission.

In December 2003, Morley filed a suite against the CIA, asking them to release all their records on George Joannides. The motion was denied by the court.

George Joannides died on March 9, 1990, at age 67.

10). Juan Almeida.

In the plots to kill Castro, beginning in 1960, many of the main figures are well known including, Johnny Rosselli, Sam Giancana, Juan Orta, Santo Trafficante Jr, to name others. However, in recent reporting by authors Lamar Waldron and Thom Hartman in the paperback edition of their book, *Ultimate Sacrifice,* they reveal another person who was not known to the general public until the present day. The man in question was the third ranking member of Castro's inner circle, a key aid to Ernest "Che" Guevara, and most importantly, a trusted source in JFK's coup planning that was scheduled for December, 1963, Juan Almeida.

The only reason that the identity of Juan Almeida was revealed was because the CIA brought it to the attention of the public, a reversal of the first magnitude as far as keeping secrets is concerned.

Like many of Castro's early followers, Juan Almeida was an ardent supporter of Castro's revolution and took part in the abortive raid on the Moncada Army Barracks along with Castro, and 123 other insurgents on July 26, 1953.

Juan Almeida was born on February 17, 1927 in Cuba. He attended the University of Havana where he first met Fidel Castro. Almeida joined up with Castro's slowly emerging Cuban Peoples Party which was vying for power against the dictator, Fulgencio Batista. Their hopes were dashed as Batista won the election and Castro and his small band of followers began plotting his demise.

In the wake of the failed attempt on the Moncada Army Barracks, both Castro and Almeida were imprisoned but were released by the government in 1955. They fled to Mexico where they planned the overthrow of the Batista regime.

In what seemed like a fools errand, Almeida , Castro and a band of eighty revolutionaries arrived back in Cuba and headed for the rugged Sierra Maestra mountains where they made alliances with the local villages who provided them with aid and comfort. Soon, many of the local's joined the cause, and despite many setbacks, were eventually successful in routing Batista from power. Almeida held the position of Commander of the Santiago Column of the Revolutionary Army and joined Castro when he finally seized power in new years eve, 1959.

As one of the few Black men in the Cuban government, Almeida held a unique position of power. He was appointed a General in the Revolutionary Armed Forces and in 1966 was appointed a member of the Central Committee and the Political Bureau. He later assumed the job of head of the Directorate of Logistics of the General Staff of the Ministry of the Revolutionary Armed Forces.

As time went on, Almeida solidified his position of power in the Cuban Revolutionary regime, cementing a solid relationship with Che Guevara, and was third in the pecking order after Fidel and his brother Raul.

U.S. government documents that have been recently declassified show that the CIA was keeping a close watch on Almeida during the early 1960's. In a document dated February 20, 1961, regarding the rebel leaders in Oriente Province in Cuba, has a revealing comment regarding Juan Almeida. The pertinent sentence reads as follows: "It also has been reported to me that Commander Juan Almeida, who is Chief of Fidel's army actually is very much disgusted with the Communist situation, and is about to defect. This Almeida told to Manual Ray, who is head of an anti-Castro Movement inside Cuba."[122]

Another CIA memo dated March 17, 1961, corroborates the previous message regarding Almeida's distaste for the Cuban regime. The subject of the memo is "Possible Defection of Army Chief Almeida." The source is an unnamed Cuban national exiled in the United States. The source is further revealed as "one of the top leaders of the Electrical Workers Union in Cuba. He was a

122 RIF No. 104-10400-10200.

political analyst in the Brazilian Embassy in Havana." The text of the message reads: "On March 7, 61, the wife of the Chief of a Latin American diplomatic mission in Havana arrived in Miami and advised me that Major Juan Almeida, Chief of Staff of the Cuban Army, has been approaching certain Latin Ambassadors in Havana to determine whether he would be accepted as a political asylee. She also advised that several high ranking personalities of the Cuban government are sounding out the Latin diplomats in order to request political asylum."

In December 1962, another US intelligence document revealed yet more dissent among certain members of Castro's government, including Juan Almeida. This January 7, 1963, memo was from a "Resident of Havana whose employment entails considerable travel in Havana Province and brings him into contact with government officials."

The memo talks about the discord among the high ranking members of Castro's inner circle, the so called "26 July Movement" regarding Soviet-American relations affecting an agreement in Cuba. The main point of interest is as follows:

"The delay of the Soviet and Americans in reaching an agreement on Cuba, as promised by the Soviet's, has caused an increase in anti-Communist pressure within the leadership of the 26 of July Movement. Prominent behind the pressure is Juan Almeida, commander of the Central Army, and Celia Sanchez, secretary to the Presidency. As a result, a number of high-level consultations have been held by Fidel Castro, Raul Castro, Ernesto "Che" Guevara, Ramino Valdes, and Celia Sanchez. President Osvaldo Dorticos, however, has not attended these meetings."

What we see here is a change of heart by Almeida towards Fidel Castro and the Cuban revolutionary cause in general. His dissatisfaction however is not backed up by US authorities in a memo called an "Intelligence Informant Report" called Significance of the Appointment of Juan Almeida as National Coordinator of Construction Activities. After describing his new positions the national coordinator for construction, the memo goes on to say, "Almeida is not a man of outstanding ability. His principal qualifications for the position is his absolute loyalty to Fidel Castro."[123]

We now see two different interpretations of Almeida's role in the Castro government. It seems that Almeida was keeping his rather large reservations about where Castro was taking the Cuban revolution to himself, most likely, to ensure his physical safety. He did not want his long time friend Fidel Castro, from gaining knowledge about his sudden change of heart. If he was going to somehow alter the way Cuba was being run, it would have to be from the inside, near where the levers of power were, not from some jail cell where his only future was at the end of a rope.

A CIA memo dated January 5, 1965, two years after the Kennedy assassination, sheds new light on Almeida's role in the Cuban government pecking order.

"Although Major Juan Almeida Bosque is designated First Deputy Minister of the Revolutionary Armed Forces, he might more properly be described as Chief of the Office of Armed Forces Minister Raul Castro Ruiz. Almeida's primary function is to receive all telegrams that do not require Raul Castro's personal attention.

"Almeida has no real influence in the armed forces and he has so stated publicly. He owes his appointment as First Deputy to his bravery during the anti-Batista struggle and to the fact that he is a Negro. Almeida is popular with his men in the Armed Forces and throughout the country as a whole.

"Almeida is not a Communist and he has no inclination of become one. Almeida is the only Armed Forces Major who wears civilian clothes after working hours. He drives his own car and refuses to have a bodyguard assigned to him."[124]

123 RIF No. 104-10102-10041.

124 RIF No. 104-10102-10044.

A fuller picture of Juan Almeida's covert association with the Kennedy administration has been brought to life in the paperback edition of Waldron and Hartman's book, *Ultimate Sacrifice.* This new material on Almeida and his covert links to the coup in Cuba planned by JFK in December 1963 shows just how deep he was trying to oust his former mentor, Fidel Castro.

According to *Ultimate Sacrifice,* Almeida was in contact with both JFK and RFK in November 1963. He was going to lead JFK's "palace coup" against Castro and received cash payments from JFK and the CIA on November 22, 1963, the same day that the president was killed in Dallas. While preparations were going on involving Almeida, his family was taken out of Cuba and sent to a safe country (*Ultimate Sacrifice,* Page 2, paperback ed). With Almeida on board, the Kennedy administration now had two, deep cover agents on their payroll who were ready to eliminate Castro; Juan Almeida and Rolando Cubela, a.k.a. AMLASH.

With political tensions running high in Havana in late November 1963, Castro's alter ego, "Che" Guevara, was arrested for plotting against Castro. A CIA memo dated 12-3-63 says of the "despair expressed by Major Juan Almeida," probably due to the fact that JFK had been killed only a few days before, and that Che was in jail.

As the years passed, Juan Almeida continued to serve the Castro government. In 1978, he met with the United States Ambassador to the United Nations, Andrew Young in New York. For all intents and purposes he was now rehabilitated and back in Castro's good graces. However, Castro was well aware of Almeida's past indiscretions but took no action against him. Over time, his sons prospered, with one living in Madrid and the other in Cancun.

Looking back at the "what if" of this incident, if the coup against Castro had succeeded in December 1963, Almeida would have been part of the new provisional government and would then have asked for US assistance in shoring up their new regime.

According to Waldron and Hartman, Almeida's role in the planning of the coup was backed up by Harry Ruiz Williams, a prominent Cuban exile and a personal friend of Robert Kennedy. Williams said that he stopped contact with Almeida in December 1963 but that he learned that Almeida's family continued to receive money from the United States government (*Ultimate Sacrifice,* Pg. 810, new edition).

The public did not know if Almeida was still living until the 1990's, when it was revealed that he was back in the good graces of Fidel Castro.

Waldron and Hartman purposely left out Almeida's name in case he was still alive so as not to harm his safety. In a rare turnaround, it was the United States that first announced that their once prized agent of the cold war was among the living, even if he still refused to go public with his most remarkable story.

Juan Almeida, the spy whose identity the United States kept secret for so long, died on September 11, 2009 in Havana of a heart attack at age 82.

11). Winston Scott.

Winston Scott was one of the most promising and influential members of the CIA in the decades of the 1950's and 1960's. He was a poet, a writer, a veteran of the OSS, and served as CIA Station Chief in Mexico City from 1956-69. He also wrote a personal memoir of his life in the CIA which mysteriously disappeared within days of his sudden, and premature death.

Winston Scott was born in Alabama in 1909. Well built, and very athletic, he played football and baseball at the University of Alabama. He later graduated from the University of Michigan where he got his PhD in mathematics. He was such a talented baseball player that the New York Giants even offered him a professional contract as a catcher. He declined the offer, and instead, joined the FBI at the beginning of America's entry into World War 2.

During his stint at the Bureau, Scott found time for his passion; writing. He published poetry and wrote a few math text books under the pen name "Ian Maxwell."

His first overseas posting for the FBI was in Havana, Cuba. As the war progressed, Scott transferred to the US Navy and he was commissioned as a lieutenant commander. Finding his interest lay in the mundane tools of the intelligence craft, he was sent to the OSS office in London where he was given detailed instructions by the British secret service.

After the war ended, Scott returned to London to become the CIA's first station chief (from 1947-50). This was at the height of the cold war in Europe and Scott was on the firing line of some of the most important CIA operations of the day. He divorced his first wife and remarried a woman named Mave Paula Murray. Returning to the United States, he was appointed to the position of CIA Inspector General. In 1956, Scott was given one of the top assignments the CIA could hand out. He left for Mexico City as the new station chief.

As Station Chief, Scott was politically well connected in the capital city, making personal friends with some of the top leaders in the Mexican government. Among his associates were Gustavo Diaz Ordaz, who would later become president of Mexico, Alolfo Lopez Mateos, Mexico's president from 1958-64, and Luis Escheverria, at the time the minister of government.

Using his considerable political ties, Scott was able to learn from one of his Mexican political sources that the Soviet Union was contemplating an intervention in Czechoslovakia (they invaded that country in 1968).

It was during Scott's tenure as Station Chief in Mexico City that he became embroiled in the secret machinations of Lee Harvey Oswald, the alleged assassin of President Kennedy. In late September and early October 1963, Oswald came to Mexico City seeking a visa to return to the Soviet Union. The CIA later learned that Oswald, or someone pretending to be him, went to the Cuban and Soviet embassies, loudly demanding that he be given travel permits for him and his family to leave the United States, via Cuba.

It has been speculated over the years that the CIA had a

recording of Oswald's voice at the Soviet embassy, although it has never turned up. How then, does Win Scott fit in with all these speculations?

Intriguing information concerning Winston Scott's role in the pre-assassination maneuvering in September 1963 comes from a book by Michael Kurtz called "The JFK Assassinations Debates: Lone Gunman verses Conspiracy." According to author Kurtz, Scott told a CIA contract officer named William George Gaudet to tell Oswald to travel to Dallas, Texas on September 27, 1963 "to meet a couple of anti-Castro Cubans and accompany them to the home of a Cuban woman who might invest money in the anti-Castro crusade."[125]

The woman in question was Sylvia Odio, whose family took a leadership role in the anti-Castro cause. Oswald was to meet with two other men and visit the Odio home in Dallas in order to raise funds for the anti-Castro cause. The Odio story is well known to JFK assassination researchers and therefor it is not necessary to retell the entire incident. Suffice it to say that the Warren Commission was well aware of the Odio story and found it troubling, if not dangerous to its preconceived findings as Oswald as the lone gunman. (For those not aware of the Odio story, Oswald was supposed to be in Mexico City when three unidentified men paid a visit to the Odio home asking for help in the anti-Castro crusade. After the assassination, Sylvia Odio saw a picture of Oswald on TV and realized that he, or someone who looked just like him, was at her home in September of that year).

It is interesting to note that William George Gaudet was issued a Mexican tourist card to enter Mexico on the same day as Oswald (September 17, 1963), and at the same location. The number of Gaudet's tourist card was one number before that of Oswald. Over the years, Gaudet was associated with the CIA but denied that he had met Oswald in Mexico City.

---

125 Michael Kurtz. "The JFK Assassination Debates: Lone Gunman verses Conspiracy," University Press of Kansas, 2006. Page. 190.

In his book, author Kurtz tells another interesting story about a possible Oswald-Gaudet connection. He writes that he interviewed Gaudet and that "Gaudet stated that he and Oswald were sent to Mexico City to survey the scenes at the Cuban and Russian embassies and to report their findings to the CIA."[126]

The CIA had a security file on Gaudet for many years. He was the publisher of a magazine called, *The Latin American Report* and the CIA first approved contact with him in 1948. In 1950, the CIA began paying Gaudet for information he provided to them relating to Latin American affairs. By 1953, the CIA upped Gaudet's security clearance to "Secret." However, there is nothing in his CIA file that says Gaudet was used by the agency for any undercover assignments.

On November 23, 1963, President Johnson met with CIA Director John McCone who told the new president that according to Win Scott, Oswald had met in Mexico City with KGB officer, Valery Kostikov. McCone informed Johnson that Kostikov was a member of the KGB's Department 13, which dealt in assassinations. This meeting began a high tension mind set inside the new administration that tried to link Oswald to the Soviet Union.

The previous day, on the afternoon of the assassination, a high level meeting took place at the United States Embassy in Mexico City. In attendance were Winston Scott, U.S. Ambassador to Mexico Thomas Mann, and Clark Anderson, who was the FBI's legal attaché. Their discussion concerned new information that Oswald visited the Cuban and Russian embassies. Clark Anderson fumed at Scott because Scott had not told him of the Oswald visit. Anderson was given the photos and tapes of Oswald's visits to the two embassies. These materials were then flown immediately to Dallas where FBI agents were in the process of interrogating Oswald. The agents were surprised to learn that the photos of the man who visited both embassies was not Oswald. "The photographs depicted a man about forty years old,

126 Ibid. Page 162.

around six feet tall, with a stocky, muscular build, and sporting a receding hairline and a square jaw." This was the picture of the so called "Unidentified Man" who was impersonating Oswald (the identity of his man has still not been verified).

Scott, as well as Ambassador Mann, also tried to tie Oswald with pro-Castro forces. They championed a version of events that centered on Gilberto Alvarado, Nicaraguan intelligence agent who said that he had seen Oswald meeting in Mexico City with a "tall, thin Negro with reddish hair," and a "blonde haired girl with a Canadian passport" named Maria Luisa. Alvarado said that the Negro gave Oswald $6,500 as a payment to kill JFK.

When LBJ was preparing to organize a commission to look into the president's murder, he ignored pleas from Scott and others to at least consider the fact that Oswald might have been involved with Cuba.

In his testimony to the HSCA, former Ambassador Mann gave his reservations about what took place in Mexico City on the weekend of the assassination. He said that "instructions were received from Washington to stop investigative effort to confirm or refute rumors of Cuban involvement in the assassination. Mann said his instructions came from Dean Rusk and he believed that Scott, CIA Station Chief, and Anderson, FBI Legat, had received similar instructions from their respective directors."

New, historical information regarding CIA covert activities in Mexico at the time that Win Scott was in Mexico working for the CIA, give us a deeper understanding just how much Scott was involved in undercover machinations in the Mexican capital. The new material was provided by Jefferson Morley and posted on the web site of the National Security Archive, a private watchdog group that has been pioneering, and reporting on the secret side of American history during the cold war years.

The article called *Litempo: The CIA's Eyes on Tiateloioc CIA Spy Operations in Mexico,* shows just how far the Agency went in developing high level sources inside the Mexican government in its clandestine activities between 1956 and 1969.

Among the high level recruits whom the CIA used for espionage-political purposes were President Gustavo Diaz Ordaz and the future president Luis Echeverria. During those hectic years, Win Scott ran a secret intelligence network out of Mexico City that he called LITEMPO. Its agents worked out of the US Embassy in Mexico City and was far ranging in its scope. According to the report, "Scott used the LITEMPO project to provide an unofficial channel for the exchange of selected sensitive political information which each government wanted the other to receive but not through public exchanges." [127]

Scott used these two powerful people, as well as other sources, to gather information on the student protest movement that was taking place in Mexico whose leaders were challenging the government's rule in that nation.

In his article, Jefferson Morley writes that Scott hired 12 agents to report to him on the ever growing unrest among the student protests that would culminate in the October 2, 1968 student massacre. "As a result, the CIA helped to protect Mexico's ruling party from bearing responsibility for the massacre, and delivered a muddled and misleading account of it to Washington."

In CIA parlance, the letters LI represented the Agency's code name for Mexican operations; TEMPO was Scott's term for a program that was "a productive and effective relationship between the CIA and select top officials in Mexico." Scott's spy network began in 1960 and LITEMPO "served as an unofficial channel for the exchange of selected sensitive political information which each government wanted the other to receive but not through public protocol exchanges."

Among Scott's agents were LITEMPO-1, Emilio Bolanos, a nephew of Gustavo Diaz Ordaz, then the Minister of Government, LITEMPO-2 Diaz Ordaz. It is not known how much money

127 "Litempo: The CIA's Eyes on Tiateloico: CIA Spy Operations in Mexico." The National Security Archive Electronic Briefing Book No. 204. Posted October 18, 2006.

Scott paid this agents but one member of the CIA's clandestine staff in Mexico said that "the agents are paid too much and their activities are not adequately reported." Another colleague of Scott's said regarding his agents that they were "unproductive and expensive."

In October 1963, Scott, who befriended his agents, gave Bolanos,-LITEMPO-1, a "personal gift" of 1,000 rounds of .223 Colt automatic ammunition to pass on to Diaz Ordaz." In his memos to Washington, Scott said that the work of his spy network was necessary and that "changes to the LITEMPO program may be necessary when LITEMPO-2 becomes the presidential candidate."[128]

When Scott retired from the CIA in 1969, he remained in Mexico City and went into private business, creating a firm called Diversified Corporation Services. He also kept most of his private files that he had accumulated over the years. He told many of his colleagues that he was writing his memoirs, but most of them did not really know what was going to be included in the book. Some people who knew about Scott's book said it contained information about his life in the OSS and the FBI. The book was referred to as an autobiographical "novel" about Scott's life.

The working title of the book is called *Four Foe* (another title was said to be *It Came to Little).* The manuscript, which was never released to the public, has numerous, candid references to the CIA's relationship with Oswald during the September-October 1963 time period. Furthermore, after Scott's death, his manuscript was seized, along with all of his personal papers.

Shortly before his untimely death in 1971, Scott contacted Richard Helms who by then had been appointed Director of the CIA by President Johnson. Scott ostensibly wanted to see Helms in order to give him his book as a courtesy. Right before his trip (which he never made), he fell from a ladder in his home, fell off the roof, and received a number of cuts and bruises. He didn't

128 Ibid.

seem to fazed with the injury and resumed his normal activities. On April 26, 1971, one day after his fall, his wife found him dead in their home.

In the wake of Scott's mysterious death, the CIA, which had been notified of the event shortly after it happened, moved quickly. In circumstances that are still unknown today, James Angleton, the agency's legendary counterintelligence chief, made a hurried trip to Mexico City to retrieve all of Scott's personal papers, including the cryptic manuscript he had written. What could have made Angleton go to Mexico in such a hurry? Could it have been Scott's very knowledgeable information that he learned about Oswald's visit it Mexico, and any potential CIA involvement?

Thomas Mann, who served as JFK's ambassador to Mexico at the time of Scott's residence as CIA Station Chief, had some rather interesting remarks concerning Scott's death. In an interview Mann gave years alter, he said, "But that (his death) was one of the things that makes me a little bit suspicious about Win Scott dropping dead like that. Well, I always suspected that he might have been murdered. He started running some kind of his own personal intelligence organization (the aforementioned LITEMPO). They wanted to use his expertise and knowledge of Mexico, especially the intelligence side of it. When you get involved in that sort of thing, one is not surprised, if you know that world, when people drop dead real quick. I wouldn't want to write a life insurance policy on some of the people I've known connected to that organization."

In 1985, Michael Scott, Winston's son, tried to get the CIA to allow him to access his father's papers, as well as the secret report. The younger Scott paid a visit to CIA headquarters in Langley, Va. There, he was treated with respect by the people he talked to. However, they refused to release any of his father's materials to him. According to Michael Scott, one of the CIA men whom he met told him that, "There may be information you know from outside sources that might seem to be public knowledge, but we can't officially release it to you."

To this day, Winston Scott's unpublished manuscript and any explosive material it may contain regarding the Oswald trip to Mexico City (and other hot topics), is still under wraps.

12). David Atlee Phillips.

The name of David Atlee Phillips is know to all serious researchers of the Kennedy assassination. Phillips was a veteran CIA case officer, a writer, playwright, and possibly, the elusive "Maurice Bishop" who has been linked to the accused presidential assassin, Lee Oswald.

David Phillips was born on October 31, 1922 in Fort Worth, Texas. He attended William and Mary College and Texas Christian University. After college he got a job as an actor and then joined the Army in 1943. He served as a bomber pilot crew member on flights over Germany. He was shot down and served a brief time as POW before making a successful escape. After the war ended, Philips again went into acting and later got a job as a playwright and radio announcer. By 1948, Phillips left the United States for Chile where he continued to write and in 1949, founded an English language newspaper called *The South Pacif Mail.* It was during this time that the CIA station in Chile began to take notice of this young David Phillips and began covert contact with him. In 1950, the CIA made him an offer and Phillips became a contract officer for the agency. He started out as a part time employee in the agency's Clandestine Service, that part of the CIA that was responsible for dirty tricks, among others. By 1954, he left Chile and teamed up with another up and coming CIA man, E. Howard Hunt. In 1954, the CIA was planning a coup against the elected government of Guatemala and Phillips joined Hunt in the overthrow of the Arbenz regime. His job was as the propaganda chief for the operation called "The Voice of Liberation." In the end, the insurgent CIA backed leader, Castillo Armas, took power.

After the successful Guatemala coup, Philips returned to Washington and worked as a full time employee of the CIA in its psychological warfare department. By 1960, he was sent to Havana where he came face to face with the newly arrived government of Fidel Castro. It was from this vantage point that David Phillips would make a name for himself in the continuing CIA war against Castro. While in Havana, Philips' cover was that of the owner of a public relations company, all the time, being a deep cover agent for the CIA. He got to know many of the top people in the Cuban government, as well as the top political and military men assigned to the US embassy. While Phillips put out his single, there was little or no "public" business to be had. One of his real clients was the Berlitz Language School.

In 1960, the Eisenhower administration began its first clandestine attempts to get rid of Castro. They decided on an exile raid into that country that would be known as the Bay of Pigs affair. In preparation for that assault, Phillips was given the task of coordinating the propaganda for the invasion. He made frequent trips to Miami to meet with his CIA and Cuban contacts and began an intensive radio propaganda effort to destabilize the Castro regime.

After the failure of the CIA's operation, Phillips was assigned to his next duty post; Mexico City, from 1961 to the fall of 1963. What has intrigued many in the research community is that it was during this time that David Phillips was Chief of the Covert Action Station in Mexico City that Lee Harvey Oswald allegedly came to Mexico City in September 1963, supposedly to obtain a visa back to the Soviet Union via Cuba. If indeed Oswald was in the Mexican capital during this time, it would be quiet obvious that Phillips would have known about the ex-Marine's whereabouts.

In the early 1960's, while David Phillips was stationed there, Mexico City was one of the most important espionage posts in all of the Americas. The CIA had its largest foreign station there, and spies from all over the free and communist worlds roamed its byzantine streets, trying to "turn" each others agents, and gather as much information on the enemy as possible.

With the advent of the Kennedy administrations's Operation Mongoose, following the Bay of Pigs invasion, David Phillips was made Chief of Cuban Operations. Operating out of the US embassy, Phillips' job was counter intelligence against both Cuban and Soviet spies operating in Mexico City, propaganda, and dirty tricks. One of his main jobs was to observe the many intelligence agents of the Cuban government that were prevalent in that city.

One of the lingering questions concerning the activities of David Phillips as it relates to the assassination of JFK, concerns his testimony before the HSCA in 1976, and the information he told regarding Lee Oswald and the Cubans. Besides talking to the House Committee, Phillips gave an interview to the *Washington Post* that Oswald offered information to the Soviet Embassy in exchange for money. If this information could be corroborated, then it would add an entire new meaning to the assassination of the president. But in reality, Phillips's statement proved to be unfounded. In his testimony to the HSCA, Phillips said, "Oswald indicated in his discussions with the Soviet embassy that he hoped to receive assistance with the expenses of his trip." This is a long way from offering information in exchange for cash. Phillips further said that Oswald was overheard saying that, "I have information you would be interested in, and I know you can pay my way to Russia." Phillips failed to tell the reporter for the *Post* where his story came from or if it could be verified.

In his own book called *The Night Watch,* an account of his years in the CIA, Phillips tells a rather different story concerning the Oswald-selling-information tale. He wrote the following, "I know of no evidence to suggest that any aspect of the Mexico City trip was any more ominous than reported by the Warren Commission."

Phillips flip flopping on his knowledge of Oswald's stay in Mexico City and the CIA's interest in him, concerns Oswald's affair with Sylvia Duran, a woman who interviewed him in the Cuban consulate in that city. With the release of new documents on the Kennedy assassination, it is now clear that Oswald was having an affair with Sylvia Duran, that the CIA knew of it and tried to use that information against her. As Phillips was Chief of Cuban operations at the time of Oswald's supposed visit, he must have known about the Duran-Oswald link. But in his testimony by the committee, he backtracked by saying that he doubted the agency would "pitch" Duran because "the station could not identify her weakness."

David Phillips also had a wide ranging relationship with one of the most important anti-Castro exiles of the 1960's, Antonio Veciana. Veciana founded the militant anti-Castro group called ALPHA 66, which operated at the behest of the Kennedy administration. His name was also prominent in the aftermath of the Kennedy assassination, having been in close contact with his CIA case officer, one, "Maurice Bishop," who oversaw all of ALPHA 66's operations, and may have known the president's alleged assassin, Lee Oswald.

The CIA's file on Antonio Veciana reads like a good spy novel, full of covert activities and vital information on him that the Agency found useful.

The CIA files state that on December 7, 1960, Veciana made contact with the Agency's COS Havana station with a friend, Justo Carrillo Hernandez to inform them of a plot against Fidel Castro. The file states that Veciana had spoken to an unnamed State Department officer concerning this information. On October 7, Veciana entered the US at Key West, via small boat, carrying a passport but no visa. He was allowed to stay in the country, and was given $100 a month in refugee assistance.

By December 1960, the CIA and Veciana had become mutually acquainted, and a mutual relationship began. During that time, the CIA's JMWAVE station in Miami, agreed to use him on sabotage missions into Cuba.

The files report that by July 1962, Veciana and a friend named Emelio Fuentes, went to Puerto Rico to solicit funds form forty people for the anti-Castro cause. "Veciana's pitch was a demand, rather than a request for funds with inference reprisals against any who failed to full his duty." He said that he needed to do this outside of US control. He said that the group was in contact with a man named "Joe" (possibly Santo Trafficante-Joe the courier) and that his group was not going to confide in the CIA and were taking precautions of avoiding CIA penetration. From Puerto Rico, they returned to Chicago.

On July 23, 1962, Veciana met with CIA agent Harry Real who was an officer of the New York Contract Division. Veciana said that he needed CIA help but under no circumstances would he ask the CIA to become identified with his group. He told Real that he had up to $50,000 in the bank and "wanted someone in the Agency sufficiently highly placed to make commitment."

Veciana's 201 file now skips to 4 January, 1974. A report from the US Attorney's New York Office, makes mention of the fact that Veciana and another man, Airel Powers, are involved in "the unlawful importing of cocaine or other narcotics." The file ends with this remark; "Veciana had allegedly been involved in several assassination attempts on Fidel Castro which, for one reason or another, never came off. They were not connected with the Agency."

Despite Veciana's rabid anti-Castro proclivities, the CIA wanted no official association with him. A May 13, 1977 memo spells out the CIA's lack of interest this way. "According to our records, he contacted this Agency on three occasions (December 1960, July 1962 and April 1966 to discuss his plans to assassinate Fidel Castro. On these occasions, our officers listened to Veciana but expressed no interest in and offered no encouragement to him and never re-contacted him on this matter."

David Phillips has also been linked to a mysterious CIA agent known as "Maurice Bishop." Bishop's name was given to the HSCA by Antonio Veciana. "Bishop," according to Veciana, was 6'2 tall, of an athletic build, 200 pounds, grey eyes, light brown hair, and at that time, in his mid-sixties. Veciana said that Bishop was his spymaster in Havana. Bishop told Veciana to contact a number of CIA officers then working in the US embassy in Havana who might be helpful in aiding the anti-Castro cause. One Army intelligence officer working in the Havana station, a man named "Sam Kail," said that he remembered a man by the name of Bishop but couldn't identify him.

Another top CIA official to have known of "Bishop," was Director John McCone. When asked if he knew a Maurice Bishop, McCone said yes. He also remarked that he believed Bishop was a CIA employee. McCone however, said he did not know what kind of work Bishop did.

A second operative who knew Bishop was a CIA employee who went by the name of "Cross." "Cross" said that he knew Bishop and that he used that as a cover name in his capacity as a headquarters officer who frequently came to the JMWAVE station in Miami. He also said that he thought Howard Hunt used the code name "Knight" and Phillips used the code name "Bishop" (both are terms in chess).

The HSCA tried to find out the identity of Bishop as relayed to them by Antonio Veciana but was unable to do so. However, when they looked deeply into the long career of David Atlee Phillips, their interest in Bishop got even more intriguing. According to the record, Phillips, and that given by Veciana, Phillips was in all the same spots, did all the same jobs for the CIA that Veciana said he did.

In later years, Veciana and Phillips met at a meeting of former CIA veterans. According to people who were there, Phillips did not recognize Veciana. This would be a rather remarkable thing, given the fact that Phillips//Bishop and Antonio Veciana were old colleagues in the war against Castro. Later, Veciana said that the man he met at the party was not Bishop.

The HSCA however, took a rather different view of the Phillips/Veciana meeting. The report stated in part, "the Committee suspected Veciana was lying when he denied that the retired officer was Bishop."

All this pales in comparison to a remark by Veciana

concerning Bishop and Oswald. Veciana said that in the summer of 1963, he saw his old CIA contract agent, "Maurice Bishop," meeting with Lee Harvey Oswald on a Dallas street. If Veciana is right regarding the supposed Oswald/Bishop/Phillips meeting, then the entire question of CIA involvement in the murder of JFK (if there was any), takes on a new, and important meaning. David Phillips died in July 1988.

13). Santo Trafficante and Cuba.

Santo Trafficante Jr was one of the three Mafia leaders whom the CIA recruited to assassinate Fidel Castro (the others being, Carlos Marcello and Johnny Rosselli) during the last days of the Eisenhower administration. He was one of the major players in the mob operations in Cuba, the owner of such influential casinos/hotels as the Sans Souci and was responsible for overseeing most of the mob related business in Batista's Cuba. Besides running the Sans Souci, Trafficante had interests in other hotels such as the Rivera, the Tropicana, The Sevilla Biltmore, the Cabri Hotel Casino and the Havana Hilton. Besides having a controlling interest in these Cuban hotels, at that time, Trafficante also had investment interests in Florida establishments such as the Columbia Restaurant and the Nebraska, Tangerine and Sands Bar in Tampa. He also had a tangential relationship with the killer of Lee Oswald, Jack Ruby.

Trafficante's Cuban mob connections were cemented in the late 1950's, when, in 1956, Meyer Lansky moved his lucrative casino operations to Cuba. Once ensconced amid the open arms of Batista, the two men arranged a powerful alliance whereby they both controlled most of the gambling establishments on the island.

Trafficante and Lansky made a deal with Batista whereby all sides would be winners in the lucrative Havana casino operations. In order for a casino to operate in Cuba, they had to pay a license fee of $25,000 to $50,000, and a casino was not allowed to operate on the property unless the hotel was worth at least one million dollars. Once these various hotels were fully operational, the Cuban Treasury Department got 20% of the profits. This was not the actual payment however, as may middlemen got their cut and the end result was that the Cuban government netted much less.[129]

During the reign of Batista, Trafficante's second-in-command in Havana was James Longo, who, according to records, was "a lieutenant and enforcer for Santo Trafficante Jr."

In those days it was easy for Americans and others to travel openly to and from Cuba. While Trafficante controlled events in Havana, outside circumstances would play an intricate part in Trafficante's further role in Havana.

In 1957, the so called "Apalachin Conference" took place in upstate New York. This was an unprecedented gathering of all the top mafioso from all the prominent families in the United States. This meeting of 60 of the top mafia leaders met in the hide-away town of Apalachin, New York at the home of Joseph Barbara. Barbara was known in mob circles as the "Underworld Host" for allowing his home to be used as the site of the meeting. Barbara's crime spree lasted for thirty years, and he was the owner of several beer liquor distributor ships in upstate New York.

Among the mafia big-wigs who showed up at Barbara's home were in no certain order, Santos Trafficante, Vito Genovese, Joseph Bonanno, Joseph Profaci, Carlo Gambino, Frank DeSimone, Nicholas Civello, among others. Mob families from across the United States including New York, New Jersey, Florida, Texas, California and Illinois, made the long trek to Barbara's mansion.

Since no "record" of what went on in the meeting exists, the historians who have studied this incident say that the reason for the conclave was to discuss the assassination a few weeks prior to the event of mob boss Albert Anastasia, and the ascendancy of

---

129 Santo Trafficante Jr. 1961. Cuban Information Archives. Document 0126. See-Gordon Winslow's website.

Vito Genovese as the planned number one man in the American mob.

The secret gathering of cars at the Barbara home was noticed by the vigilant eyes of a passing New York State trooper who called in for reinforcements. At the sound of police sirens at the Barbara home, the mobsters fled like lemmings, trying to elude capture.

Trafficante and a number of his fellow cohorts were arrested but were soon released. To this day, it is not certain if the police were tipped off as to what was going on inside the home, but conspiracy theories abound.[130]

Following the Apalachin Meeting, a Grand Jury was empaneled to look into what went on at the Barbara home and a subpoena was issued to Trafficante to appear before the panel. In order to evade the subpoena, Trafficante fled the US and returned to Cuba where the could not be extradited (When Trafficante was arrested at the conference, he gave his name as "Louis Santos"). Upon his return to Cuba, Trafficante was interviewed by Cuban police and was subsequently arrested. During his interrogations he denied having used the name Santos and said he never took part in the New York meeting. He did say he knew Albert Anastasia but repeated that he had no part in his murder.

During this time, reports circulated among the Cuban mobsters that Trafficante was losing large amounts of money from the "bolita," or numbers game in Cuba. It was said that he was "completely broke" but there was no way to verify that charge.

The Trafficante family had its roots in Italy where his father. Santo Trafficante Senior, was born in the town of Cianciani, Sicily on May 28, 1886. His mother, Maria Giuseppa Cacciatore was born in Italy, date and place unknown.

Santo Trafficante Junior was born on November 15, 1914. He lived as a young man mostly in Tampa, Florida, where, over

130 Carl Sifakis, "The Mafia Encyclopedia: From Accardo to Zwillman." Facts on File, 1987, Page 18-20.

time, he would command the influential Mafia in the city and its environs. While he lived in Cuba, his residence was located at Calle 12, No. 20 Vedado in Havana. His wife's name was Josephine Marchese and they were married in Tampa on April 17, 1938. Two daughters were born, Mary Josephine and Sara Ann. Santos' siblings were a brother Frank, Salvatore (known as Sam), Epifanio and Encrico. An uncle named Joseph Caccatore was a convicted narcotics trafficker.

While living in the United States, Santo amassed quite a rap sheet, mostly in Florida, on charges that ran from general investigation, vagrancy, bribery, bolita operations, conspiracy in operating a Wagering Act, among others. He was charged by local police departments all across Florida, from Tampa to St. Petersburg, sometimes, more than once. On May 20, 1954, he was arrested by the Sheriff's Office in Clearwater, Florida for bribery and was sentenced on September 27, 1954. However, the charge did not stick and Trafficante's conviction was reversed by the Florida State Supreme Court in January 23, 1957.

As mentioned before, when Trafficante returned to Cuba after his subpoena in the killing of Albert Anastasia, he was arrested by the Department of Investigation of the Cuban National Police.

Upon taking over the power as the undisputed mob boss in Tampa, Trafficante followed in his father's footsteps, taking a firm grip on the gambling, vice, loan harking, and most important of all, the lucrative narcotics business that the mob was branching into. Over time, Florida became one of the most important entry points of illegal drugs, especially heroin, into the United States. Over the years, Trafficante would be one of the major narcotics kingpins in the distribution of heroin into the U.S. He allied himself with the major heroin traders of the Golden Triangle of Southeast Asia, notably Burma, Thailand, and Laos. His actions in the illegal drug trade made Trafficante's name well known to the intelligence services in the US, especially the CIA and the Bureau of Narcotics (as it was called then). In 1969, Trafficante went to Saigon where he made contacts with the Corsican Mafia leaders who had control over the vast heroin business in Southeast Asia. Trafficante and the Corsican mob made a deal whereby Trafficante would be allowed to control the shipment of Indochinese heroin into the United States.

But Cuba was never far from Trafficante's mind and in 1946 he moved from Tampa to Havana where he oversaw his fathers one time gambling interests. It was while he was in Havana that Trafficante made a covert deal with the island's pro-American dictator and president, Fulgencio Batista.

When Batista fled the country in 1959 after the successful Castro revolution, Trafficante remained in Cuba for a while, even when the majority of his fellow mobsters had fled with their ransom to Florida. On June 6, 1959, Trafficante was arrested by Cuban authorities and was placed in the Trescornia prison, a minimum security facility. Trescornia was not your ordinary jail, as Trafficante would soon find out. Due to his status in Cuba, he was given special treatment by his guards, and was even allowed his own food and drink to be sent to him.

One of the men whom Trafficante met in Trescornia was another American soldier of fortune, Loran Hall. Hall was an associate not only of Frank Sturgis, but Gerry Patrick Hemming, an American fighter who once worked for Castro in a post Batista Havana. Later, after souring on the Cuban revolution, Hemming would ally himself with any anti-Communist, anti-Castro group whom he could link up with. The CIA and FBI had a huge file on Hemming and his anti-Cuban brigade, whose members flocked to Florida and Louisiana to train for the day when they would forcefully liberate Cuba from Castro's clutches. Hemming would soon found an organization called the Intercontinental Penetration Force that operated both openly and clandestinely out of bases in south Florida and made numerous hit and run raids into Cuba.

During his heyday as a mercenary, Hall was arrested by the Cuban government on April 21, 1959, two months prior to the arrest of Trafficante for planning an invasion of Nicaragua that was to be launched from Cuba. At that time, Hall was a captain in Castro's army and the raid was to be an embarrassment for the regime. Hall, along with a number of other people involved in the presumptive raid, were arrested and placed in jail.

In the documents released on Loran Hall by the House Select Committee on Assassinations, (HSCA), the government panel wrote that the Nicaraguan connection is important to the events of November 22, 1963 because of a report given to the CIA by a British journalist named John Wilson Hudson. Hudson, if the story is to be believed, said that he was in the same prison as both Hall and Trafficante. He further said that while he was in jail, Jack Ruby arrived at the prison and met Trafficante. Wilson-Hudson was arrested in connection with a large arms cache to be used for Hall's planned attack on Nicaragua.

It has been alleged that Hall and Hemming both trained at a para-military camp in Lake Pontchartrain outside of New Orleans and that possibly Lee Oswald tried to infiltrate the group. Hemming told investigators that both he and Hall made a trip to Dallas in November 1963, prior to meeting Trafficante in October in Florida. If this meeting took place, and what they discussed, is not known.

Hall was also deeply involved in a much disputed event that took place in September 1963 as the same time that Lee Oswald was supposed to have been in Mexico City. During that time period, three unidentified men came to the Dallas, Texas home of Silvia Odio, a wealthy and prominent anti-Castro family. Odio's father was involved in the anti-Castro cause. Two of the men who came to the Odio home were Cuban looking men. The other was an American who was introduced as "Leon Oswald." At this time, the real Lee Oswald was supposed to be on his way to Mexico City. Later, when the Warren Commission was investigating this incident, Hall said that he was one of the men who came to Sylvia Odio's home. That proved to be false and Hall subsequently retracted his statement.

If indeed it can be proved that both Ruby and Trafficante did in fact meet at Trescornia, the implications are enormous.

While it is an historical fact that the Kennedy assassination was not planned at this time, (JFK was not elected president until November 1960), then it is not out of the possibility that Trafficante could have enlisted Ruby's services when Ruby killed Oswald as part of a Kennedy assassination conspiracy.

In the final report on a possible Ruby-Trafficante relationship, the committee said that "The importance of a Ruby-Trafficante meeting in Trescornia should not be overemphasized. The most it would show would be a meeting, at least a brief one. No one has suggested that President Kennedy's assassination was planned at Trescornia in 1959. At the same time, a meeting or association even minor, between Ruby and Trafficante would not have been necessary for Ruby to have been used by Trafficante to murder Oswald. Indeed, it is likely that such a direct contact would have been avoided by Trafficante if there had been a plan to execute the President or the President's assassin, but since no such plot could have been under consideration in 1959, there would not have been a particular necessity for Trafficante to avoid contact with Ruby in Cuba."[131]

The fact that Santo Trafficante made two trips to Cuba after his release from Trescornia begs more questions than it answers. Why was Trafficante, one of the most important leaders of the anti-Castro cause, a known mob leader who was no friend of Castro's, allowed safe passage back to Cuba? The HSCA felt that this question was so important that they wrote the following in this regard:

"Location of Trafficante.

To support the description of Trafficante as a courier the IGR states that, "At the time the gambling casinos were still operating in Cuba, and Trafficante was making regular trips between Miami and Havana on syndicate business.

131 The Final Assassinations Report, New York Times Edition. Bantam Books, 1979. Page 187-188.

The Committee has obtained some evidence which indicates that Trafficante was not traveling to Cuba during this period. No records available to the Committee from INS, State Department, or the FBI reflect any travels after February 1960. During this time, the FBI maintained physical surveillance on Trafficante. Trafficante testified before the Committee that he only made two trips to Cuba after his release from the Trescornia prison in Cuba in August 1959, and that these trips occurred within two to three months of this release. Additionally, considering Trafficante's reputed top position in the La Cosa Nostra, it seems more reasonable that Trafficante would send a representatives to Cuba to conduct any business rather than being detained by Castro again."

"If Trafficante was actually traveling between Miami and Havana, the implications are interesting. He was either willing to risk being detained again or had acquired assurances from the Cuban government regarding his safety. In any event the presence of Trafficante during the fall of 1960 in Cuba raises the possibility of a more cooperative relationship between himself and the Cuban government than believed previously. Such a relationship during the period when Trafficante was scheming to assassinate Castro invited the theory that Trafficante was possibly informing the Cuban government of activities in the Miami area in general and of the plots in particular. In return for such information, Trafficante could have been promised lost gambling operations as well as support and a Cuban sanctuary for the smuggling of contraband into the United States.

"There are enormous ramifications to such a theory and the Committee cautions that it has not received any information or evidence in this regard. In addition, the available evidence indicates Trafficante was not traveling between Miami and Havana although it is recognized that Trafficante could make such trips and not disrupt his normal routine in Miami and Tampa, thus possibly undermining the effect of any surveillance."[132]

132 RIF # 180-10142-10486.

Before Santo Trafficante's testimony to the HSCA, the panel members wrote a detailed outline of questions they wanted to ask him. Thanks to the declassified JFK files, we now have a verbatim list of the points the members of the committee were interested in.

Entitled "Basis For Questioning," the committee members listed four general areas they wanted answers to. 1. Mr. Trafficante's Activities in Cuba Prior to 1960, 2. Participation in Assassination Plots, 3. Knowledge of the Kennedy Administration's Proposed Crackdown on Organized Crime and 4. Exploration in Depth of a Possible Ruby/Trafficante Meeting or Ruby/Trafficante/Affiliation.

As far as Santo Trafficante's activities in Cuba were concerned, the committee asked the following questions:

"It is significant to determine his activities and his relationship with the Cuban government so that an assessment may be made as to why Mr. Trafficante would participate in assassination plots against Fidel Castro. His relationship with a Cuban official and a Cuban exile leader is important since it is believed that these individuals participated in some of the anti-Castro plots. His associates in jail are relevant both because they may have had a motive to participate in anti-Castro plots and it is possible that Jack Ruby visited the jail during his stay in Cuba."

The role that Trafficante played in the US.-mob connected plots to kill Castro was viewed as particularly significant. In "Participation in Assassination Plots," the Committee wanted to know why "Mr. Trafficante's participation in the plots is relevant. It would establish he had the means to kill a national leader, and his motivation for doing so is very important. His relationship with Mr. Rosselli and Mr. Giancana are of interest since they not only knew of the Castro assassination plots, but were members of organized crime. Organized crime may have had an independent motive to kill either Castro or Kennedy or both. Mr. Trafficante's participation with anti-Castro exiles living in the United States also relates to possible activities that may have undertaken against either Castro or Kennedy."

Since Trafficante had a long history of being one of the top hoodlums in the United States and the Kennedy Justice Department was hot on his tail, the committee paid particular attention to this area. Under the heading "Knowledge of the Kennedy Administration's Proposed Crackdown on Organized Crime," the panelists said that, "Mr. Trafficante's awareness of Attorney General Kennedy's crackdown on organized crime is extremely relevant to the Committee. Mr. Trafficante himself was a target of this program and will still be inquiring as to his dealings with several other individuals who were targets of the program or associates who were targets. This line of questioning is highly relevant as establishing a possible motive for Mr. Trafficante to kill President Kennedy, given the effect the Attorney General's program had on organized crime."

As mentioned before, Trafficante, while in jail in Cuba, as well in his casino business, had run into two men whom the HSCA wanted to learn more about; Lewis McWillie and to a lesser degree, the British journalist John Wilson-Hudson. In the heading called "Exploration in Depth of a Possible Ruby/Trafficante meeting or Ruby/Trafficante Affiliation," the committee said, "This area of questioning will concentrate on Mr. Trafficante's jailing in Cuba, and his relationship with Mr. Lewis McWillie. It has been alleged by John Wilson-Hudson that an "American gangster type" named Ruby or Rubenstein met Mr. Trafficante when Mr. Trafficante was in jail. Furthermore, independent sources the Committee has obtained access to have indicated that this meting is possible. Mr. Lewis Mcwillie is an acknowledged associate of Jack Ruby and his relationship with Mr. Trafficante must be explored in detail."[133]

Among the people whom the committee was interested in exploring as far as having a relationship with Trafficante were mob fixer Johnny Rosselli, mobster and CIA plotter Sam Giancana, ex-FBI cut-out, Robert Mahue, and a Cuban called "X"

133 RIF No. 180-10118-10142. General Guidelines.

who was a "Cuban official to be used in the CIA-Mafia plots to administer the poison pills to Castro."

The person called "X" was probably Juan Orta who was the man who was designated by the CIA and the mob to take the poison pill and slip it into Castro's favorite food in a restaurant that he frequently attended.

Juan Orta was the Office Chief and Director General of the Office of the Prime Minister in Cuba (i.e. Castro). Castro and Orta got along well and it was only after Castro became a Communist and in Orta's belief, betrayed the Cuban revolution, that he turned on his old comrade.

Before Orta had the chance to slip the poison into Castro's food, his personal circumstances changed for the worse. On January 26, 1961, only six days after JFK was inaugurated as president, and while the planning for the poison pills escapade was going on in Washington and Miami, Orta lost this job and his access to Castro. In April 1961, at the time of the Bay of Pigs invasion, Orta fled to the safety of the Venezuelan Embassy and was given safe haven. He stayed under the protection of the Venezuelan's until October 1964, and was then given a safe conduct pass by the Castro government to leave the country. He fled to Mexico City and then came to the U.S. in February, 1965.

The HSCA panelists were also interested in finding out as much as they could regarding any possible relationship between Trafficante and some of the most influential Mafia figures in the country, including: New Orleans crime boss Carlos Marcello (who was also in the original CIA-Mafia plots), Joseph Colombo, the reputed leader of the New York crime family, Thomas Eboli, "reported organized crime figure in New York," Joseph Stassi, who "had a share in the Sans Souci Casino in Havana, along with Santo Trafficante," Vito Genovese, who was one of the participants in the Apalachin meeting in 1957, Carmine Galante, "Reputed organized crime figure from New York who attended the Apalachin meeting," John Ormento, another mafia leader of high esteem, John Henry Dolan, who was "active in criminal activities in the 1950's and early 1960's in the Dallas, Texas area-associate of Jack Ruby-allegedly worked in a few operations for Santo Trafficante," and Jackie Cerone, another mafia figure from New York, who was "observed several times with Santo Trafficante in the Miami area."[134]

Other people of interest who the committee wanted to investigate were: Jose Aleman, the son of a wealthy and powerful Minister of Education of the Cuban Government whose name Jose Aleman Sr.

The committee wanted further information on a comment allegedly made by Jose Aleman, a leading anti-Castro organizer, after a discussion with Trafficante about the Kennedy brothers. When the two men met in September 1962, it is alleged by Aleman that when the topic of the 1964 election came up, Aleman said that in his opinion, Kennedy would be easily re-elected. Trafficante, according to Aleman, said that JFK would not make it to the next election, he was to be "hit."

Aleman further said that he was certain that Trafficante himself would not be the one to carry out the assassination, and stated that the name of Jimmy Hoffa, the powerful President of the Teamsters Union, was discussed in that meeting. According to Aleman, Hoffa said that Kennedy "would get what's coming to him," because of the Attorney General's ruthless pursuit of Hoffa.

Aleman further testified before the HSCA that it was his impression from his brief conversation with Trafficante that the Tampa boss was not kidding when he said that the president was to be killed. "Rather, he did in fact know that such a crime was being planned." Aleman further stated that "Trafficante had given him the distinct impression that Hoffa was to be principally involved in the planning of the president's murder."

Later, Aleman changed his mind regarding Trafficante's statement to him about Kennedy being "hit." He later said that

134 Ibid.

Trafficante meant that Kennedy was going to be "hit" by a lot of Republican votes. Obviously, someone had gotten to Aleman, most probably Trafficante, who, it can be assumed, threatened bodily harm against Aleman if he stuck to his story. If that is the case, Aleman must have been scared out of his wits and would do and say anything to get back in the good graces of Trafficante.

On September 28, 1978, Trafficante testified before the committee and denied ever talking with anyone about assassinating President Kennedy, and further said that he played NO role in the event (JFK's murder). He also said that he did not remember talking with Aleman but denied that a planned "hit" against JFK was ever discussed.

In its final report, the HSCA wrote the following regarding the Trafficante-Aleman story. "The committee found it difficult to understand how Aleman could have misunderstood Trafficante during such a conversation, or why he would have fabricated such an account."

Another person with direct links to Trafficante was Frank Ragano, an attorney who represented Trafficante. Another long time client of Ragano's was Jimmy Hoffa, no friend of either of the Kennedy's. In January 1992, an article appeared in the *New York Post,* in which Ragano said that a plot between Hoffa, Trafficante, and Carlos Marcello was hatched to kill the president. They story made instant nation-wide headlines but in the decades to come, all the major participants in the alleged meeting, Trafficante, Marcello, Hoffa and Ragano have since died an no one can absolutely be sure that the supposed conversation ever took place.

Besides these individuals, according to the newly released documents, the committee members were very interested in any possible Trafficante-Ruby connection. The topics they wanted to further investigate were:

- Did Ruby see Trafficante in jail, possibly accompanied by McWillie?

- British journalist John Wilson Hudson story.
- Fully explore other jail associates; possibly casino owners used (Ruby for Trafficante) to get money out of Cuba after Castro's takeover.
- Relationship of McWillie to Trafficante.

One hopes that the remaining files that are still classified by the CIA will someday reveal the entire story of Santos Trafficante's role in the Kennedy assassination.

14). "Harry" Ruiz-Williams.

"Harry" Ruiz-Williams was a veteran of the Bay of Pigs invasion, one of the many men who were captured by Castro's forces and served time with the other unlucky brigade members. When the Bay of Pigs exiles were finally released from Castro's jails and returned to the United States, it was Harry Williams who was the last out of the plane. He was met at the airport by his long time friend and fellow anti-Castro leader, Pepe San Roman. After many hugs and warm solicitations, San Roman took Williams aside and told him that he had to make an important call to a man in Washington who was on their side. That man was Attorney General Robert Kennedy. After a few minutes on the phone, both men made their way to Washington, D.C. to meet with their new benefactor.

Harry Williams was a geologist by trade, having gone to the prestigious Colorado School of Mines. While in Cuba, Williams lived in Oriente Province and soon made contact with Castro's revolutionary band, including Raul Castro and Che Guevara. He supplied them with ammunition and worked for the cause. Before Castro took over, Williams went to the United States and returned home after Batista took over. But once Castro proclaimed his Communist intentions, Williams took up the cause of getting rid of his old friend.

During the Bay of Pigs invasion, Williams was wounded

numerous times but managed to survive. While he lay gravely wounded on the shores of Cuba, Harry woke up one day to see a familiar figure standing over him. It was his old nemesis, Fidel Castro. Instinctively, Harry reached for a .35 pistol that he had concealed under his bed and pointed it at Castro. From what others who were in the room later told Harry, Castro leaned over to him and said, "What are you trying to do, kill me?" Harry is supposed to have replied, "That's what I came here for." Now home, he was ready and willing to do anything to see Castro go.

The first time Robert Kennedy met Harry Williams, the first brother took an instant liking to the young Cuban. RFK told Williams in that initial meeting that "we've selected you to be, let's say, the man we trust most in the exiles." Williams, ever distrustful of the Kennedy's because of the Bay of Pigs failure, was less than enthusiastic and initially turned down frequent requests from Robert Kennedy to visit him at his Hickory Hill, Virginia home. Later though, as Williams got to know Bobby better, and understood the dominant role he played in the Castro plots, the more he came around to trusting the president's sibling.

Williams, at one point in a conversation with RFK said that, "It was my idea to physically eliminate Castro." Robert Kennedy agreed and said that the administration was ready to proceed in that regard.

Williams said this concerning his relationship with RFK, "I worked for Bobby. I was his number one man in Cuba. He was my friend. I got into a lot of trouble with the Cubans who hated the Kennedys. They called me 'Bobby's Boy.'" The closeness between the two men is shown in the logs of Robert Kennedy's Justice Department's phone conversations in which 36 calls were made between the two men.

Recalling the control Robert Kennedy had over the Cuban situation, Williams recalls, "Bobby called the shots in the Cuba Project. In my opinion, Bobby ran the CIA. Bobby's anti-Castro campaign continued right up until the assassination. We had camps in the Dominican Republic, in the jungles of Guatemala, in Costa Rica. At the camps, the CIA guys would try to give me orders, but I would laugh and say, I don't work for you. You work for me."

Williams's CIA case officers were E. Howard Hunt and Bernard Barker, who would later be involved in the Watergate affair. All three men met many times in Washington in the later summer, early fall of 1963 to plan another exile invasion of Cuba. In was Williams' job to unite the other members of the exile community into a cohesive force when the new invasion which was scheduled to take place in December 1963. Somehow, this meeting got the attention of the Associated Press which ran an article concerning the new invasion and Williams' close association with RFK. The late author and CIA man Robert Morrow, says that Robert Kennedy promised Williams's exile brigade CIA money, guns, and other means in this new invasion (in December 1963) to topple Castro.

On the morning of November 22, 1963, the day JFK was killed, Robert Kennedy met with a number of his closest associates, including Harry Williams to plan Castro's demise. A source close to the meeting says that a Castro official offered – in return for a large cash payment – that he would initiate a coup directed against Castro (probably Juan Alameda). Robert Kennedy agreed, and put a large sum of money into a foreign bank account. The only reason that the operation did not go into effect was the president's murder.

As mentioned before in this book, the Kennedy's top Cuban spy in Havana was Juan Almeida, whose task it was to lead the coup against Castro. In May 1963, Commander Almeida contacted Harry Williams and told him that he would be willing to initiate a coup against Castro if the Kennedy administration would give him the backing he needed. Harry and Almeida were old comrades in arms, dating back to the time when Castro and his band of revolutionaries were camped out in the mountains of Cuba, battling Batista's troops. Williams was one of many people who supplied the rebels with much needed military supplies.

During the spring of 1963, as the first stages of the new coup against Castro took shape, Harry Williams was the intermediary between Bobby Kennedy and Juan Almeida, bringing messages between the two parties. The CIA gave Williams the sum of $50,000 which he gave to Almeida to use for the much needed supplies for the coup. They also helped get his wife and family out Cuba.[135]

Robert Kennedy told Harry to tell Juan Almeida that the CIA would insure his families safety in the event of his death. Almeida must have been gratified and plunged deeply into the planned coup against Castro.

The date for the coup was scheduled for December 1, 1963, and in the weeks leading up to the date, Bobby and Harry, along with his other, trusted Cuban aids, held frantic meetings in Washington to iron out the details. On the morning of November 22, 1963, the day of the assassination, Robert Kennedy held a strategy session in D.C. with Harry and the others involved in the coup planning. It was later reported by the *Washington Post,* regarding this meeting that, Harry Williams was "having the most crucial of a series of secret meetings with top level CIA and government people about the problem of Cuba at a safe house in Washington."

According to the plan outlined by Robert Kennedy, Harry Williams was supposed to leave Washington for Miami in the coming days and then make his way to the American naval base at Guantanamo. From there, he was to enter Cuban territory and secretly meet with Juan Almeida to make final preparations for the coup against Castro, which included the "elimination" of the Cuban leader.

According to authors Hartman and Waldron, the December 1, 1963, coup date was not written in stone. If circumstances called for it, the date could have been changed by a day or two

135 Lamar Waldron With Thom Hartman. "Legacy of Secrecy: The Long Shadow of the JFK Assassination." Counterpoint, Berkeley, 2008, Page. 14.

earlier because of friction between the Kennedy administration and Manuel Artime, one of the most powerful of the anti-Castro leaders of the day. The authors write that in October and November of that year, Artime was feuding with Harry Williams and making contact with Robert Kennedy behind Harry's back. Artime did not trust the other, mostly liberal members of the anti-Castro cause and friction was brewing between them. For years, the CIA had lavishly funded Artime's anti-Castro group and he was referred by some at Langley headquarters as the CIA's "Golden Boy." Artime saw himself as the new president in a post-Castro Havana and he did not relish playing second fiddle to any one else who might take his place.

Harry was intimately involved in the coup planning and with his close ties to Robert Kennedy, the Attorney General asked him to select a few exiles who would take part in the coup. Among those selected by both Bobby and Harry were, Manuel Artime, Tony Varona, (head of the CRC-Cuban Revolutionary Council), Manolo Ray (head of JURE), Eloy Menoyo (head of SNFE-Second National Front of the Escambray), and a number of ex-Bay of Pigs veterans who were then taking training at the U.S. Army base at Fort Benning, Georgia.

Despite much bickering between them, an accommodation was arranged and all of the leaders reluctantly agreed to work with each other in one common end-the removal of Castro.

While the planning for the coup was underway, Harry was facing all sorts of problems. At one point, he traveled to Guatemala for a meeting with Manuel Artime. While in Guatemala, Harry was attacked by two men in restaurant and barely escaped with his life.

Harry was in Washington D.C. on the morning of November 22, 1963, staying at the Ebbit Hotel. While Bobby Kennedy was meeting at his Hickory Hill home in Virginia with his top Justice Department colleagues, Harry Williams was in secret meeting to finalize the coup plans set for the following week. Among those in attendance with Harry at the fateful meeting were E. Howard

Hunt and Lyman Kirkpatrick, the CIA's Executive Director. In their interview with Harry, authors Hartman and Waldron write that Harry told them that Robert Kennedy asked Harry to specifically attend the November 22 meeting and said that "we were really advancing" (the coup plan). One of the topics of the day's meeting was looking at "all the ways of eliminating Castro." When the topic of killing Castro came up, Harry said, "I am sure that you guys know more people, a hell of a lot more people that could, you know, could do these things." Harry also said that he knew a few people who could to the Castro hit.

The meeting was in their afternoon session when word came in that Kennedy had been shot. For Harry, it was a personal shock. He was close to Robert Kennedy and it can be logically assumed that Bobby told his brother of his close relationship with Harry. Harry showed little outward emotion when the news of the president's death reached the group. He was later criticized by some in the room of being to "cool" when he heard the terrible news. Harry said it was not his style to show outward emotion in public, but underneath, he was probably seething with resentment at what had transpired.

Harry called Robert Kennedy at the DOJ office and offered his most profound sympathy. Harry was meeting with writer Haynes Johnson who was well connected with all the leaders of the anti-Castro cause. As per RFK's request, he asked to speak with the writer. Haynes would later write that as he spoke to a grieving Bobby Kennedy, the Attorney General was lucid and in control of his thoughts, Bobby said to Johnson that, "One of your guys did it."

What did RFK mean by this statement? Robert Kennedy knew too well all the facets of the plans to kill Castro-Operation Mongoose, the Bay of Pigs, the efforts by the various anti-Castro exile groups, and the CIA-mob plots to kill Castro. What is still in dispute is did RFK know of Lee Oswald and his double dealing in New Orleans in the summer of 1963? RFK could not have known all the machinations of all the players in the drama then unfolding vis-a-vi Cuba – the Almeida coup plans and all that it entailed. In later years, Bobby would talk privately about the fact that his brother might have been killed because of the CIA plots to kill Castro and if, somehow, the act could have been prevented.

Among the files still held by the CIA and other government departments in the JFK case, are those that pertain to Harry Williams, his relationship with Robert Kennedy, and his role in the anti-Castro cause that so dominated his life.

The End

BIBLIOGRAPHY

BOOKS

Beschloss, Michael. *The Crisis Years: Kennedy and Khrushchev 1960-1963.* Harper Collins, 1991.

Brown, Walt. *Treachery in Dallas.* Carroll & Graf, 1995.

Blakey, Robert G., and Billings, Richard. *The Plot to kill the President.* Times Books, 1981.

Callahan, Bob. *Who Shot JFK? A Guide to the Major Conspiracy Theories.* Fireside Books, 1993.

Earley, Pete. *Confessions of a Spy. The Real Story of Aldrich Ames.* G. P. Putnam's Sons, 1997.

Fursenko, Alexander and Naftali, Timothy. *One Hell of a Gamble: The Secret History of the Cuban Missile Crisis. Khrushchev, Castro & Kennedy. 1958-1964.* W.W. Norton & Co. 1997.

Hinkle, Warren & Turner, William. *The Fish Is Red: The Story of the Secret War Against Castro.* Harper& Row, 1981.

Hinkle, Warren & Turner, William. *Deadly Secrets: The CIA-Mafia War Against Castro and the Assassination of JFK.* Thunder's Mouth Press. 1992.

Hurt, Henry. *Reasonable Doubt: An Investigation Into the Assassination of John F Kennedy.* Henry Holt & Co., 1985.

Kross, Peter. *Traitors, Moles & Spies: An Espionage and Intelligence Quiz Book.* Illuminet Press, 1997-98.

La Fontaine, Mary and Ray. *Oswald Talked: New Evidence in the JFK Assassination.* Pelican Press, 1996.

Marrs, Jim. *Crossfire; The Plot That Killed Kennedy.* Carroll & Graf, 1989.

O'Toole, G.J.A. *The Encyclopedia of American Intelligence and Espionage: From the American Revolution to the Present Day.* Facts on File, 1988.

Polmar, Norman and Allen, Thomas. *Spy Book: The Encyclopedia of Espionage.* Random House, 1997.

Roberts, Craig and Armstrong, John. *JFK: The Dead Witnesses.* Consolidated Press International, 1995.

Russell, Dick. *The Man Who Knew Too Much.* Carroll & Graf, 1992.

Schiem, David. *Contract On America.* Shapolsky Books, 1988.

Schleslinger, Arthur, Jr. *Robert Kennedy And His Times.* Ballentine Books, 1978.

Scott, Peter Dale. *Deep Politics 11: Essays on Oswald, Mexico, and Cuba. The New Revelations In US Government Files: 1994-1995.* Green Archive Press, 1995.

Stone, Oliver, and Skiar, Zachary. *JFK: The Book of the Film.* Applause Books, 1992.

New York Times. *The Final Assassinations Report.* Bantam Books, 1979.

New York Times. *Report of the Warren Commission; The Assassination of President Kennedy.* McGraw Hill Book Co., 1964.

Ocean Press. *CIA Targets Fidel: The Secret Assassination Report.* Melbourne, Victoria, Australia, 1996.

MAGAZINES / JOURNALS

Fonzi, Gaeton. *The Last Word (Hopefully) On AMLASH.* AARC Quarterly. Spring/Summer 1996.

Gest, Ted, and Shapiro, Walter. *JFK: The Untold Story of the Warren Commission.* US News & World Report, August 17, 1992.

Kross, Peter. *JFK And the French Connection.* Back Channels. Vol 1 #1. Pg. 34 October 1991.

Kross, Peter. *Oswald's Military Investigation.* Back Channels. Vol 2. No. 1. Pg. 12-13.

Kross, Peter. *Project ZR/RIFLE & JFK.* Back Channels. Vol 3. No. 1 & 2. Pg. 9-11.

Kross, Peter. *The Ferrie Flight Plan Document.* Back Channels. Vol 3 No. 1& 2. Fall-Winter 1993-4.

Kross, Peter. *Back Channels Talks to Gerry Hemming.* Back Channels. Vol 1 No. 2. Pg. 22.

Malone, W. Scott. *The Secret Life of Jack Ruby.* New Times, 1/23/78.

Schulz, Donald. *Kennedy And the Cuban Connection.* Foreign Affairs (no date or issue #).

No Author. *Was Lee Harvey Oswald Working For The CIA? An Insider's View.* Clandestine America. #5.

DOCUMENTS

"CIA Briefing on (Alleged) Soviet/ Cuban Assassinations." Record No. 157-10011-10029. Date: 1/15/76.

"Scelso Report." Record No. 180-10131-10330. File No. 014728.

US Senate Select Committee on Intelligence. Draft. - "Assassination Report" 1975.

***NOTE: Footnotes have been made throughout the text referring to specific documents and information.**

About the Author

Peter Kross is a native of the Bronx, New York. He has a B.A. in history from the University of Albuquerque. He was the former editor of "Back Channels" magazine. His three published books include: "New Jersey History," "Spies, Traitors and Moles: An Espionage and Intelligence Quiz Book," and "The Encyclopedia of World War 2 Spies." He has been published in magazines such as "World War 2," "World War 2 History," "Military Heritage, Military History" and the "History Channel Magazine." He lives with his wife and twin daughters in New Jersey.

www.ingramcontent.com/pod-product-compliance
Lightning Source LLC
Chambersburg PA
CBHW062153270326
41930CB00009B/1516

* 9 7 8 0 9 8 4 4 7 3 3 6 6 *